Trade and Globalization

Trade and Globalization

An Introduction to Regional Trade Agreements

David A. Lynch

ROWMAN & LITTLEFIELD PUBLISHERS, INC.
Lanham • Boulder • New York • Toronto • Plymouth, UK

To, from, and with Ann,
First Calvin and now Hobbes;
My heartfelt gratitude,
My heartfelt apology,
And always, love.

Published by Rowman & Littlefield Publishers, Inc.
A wholly owned subsidiary of The Rowman & Littlefield Publishing Group, Inc.
4501 Forbes Boulevard, Suite 200, Lanham, Maryland 20706
http://www.rowmanlittlefield.com

Estover Road, Plymouth PL6 7PY, United Kingdom

British Library Cataloguing in Publication Information Available

Library of Congress Cataloging-in-Publication Data

Lynch, David A., 1966–
  Trade and globalization : an introduction to regional trade agreements / David A. Lynch.
     p. cm.
  Includes bibliographical references and index.
  ISBN 978-0-7425-6688-0 (cloth : alk. paper) — ISBN 978-0-7425-6689-7 (pbk. : alk. paper) — ISBN 978-0-7425-6690-3 (electronic)
  1. Commercial treaties. 2. International trade. 3. Regionalism—Economic aspects. 4. Trade blocs. 5. Foreign trade regulation. I. Title.
  HF1721.L96 2010
  382´.91—dc22

                                                            2010014730

♾ ™ The paper used in this publication meets the minimum requirements of American National Standard for Information Sciences—Permanence of Paper for Printed Library Materials, ANSI/NISO Z39.48-1992.

Printed in the United States of America

Contents

Since globalization is so dynamic, *Trade and Globalization* has a companion website with additional original content including RTA maps, tables, updates of key developments, and coverage of non-RTA international organizations relating to trade and globalization such as the Organization of Petroleum Exporting Countries (OPEC) and the UN Conference on Trade and Development (UNCTAD). The website will also have links to RTAs and other trade and globalization resources.

   Go to http://www.rowman.com/isbn/0742566897.

Boxes, Figures, and Tables

BOXES

FIGURES

TABLES

Preface

The explosion of regional trade agreements (RTAs) has led to a similar explosion of literature on the subject. This book is not an overview of that scholarship; rather the book draws upon the literature and fulfills a number of gaps in the literature regarding scope and focus, technical language usage, and, to a lesser extent, ideological perspective. RTA studies' scope and focus are the primary gaps in the literature: scholars tend to use either microscopes or binoculars as they examine RTAs. Studies using a microscope might examine one sector of one RTA, for instance. It is common to employ a microscope to numerous facets of a single RTA or to compare one facet of numerous RTAs. Without question, these studies are important, but it is difficult to learn much of the broader terrain using a microscope. Conversely, it is also common for studies to stand far from RTAs to survey their broad terrain: examining how large are they and who the members are and giving details about their formation and organization. While these issues are important and worthy of examination, too often they miss what is truly important about a given RTA; the gullies and crevasses that are revealed upon somewhat closer inspection might make a smaller mountain more difficult to climb than a larger one. A lack of political will, divergent agendas, or distrust between leaders might render an RTA that is large in economic weight insignificant in reality. A simple overview of RTAs comparing only their economic weight would find that the Free Trade Area of the Americas (FTAA) is dramatically important: it encompasses nearly every country in the Americas. But it is also, at the time of this writing, stalled over divergent views for hemispheric trade among some of the hemisphere's largest economies—Brazil and the US, for instance—and over divergent ideological perspectives—Venezuela and Bolivia on the one hand and the US and Mexico on the other. These divisions ensure that the

FTAA's current importance is far less than suggested by examining its economic weight alone. In short, RTA literature that is overly microscopic or macroscopic is more apt to miss some of these important features. This book takes a middle ground. Its scope is wide—RTAs the world over—but draws upon more focused scholarship to add depth.

A second gap in the literature stems from a dichotomy in language usage. Much of the literature on RTAs is highly technical and filled with jargon. There is a reason to use technical terminology; it helps those who are familiar with it to more rapidly describe and analyze a given subject matter. But jargon-laden studies are less accessible to the uninitiated. Other RTA literature errs on the side of simplicity. Such an approach helps a wider audience understand the subject matter, but sometimes simplicity misrepresents reality. This book attempts to modestly bridge this technical jargon gap by drawing on highly technical literature and explaining it when needed, but not losing sight of the larger picture. The book aims for the middle terminological level.

There is also an ideological divide regarding RTAs that parallels the ideological divide surrounding globalization. Some of this divide is based upon the distinctive approaches that authors and readers bring to the subject. Economists, for instance, tend to focus on markets and efficiency, and this is sometimes mistaken by non-economists as a lack of empathy. Economists would argue that efficiency and increased productivity are the primary way that humans lead better material lives. Antiglobalization activists are concerned that globalization worsens inequality and leads to social ills such as pollution.

Economics stresses a marginal view of the world while other perspectives—various environmental sciences, for instance—fear there are thresholds that make marginal thinking dangerous. Both types of thinking are useful. Marginal thinking leads to insights over what seems to be obvious. For instance, which is more valuable, a gallon of water or a gallon of diamonds? The quick answer is diamonds, naturally. Economists would argue a better question is which is more valuable, an additional gallon of water or an additional gallon of diamonds. If one has no water, that first gallon is infinitely more valuable than the diamonds. If one is in Bangladesh during the monsoon season amid flooding, an additional gallon of water is damaging. Many environmental sciences and environmental groups are concerned that this marginal thinking might mislead policymakers in some contexts. A marginally more diminished fishery stock, for instance, may be only moderately worse, or it may cause the fishery to collapse if a threshold of insufficient genetic diversity is crossed.

These differences should not be overstated. Among the most respected economists in modern times is Nobel Prize–winning economist Paul Samuel-

son, who said, "My belief is that every good cause is worth some inefficiency."[1]
This is hardly the language of a doctrinaire black-and-white thinker closed to
other ideas and values. This book does not purport to solve any of these ideological or intellectual divisions. Instead the book will illuminate them to better
understand how well-intentioned observers can speak past one another.

There is some danger in straddling separated communities. As the Texan
political columnist Jim Hightower colorfully described what might happen
to those standing in the middle of the ideological divide in the US, "There's
nothing in the middle of the road but yellow stripes and dead armadillos."
But in the words of another famous Texan, Lyle Lovett, "What would you
be if you didn't try?" This book hopes to explain RTAs and, in the process,
modestly bridge the divergent communities outlined above while avoiding
becoming a metaphorical dead armadillo.

Acknowledgments

I have incurred many debts in writing this book, many of which I cannot pay back. I can however, express a small portion of my gratitude.

Thanks to Saint Mary's University of Minnesota for granting me a sabbatical to work on the book and for providing me with resources such as conference attendance, specialized books, and software. The sabbatical reminds me of a friend's description of oxygen tanks during his successful climb of Mt. Everest as the "greatest disappointment." He went on to explain how the oxygen tanks were both "great"—they helped—and a "disappointment"—their help was barely noticeable; they led to no burst of energy to get him to the top. He added they must have helped enough because he made it. A sabbatical wasn't anywhere near enough and I had much further to go, but it was and is nevertheless appreciated.

Thanks to Jim Rodgers who chaired the department in my absence and showed me that one could write books despite a heavy teaching load. No thank you to him, however, for tricking me into believing that it could be done gracefully. Thanks to my dean, Marilyn Frost, for supporting my sabbatical and helping orchestrate its implementation, and to Theresa DeGeest, who taught some of my courses in my absence. Thanks to Stan Pollock, who mentored me in statistical research methodology (and in teaching pedagogy and in keeping one's sanity). Thanks to the Saint Mary's students on whom many of these ideas and some earlier drafts of this writing were tested and to a number of Saint Mary's student workers who helped track down many references for me. Thanks to Dave McConville and the excellent Geographic Information System (GIS) program at Saint Mary's University that assisted me in getting up to speed on GIS software.

Thanks to the United Nations Association of the United States of America (UNA-USA) both for permission to use "NAFTA, 10 Years Later," from *A Global Agenda: Issues Before the 59th General Assembly of the United Nations,* 2004–2005 edition, Angela Drakulich ed. (New York: UNA-USA, 2004) and for editorial guidance during my ten years writing the trade chapter for *A Global Agenda.* Special thanks must go, posthumously, to my first editor there, Susan Woolfson, who made editing enjoyable and helped me sharpen my writing (although I admit, not quite enough).

Thanks to my editors at Rowman & Littlefield—Susan McEachern and Carrie Broadwell-Tkach—and to anonymous reviewers for Rowman & Littlefield. Their constructive criticism was both thoughtful and helpful. Thanks also to Timothy Shaw, who provided me with valuable feedback and encouragement.

Thanks to Michael Gordon, Benjamin J. Cohen, and M. Stephen Weatherford from the University of California, Santa Barbara. They did not directly review this book but mentored me on work I did previously that the book draws upon. Their mentoring still guides me.

Thanks to my family for their support. Thanks to Ethan and Megan Lynch, whose pride in their dad has made me smile when a smile was needed. They help me keep my life balanced.

And Ann. We both know I will never be able to thank you enough, but I'll try. Thanks for your support in so many ways. Thanks for the extra hours of parenting, household tasks, and patience this book required of you, for your scheduling skills (despite my less-than-gracious response to them), for my office makeover (a.k.a. organizational intervention) and the organizational tools that you've taught me (despite my questionable success in using them), for your ability to develop metaphors and analogies as good as the day is long that wore off on me (okay, they didn't wear off on me enough), for your considerable communication skills and ability to teach them (again, my questionable learning), and for your encouragement to have fun, especially in the face of work and stress. They say that behind every successful man is a surprised woman; so thank you for hiding any surprise relating to my success and, beyond merely hiding surprise, thank you for your encouragement and your belief in me.

Introduction to Regional Trade Agreements

Making Sense of the RTA Spaghetti Bowl

THE IMPORTANCE OF RTAs

Regional Trade Agreements (RTAs) are not new, but their importance in global economics and politics is growing.[1] Indeed, there have been distinctive waves of RTAs over time. The most recent wave began in the 1990s and will be the primary focus of this book, although historical antecedents to modern RTAs are also important and will be examined. Compared with preceding regional trade groupings, this modern wave of regionalism is characterized by RTAs that tend to be less discriminatory in trading with nonmembers, cover more economic sectors, and address trade barriers beyond tariffs. Despite the nondiscriminatory nature of this new regionalism, RTAs have become increasingly controversial because the number, scope, and cross-cutting memberships of the web of RTAs has become so complex that many fear it challenges the WTO's multilateral trading system. One prominent observer, Columbia University economist Jagdish Bhagwati, has likened the rise of RTAs and the complexity they bring to trade to a spaghetti bowl. This culinary theme has now been widely used and expanded upon with Asian RTAs called a noodle bowl.[2] RTAs are also curious constructs with so much variation among RTAs in just one country that one is reminded of an aphorism used to explain how bureaucratic negotiations produce strange end products: a camel, it is said, is a horse created by a committee. Each committee member requires there be a particular characteristic in the animal under construction with the end result being a camel; no rational design would create such an odd-looking animal. The array of unique features in RTAs—though not without patterns and similarities—certainly are curiosities, and economic liberal observers increasingly fear that RTAs add sufficient confusion to policymakers, administrators, and businesses that they pose a threat to the global trading system.

Not all RTAs are of significant economic or political importance; some RTAs appear to foster integration in both their written provisions and governmental press releases but in reality are ignored by their own members. Much like "paper constitutions," which pledge to give rights to all but are ignored by dictators, some RTAs pledge much but deliver little. It is therefore important to explore both what is inside an RTA and how that is interpreted and implemented. As long-serving Australian prime minister John Howard said, defending his lack of bilateral free trade agreements in Asia, "It's the substance of the trade relationships that matters, rather than formal documents and formal processes. Documents are process, trading relationships are the substance of an association between countries."[3] He is right, up to a point. Just as once ignored constitutional provisions can come to life with a change in context—from new judges or a new ruling party—once obsolete RTAs can become relevant if the political interests and will of relevant leaders change. In 1989 the Asia Pacific Economic Cooperation Forum (APEC) was simply a forum for Pacific Rim countries to discuss relevant issues. But in 1993, President Clinton called for APEC to be more than just a forum; when other APEC members followed, APEC suddenly mattered. RTAs can also fall out of favor when one or more important members formally withdraw, drag their heels, or simply put their energies for trade relations elsewhere.

WHY RTAs?

The reasons behind the rising number of RTAs are many and are overlapping. Box 1.1 lists the primary reasons why countries form RTAs.

BOX 1.1. WHY RTAs?

To increase market access
To promote investment
To shield against unfair use of trade remedies
To guard against slowed multilateral liberalization
To increase support for multilateral liberalization
To achieve "WTO-plus" levels of integration
To solidify domestic reforms
To increase competitiveness in global markets
To increase clout in international negotiations
To achieve economic stability
To meet other strategic goals

To Increase Market Access

Greater access to foreign markets is perhaps the most typical reason for entering into an RTA. Lower tariff barriers are the type of market access that is easiest to see and measure. The degree to which an RTA grants preferential access—the margin of preference—can be substantial: the US imposes a 25 percent tariff on imported light trucks, but qualifying light trucks made in fellow NAFTA countries Canada and Mexico face no tariff.

But market access can also come from reduced nontariff barriers such as reduced regulations. It should be noted that the margin of preference varies among RTAs, among economic sectors in an RTA, and even within one sector over time (the more multilateral liberalization spreads, the lower the margin of preference). Some RTAs do not liberalize trade substantially and thus are less economically consequential for their members.

To Promote Investment

Better access to foreign markets also makes a country a more attractive investment site. This is especially the case given the preferential nature of the market access. Given margin of preference in light truck production noted above, the economic incentive to produce within one of the NAFTA countries is therefore quite clear to manufacturers.

In many cases, RTAs do spur investment. Investment flowing to Spain and Portugal after their entry to the European Community—now called the European Union (EU)—helped to make EU membership coveted. EU assistance to help acceding members with the transition to membership and, with membership achieved, EU regional assistance, agricultural subsidies, and other programs increase the financial gains to membership. It should be noted that the EU scale of this assistance is atypical. While the scale of EU assistance is atypical, increased investment is not. In fact, serious negotiations themselves can sometimes lead to increased investment before negotiations are final, as was the case with Mexico during the NAFTA negotiations. But again, because not all RTAs have significant economic consequences, this is not universal.

Another reason that RTAs can increase investment is that they may include specific investment provisions designed to make foreign investors feel secure: prohibitions on expropriating property without due compensation, due process regarding investment disputes (sometimes including arbitration and adjudication of disputes outside shaky domestic legal systems), equal treatment between foreign and domestic investment, and reduced bureaucratic hurdles. For instance, investment in Mexico's auto industry used to be subject to a series of periodical auto decrees that were issued by Mexican presidents.

These required a specific amount of production to be exported and a host of other requirements and, more troubling to potential investors, could be changed easily by a Mexican president. NAFTA's investment and auto provisions cannot capriciously be changed.

To Shield against (Perceived) Unfair Use of Trade Remedies

One reason for RTAs is their use as a shield against purported abuse of trade remedies such as antidumping measures, countervailing duties, and safeguards. For example, when President George W. Bush announced safeguard tariffs of up to 30 percent against steel imports in 2002, he exempted 80 developing countries and Canada and Mexico, partners with the US in NAFTA.[4] Thus, Brazilian steel, for instance, faced US safeguards while Mexican and Canadian steel did not. The message received was clear: RTAs can shield against questionable use of trade remedies. In fact, it was mercurial trade remedy usage by the US against Canada that propelled Canada toward NAFTA, which had initially been discussed as involving only Mexico and the US. Receiving improved treatment under US trade remedy provisions than provided for in the Canada-United States Free Trade Agreement (CUS-FTA, or sometimes the more phonetically appealing "CUFTA") was one of Canada's primary reasons for entering into NAFTA and was something they successfully achieved.

To Guard against Slowed Multilateral Liberalization

Another reason for RTAs is to promote liberalization, especially when multilateral trade negotiations are stalled, as has been the case in the DDA negotiations. Specifically, the discord exhibited at a DDA meeting in Cancún in 2003 seems to have made countries more interested in RTAs. For example, Australian prime minister John Howard cited the "glacial pace" of liberalization in the WTO as one rationale for Australia pursuing bilateral free trade agreements.[5] Australia is not alone in this line of thinking. Nor is it alone in acting upon it. As then candidate Bill Clinton said of NAFTA in 1992, "While we don't know what will happen to these other regional trading blocs [the EU and "yen" bloc], we know enough to know that we need stronger ties to our neighbors, both for the positive opportunity and to protect us in the event that other countries become more protectionist."[6]

To Increase Support for Multilateral Liberalization

As former US trade representative Robert Zoellick put it, promoting "competitive liberalization" was a key reason the US shifted toward bilateral

RTAs. The logic behind this strategy was that as more countries signed liberalizing RTAs with the US, others would be compelled to also form liberalizing RTAs with the US. As this network of liberalization spread, multilateral liberalization would become more palatable to these countries because they would have already made difficult choices in liberalizing their trade regimes relative to one of their most significant trading partners.

To Achieve "WTO-Plus" Levels of Liberalization

Some countries want liberalization beyond what the WTO has currently established, and joining together with like-minded countries for deeper liberalization is much quicker than waiting for the multilateral system to increase its liberalization. On some issues, it does not take much to move to deeper levels of liberalization than offered by the WTO: intellectual property rights (IPRs), trade in services, and coverage of the so-called Singapore issues. Many developed countries argue the WTO's level of protection for IPRs such as patents and copyrights is insufficient. Trade in services is far less liberalized in the WTO than trade in goods, and those RTAs that include services—more common in 1990s onward–era RTAs—tend to go well beyond the WTO standards set in the General Agreement on Trade in Services (GATS), established under the Uruguay Round of WTO negotiations. The so-called Singapore issues—trade and investment (e.g., policies on foreign investment), trade and competition policy (e.g., antitrust laws), transparency in government procurement (e.g., anticorruption laws), and trade facilitation (e.g., customs administration)—are areas where WTO rules are insufficiently liberal, according to many developed nations.[7] For more on these subjects, see "RTA Variation: IPRs—TRIPS Plus or Minus?" and "RTA Variation: Services—GATS Plus or Ignored?"

To Solidify Domestic Reforms

Often a country's leadership knows it needs to liberalize the economy but cannot successfully create the political support needed to carry out these reforms. RTAs offer a way to change the political support for reform within a country. For example, Mexican president Carlos Salinas de Gortari—who proposed NAFTA—had already taken significant steps toward liberalizing the Mexican economy. He met with much success in his drive to reform Mexico's economy, but full liberalization in some industries—textiles and apparel, for instance—dragged because of domestic opposition. Salinas used NAFTA to change the political equation. NAFTA linked further liberalization of the Mexican textile and apparel industry with greater access to the US textile and apparel market—an issue that had wider support within the Mexican textile and apparel industries and in Mexico more broadly.

Some have argued that China's entry into the WTO was used in a similar manner by Chinese leaders.[8] Reforms—such as modernizing China's legal system and diminishing provincial and local leaders' ability to capriciously and corruptly impose taxes, make regulations, and restrict trade *within* China—were actions the Chinese leadership had been calling for but had difficulty obtaining due to resistance from provincial and local leaders. These same provincial leaders, however, also recognized the benefits of WTO membership, which included better and more stable access to foreign markets. For China to successfully obtain WTO membership, it needed to ensure that regulations on taxation, the distribution of goods, and numerous other matters were transparent to companies (and their governments) exporting to or investing in China.

But using accession to the multilateral pressure such as the WTO to foster domestic reforms is not quick. China's WTO entry took more than 15 years and required every other WTO member to be satisfied with its adherence to WTO rules during the phase-in period for those rules. Most countries could and do complete this process more rapidly—typically it takes less than five years—but it is always the case that any one WTO member has the right to withhold support and stop the accession process. RTAs offer a more rapid and manageable way of achieving the same objective.

To Increase Competitiveness in World Markets

Increasing competitiveness in world markets can sometimes be enhanced through regional production strategies. Central to this goal is to often include using cheap labor—as the US does with Mexico and as Western Europe does with Central Europe, Turkey, and North Africa. The model for this "integrated regional production" is to use the capital-intensive high-skill portion of production in a developed nation and the lower-skill portion where wages are less expensive. In other words, RTAs may enhance companies' ability to "source globally, produce regionally, and sell locally."[9] China is increasingly interested in achieving stable sources of inputs for its massive industrial production boom, and RTAs assist in this goal.

Critics argue that regional production leads to exploitation in developing countries and places downward pressure on wages in wealthy countries, thus also weakening labor unions and the rights they promote. Supporters argue that greater efficiency means regional production can more effectively compete in an increasingly global economy and that without regional production, manufacturing jobs would still flow out of relatively wealthy countries and the so-called exploited workers in poor countries would find themselves jobless.

To Increase Clout in International Negotiations

There are two ways in which countries join an RTA to increase negotiating clout. The first is by pooling representation. Countries in an RTA can have more clout in international negotiations than the countries would have separately, assuming the RTA is sufficiently integrated and cohesive. In fact, it is quite common that poorer countries cannot send permanent representatives to the secretariats of important multilateral organizations such as the WTO or to some other important negotiations. An RTA can help countries' clout by creating institutionalized channels for coordinating RTA representation at other institutions or in other negotiations. The importance of banding together for greater international clout is particularly true of smaller and poorer states. They often view such coordinated action as a necessity. Examples include the 15 CARICOM states in the Caribbean and the 14 Pacific Island countries (PIC) of the Pacific Island Forum (PIF).[10]

Being in an RTA or ongoing RTA negotiations also creates a degree of negotiation enhancement in other negotiations. How so? Countries in an RTA may be able to claim the RTA is a plausible alternative to other negotiations, should those other negotiations not go well. This may change the negotiating power of the countries, or at least change perceptions about that negotiating power. How so? If one is negotiating about the price of a car, it will be a different negotiation if one walks rather than drives to the dealership. The car buyer who drives to the dealership has greater credibility to "walk away" from a bad deal. Importantly, the car salesperson knows this. Like the car buyer who drives to the dealership, the country with an RTA will appear less desperate, other things being equal. This line of thinking was seemingly at work after the Asia Pacific Economic Cooperation forum (APEC) announced it was moving toward freer trade at a time when the EU had been resisting further agricultural liberalization needed to complete the then-stalled Uruguay Round GATT negotiations. One month later, European negotiators softened their position and attributed their change to APEC's new and credible ambition, saying it "showed us you had an alternative that we did not."[11]

It should be noted, however, that RTA membership also constrains a member country's freedom to choose its negotiating strategy. Examples of this abound. One week before the 2006 annual EU-Russia summit, Poland prevented a united EU negotiating stance with Russia over a new framework for EU-Russian relations. Some of Poland's concerns were local—it wanted to delay the framework agreement until Russia lifted bans on Polish meat and plant imports—while other concerns were broader; Poland wanted the EU to require Russia to open its energy markets significantly before agreeing to a new EU-Russia framework.[12] No matter the motivation, Poland's position limited the array of possible negotiating positions for the other EU members.

The EU's position in the DDA negotiations provides another example. Germany and Great Britain would readily jettison EU farm subsidies in exchange for greater access to industrial markets abroad, but to do so, they have to convince France. The EU's top trade negotiator, Great Britain's Peter Mandelson, was publicly chastised by French officials for suggesting a greater willingness to abandon EU agriculture support than they felt he had been mandated. Mandelson may have knowingly gone beyond his mandate in a calculated effort to move the French, and therefore EU, position. France's public reprimand of Mandelson also highlights the increased complexity required to coordinate among RTA members attempting to jointly negotiate.

Sometimes the call for integration is intended to increase clout in a more diffuse way, not attached to any specific set of negotiations. An important rationale for the African Union given by AU Commission chairman Jean Ping is for a stronger voice for Africa more generally. Africa "is divided by 165 borders into 53 countries. Even the voice of a larger country like Nigeria or South Africa by itself is inaudible in international negotiations on world trade or climate change. But collectively it's impossible to ignore 53 countries with almost one billion inhabitants."[13]

To Achieve Economic Stability

Unstable economies hope to gain stability by forming RTAs with more stable economies. Typically, this means developing countries forming an RTA with developed countries, although it has been an increasing trend to see developing countries form RTAs with other developing countries. Some of the sought-after stability may come from increased market access and investment, and some may come from having a larger economic pool; larger bodies of water take longer to change temperature when the weather changes and thus fluctuate less than smaller bodies of water. Certainly the EU's newer entrants have seen greater levels of economic stability since membership. Currency stability has been the primary goal behind the monetary integration of the Central African franc zone (CFA franc zone), which consists of two regions: the Economic and Monetary Community for Central Africa (CAEMC), and the West Africa Economic and Monetary Union (WAEMU) and the Comoros.

To Meet Other Strategic Goals

Countries enter into RTAs for reasons having little to do with economic integration. The US has called for bilateral RTAs across the Middle East and, by 2013, the formation of the Middle East Free Trade Agreement. Why? This is part of a broader initiative. The George W. Bush administration proposed the US-Middle East Initiative (MEPI) in 2002, of which economic success in the region, fostered by economic integration and the liberalization it brings, is one pillar.[14] Why, then, this broader initiative? The Bush administration hoped to spread economic liberalization and democracy to the Middle East (and assumed they go together). Moreover, it wanted the US to be perceived by those in the Middle East as having altruistic goals, not just the goals of oil and Israel's survival, as is commonly believed in the region.

The European Union seeks trade agreements with North African and Middle Eastern countries for many reasons, some of which are altruistic. One reason—even before the riots in France over treatment of Muslims and across Europe over the Danish Muhammad cartoons—is the hope that stronger economies in North Africa and the Middle East will slow future immigration. The strategic goals that drive RTAs are varied, but it is clear that they are an essential reason that countries seek RTAs.

CONTROVERSIES ABOUT RTAs

The many controversies about RTAs can be categorized by the perspectives from which the criticism emerged. There are three broad schools of thought associated with divergent criticism of RTAs: economic liberalism, economic nationalism, and the critical IPE perspective—which is associated with the antiglobalization movement, which is, in turn, associated with economic structuralism or economic radicalism. A brief understanding of these three schools of thought is necessary to understand the debates associated with RTAs, and a brief overview of each school of thought is given directly before coverage of the RTA controversies associated with it.[15]

RTA Controversies Associated with Economic Liberalism

Economic liberalism is associated with Adam Smith and generally believes in markets and relatively little government intervention in the economy: the government's primary role should be to enforce contracts and to prevent or correct market failures. Economic liberals themselves hotly debate the proper scope of government intervention in the economy but generally call for government to prevent anticompetitive business practices (e.g., prevent monopolies), prevent abuses that flow from asymmetrical information (ranging from insider trading to lemon laws), and ensure that various public goods are provided (lighthouses, firefighters, police, education, and national defense). Core to economic liberals is the general belief in the efficacy of the "hidden

hand" of the market. Nevertheless, economic liberalism also includes those
who call for somewhat wider government intervention in the economy than
the laissez-faire economics of Adam Smith. John Maynard Keynes, who
called for government intervention to minimize the swings of the business
cycle, therefore also falls within economic liberalism.

In trade, economic liberalism stresses gains that flow from economies
focusing on what they do *relatively* most efficiently, as described by David
Ricardo's theory of comparative advantage. Absolute advantage is easy to
understand: Canada and tropical countries are both better off by specializ-
ing in what they are efficient at producing—wheat for Canada and bananas
for tropical countries—and trading with one another than if Canada tried to
produce its own bananas and tropical countries their own wheat. One can
envision the massive number of greenhouses on the Canadian prairie in what
are now wheat fields to understand the scale of inefficiency. Comparative
advantage is a bit more difficult to understand. It too calls for specialization,
but specialization should be in areas in which a country is *relatively* more
efficient. This is why a surgeon who also happens to be an excellent typist is
better off hiring an assistant to turn his or her dictation into written medical
records. The surgeon has an absolute advantage in both surgery and typing
compared to the assistant, but the difference in efficiency between the surgeon and the assistant is enormous in surgery, while the efficiency difference
in typing is modest. Both the surgeon and the assistant are better off economically if they specialize in what they are relatively better at and "trade" with
each other. The surgeon can see more patients and generate sufficient income
to pay the salary of the assistant and then some. Notice that the surgeon is
gaining more than the assistant in economic terms, but also notice that the
assistant does not have to perform surgery on his or her own family members.
Rather he or she can specialize to earn money to exchange for competency
in surgery. Society as a whole benefits from the greater efficiency that trade
brings: the surgeon can see more patients and keep the cost of surgery down
compared to a world in which surgeons do their own typing.

From the perspective of economic liberalism free trade is, then, in the aggregate an unquestioned benefit for participants. Because countries do not
open all their borders to all trade, these barriers to trade reduce overall welfare enormously. To economic liberals, the fewer the barriers there are to free
trade, the better the overall welfare. Freer trade may harm some in the short
term (and fewer still in the longer term), but far more will be helped. Besides
some of the more obvious advantages to trade—a larger market for producers to sell into and greater consumer choice—there are less obvious benefits,
such as greater efficiency from increased competition, reduced inflation, and
greater economies of scale.[16]

The most efficient path to free trade is multilateral trade liberalization, where numerous countries lower their barriers to trade and let comparative advantage go to work. Where do RTAs fit into the multilateral system, and what impact do they have on the natural efficiency? RTAs, after all, lower barriers to trade among participants, so doesn't this allow for comparative advantage to work? To a point, yes; RTAs do lead to trade creation—greater efficiencies flowing from reduced barriers to trade. But RTAs are clearly a second-best alternative to multilateral free trade in terms of efficiency, and thus RTAs also lead to trade diversion—production patterns set because of RTA trade rules, not because of natural comparative advantage among a larger group of nations. With trade creation, as trade barriers are removed among RTA members, inefficient domestic production is replaced by more imports by efficient production from other RTA members. With trade diversion, the inefficient domestic production is still replaced, but it is not replaced by the most efficient foreign production found in non-RTA member countries, but rather by the somewhat more efficient production from other RTA members.[17] In other words, increased trade in an RTA may not stem from greater efficiency and specialization from lower barriers to trade, but instead may be trade diverted from elsewhere simply because trade rules are less restrictive among RTA members than between the RTA members and the rest of the world. A hypothetical example with Canada producing its own bananas illustrates this trade creation and trade diversion. In the extreme, Canada without any trade must produce its own bananas. This would obviously be extremely inefficient. If Canada were in an RTA with only the US, it would have overall economic gains by importing bananas from the US, which has more efficient banana production (thanks to Hawaii), and it could concentrate its production more fruitfully elsewhere.[18] This is trade creation. Trade diversion compares the above situation—an efficiency improvement compared to domestic Canadian banana production—to the *most* efficient possibility. Canada would be better off still if it imported bananas from the world's most efficient producers, found in Latin America. But because of the hypothetical RTA, Canada has lower barriers to trade with the US and thus consumes Hawaiian bananas. With this trade diversion, Canada is less well off economically than it would be if it were open to Latin American bananas.

Given both trade creation and trade diversion, do RTAs promote or hinder free trade? Or, as one scholar memorably put it, are RTAs building blocks to free trade or stumbling blocks?[19] The answer also depends upon administrative burdens created in RTAs and the political capital and energy consumed by—or created by—RTAs. Those economic liberals answering "stumbling blocks" are deeply suspicious of RTAs because they fear RTAs will harm the multilateral trading system and the free trade it represents through additional administrative hurdles, trade diversion, and "political diversion"—diverting the energy and political capital necessary to keep multilateralism moving forward to RTA negotiations. Those economic liberals answering "building blocks" believe that RTAs can build political support for multilateral trade and can establish trade policy standards in new areas of trade that are not yet sufficiently covered by the WTO.

Ardent free traders have sometimes been accused of being evangelical in their devotion to the religion of free trade. "Fundamentalist" free traders have always viewed regional trade agreements (RTAs) as sinful because they divert trade from its most efficient or "godly" path to less natural paths established by governments through politics, the equivalent to "pagan worship." Yet some free trade proponents have dissented from this fundamentalist free trade line, largely on pragmatic grounds. The pragmatist free traders argue that one can never be sure whether global trade barriers will continue to fall, so increasing free trade within a regional grouping promotes free trade overall. Indeed, many pragmatic free traders argue that free trade within regional groupings can help build support for multilateral free trade by building coalitions of countries willing to further liberalize their economies and by creating models upon which multilateral negotiations can build.

One argument that RTAs are building blocks to free trade relies on RTAs as incubators of trade policy norms in areas not yet covered or insufficiently covered by the WTO. For instance, important elements of the 1988 Canada-US FTA became central to the WTO's text that covered trade in services for the first time: the Uruguay Round's General Agreement on Trade in Services (GATS).[20]

Building block economic liberals who support RTAs emphasize that the recent wave of regionalism has been quite nondiscriminatory in comparison to RTAs from earlier eras. Thus some economic liberals—those who believe in the efficacy of free markets—have been less suspicious of modern RTAs than they would have been otherwise. Nevertheless, RTAs make economic liberals either nervous or more outwardly hostile. Why? The challenge they pose to the cherished WTO principle of nondiscrimination, also called most-favored-nation (MFN) status.

What is MFN and why is it under attack, according to many economic liberals? Most-favored-nation status requires WTO members to extend to other WTO members their lowest tariff level offered to any member (with exceptions). Thus, if Canada were to lower its tariffs on cars imported from India, that lower tariff rate would automatically be extended to all other WTO members. This rapidly expands liberalization around the globe and has led to significantly lower tariffs since the inception of the GATT/WTO system. RTAs are an allowed exception to MFN status in the WTO[21] under GATT Article XXIV. As RTAs expand in number, varied scope, and membership, they increasingly weaken MFN. For instance, a 2005 WTO consultative board report warns that the WTO's core principle of most-favored-nation (MFN) status has been severely endangered by RTAs (of all types).[22] The WTO has been concerned about RTAs for some time, but its concerns have become increasingly alarmist in recent years:

> When fully in line with WTO provisions, regional trade agreements (RTAs) can complement the strengthening and liberalization of world trade. But by discriminating against third countries and creating a complex network of trade regimes, such agreements pose systemic risk to the global trading system. Around 240 such agreements are currently in force and there could be close to 300 by 2005. A noteworthy development in this regard during the past year or so has been the pursuit and conclusion of regional agreements by some Asian countries that had previously eschewed them, notwithstanding the successful launching of new multilateral negotiations.[23]

There are three reasons that RTAs endanger the MFN principle: the number of RTAs, their increasing complexity, and their cross-cutting and varied memberships. While the precise number of RTAs currently in existence is uncertain, for reasons noted below, there is no question that the number of RTAs has increased significantly.

Between January 2005 and December 2006, 55 RTAs were notified to the WTO, raising the number of RTAs notified and in force to 214.[24] The number of RTAs in force but *not* notified is approximately 70, with approximately 30 more signed but not yet in force, approximately 65 under negotiation, and approximately 30 more proposed.[25] Thus, there are currently probably 300 RTAs. The WTO secretariat notes that if these are all implemented, there will be approximately 400 RTAs in 2010.[26] (A word of caution on these statistics: one cannot merely add the number of currently notified and in-force RTAs with those signed but not in force because some new agreements will supersede previously notified agreements. The EU's expansion from 15 to 25 members, for instance, repealed 65 RTAs on the WTO's list of ratified and in-force RTAs.[27]) The WTO secretariat calls the pace of RTA proliferation over the past decade "unprecedented" and, with the Doha Development Agenda (DDA) negotiations at a stalemate, interest in RTAs has increased.[28] While the precise number of RTAs is not known, no one disputes that the number of RTAs is high and rising.

Second, many of today's RTAs are more complex than earlier generations of RTAs, and there is a great deal of variation in the scope of RTAs. Some RTAs use so-called variable geometry, in which different members agree to different levels of integration according to their own needs. This may decrease pressure countries feel to sign an agreement they do not like; it gives them the option of signing a less-demanding version of the RTA. Without question, however, it adds complexity when member countries in an RTA have different provisions with different countries within an RTA. Even when variable geometry is not employed as an organizing principle, RTAs typically still have different provisions for different members. Few RTAs can survive negotiation and ratification in multiple domestic political systems without making exceptions to placate vulnerable or politically powerful industries. It has been said that a camel is a horse created by a committee; much the same thing can be said of RTAs.

RTAs vary enormously in their level of integration and in their complexity. Free trade agreements in goods are the most common, but many also include services. Provisions may address investment, cover intellectual property rights such as patents and copyrights, and have varied "rules of origin." Rules of origin (RoO) are trade provisions that determine whether a sufficient percentage of a given product was produced within a given RTA to allow the product to receive the RTA's tariff rate, presumably lower than the MFN tariff rate. One can imagine the immense challenge businesses and customs officials face having to learn multiple and very detailed rules of origin to know what tariff a given item will receive. For instance, an auto assembled in Mexico may or may not qualify as "North American" under NAFTA. It must have 63.5 percent North American content—with precise rules about what aspects of production count in the origin calculations and whether these will be rounded up at various prefinal assembly steps of production—in order to be considered North American. Other autos coming into the US market may receive favorable (yet different) tariff treatment under other agreements, but using different RoO. Other RoO may also apply for other purposes. US Corporate Average Fuel Economy (CAFE) regulations require automakers to meet mileage standards on both their domestic production and their foreign production that is imported into the US. To determine whether production is domestic or foreign for CAFE purposes, yet another RoO is used. The confusion from multiple agreements does not end when products are brought into a country. If there is a dispute over trade rules, countries may adjudicate the disagreement in multiple settings. For instance, the US and Canada took their softwood lumber dispute to the dispute resolution mechanisms of both NAFTA and the WTO.

Cross-cutting membership in RTAs is the third reason RTAs pose an increasing challenge to MFN status. Cross-cutting RTA membership is when some, but not all, members of a regional group form a bilateral or regional FTA with countries outside their group, while other countries in the grouping do not. The result is that there are different trade rules for different countries within an RTA. Given the number of RTAs and the number of RTAs engaging in RTAs with other countries or groups of countries, again, the situation is confusing and thus a challenge to MFN. Africa provides the best examples of the cross-membership tangle: in 2004 only six of 53 African countries were in only one RTA, with 26 countries being in two RTAs, 20 countries in three, and one country in four.[29] Figure 2.1, "African RTA Spaghetti Venn Diagram"—which shows a *simplified* version of overlapping membership in African RTAs—demonstrates this complexity.

The sum of these challenges has led the WTO Consultative Board Report to lament that "MFN is no longer the rule; it is almost the exception." The report blames the "'spaghetti bowl' of customs unions, common markets, regional and bilateral free trade areas, preferences and an endless assortment of miscellaneous trade deals." For instance, the EU's array of trade agreements is so extensive that its MFN tariffs are fully applicable to only nine countries.[30] Thus the WTO Consultative Body Report calls for the DDA to reduce tariff barriers and nontariff barriers in order to minimize RTA-created market distortions and confusion.[31]

Given the role that multilateralism plays in minimizing the negative effects of RTAs, the floundering DDA is doubly problematic according to economic liberals. If the DDA negotiations fail—as well they might; they were suspended in July 2006—look for a dramatic rise in RTAs of all sorts. Rodrigo de Rato, managing director of the International Monetary Fund, and Paul Wolfowitz, former president of the World Bank, succinctly described the interactions between RTAs and multilateralism in their call for the completion of the stalled DDA:

> Blockage of the multilateral process will trigger an even more pronounced shift toward bilateral or regional free trade agreements (FTAs). FTAs cannot substitute for multilateral liberalization. If properly designed, they can benefit their members, especially if combined with reduced trade barriers for all trading partners. If designed badly, the cost of such agreements—in terms of trade diversion, confusion and demands on limited administrative capacity—often exceeds the benefits. More broadly, the growth of FTAs undermines the central principle of the multilateral trading system: trade opportunities should be offered to all countries equally.[32]

Thus, despite the hesitation expressed by economic liberals, interest in RTAs of all sorts shows no signs of slowing and is likely to continue.

RTA Controversies Associated with Economic Nationalism

Controversies surrounding RTAs also flow from the economic nationalist perspective. Economic nationalism calls for a more robust intervention in the economy in order to ensure that production and employment are maximized and that states maximize their economic autonomy and security. Specifically, economic nationalists stress that comparative advantage is dynamic and that government policies can alter comparative advantage; policies can concentrate expertise and resources so that a given country's producers can become *relatively* more efficient than producers elsewhere. Economist nationalists note that economic liberalism is fragile and dependent upon the security of nation-states and therefore upon the international political system.

A little trade diversion is fine as long as it helps one's balance of trade. Economic nationalism stresses the benefits of exports—and the jobs, national wealth, and industrial strength that come with them—over imports—which are often seen as lowering jobs, wealth, and industrial strength. Economic liberals care about a negative balance of trade only when it becomes unsustainable.

RTA Controversies Associated with the Antiglobalization Movement, Including Economic Structuralism/Radicalism

Antiglobalization criticisms of RTAs are diverse but include a significant skepticism of the efficacy of markets. More specifically, antiglobalization criticisms of RTAs echo criticism of the global economic order and particularly focus on the massive inequality—between and within countries—that prevails and, in their view, is perpetuated by globalization. This school of thought is sometimes characterized as leftist, and certainly there are communists within the school of thought, and the concern about capitalism's inequality is rooted in the thinking of Karl Marx. Some dismiss this school of thought because of its links, however distant, to communism. These critics ignore that much of the school of thought does not call for communism. Rather this school of thought argues that the international economic structure—its markets, institutions, and laws—unfairly favor the wealthy over the poor. There are variations among economic structuralists in their views about the primary mechanism of inequality—international finance, trade rules, intellectual property rights rules, ineffective labor rights, or others—and about the primary beneficiaries of the exploitation—corporations, consumers, classes, or countries. But they are united by their skepticism of markets and their belief that free market globalization is inherently unfair and exploitative.

Many in this camp argue that RTAs do too much to perpetuate the worst elements of globalization and facilitate corporations escaping domestic rules designed to protect the public. For instance, too often RTAs facilitate what economists call competition in laxity—where corporations produce in whichever jurisdiction offers them the most lax regulatory framework for them to pollute and pay low wages. Many on the left also complain that RTAs do not facilitate economic development, even when they successfully facilitate economic growth. Growing more food for export might earn more hard currency for a country—an important goal—but it also might decrease the number of poor people with access to land and thus increase hunger for subsistence farmers. This is not a recipe for economic development.

It is not surprising that RTAs' influence on trade and investment can be significant, and thus their effect on employment and development is often considerable. Since the early 1990s RTAs' influence on issues that used to be considered separately from RTAs—the environment, labor rights, and human rights are prominent examples—has received more attention from activists, scholars, corporations, and governments.

Another related controversy in RTAs is that developing nations have less bargaining power relative to developed nations than in multilateral negotiations. Jagdish Bhagwati, the most prominent proponent of the multilateral trading system and a leading economically liberal voice against RTAs, argues that developing nations negotiating bilaterally tend to get worse deals.[33] For instance, bilateral and regional RTAs between developed and developing countries—so-called north-south RTAs—more likely include the so-called Singapore issues than in previous multilateral north-south negotiations.[34] The Singapore issues are of no interest to developing nations at best, and many developing nations are openly hostile about the Singapore issues. Examples of both the Singapore issues and of developing countries receiving worse deals than they would get in a multilateral setting can be found in US bilateral agreements in the Americas. The US insisted on stronger intellectual property rights (IPR) protections in its RTAs with Central and South American countries (in the CAFTA and various bilateral FTAs) than it has achieved—or realistically could achieve—at the multilateral level. This is echoed in negotiations on trade in services in RTAs compared to WTO multilateral services negotiations. South-south RTAs have lower levels of liberalization in services trade than do south-north RTAs. South-south RTAs services liberalization tends to be close to that found in the WTO's General Agreement on Trade in Services (GATS), while north-south RTAs are more likely to be GATS plus—offering greater liberalization than found in GATS—suggesting that richer countries, which called for trade in services to be included in the WTO in the first place, are better able to win arguments in the RTA setting than in the multilateral setting.[35]

Many RTA critics fear excessive privatization of what are currently government services. They fear that RTAs that cover trade in services—increasingly common in modern-era RTAs—will create an additional venue for the privatization of basic services such as water, delivery, health care, and education. Furthermore, they complain there is an element of stealth in services privatization through RTAs because it is not always clear services will be covered in services trade and which will be excluded, depending upon how language in a given RTA is interpreted by member governments and by any dispute mechanism system set up by that RTA. These criticisms are leveled both at RTAs' and the WTO's efforts to liberalize trade through the General Agreement on Trade in Services (GATS). Liberals argue efforts to liberalize trade in services are, if anything, inadequate because GATS signatories choose for themselves what services they will offer for what level of liberalization. Moreover, liberals argue that there are specific provisions in the GATS excluding coverage for government services. Specifically, GATS excludes services that are considered "supplied in the exercise of governmental authority," meaning they are supplied on a noncommercial basis and do not have competition with other suppliers. Examples of this are police, fire, mandatory social security systems, and administering tax and customs policy.[36] Structuralist critics argue once an agreement is signed and implemented, the meaning of such language may be reinterpreted to allow for additional privatization, which has, in any case, gone too far already. Their fears of privatization include privatization's alleged overvaluing efficiency at the expense of equality—for instance, will all regions receive services, or only more profitable regions; will service prices be affordable for the poor?—and they fear insufficient citizen control over the services provided and the governance of the service providers.

TYPOLOGY OF RTAs AND OTHER ECONOMIC AGREEMENTS

The language used to describe regional trade agreements (RTAs) can be confusing because it is used inconsistently and with varying levels of precision. The term *regional trade agreement* reminds one of the memorable description of the Holy Roman Empire: it was neither holy, nor Roman, nor an empire. Regional trade agreements are not (necessarily) regional, nor are they solely, or even primarily, about trade, and RTAs are often an agreement on paper more than in reality. Another term used to describe the same sort of agreements—free trade agreements (FTAs)—is a similarly misleading term: FTAs may or may not promote free trade. Because FTAs have a specific meaning in economics and because the term is value laden (who would be against freedom?), the term *regional trade agreement* will be used to broadly include all types of economic integration agreements that grant some level of preference beyond MFN for their members.[37] This includes nonreciprocal preferential trade agreements, noncomprehensive free trade agreements, free trade agreements, customs unions, common markets, monetary unions, and political unions, all of which can be between two or more countries that may or may not be within a region. See box 1.2, "Levels of RTA Integration," and table 1.1, "Functions Performed by Various RTA Types (Ideal Types)." While most observers include only full monetary union (a shared currency and central bank) and formal exchange rate unions (multiple currencies and central banks with virtually no currency fluctuation) in the category of "monetary unions," there are other levels of monetary integration with trade-offs involving autonomy, credibility, and coordination difficulties, as demonstrated in table 1.2, "Types of Monetary Integration."

BOX 1.2. LEVELS OF RTA INTEGRATION

1. *Nonreciprocal preferential trade agreements*—Unilateral trade preferences given by more developed countries to developing countries, typically as part of the General System of Preferences.
2. *Sectoral preferential trading arrangements*, also called *partial scope preferential trade agreements*—These agreements give preferential tariff rates between two or more countries in a limited number of sectors.
3. *Free trade agreement, or free trade area (FTA)*—FTAs include the removal of tariffs and other trade restrictions on a comprehensive array of either goods, services, or both. FTAs are more likely to be on goods than services. FTAs do have exceptions; some have so many exceptions that they look a lot like partial-scope preferential trade agreements/sectoral preferential trade arrangements. *Comprehensive FTAs* include removal of tariffs and other trade restrictions in goods, services, and investment.
4. *Customs unions (CU)*—Remove tariffs and other trade restrictions, as with an FTA, but also adopt a *common external tariff (CET)* and harmonized trade regulations for imports coming from outside of the CU. For instance, there are EU-wide tariffs on imports from a given non-EU country. An exporter of a given product will face the same EU tariff no matter where in the EU the product enters. Again, there are exceptions in CUs, and again, there may be a CU for goods or services or both.
5. *Common* market—FTA in goods, services, investment, and labor. It eliminates internal trade barriers that limit trade (or mobility) of goods, services, investment, and labor. Again, there are always exceptions. In its fullest form—called a *single market*—member countries harmonize all laws and regulations that affect market prices. In practical terms, this is difficult; even economic relations within one country have difficulty living up to this standard. For instance, in the US, some, but not all, states allow wine to be mailed from other states. Alcohol and gasoline taxes vary widely from state to state, and there are different formulas for gasoline in different regions.

6. *Economic* union—This is a common market in which economic institutions are unified by supranational policymaking institutions to promote economic policy coordination.

7. *Monetary* union—In its fullest form, a monetary union includes two or more countries with a single currency and a single central bank. There are, however, other levels of monetary integration. (See table 1.2, "Types of Monetary Integration," for more.)

8. *Political* union—Political decision making is primarily at the supranational level.

Source: Entries 1–7 are adapted from Mari Pangestu and Sudarshan Gooptu, "New Regionalism: Options for China and East Asia," *East Asia Integrates*, World Bank, June 2003.

Note: The lineage of typologies such as that in entries 1–7 is long indeed. Some typologies of RTAs would exclude categories 1 and 2 from being classified as "RTAs" because of the insufficient integration they bring. They are included here because they typically move beyond MFN, albeit unilaterally, in a limited number of economic sectors or for a limited volume of trade (or with all of these qualifications). Pangestu and Gooptu categorize a single market distinctly from a common market. Others, such as Glania and Matthes, have an intermediate stage between a CU and common market, called a *common economic area*, where "rules and technical standards are partially aligned." Guido Glania and Jurgen Matthes, *Multilateralism or Regionalism? Trade Policy Options for the European Union* (Brussels: Centre for European Policy Studies, 2005), 5. Note that the *fiscal union* category (complete nondiscrimination and equality in the tax treatment of people and companies from other RTA members) used by Pangestu and Gooptu is subsumed within the *economic union* category for practical purposes.

Non-RTA Economic Agreements: Economic Cooperation Agreements and Framework Agreements

There are also numerous types of agreements that fall short of being an RTA. One set of non-RTA economic agreements fall under the heading of economic cooperation agreements. Included within this rubric—also sometimes called trade and economic agreements—are treaties and other agreements that encourage trade or investment between two or more countries, establish most-favored-nation status, and specify customs or other similar trade facilitation rules. These agreements are aimed at fostering economic cooperation, not economic integration. Often, they aim at cooperation in just one economic sector. Increasingly common examples are bilateral agreements on investment—called bilateral investment treaties (BITs) by the US—or bilateral agreements on intellectual property rights (IPRs). The US has BITS with nearly 40 countries and bilateral IPR agreements with 19 countries.[38]

Table 1.1. Functions Performed by Various RTA Types (Ideal Types)

RTA Type \ Function:	Tariffs and Barriers Removed/ Reduced in Some Sectors	Tariffs and Barriers Removed/ Reduced in Most Sectors	Common External Tariff (CET)	Eliminate Barriers to Goods, Services, Capital, and Labor	Supranational Policymaking Institution(s) to Promote Economic Policy Coordination	Monetary Union: A Single Currency and Central Bank	Political Decision Making Is Primarily at the Supranational Level
Partial-Scope or Preferential Trade Agreement (PTA)	✓						
Free Trade Agreement FTA	✓	✓					
Customs Union (CU)	✓	✓	✓				
Common Market	✓	✓	✓	✓			
Economic Union	✓	✓	✓	✓	✓		
Monetary Union	✓	✓	✓	✓	✓	✓	
Political Union	✓	✓	✓	✓	✓	✓	✓

Table 1.2. Types of Monetary Integration

	Separate or Shared Currencies (and Central Banks)?	Degree and Method of Currency Parity	Example	Level of Symmetry	Coordination
Informal Exchange Rate Union	Separate currencies and central banks	Rates fluctuate in (relatively) wide margins. Margins can be changed. Central parity can be changed.	European Monetary System's Exchange Rate Mechanism (ERM) after August 1993.	Symmetry varies	Bilateral or multilateral, depending upon the number of members
Formal Exchange Rate Union	Separate currencies and central banks	Rates fluctuate in narrow or zero margins.	Common Monetary Area (CMA) in Southern Africa	Symmetry varies	Bilateral or multilateral
Full Monetary Union	One currency and central bank	N/A, one currency	Eurozone, CFA franc zones Eastern Caribbean dollar	Symmetry varies	Bilateral or multilateral
Adoption of Another Country's Currency	One currency and central bank	N/A, one currency	Panama, El Salvador, and Ecuador have "dollarized"	Completely asymmetrical	Unilateral
Currency Board	Two currencies, but, in effect, one central bank in the "adoptee's" country	Pegged to another country's currency with handcuffs: supply of local currency matches reserves held in the other currency.	Bulgaria Djibouti Estonia	Completely asymmetrical	Unilateral

Source: Paul R. Masson and Catherine Pattillo, *Monetary Geography of Africa* (Washington, DC: Brookings, 2003), 2, www.brookings.edu/views/papers/masson/20030410.htm. See also Benjamin J. Cohen, *The Geography of Money* (Ithaca: Cornell University Press, 1998).

Non-RTA Economic Agreements: Framework Agreements

Also within the non-RTA economic agreements category are framework agreements, which are agreements to explore or negotiate the formation of an RTA.[39] They establish the parameters of the negotiations and therefore, to some extent, the parameters of the eventual RTA. For instance, a framework agreement will say whether the signatories' subsequent negotiations will include services and investment or just goods. They also can give skeletal structure to other matters in negotiations, such as whether there should be special treatment for poorer signatories in the eventual regional trade agreement. Framework agreements commonly set out target dates to negotiate various elements of the eventual RTA. A framework agreement is no guarantee of success in the negotiations, and a country is free to not sign the RTA that emerges from the framework agreement. Framework agreements turn into future integration only if the countries' economic and political interests coalesce.

The US uses what it calls trade and investment framework agreements (TIFAs) to serve this purpose. TIFAs do not ensure that there will be an RTA formed; rather they set up the process to "establish whether there is sufficient agreement on goals to move forward on an FTA."[40] The US has 15 TIFAs with a total of 45 countries (some TIFAs are with groups of countries).[41] If no RTA is formed, the TIFA can itself be influential in fostering economic cooperation between the US and other countries.

Some economic cooperation agreements and framework agreements will also receive coverage in this book, but largely as their potential to lead to RTAs.

RTAs: Sectoral Preferential Trade Agreements

Sectoral preferential trade agreements are the first category of agreements that warrant inclusion in regional trade agreement rubric. These move toward integration because they grant greater than MFN status, but only in a single (or several) economic sector(s). Sectoral preferential trade agreements are also called *partial-scope preferential trade agreements* or *noncomprehensive free trade agreements* (although it should be noted that the latter often implies numerous economic sectors but excludes free trade in services). An example of a sector-specific integration agreement was the 1965 US-Canadian Auto Pact, which eliminated tariffs on auto trade between the US and Canada for qualifying production—production that met Canadian value added and other requirements—and led to increased bilateral auto trade and significantly increased integration of the US and Canadian auto markets.

The Importance of Economic Cooperation Agreements, Framework Agreements, and Sectoral Preferential Trade Agreements

Economic cooperation agreements, framework agreements, and sectoral preferential trade agreements vary in importance, but all can possibly be significant in two ways: their rules may directly encourage trade and investment, and they may build political and economic support that facilitates more comprehensive RTAs (or, conversely, create a political and economic backlash against greater integration). The US-Canadian Auto Pact influenced more trade than most comprehensive bilateral free trade agreements involving nonindustrialized countries. Another economic impact involves the dynamism that may be facilitated (or hindered) by economic cooperation agreements and sectoral-specific PTAs. Larger markets lead to larger economies of scale and thus to greater efficiency. Indeed, after the US-Canadian Auto Pact, Canadian automakers reduced the number of models produced but increased auto production. So too did the Auto Pact–qualifying companies producing in the US. Instead of making a given model in both the US and in Canada—which required duplicating many fixed costs—car companies could concentrate the production of a given model in the US *or* Canada and produce as many cars with fewer costs.[42] Just as comprehensive integration increases dynamism in a market by increasing competition and economies of scale, so too might economic cooperation agreements and sectoral-specific PTAs.

Second, economic cooperation agreements, framework agreements, and sectoral PTAs often pave the way for deeper cooperation and integration. How so? The changes needed in a developing nation to have a bilateral FTA with the US include granting US investment at least most-favored-nation status (treating US investment at least as favorably as investment from elsewhere). Thus a BIT with the US is like having one portion of a US FTA already agreed upon, notwithstanding that all issues can be revisited in future negotiations. Also, a BIT with the US demonstrates the will to make commitments that US policymakers consider essential to having a bilateral FTA with the US. A similar dynamic can be found with bilateral intellectual property rights agreements. The treatment of IPRs, like patents on medicines, is increasingly important to the US in its RTAs negotiations.

Nonreciprocal RTAs

Nonreciprocal RTAs involve one country unilaterally offering lower tariffs on trade for another country, usually a least-developed country and usually as part the General System of Preferences (GSP). These are a GATT/WTO-approved violation of the MFN principle and are created by each preference-granting country with sectoral coverage, depth, and specific preference-receiving membership varying. There are 13 countries with GSP programs officially notified to the UN Conference on Trade and Development (UNCTAD), which first established the GSP program in 1968 (counting the EU as one country).[43] In 1971 the GATT approved of a waiver to the MFN principle for the GSP, and in 1979 this waiver was made permanent.[44] The US and the EU have the most extensive GSP programs. Some programs are specific to a given region: the US offers the African Growth and Opportunity Act (AGOA), the Caribbean Basin Initiative (CBI), and the Andean Trade Preference Act (ATPA) as well as its nongeographic-specific GSP. The EU offers the Africa, Caribbean, Pacific-EU Partnership Agreement (ACP) for 78 countries, the Everything but Arms program for least-developed countries, and a GSP program. Nonreciprocal preferences do raise issues of "GATT compliance," which is to say, WTO rules. (See the discussion of the Africa, Caribbean, Pacific-EU Partnership Agreement in chapter 3 for more coverage on this point.)

Of the RTAs notified to the WTO, approximately 66 percent are FTAs on goods, and 15 percent are FTAs on services, with an additional 20 percent coming from the following three categories: customs unions, PTAs among developing nations, and accessions to existing agreements. RTAs moving to the level of customs unions are rare, as table 1.3, "Customs Unions Notified to the GATT/WTO," demonstrates. The vast majority of RTAs—80 percent—are bilateral.[45]

COMPARING RTAs/VARIATION IN RTAs

Besides the basic typologies about depth of integration, RTAs vary along numerous other fronts, and there are patterns that are more common in particular eras and in particular geographic regions. Recent RTAs are less likely to discriminate against third parties than in previous eras of RTAs. Asian RTAs are led by the desire for financial integration more than trade integration. Some African RTAs have high levels of monetary union but lower levels of trade integration. Both of these are not the typical order of integration. Newer RTAs are more likely to involve developing nations than in earlier eras. Newer RTAs are more likely to be comprehensive, that is, having coverage for trade in services, investment, and intellectual property rights.

Besides varying in depth of integration along the various categories, as explored above, RTAs vary in the degree to which they are comprehensive in their sectoral coverage and the degree to which they address related issues of economic and other governance. Following is some explanation of a few of the more important ways in which RTAs vary along these fronts.

Table 1.3. Customs Unions Notified to the GATT/WTO and in Force as of March 1, 2006

Acronym	Name of Customs Union	Entered into Force	Membership	
EC (now EU)	European Community	1958	In 1958, the members were the founders of what is now the EU: Belgium, Luxembourg, France, Germany, Italy, and the Netherlands. Now 27 members.	
EU-Andorra		1991	27 EU members and Andorra	
EU-Turkey		1996	27 EU members and Turkey	
CARICOM	Caribbean Common Market	1973	Antigua and Barbuda Bahamas* Barbados Belize Dominica Grenada Guyana Haiti Jamaica Montserrat	Saint Kitts and Nevis Saint Lucia Saint Vincent and the Grenadines Suriname Trinidad and Tobago
CACM	Central American Common Market	1961	Costa Rica, El Salvador, Guatemala, Honduras, and Nicaragua**	
MERCOSUR	Common Market of the South	1991	Argentina, Brazil, Paraguay, Uruguay, and Venezuela	

Source: WTO, "Regional Trade Agreements Notified to the GATT/WTO and in Force as of March 1, 2006," WTO website. There are other CUs in operation that have not been notified to the WTO.
* The Bahamas is a CARICOM member but does not take part in the Caribbean Community.
** There are other CACM members that take part in the CACM's political institutions but not its customs union.

RTA Variation: Market Size and Trade Intensity

RTAs vary greatly in their market size and in the intensity of their intra-RTA economic interactions. Economic interactions include trade, of course, but also include the movement of labor—both the legal and black market varieties—and investment. Sometimes RTA members may have massive markets but may not be significantly intertwined with one another's economies. One measurement of an RTA's trade weight is the overall level of exports from its members, as figure 1.1, "Selected African RTAs' Merchandise Exports," demonstrates. At the same time, however, this can be misleading for a number of reasons. First, the RTA may be dominated by

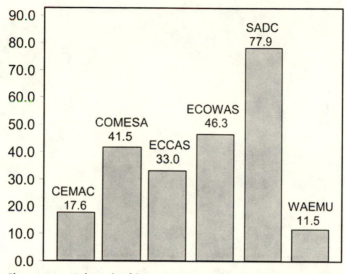

Figure 1.1. Selected African RTAs' Merchandise Exports, Billions of US$, 2004

a larger anchor nation within the RTA, as is the case in the SADC, which is dominated by South Africa, and in ECOWAS, which is dominated to a lesser extent by Nigeria. Second, high levels of RTA trade may not represent intense intra-RTA economic activity. Intra-RTA trade may comprise only a small percentage of an RTA's overall trade. The subsequent figure— figure 1.2, "Measuring RTA Depth (Intensity) and Width (Size)"—examines the extremes of both market size—measured by level of merchandise exports—and RTA trade intensity. The larger the circle is in the chart, the higher the RTA's level of overall merchandise exports. The higher and more to the right the circle, the higher the percentage of imports and exports, respectively, are with fellow RTA members. The European Union member nations set the standard for having both massive overall trade and high intra-RTA trade intensity. The Andean Community of Nations (CAN) is hardly visible, a sign of its low overall export levels, and is far to the left and bottom, a sign of low-intra RTA trade intensity.

RTA Variation: Degree of Institutionalism

RTA institutionalization—the formation of RTA organizations with the capacity to implement and, more strongly, to make decisions—varies enormously.

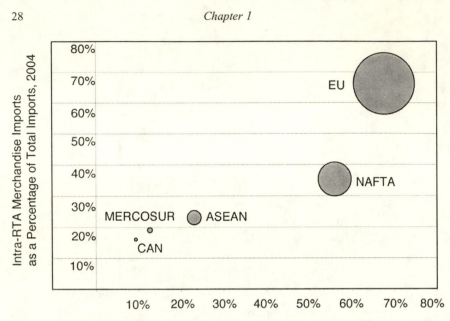

Intra-RTA Merchandise Exports as Percentage of Total Exports, 2004

Figure 1.2. Measuring RTA Depth (Intensity) and Width (Size), Intra-RTA Merchandise Imports and Exports, 2004
Key: See list of abbreviations.
Note: Depth (Intensity) = Intra-RTA merchandise trade as percentage of overall merchandise trade (X and Y axes)
Width (Size) = Overall merchandise exports (circle size)

There are numerous elements of institutionalization: resources, expertise, and legal authority are the most concrete; legitimacy—the belief that an organization rightfully has the authority to make and carry out decisions—is more abstract. Legitimacy flows from and leads to the other elements of institutionalization.

The European Union is the undisputed champion of RTA institutionalization, a point of pride and derision to EU backers and detractors, respectively. The number and scope of institutions in the EU is considerable, and many do have real decision-making power, although this is regularly checked by the EU member governments directly or through various other EU institutions. Real money flows to and from the various EU institutions, massively overshadowing any other RTA's budget. On some issues, the EU's institutionalization moves beyond intergovernmental to supranational, where the member governments have ceded a degree of their sovereignty in a given issue area. The EU, however, remains primarily intergovernmental, where governments keep a more direct check on EU authority.

Moreover, many deride EU institutionalization as overly "bureaucratic" in the pejorative sense of the word: inefficient, confusing, and meddling in matters best left to other levels of government or to private citizens. Some argue, in fact, that the EU is facing a legitimacy crisis, despite having high levels of legitimacy compared with other RTAs. The EU faces a so-called democratic deficit—a charge that EU decision making is too confusing and insufficiently accountable. EU citizens either cannot "throw the bums out," because they are unelected, or are not sure which bums to throw out. The EU's democratic deficit is a chronic problem that will require continual effort to sort out. Efforts to diminish the democratic deficit through the passing of the EU charter, sometimes called the EU's constitution, led to another crisis when voters in France and the Netherlands, two founding EU courtries, rejected the charter in referenda. It was renegotiated as the Lisbon Treaty, a charter with only slight variation to make it more palatable to EU voters. Even so, it had a tough time being ratified in EU member-nations: Ireland rejected it initially, and it took the financial crisis with the EU's financial assistance to make Irish voters support it. Lisbon's changes may minimize the democratic deficit somewhat, but few observers believe it will eliminate it. Despite these problems, the capacity of the EU institutions to act—however much hand wringing it causes—is significantly larger than that of other RTAs.

At the other end of the spectrum are RTAs with no permanent secretariat. With no staff to facilitate studies or help implement policies, national governments are left to do these tasks. They may or may not have the capacity—expertise and money—to make this work. RTAs with a weak secretariat may also be more tethered to national interests than those having a permanent secretariat.

RTA Variation: Dispute Resolution Mechanisms

RTAs vary in their dispute resolution mechanism, as indeed do all international agreements. In fact, many RTAs have varied dispute resolution mechanisms from issue to issue within a single RTA. Some RTAs' dispute resolution mechanisms are intentionally quite vague, leaving resolutions to be handled "politically"—through consultations by either heads of government or their representatives. A political or diplomatic-style dispute resolution body would have little independence from the states involved and could easily either block the process or allow it and block any possible sanctions that may come from the process. Many international organizations and RTAs in Asia have chosen these less formal mechanisms to resolve disputes.[46] Other RTAs have developed dispute resolution mechanisms that are far more detailed and more "judicialized" or "legalized," meaning that the dispute resolution process more closely resembles the court system in the domestic setting. This is a continuum. A legalized dispute resolution mechanism would have the dispute resolution body that resolves the dispute independent of the parties involved, following procedures that are known to all before a dispute arises, being difficult to block, and binding upon the parties involved. The dispute resolution body—a court or panel, for instance—could authorize or even mandate sanctions for violations of rules or noncompliance with rulings.[47] Many scholars have employed a simply typology across three criteria to determine depth of legalization: the degree to which rules are *obligatory*, the level of *precision* of those rules, and the level of *delegation* to a third party of the interpreting, monitoring, and implementing of these rules. More obligation, precision, and delegation create more legalization, also called hard legalization, while less obligation, precision, and delegation create less legalization, also called soft legalization.[48] Harder legalization implies that a given dispute resolution mechanism has teeth. See table 1.4, "Continuum of Diplomatic to Judicial Dispute Resolution Mechanisms."

The trend in the modern era of RTAs, as is the trend in the multilateral trading system, is toward the latter. The GATT's dispute resolution mechanism, which was in place from 1947 until the GATT was transformed into the WTO in 1995, was far toward the political/diplomatic end of the spectrum. Until the late 1980s, GATT rules allowed any one party to stop a complaint panel from being formed. That changed, but throughout the GATT's dispute resolution mechanism's tenure, any one party could stop punishment against any

Table 1.4.   Continuum of Diplomatic to Judicial Dispute Resolution Mechanisms (DRM)

	Diplomatic DRMs (soft legalization)	Judicial DRMs (hard legalization)
Political Independence of DRM	DRM comprising representatives of member governments.	DRM independent of member nations. Standing body of independent judges.
Legal Mandate of DRM	Governments negotiate a settlement. Nonbinding procedures.	Binding procedures result in legal recommendation, or more strongly, in a legal decision.
DRM Authority to Decide	Procedure and/or ruling can be blocked by parties involved.	Procedure and ruling cannot be blocked. Compulsory jurisdiction.
DRM Authority to Sanction	Sanctions can be blocked by recipient of sanctions.	Sanctions authorized and, more strongly, mandatory.

Source: Adapted from Bernhard Zangl, "Judicialization Matters! A Comparison of Dispute Settlement under GATT and the WTO," *International Studies Quarterly* (2008): 828.

noncompliance with a dispute panel ruling.[49] Clearly this dispute resolution mechanism was flawed, and thus the WTO's dispute resolution mechanism has been more robust: compliance with panel rulings is required unless all WTO members agree. The final appeals panel in the WTO consists of experts chosen by WTO members as a whole, not just the parties to a dispute, and they are chosen before any specific dispute arises. Moreover, the WTO can authorize the injured country to impose trade barriers of equivalent value against countries that have failed to comply with rulings. This created a dispute resolution process more closely resembling a domestic justice system than was the case under the GATT. Modern RTAs are more likely to have dispute resolution mechanisms that are more legalized than in previous eras of RTAs, but to be sure, they vary greatly along the political/diplomatic to legal/judicial continuum. Toward the less legalized end of the spectrum is APEC, with low levels of precision, obligation, and delegation, and toward the more legalized end of the spectrum are NAFTA and the EU. Even here there is variation in the nature of the legalization. NAFTA dispute resolution mechanisms—plural because they vary from issue area to issue area—tend to have high levels of precision and obligation but lower levels of delegation to third parties (panels and courts), while the EU has a great deal of obligation and delegation but has "moderate" level of precision.[50]

Another significant difference in RTAs' dispute resolution mechanisms is who has access to the process. Most international law is state to state; the only parties to it are countries, not their citizens nor any other entity wishing access. Some RTAs, however, allow "investor-to-state" access, in which companies may be parties to the dispute resolution mechanism. In contrast, a few also have limited citizen channels for input, but this is far short of true access because such systems, where they exist, typically include the government playing the gatekeeper role over who gets this limited input and even more control over whether a case can go forward or not (NAFTA's dispute resolution associated with environmental laws, for instance, allows public comment but little other input). Structuralist critics highlight how this creates unequal access to the dispute system: corporations having access and workers and/or citizens denied that access. And, with corporations being able to sue governments for noncompliance with an RTA, corporations have a venue with which to roll back policies set through more transparently democratic procedures.[51]

Economic liberals argue that there are legitimate reasons for such provisions. Because developing nations' legal systems are typically less robust than those of developed nations, property rights are more tenuous. Or, more negatively, many developing nations' legal systems are riddled with corruption, and a hearing based on simply the law is less than assured. Developed-country corporations often seek investment protections that go beyond those offered in developing nations' domestic courts. To those critical of globalization, these are viewed as an attempt by corporations to evade punishment for irresponsible and potentially illegal behavior such as pollution. To corporations, RTAs' dispute resolution mechanisms can shield them from capricious and often corrupt legal systems.

Controversies over NAFTA's various dispute resolution mechanisms exemplify the debate over access to the dispute resolution process and the increased legalization of dispute resolution. NAFTA's so-called Chapter 11 dispute resolution mechanism for investment has been the most controversial element of the NAFTA dispute resolution mechanisms (there are other dispute chapters for the financial sector, for trade remedies [anti-dumping and countervailing duties], environmental laws, and labor laws).[52] Mexico's willingness to agree to investment-specific dispute resolution mechanism provisions in Chapter 11 signaled it was eager to court foreign investment. To critics, Chapter 11 is a subversion of democracy because governments—local, state, and national—can be sued by corporations for violations of NAFTA's investment provisions. In the words of the anti-globalization activist group Public Citizen, the "investor-to-state" dispute resolution mechanism "empowers private investors and corporations to sue NAFTA-signatory governments in special tribunals to obtain cash compensation for government policies or actions that investors believe violate their new rights under NAFTA."[53]

Other elements of NAFTA's dispute resolution mechanism have been challenged as unconstitutional. US lumber producers filed suit in the US Court of Appeals in Washington, DC, claiming NAFTA's Chapter 19—a dispute resolution process that had ruled unfavorably toward the claims of US producers—was unconstitutional for a number of reasons, but primarily because its binational review panels that rule on trade remedies cannot (somewhat ironically) be challenged in US courts.[54] Despite these controversies, the NAFTA dispute provisions have become a template for other US trade negotiations.

RTA Variation: The Degree of Discrimination toward Nonmembers

At one end of the spectrum, some RTAs attempt to avoid discrimination as much as possible. The Asia Pacific Economic Cooperation Forum (APEC), for instance, follows "open regionalism," which is designed to support multilateralism by the "extension of regionally agreed preference to all . . . WTO members."[55] Many more RTAs, however, do strongly distinguish between members and nonmembers and do so through highly restrictive rules of origin (RoO).

RTA Variation: Rules of Origin (RoO)

Rules of origin are rules that determine which products receive preferential treatment in an RTA. At a minimum, many RTAs' rules of origin require complex administrative gymnastics for businesses and governments alike. Others attribute more sinister motivations behind complex RoO: to more effectively discriminate against nonmembers. Whatever their motivation, RoO surely have added enormous complexity to world trade.

Variation in Types of RoO

There are massive variations in RoO between RTAs and even within a single RTA. Rules of origin may be sectoral, be product specific, or apply to an entire RTA. The World Customs Organization and its Revised Kyoto Convention recognize two standards for RoO: that the product is "wholly obtained" or that the product goes through a "substantial transformation."[56] There are various standards that can be followed that define what specifically entails a "substantial transformation"—a change in the product's tariff classification (in a standardized product classification system), for instance, or requiring that a certain percentage of the production of a good must take place within the RTA's borders, or that specific steps in the production process take place within the RTA's borders. Typically RoO are designed so that no one country in the RTA is able to serve as an "export platform" into the others. For instance, NAFTA's automotive rules of origin ensure that cars produced primarily in Japan won't have some trivial change made to them in Mexico in order to receive NAFTA's preferential tariff treatment as they are exported to the US or Canada. To receive NAFTA's preferential tariff treatment, autos must be made with 62.5 percent North American production. Rules of origin also ensure how that number is calculated. For instance, should only the "direct costs" of production be used to determine production costs, or should the "net costs" of production, such as insurance on a production facility or research and development spending, be included in RoO calculations? If a component is made of North American and non-North American production, which method should be used to calculate the level of "North American" content for a component as it is used in a subsequent component—roll up, roll down, or tracing? Roll up would count a component that makes some threshold of North American content—say the 50 percent threshold found in the CUSFTA—to count as 100 percent North America in subsequent production. Roll down rounds downward, as its name suggests, while tracing tracks the precise North American level of the component as it used in the auto. NAFTA's auto provisions use tracing and the net cost of production.[57] This is dizzying, and this is only one portion of one economic sector.

Other rules of origin require that certain steps in the production process be within the RTA for preferential tariff treatment. In NAFTA's textile and apparel sector, for instance, the general RoO is "yarn forward"—requiring textile products to be cut and sewn in North America from fabric woven or knit in North America with North American–spun yarn from either North American or non-North American fibers. But even this level of specificity is a vast simplification. There are significant deviations from this RoO within the textile and apparel sectors, including both more stringent requirements to use only North American fibers for some products and more lenient requirements for others. And there are numerous other caveats to add to NAFTA's RoO requirements: tariff preference levels (TPLs), which allow a quota of a product to receive preferential NAFTA tariff rates while imports beyond this quota face higher (MFN) tariff rates.[58] Yet another RoO provision for textiles and apparel production in NAFTA is the *de minimus* standard. If textiles and apparel products do not otherwise meet NAFTA's RoO, they will still receive NAFTA's preferential tariff rates if less than 7 percent of the weight of a given product is non-North American.[59] Thus, an import could be subject to more than one RoO ruling.

As this hopes to make clear, those seeking evidence that RTAs make trade very complex for importers, exporters, and governments alike need only examine RoO.

Variation in Stringency of RoO

As is clear from the previous discussion, RoO may be more or less strict in requirements for production to receive preferential treatment in an RTA. Scholars have developed indices to calculate which methods are more or less stringent. RoO that require only a change in tariff classification are the least restrictive, those requiring a particular percentage of "local" production are more stringent than those that require only a change in tariff classification, those that require both are still more restrictive, and those requiring that specific production steps take place "locally" are the most strict.[60] Scholars have created indices of average RTA restrictiveness, but even with these it is difficult to generalize about the restrictiveness of an RTA's RoO because there is so much variation from product area to product area within a given RTA and because the more restrictive RTAs are within product areas, the more likely they are to have alternative RTA-wide RoO that increase flexibility and therefore reduce restrictiveness.[61]

RTA Variation: Trade Remedies

Many RTAs include provisions on trade remedies—which are government protections against some unfair trade practices and against damaging surges of imports in which no unfairness is alleged.

The GATT/WTO's Uruguay Round also established rules of trade remedies, but many countries want additional assurances about how the remedies will be applied to their exports to a given market; thus trade remedy provisions serve as a motivation to enter into RTAs and are an important element by which RTAs can be differentiated. Trade remedies include antidumping provisions (AD), countervailing duties (CVDs), and import safeguards. Dumping—the selling of goods at less than the cost of production or for less than they are sold in a domestic market—is illegal under the GATT/WTO and allows countries to use antidumping provisions to punish companies that undertake such actions. CVDs are increased tariffs used to offset subsidies to industries given by foreign governments, and import safeguards are temporary tariff barriers to protect surges of imports that have harmed an industry.[62] These trade remedy laws are seen by many as widely abused. Thus, coverage of trade remedies in RTAs is of particular importance to many countries. For instance, it was the primary reason that Canada took part in NAFTA negotiations when it already had an RTA with the US, the CUSFTA.

RTA Variation: Intellectual Property Rights (IPRs)— TRIPS-Plus or TRIPS-Minus?

RTAs vary in the degree to which they protect intellectual property rights (IPRs). IPRs are defined as the "rights to control use of intellectual property— an invention or creative work."[63] IPRs use various terms and mechanisms such as patents (for inventions), copyrights (for literary and artistic works such as music and computer software), and trademarks (for distinguishing characteristics of a company and other industrial property) to grant the owners of IPRs exclusive (or at least preferential) rights over the protected item in order to ensure that profits go to the inventor/creator.[64]

Economic liberals tend to want strong IPR protections as an incentive for innovation, although some also note that if IPRs are too stringent, they will stifle adoption of new technologies and creative works. There are numerous and varied levels of IPR protection in the global trading system. Since developed nations' firms are far more likely to own IPRs than developing nations' firms, developed nations tend to argue for stronger IPRs in trade negotiations.

There have long been international treaties to protect IPRs, many dating to the late 1800s. In 1967, the World Intellectual Property Organization (WIPO) was established to enforce IPRs in two previous conventions (the Berne Convention and the Paris Convention).[65] But developed nations and developed nations' firms are highly suspicious of the WIPO's ability to adequately protect their IPRs. Membership in the WIPO is nearly universal—there are 183 members—but this does not guarantee enforced IPRs.[66] Thus, in the Uruguay Round of the GATT negotiations, which also created the WTO itself, developed nations successfully included IPRs in the GATT/WTO with the Trade-Related Aspects of Intellectual Property Rights Agreement (TRIPS). One scholar notes the difference:

> Unlike prior international intellectual property agreements negotiated under the auspices of the World Intellectual Property Organization (WIPO), TRIPS has teeth. It contains detailed, comprehensive substantive rules and is linked to the WTO's comparatively hard-edged dispute settlement system in which treaty bargains are enforced through mandatory adjudication backed up by the threat of retaliatory sanctions.[67]

There has been considerable dissent against these stronger IPRs. As noted earlier, developing nations in particular do not care for the TRIPS provisions. This became increasingly true as the phase-in period for TRIPS ended and the TRIPS provisions became fully in force. In addition to being administratively costly, many developing nations fear that strong IPRs will lead to increased royalty payments to wealthy countries, to less widely disseminated technology and creative works, and to another way for developed nations to exclude developing nations' exports through trade remedy procedures that are very rigorous against IPR violations compared with other trade remedies (such as antidumping procedures).

Thus there has been a movement to resist TRIPS levels of IPR protection. This movement has been especially active at the multilateral level in ongoing DDA negotiations of the WTO. Specifically, there has been a movement— led by NGOs and developing nations—to weaken patents on medicines for poor countries. Patents, activists and others argue, make medicines more expensive for patients and governments to buy. Activists have long wanted easier authorization for countries to generically produce drugs still under patent. They became more vocal and organized, as box 1.3 notes. Developed countries, especially the United States, however, have feared that this would weaken the TRIPS agreement and destroy the incentives under which many of the HIV/AIDS medicines that are sought were invented.

BOX 1.3. NONPATENT HURDLES TO AFFORDABLE MEDICINES

There are numerous other hurdles to medicine access. As WTO director-general Pascal Lamy noted, "We have solved about 10 percent of the problem of access to medicines by developing countries." The agreement does not guarantee that generic drugs will be produced and exported cheaply to those poor countries with medical emergencies. In fact, there are other outstanding nonpatent issues that stand in the way of medicine delivery. As WIPO notes, 95 percent of the medicines on the WHO's essential drug list are off patent, yet many remain unavailable in poor countries. The reason: even priced at one dollar per day or less, medicines remain too expensive in countries where annual incomes average a dollar a day per person. Moreover, there is often a lack of physical and medical infrastructure to effectively distribute and administer the medicines. Patents alone are not to blame.

Source: "Poor Countries Fail to Take Advantage of WTO Accord on AIDS Drugs," *Agence France-Presse*, March 7, 2004.

As the movement gained publicity and followers, the HIV/AIDS pandemic continued in the late 1990s, just as developed nations wanted to convince developing nations to engage in a new round of WTO talks. One price of the talks would be concessions on medicines' patents. As a result, drug companies and their governments conceded on drug patent rules for medical emergencies at the 2001 Ministerial Conference in Doha, Qatar, or so it was thought.

In Doha, developed nations agreed to allow poor countries to domestically produce medicines still under patent without violating trade and patent law, provided they faced a medical emergency. This certainly helped some countries with sizable pharmaceutical capacity, but it offered no help to the majority of least-developed countries without the ability to produce the medicines. Developing nations and activists wanted to import generically produced medicines under patent law without running afoul of trade and patent law. Countries like India and Brazil have sizable generic industries and could export generic drugs to developing countries facing medical emergencies. The US was the lone holdout on the issue. It feared the generic drugs could be easily diverted to developed countries in a violation of patent law and a reduction of pharmaceutical industry profits. The US was concerned about which countries would qualify for patent waivers for traded medicines and for which diseases and medicines. The issue was supposed to be resolved by a December 2002 deadline that came and went. Finally, as the September 2003 Cancún meeting drew near, negotiators found a compromise palatable to the US and its pharmaceutical industry. The compromise allows patent waivers for traded medicines for any disease. It applies only to medicines used for noncommercial reasons, and importation must be under government control.[68] As box 1.4 demonstrates, this will not be enough to guarantee poor countries access to these medicines.

BOX 1.4. LEADING THE ANTI-IPR CHARGE

Some countries are getting more aggressive in negotiations with drug companies to supply low-cost medicines. The Brazilian government, for instance, is giving AIDS medicines to all Brazilians that need them and has threatened to produce generic versions of those AIDS drugs that it does not already produce generically. But this is not a viable option for most developing nations. On the NGO front, Doctors without Borders has been among the most vocal of groups calling for changed IPR rules on medicines. Their experience on the frontlines of disease, development, and war—including winning a Nobel Peace Prize—increases their ability to be heard. However, grassroots activism in developing nations has increased pressure on those developing nations to take a harder stance in negotiations.

Source: "Brazil to Stir Up AIDS-Drug Battle," *Wall Street Journal*, September 5, 2003.

This was a victory for developing nations in their efforts to gain access to affordable medicines, but it was also an important victory for those that seek weaker or at least more flexible IPRs. There was another important repercussion to this multilateral victory to weaken IPRs: the US increased its efforts to include IPRs in its RTAs. To be sure, the US already had won numerous TRIPS-plus provisions in RTAs, but the weakening of medicine patents certainly confirmed the fact that RTAs could be useful to the US on two IPR fronts. First, RTAs could strengthen IPRs for US companies in important developing markets even if the DDA and US efforts to increase IPRs in multilateral settings failed. Second, RTAs abroad with TRIPS-plus provisions could also ease the way toward multilateral gains in IPRs.

RTA Variation: Services—GATS-Plus or GATS-Ignored?

A very common way for RTAs to vary is in whether they address trade in services and, if so, whether they move beyond the liberalization of services found in the WTO General Agreement on Trade in Services (GATS). Before 2000, only five RTAs notified to the WTO contained services, while between 2000 and 2007, 42 RTAs notified to the WTO had services provisions.[69] By

2006, the top 25 services exporters were all in or negotiating at least one RTA with services.[70] The increase should not be surprising given that services trade is a rapidly growing area of trade and is far more economically important and traded than is widely understood. Over half of all foreign direct investment (FDI) flows are now in services, "measured" services trade accounts for 20 percent of all trade, and services account for 50, 54, and 72 percent of gross domestic product (GDP) in poor, middle-income, and rich countries, respectively.[71] As this suggests, service sectors tend to be more developed in more wealthy countries, many of which run service trade surpluses and are thus keenly interested in expanding trade in services. Indeed, it was the US that insisted that services trade be covered by the WTO. Developing nations tend to be less interested in expanding services trade, although there are some important exceptions to this—they generally support liberalizing outsourcing services and easing regulations on so-called mode 4 services trade, which regulates the "mode" of services delivery through temporary foreign workers.[72]

The WTO's Regulation of Services Trade: The General Agreement on Trade in Services (GATS)

The WTO's Uruguay Round included the General Agreement on Trade in Services (GATS), which brought trade in services into the GATT/WTO system for the first time. GATS allows WTO members to choose the degree of openness more à la carte than is the case for traded goods, and thus trade in services is less open than trade in manufactured goods. Specifically, GATS allows countries make their own "schedule" of "commitments" that they must abide by in some 160 sectors/subsectors (12 sectors [e.g., business services, tourism services, etc.] broken down into subcategories, creating 160 overall categories) and in four "modes" of services delivery. Thus the degree of service trade openness varies widely. Countries may offer "full commitments" (renouncing any limitations on a sector or subsector of services trade), "partial commitments" (some limitations on a sector/subsector), or "unbound" (allowing any limitations on trade in a service sector/subsector). GATS allows a country's schedule of commitments to include great variation within a services sector or subsector by modes of delivery.[73]

The four GATS modes of services delivery are

Mode 1, cross-border supply—Similar to trade in goods, the services producer delivers (exports) the service to the foreign consumer by telecommunications or mail. For instance, banking services in one country are exported to a consumer in another country through the Internet. The service itself travels.

Mode 2, consumption abroad—The service consumer goes into another country to obtain the service. Examples include foreign travel, foreign medical services, or foreign study. The services exporter need not have a presence in the service consumer's country. For instance, a Thai student consumes education services by traveling to study at an Australian university, the educational service provider, which need not have a branch office in Thailand.

Mode 3, commercial presence—The service provider establishes a presence in the service consumer's country through owning or renting property, including a subsidiary branch of a foreign company. Examples would be foreign-owned retail outlets, insurance branches, or financial service branches. A Swiss bank with a branch in the US serving US customers would be a mode 3 Swiss export and US import. Most trade in services is mode 3 trade.

Mode 4, movement of natural persons—Here the service provider goes into the service consumer's country on a temporary basis to provide the service. For instance, a US medical team travels to Mexico to train a Mexican medical team on how to use a heart-assist device.[74]

The liberalization contained in countries' schedules of commitments varies greatly, but there are distinct patterns that are important in their own right and because they often set the stage for variation in RTAs. Developed countries generally liberalize services trade more than developing countries in both breadth and depth; developed countries offer commitments in more sectors and subsectors and are more likely to have fewer restrictions on those commitments (more full commitments). This developed nation desire for greater services liberalization in GATS is echoed in RTAs.

Services in RTAs

Because the GATS has *not* liberalized trade in services greatly, RTAs have increasingly included provisions for trade in services and increasingly provide deeper levels of liberalization than found in the GATS; RTAs that liberalize more than GATS are thus called "GATS-plus." Juan A. Marchetti and Martin Roy recently created an index to quantitatively compare services liberalization in countries' GATS commitments, potential GATS commitments offered in the DDA negotiations, and the average level of commitments contained in their services RTAs. On a scale of 1–100, with 100 indicating full commitments in all service sectors, actual GATS index scores were 24 and 30 for modes 1 and 3, respectively, compared with RTA scores of 59 and 67, respectively. Countries in services RTAs, in other words, tended to include coverage for many more sectors—approximately double—than they did in their own GATS commitments. RTA services coverage also went well beyond their negotiation offers in the DDA talks, which were only slightly higher than actual GATS scores.[75]

While developed nations are more likely to include services in their RTAs, they are also increasingly common in developing nation RTAs. There are, however, regional variations: Middle Eastern and North African RTAs are less likely to include services than RTAs in other regions (with the exception of bilateral RTAs between MENA countries and the US).[76]

Models for Services in RTAs: The Positive List (GATS) and the Negative List (NAFTA)

While the GATS has not significantly liberalized services trade, it has created a framework for liberalization in RTAs that many RTA follow and for which there is now a competing framework. The modes of services trade delivery and the typology of sectors and subsectors developed by GATS are all widely referenced in RTAs. The GATS also uses a positive-list system of liberalization in which there is no liberalization in a service sector unless it is specifically listed. The status quo is nonliberalization unless specified on the GATS schedule of commitments. Many RTAs utilize the GATS-style positive-list model—the EU, European Free Trade Association (EFTA), and Japan's RTAs all tend to use positive lists. But many RTAs also use an alternative approach, the negative-list system, in which services trade is liberalized except for those areas specifically listed. Under a negative-list system, the status quo is for liberalization unless an exception is placed on a list. NAFTA, a very prominent RTA, used this system, and the US then followed this NAFTA model in its numerous subsequent RTAs. Many RTAs have combined aspects of the two approaches with variation from sector to sector. There are somewhat more negative-list RTAs than positive-list, and sector liberalization tends to be greater for those RTAs that use the NAFTA-style negative list than those that use the GATS-style positive list.[77]

RTA Variation: Trade Remedies

Trade remedies—antidumping actions (AD), countervailing measures, and safeguards—are steps taken to prevent specific types of unfair and damaging trade practices (the use of safeguards alleges no unfairness, only injury). Antidumping actions are used to combat dumping, which is the exporting of goods at less than a "fair cost," determined to be lower than the price in the producer's home market, lower than the price in other markets, or less than the cost of production. Countervailing measures—sometimes identified by the most common measure employed, countervailing duties (CVDs)—are used to counter "illegal" subsidies, which are those subsidies allegedly harmful to an industry in the importing country. Safeguards are designed to temporarily protect a domestic industry from an unexpected surge in imports that has allegedly harmed that industry.[78]

AD actions are the most commonly used of the trade remedies, followed by countervailing measures, with safeguards being used the least. Each of the three trade remedies is governed by WTO provisions but also commonly covered in modern-era RTAs. In fact, the desire to protect oneself against allegedly capricious and overzealous use of trade remedies has been one of the primary reasons for many countries to enter into RTAs, as noted earlier in this chapter.

Few RTAs specifically get rid of the right to use trade remedies. In fact, only the EU specifically disallows its members using all three types of trade remedies against one another. One recent study found that only 13 of 74 RTAs examined specifically disallow at least one of the three types of trade remedies.[79] Nine RTAs disallow AD, six disallow CVDs, and five disallow safeguards. The EEA and the EFTA both disallow AD and CVD but not safeguards. MERCOSUR disallows safeguards. While generally forbidding the use of trade remedies can be seen as a deeper level of integration, some economic liberals fear that the difference between intra-RTA trade and extra-RTA trade will only add to the spaghetti-bowl effect of confusion, complexity, and trade diversion.

Antidumping (AD) Actions

Only nine of 74 RTAs studied disallow AD actions. These include the EU, EEA, EFTA, two of EFTA's bilateral agreements, China's bilateral RTAs with Hong Kong and Macao, the Canada-Chile FTA, and ANZCERTA. Twenty-seven RTAs either make no mention of AD or simply state that AD actions among members will adhere to WTO AD rules. This leaves 36 RTAs allowing some differential AD treatment between their members and nonmembers. Typically, these measures weaken RTA members' ability to engage in AD actions with one another.[80] A few RTAs—five of the 74 studied—establish a regional body to conduct the AD investigation or review a nation's AD determinations (rulings): the CACM, CAN, CARICOM, NAFTA, and WAEMU. All of these five, except NAFTA, are customs unions.

Countervailing Measures

Only five RTAs have disallowed CVDs: the EU, EEA (agriculture and fish only), EFTA (agriculture and fish only), and China's bilateral RTAs with Hong Kong and Macao.[81] Forty-seven RTAs either make no mention of CVDs (thus allowing them) or specifically allow CVDs that must be WTO-consistent (also allowing them). Twenty-two RTAs have detailed provisions on CVDs, with only four of these in which an international body either conducts the CVD investigation or oversees the national bodies that conduct it: CAN, CACM, CARICOM, and NAFTA. Why so little restriction on CVDs? Because RTAs do little to rein in the source of CVD investigations: subsidies. Subsidies have been little curtailed in RTAs (with the exception of export subsidies on agricultural), and thus states wish to keep CVDs as a way to battle what their members view as a potential threat.

Safeguards

Only four RTAs make no mention of safeguards: the CACM, the CEMAC, the GCC, and the RTA between the EU and microstate Andorra.[82] That leaves most RTAs regulating and at least allowing some safeguards. Many RTAs have safeguard provisions during transitional periods only, thereby increasing the political palatability of RTA liberalization. Sixteen have provisions that allow safeguards on specific economic sectors that usually go beyond the transition period, and this type of safeguard is usually found in agriculture and textiles and apparel, among the most protected of economic sectors having only been brought under WTO/GATT rules with the formation of the WTO itself in 1995.[83] It is also common to have RTA provisions that exclude RTA members from global safeguard actions. It is not clear the degree to which these provisions are WTO-consistent. What is clear is that it is against WTO rules to *include* RTA members in the "determination" of a *global* injury—a process by which the degree of injury and source of injury to a domestic industry are established—and then *exempt* RTA members from the safeguard restriction. Rather a nation must exclude the RTA members from both the determination of injury process and the safeguard restriction to be WTO-consistent.[84]

The EU and Trade Remedy Politics

That the EU has gone the furthest toward disallowing trade remedies should not be surprising given that the EU is the most integrated of RTAs; it includes harmonization of regulations, and it does give EU institutions a great deal of power to enforce some of these regulations. For instance, the 2009 French plan to subsidize—through better-than-market loans—French car companies Renault and Peugeot-Citroën are coming under the scrutiny of the European Commissioner for Competition, Neelie Kroes. If the EU Commission for Competition finds that France has violated EU competition policy—requiring that a member nation's government not favor its own companies in policies such as tax breaks or favorable loans—the EU Commission for Competition may authorize fines. But not all "state aid" is against EU rules. France, for instance, argues that the measures are temporary and merely assist access to credit and as such should be legal. As the EU process to internally adjudicate state aid and other competition rules continues, so too do political efforts to define what steps member nations may take to assist industries in crisis from the financial and economic crisis: the EU held a summit to discuss how to respond to the economic crisis without sparking protectionism.[85] In other words, just as the quasi-judicial process began, the political process intervened. You can take trade remedy policies out of the RTA, but you can't take the RTA out of the trade remedy politics.

RTA Variation: Agriculture

Many RTAs do not include agriculture. This is one sector that is of greatest interest to many large, agricultural exporting, developing nations as they enter into RTAs with developed nations. Why? Agricultural trade is another sector that has only recently been included in the multilateral trading system in the GATT's Uruguay Round. Agriculture is subject to higher levels of tariffs than manufactured goods, has numerous health standards that may also restrict trade, and, most significantly, is subject to massive levels of subsidies in wealthy countries. Agriculture is massively important to developing nations because agriculture represents such a significant portion of the many developing nations' economies: employment, exports, and food security make agriculture of heightened interest to developing nations in both multilateral and RTA trade negotiations. Developed nations also place great importance on agriculture, but here they largely seek to keep their farm subsidies. Agriculture is a much smaller percentage of developed nations' economies, but their political power outweighs their economic size. In the US Senate, for instance, states dominated by agriculture each get two senators, the same as more industrial and populous states. Agricultural coverage in RTAs is becoming more common, but most RTAs do not substantially lead to agricultural trade integration.

RTA Variation: The Environment

This is a new area for trade negotiations. Laws designed to shield the environment can also be used to keep out imported products, and thus trade and environmental issues have been of heightened concern. Protestors in turtle costumes at the 1999 WTO ministerial meeting in Seattle were a colorful illustration of this. NAFTA was the first RTA to specifically include environmental provisions, which were concluded in separate negotiations as promised by then candidate Bill Clinton as the price of his supporting NAFTA. NAFTA requires member nations to follow their own environmental laws and creates a process to challenge governments that do not, but most observers agree that these provisions lack the teeth found in other elements of dispute resolution. Nevertheless, that NAFTA had an environmental provision was a substantial departure from previous RTAs, and the practice is spreading.

RTA Variation: Labor

As with environmental provisions, NAFTA also included side provisions that established a process to challenge members that allow labor law violations. Like the environmental provisions in NAFTA, the labor provisions lack teeth. Nevertheless, they too are more than is found in most RTAs. Much controversy about RTAs surrounds the lack of labor provisions. Specifically, antiglobalization activists are concerned that RTAs ensure compliance with what the International Labour Organization (ILO) calls its four core labor rights. Pressure for greater labor rights provisions in RTAs is growing but faces skepticism from corporations that do not want to alter their business practices and from developing countries' governments that fear labor rights provisions in RTAs will be used as a way to protect wealthy countries' markets. Many activists in both developed and developing countries do not agree. Controversy over labor rights provisions is not likely to go away.

ORGANIZATION OF THIS BOOK

All of the remaining chapters except chapter 9 focus on RTAs in a given geographic area. Each of these chapters is organized with a combination of three sections. First is a section containing an overview of RTAs in the region. Second is a section, "context of RTAs" in the region, which examines the IPE of a given region and provides other relevant background that informs the region's integration developments. There will sometimes be multiple overview and context sections when a region is further subdivided; for example, for the Americas chapter there are sections on both context of RTAs in the Caribbean and context of RTAs in South America. Third, each chapter will have an "RTAs in the region" section that begins with a Venn diagram showing membership in the region's RTAs, followed by a description and explanation of each RTA in the region. There will be subsections for those RTAs with more substantial coverage. The membership of most RTAs will be listed in a table at the end of its coverage, although for some RTAs, membership will be listed within the narrative of the RTA's coverage. Last, the appendixes contain coverage of the WTO, EU preferential access agreements, US FTAs, and there is a list of abbreviations and a glossary of terms.

2

Africa

Africa has embraced regional trade groupings to a very high extent. There are over 30 RTAs in Africa, and African countries average four RTA memberships each.[1] (See figure 2.1.) African RTAs are diverse: some—such as WAEMU/UEMOA—are monetary unions, others—such as the EAC—are customs unions with plans for monetary union, and some—such as the CBI/RIFF—are fairly open to trade with outside countries, while many others are not. Africa has its share of "paper RTAs" that are RTAs only in the documents proclaiming their existence; these façade RTAs do not reflect the reality of African interactions. Three general commonalities do emerge from African RTAs: they tend to have very ambitious goals, their membership coverage is confusing, and they have low levels of intragroup trade. First, African RTAs are typically ambitious; they usually set out monetary union as the ultimate goal. Second, many African RTAs are overlapping. Subregional RTAs in Africa often compete with other RTAs in the same subregion. RTAs in different subregions tend to have overlapping membership. This increases the cost of doing business for the private sector and makes administering customs expensive and difficult for governments. Third, RTAs in Africa tend to have low levels of intra-RTA trade. In part, this stems from poor transport connections between African RTAs. An important implication of lower levels of intra-RTA trade is that the economic benefits of lower trade barriers are less than if intra-RTA trade were higher.

Why have African countries entered into so many regional groupings? Why are there many so-called paper RTAs that appear more in theory than reality? The two most significant reasons for African trade groupings are the need for economic development and the desire by African countries to

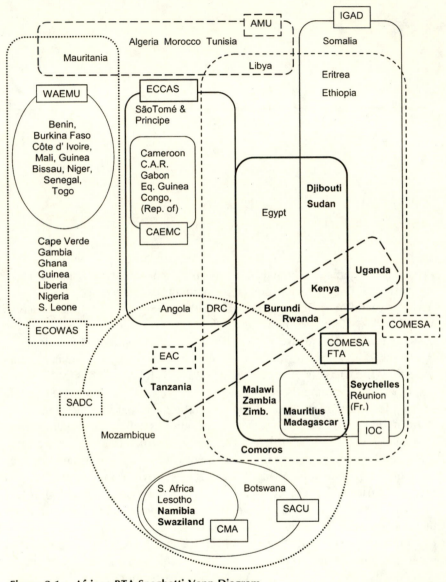

Figure 2.1.   African RTA Spaghetti Venn Diagram
Key: See list of abbreviations.
*Bold denotes RIFF membership.

pool their influence relative to outside forces such as global markets and
developed nations. Much of this can be explained by a lack of power relative
to these outside forces. Some of it can be explained by the desire to control
one's own destiny. There is an element of pan-African nationalism at work.
A well-known example from another time and place exemplifies the desire

for greater autonomy: as India fought for its independence, Mohandas "Mahatma" Gandhi advocated wearing "homespun" garments not for efficiency, but because doing so helped India avoid importing finished clothes from the colonial power, Great Britain. Just as there was symbolism in Gandhi's homespun, so too is there in African RTAs.

AFRICAN MONETARY UNIONS

Unique to Africa is the degree to which RTAs include high aspirations for monetary union and the degree to which some have actually achieved this, despite low levels of trade and other forms of economic integration. The most ambitious aspiration for monetary union is that of the African Union; it seeks to have a single currency for the entire continent. The Association of African Central Bank Governors declared that the target date for continental monetary union will be 2021. Few analysts believe that continental monetary union is obtainable in this time frame. Currently, Africa has three regional monetary unions. Two are regions of the CFA franc zone: the Economic and Monetary Community for Central Africa (CAEMC) and the West Africa Economic and Monetary Union (WAEMU). The third is the Common Monetary Area (CMA) in Southern Africa that is a subgrouping within the Southern African Customs Union and is dominated by the South African rand.

Additionally, there are numerous subregional trade groupings that have aspirations of forming monetary unions, and they are at various degrees of turning these aspirations into reality. The most common stage is to have formally stated monetary union as the goal with few concrete steps toward achieving integration. The SADC, for instance, has monetary union as a distant goal.[2] ECOWAS has taken steps toward a subregional monetary union. In 2000, six ECOWAS states—Gambia, Ghana, Guinea, Liberia, Nigeria, and Sierra Leone—agreed to create the (second) West African Monetary Union (WAMZ) with a common currency and common central bank by 2003. They had more distant plans to merge with the West Africa portion of the CFA franc zone, the West Africa Economic and Monetary Union (WAEMU), to form the West African Monetary Union in 2005.[3] Five of the WAMZ signatories—all except Liberia—became members of the WAMZ; Liberia and Cape Verde are observers at WAMZ meetings. In 2002, the WAMZ members assessed their progress toward meeting convergence criteria and decided that the January 1, 2003, date for a common currency, the ECO, and a common central bank, the West African Central Bank (WACB), was unrealistic, and they pushed the date back to July 1, 2005.[4] As the 2005 deadline approached, the WAMZ members again realized their goal was unrealistic and extended the date until 2009.[5]

There are numerous historical examples of monetary unions in Africa from the colonial and post-colonial area: three groups of British colonies each had currency boards and British colonial holdings in southern African were linked to the Union of South Africa; two French colonial groupings later became the CFA franc zone; and Spain, Belgium, and Portugal linked their colonies with each of their currencies which also often involved some currency integration in their respective colonies.[6]

CONTEXT OF AFRICAN RTAs: AFRICAN INTERNATIONAL POLITICAL ECONOMY (IPE)

Scholars of Africa often complain that Africa is such a broad and diverse continent that to use Africa as a descriptor—such as African political economy or African style of government—creates so many caveats as to render the practice unhelpful at best and misleading at worst. Indeed, Africa is exceptionally diverse in every possible way, and there are distinct regional, national, and subnational differences within Africa about which one needs to be aware. See box 2.1, "Cultural Geography of Africa," for examples of African regional differences. And yes, Africa is often wrongly and negatively stereotyped in the Western media and public perception. Nevertheless, there are commonalities through shared historical and contemporary experiences and processes that make broad characterizations a useful starting point.

The legacy of colonialism, for instance, is stronger in Africa than anywhere else in the world because it is so recent; so many African countries only recently won their independence, and only one country in Africa was not colonized: Ethiopia.[7] Besides the exceptionally high level of exploitation and personal suffering inherent in the colonial relationship, economic development becomes highly conditioned upon the colonial experience. For instance, much of Africa's transportation infrastructure was designed to get Africa's abundant natural resources to European and other developed nations' markets. To this day, Africa remains highly dependent upon raw materials exports. Economic structuralists—within the critical/antiglobalization approach to international political economy—stress that this raw materials export dependence in the very least leads to economic booms and busts and, worse still, leads to poor terms of trade (how much of a country's exports are required in order to buy a given unit of its imports). Moreover, colonial rule halted many organic economic arrangements such as local or regional trade and currency patterns, and forced economic relations with the colonial power—by colonial power rules—

BOX 2.1. CULTURAL GEOGRAPHY OF AFRICA

Africa is often described through various geographic typologies. The first geographic division is between North Africa and sub-Saharan Africa. Sub-Saharan Africa is then further divided into East, West, Central, and Southern Africa.

Already North Africa stands apart in typical descriptions of the continent. In fact, North Africa is often included as an extension of the Middle East. Arabic is commonly spoken in North Africa, and Islam is the predominant religion.

West Africa, with its strong French influence, is home to one of the Africa's two regional giants, Nigeria, and the region has been the scene of much political and ethnic unrest. Christianity and Islam are both popular here, and this can sometimes lead to conflict. Central Africa, with exceptions, has less Islamic influence than West Africa. The long-running war in the Democratic Republic of the Congo (Kinshasa, or the ex-Zaire) has dominated much of the region in the past decade and has pulled in countries from other African regions.

The tropical forests that are commonly found in West and Central Africa contrast with the scrub plains typical of East Africa. Along much of the East African coast, Arab influence—from long-standing trade routes—can be felt. In much of Southern Africa, the European toehold expanded and became more entrenched; Europeans—especially the Dutch and British—came to stay in sufficient numbers that "settler" colonialism took hold, and European ancestors became entrenched in power until very recently. Consequently, independence from the colonial powers (or, in some cases, black freedom from colonists' ancestors) came later than in much of Africa.

Southern Africa is home to the other of sub-Saharan Africa's regional powers: South Africa. South Africa is more than just a regional power; it is by far the most developed and economically powerful country in Africa, and now it is able to use that influence in Africa more than during the days of apartheid (white rule), when it was ostracized.

became paramount. The importance of the colonial legacy does not negate the importance of precolonial African influences on Africa today, whether they stem from local languages, religious practices, or leadership practices. Indeed, the colonial experience itself was varied by which colonial power dominated an area—with France and Great Britain being the largest colonizers—and by whether colonial rule included colonial settlers and, therefore, the degree to which the colonial power depended upon indigenous groups to administer the colony's governance. Keeping these warnings in mind, a political economic tour of Africa is in order to understand African regional trade groupings.

Africa's economies remain agriculturally based to a high degree, as is the case in least-developed countries (LDC) elsewhere, and this typically equates

to subsistence farming. Africans complain that their main economic ties to
the rest of the world economy are exporting primary products and loan payments to industrialized economies and importing industrialized goods. They
argue that their terms of trade—how much in a country's exports will buy its
imports—are horrible, often declining and often unstable. This is a pattern
that dates to colonialism, and few African countries have developed well following this scenario.

There are numerous economic bumps in Africa's economic development
road. The first of these is having to rely on roads or rails for trade, not ports;
many African countries are landlocked. Fourteen of the 31 countries on the
UN's list of landlocked developing countries are in Africa.[8] This adds cost
and isolation to countries that can afford neither. Another set of bumps in the
road are the actual bumps in those roads. Deteriorating roads impair links
among African economies and between Africa and the rest of the world.
Telecommunication infrastructure is also poor in much of Africa.

Africa's natural resources are considerable. The hard currency provided by
natural resource exports are important for any country and are essential for
desperately poor countries. Natural resources are a boon for many in Africa.
For instance, much of South Africa's wealth can be attributed to diamonds
and other valuable natural resources. But natural resources have also been
problematic for many in Africa. Diamonds and some other minerals are two-
edged swords because they increase the scope of graft to massive proportions
and because they often fuel wars. How so? With diamonds, the control of territory equals wealth—more so than is the case with agricultural or industrial
patterns of land use. Therefore, diamonds are an obvious goal for those willing to use violence to gain wealth. Diamonds are a "carat" for a government,
rebel groups, and predatory neighboring governments that are willing to fight
for their "cut." Second, diamonds pay for the weapons with which many
wars are fought. For instance, Sierra Leone's diamond mines paid for the
weapons used by the Revolutionary United Front (RUF) rebels—famous for
their signature atrocity, using a machete to cut off bystanders' limbs. Sierra
Leone was not the only country where diamonds fueled war, and nongovernmental organizations pressed for the identification and banning of "conflict
diamonds." The Kimberly Process, agreed upon in 2002 and in force since
January 2003, certifies diamonds as legitimately mined, but critics fear that
conflict diamonds continue to enter the diamond market through corruption
and smuggling.[9]

Another natural resource that is increasingly important to many African states
is oil. There are now nine African oil exporters: Nigeria, Angola, Congo-Brazza-
ville, Gabon, Equatorial Guinea, Cameroon, Chad, Congo-Kinshasa, and Sudan,
with many other oil producers that hope to find and produce sufficient amounts

for export.[10] For many African states with oil, it is by far the most significant part of the economy. In Nigeria, for example, oil accounted for 40 percent of its GDP, 95 percent of its exports, and 83 percent of its government revenue in 2002.[11]

Sub-Saharan Africa remains predominantly poor. The combined income of the 48 countries of sub-Saharan Africa is slightly larger than that of Belgium.[12] Nearly all of the highly indebted poor countries (HIPCs) are African. These are countries that are deemed to be so desperately poor and so far in debt that they have no realistic hopes of ever developing unless their debt burdens are lifted.

Africa's poverty and lack of economic development are exacerbated by three non-economic factors: disease, war, and bad government. First, disease exacerbates poverty, which, in turn, makes the spread of many diseases easier. Most dramatically, the HIV/AIDS epidemic has seriously hampered Africa. The cruelty brought by this disease does not stop with the deaths of so many; it is compounded by the poverty that HIV/AIDS has spread: communities already on the margins of survival cannot afford to lose so many workers nor so many moms and dads. Other diseases also have massive economic tolls. Malaria saps the energy of those who have it and survive it. Malnutrition and disease in childhood make education more difficult to obtain for cash-strapped families and can affect development in ways that slow down economies decades after the initial hardship has ended.

Second, poor governance has slowed Africa's economic development. Africa has been notably short on democracy in the postcolonial era. This often comes when leaders set one ethnic/tribal group against another, increasing instability. But it also comes from a more mundane problem that eats away at a government's effectiveness: corruption. Corruption has siphoned away much of the money generated by governments that could otherwise be spent on education, health care, and infrastructure. The contrast is sharp between the generation of East Asian leaders who were undemocratic but who did govern with personal propriety and with the country's economic development in mind with the stereotypical African leader of the same era who governed to enrich himself. Singapore's Lee Kwan Yew and Malaysia's M. Mahathir Mohamad contrast starkly with the archetype kleptocrat, Zaire's President Mobuto Sese Seko, who for over three decades plundered billions of dollars from his resource-rich country and left it less developed than when his rule began. There is also a problem with unstable leadership and violent changes of government. The Comoros Islands, for instance, have had over 20 coups or attempted coups since independence from France in 1975.[13] There has been an effort to remedy Africa's record on governance. Corruption is frowned upon more internally and by outside powers than it used to be. It is publicly attacked by African leaders and civil groups more than was once the case. Elections that lead to a true change in power from one faction to another are more common today than in the past, but still all too rare.

A third non-economic factor slowing African development has been war or, more broadly, a lack of physical security. Insecurity has halted all normal functioning in too many African societies. Borders imposed by outsiders did not always coincide with natural or cultural borders, and many African states have had difficult times with different groups in society vying for political and economic power. The formation of nation-states the world over has been violent, so this is not uniquely an African problem, but most other nation-states were formed earlier and are thus more likely to have resolved border and identity issues. Africa is unique in the degree to which its boundaries were drawn by outsiders, and this has exacerbated what is otherwise a more natural, if not less terrible, situation. Even those African countries that have largely escaped border and/or ethnic fighting often face unrest or war in neighboring countries, which can itself be destabilizing as refugees, armed insurgents, or both cross borders. Some of the most intractable wars in recent decades have been in Africa: Sudan, Angola, Mozambique, and the Democratic Republic of Congo (Kinshasa). Some of these have ended (Angola and Mozambique), but others continue in one form or another. As one Africanist recently noted,

> On one end are South Africa, Botswana, and Mauritius—the few sub-Saharan success stories in terms of both governance and economics. At the other end lie the abject failures, including Liberia, Sierra Leone and Somalia. And in between fall the majority. . . . A few, such as Uganda, have pulled themselves back from the brink of ruin. Several others—including Benin, Ghana, Kenya, Mali, Mozambique, Senegal and perhaps Malawi and Zambia—are functioning democracies that may be on the road to recovery. Still, of the African Union's 53 members, eight or nine could currently be described as war zones, and there are plenty more—such as Chad, Togo, and Guinea—that could go that way at any moment.[14]

In late 2008, there were eight UN peacekeeping operations in African countries: the Central African Republic (CAR), Chad (a joint mission with the CAR), Côte d'Ivoire, the Democratic Republic of Congo (Kinshasa), Liberia, Western Sahara, and two separate missions in Sudan, one in southern Sudan and one in the Darfur region. These peacekeeping missions comprised over 53,000 of the 88,000 uniformed military personnel in UN peacekeeping missions worldwide.[15] With insecurity such as this, economic development, let alone regional integration, is sure to be a casualty.

RTAs IN AFRICA

African Growth and Opportunity Act (AGOA)

The African Growth and Opportunity Act (AGOA) is a unilateral preferential trade agreement for qualifying sub-Saharan African countries. See box 2.2 for a list of AGOA-qualifying countries. AGOA expands the list of products that qualify for the Generalized System of Preferences (GSP) treatment of tariff-free entry into the US.[16] AGOA provides two levels of unilateral preferential access to the US market for African countries that meet eligibility requirements: regular AGOA access and textiles and apparel access. Textile and apparel imports must meet AGOA rules of origin (RoO) to avoid Africa's becoming an export platform for production elsewhere and places limits on

---

BOX 2.2. AGOA-ELIGIBLE COUNTRIES

Angola
Benin*
Botswana*
Cameroon*
Cape Verde*
Chad
Congo, Republic of (Brazzaville)
Congo, Democratic Republic of (Kinshasa)
Côte d'Ivoire*
Djibouti
Ethiopia*
Gabon
Gambia
Ghana*
Guinea
Guinea-Bissau
Kenya*
Lesotho*
Madagascar*

Malawi*
Mali*
Mauritania
Mauritius*
Mozambique*
Namibia*
Niger*
Nigeria
Rwanda*
São Tomé and Principe
Senegal*
Seychelles
Sierra Leone*
South Africa*
Swaziland*
Tanzania*
Uganda*
Zambia*

Source: "2004 AGOA Report," at http://www.agoa.gov; http://www.ustr.gov/assets/
Trade_Development/Preference_Programs/AGOA/asset_upload_file679_3741.pdf.
* Qualified for textile and apparel benefits

the levels of textile and apparel entering duty free (as a percentage of overall US imports in the sector), depending upon how much production takes place in Africa. Eligibility can be rescinded for countries not practicing "good governance" as defined by the US. This option has been used occasionally and therefore AGOA, in the US view, serves as both economic carrot and stick in promoting democracy. While many argue AGOA does not substantially improve development opportunities in Africa, some countries have been able to establish export-oriented textile and apparel production with nearly all exports going to the US market where there had been none before AGOA.

African Union (AU), Including the African Economic Community (AEC) and New Partnership for Africa's Development (NEPAD)

The African Union evolved out of the Organization of African Unity (OAU) in the Durban Summit of July 2002. The AU is ambitious; it models itself after the European Union. It has a long way to go to meet this goal. True, the AU has been more assertive in peacekeeping than its predecessor and, like its predecessor, supports continental economic integration. But it faces enormous challenges before it can effectively tackle Africa's massive development and humanitarian needs. These challenges include budgetary shortfalls, continued bad governance in most African states, and a lack of security. This section examines the AU's roots, its problems, the institutions designed to overcome some of the OAU's shortcomings, and, finally, it offers a description and evaluation of the AU's economic integration plans.

The AU's Roots: The Organization of African Unity (OAU)

The OAU, the forerunner to today's African Union (AU), was founded in 1963 and was widely criticized for slow decision making and its lack of action in addressing atrocities by African leaders. The latter problem was enhanced by the principle of noninterference in its members' internal affairs. The OAU also faced regular budgetary shortfalls.[17] The OAU strongly supported continental-wide integration using Regional Economic Cooperation (REC) agencies; the AU has also adopted this policy. The OAU created a legacy of grand statements with little actual action to back them up. Can the AU overcome this legacy and be more effective?

AU Problems: Budgets, Governance, and Security

The AU has run into budget problems early in its history and has been the subject of criticism for relying on Libya's dictatorial and volatile leader

Muammar el-Qaddafi for much of its funding.[18] This criticism won't be helped by Qaddafi's election as head of the African Union's rotating presidency. The AU pledges to be tougher on bad governance in Africa than was its predecessor, but because this allows a lot of latitude for continued bad governance, the AU must overcome considerable skepticism on this issue. The AU has institutionalized its efforts to promote good governance. Its primary mechanism for this is the NEPAD's African Peer Review Mechanism (APRM), through which a given African country's governance is evaluated by other African states in order to apply pressure for change. While the AU has earned greater credibility than its predecessor, thanks in part to increased self-policing of bad governance, this credibility has been jeopardized by an increase in bad governance in the AU secretariat's host country, Ethiopia and, more dramatically, in the face of muted African criticism of Zimbabwe President Robert Mugabe's increasingly despotic and disastrous rule. Zimbabwean inflation is among the highest in world history; this, combined with political repression and an emerging humanitarian crisis, has driven millions of Zimbabweans to flee the country.

AU Security Problems

AU effectiveness is challenged by continued tension between numerous African states. Chad, for instance, has accused the Sudanese government of supporting a Chadian rebel group that has attacked civilians within Chad and of supporting Sudanese militias that regularly cross into Chad, stealing cattle and killing civilians. Chad announced that it was in a "state of war" with Sudan after a December 2005 attack that killed 100 people in Chad. Chadian president Idriss Deby visited then AU chairman, Nigerian president Olusegun Obasanjo, to complain about the Sudanese attacks and to make his plea that Sudan should not host the January 2006 AU summit, nor should Sudanese president Omar al-Bashir become the chair of the AU. Other cross-border tensions abound. Some are relatively quiet but not fully settled, such as a dispute over oil-rich territory between Cameroon and Nigeria that twice led to fighting. The World Court ruled in favor of Cameroon in 2002, but Nigeria has not yet complied with the ruling.[19] Other disputes are far closer to substantial fighting. For example, Ethiopia and Eritrea's land dispute led to war shortly after the end of Eritrea's 30-year war of independence from Ethiopia. UN peacekeepers in the disputed territory have faced hostility, and Ethiopian troops sent to Somalia, nominally to support the official Somali government, have a deeper purpose: to ensure that those Islamic groups challenging the Somali government do not facilitate Eritrea's efforts in its dispute with Ethiopia.

One AU reaction to Africa's continued security problems is the development of AU peacekeeping capabilities. The AU plans to create the AU

Standby Force by 2010 that will have five or six 3,000- to 5,000-troop brigades stationed in various African locations ready to intervene quickly to quell unrest. This will require funding and logistical support. The G-8 pledged, in its 2002 Africa Action Plan, to assist the AU with both of these needed resources.[20]

Overcoming Poor Governance in Africa? New Partnership for Africa's Development (NEPAD)

NEPAD is the strategic framework for socioeconomic development in Africa that the AU's forerunner, the OAU, adopted in 2001 and the AU also adopted in July 2002. NEPAD was proposed in 1999 by the leaders of four initiating states: South African president Mbeki, Senegalese president Abdoulaye Wade, Algerian president Abdelzaia Bouteflika, and Nigerian president Olusegun Obasanjo.[21] NEPAD's goals are to promote sustainable development in Africa, eradicate poverty, empower women, and "halt the marginalisation of Africa in the globalisation process and enhance its full and beneficial integration into the global economy."[22] It also calls for policy reform and investment in agriculture and infrastructure. NEPAD's program of action includes the promotion of accelerated integration at both the subregional and continental scale, as called for the by the AU through the AEC. One of the more potentially significant elements of NEPAD is the peer review process, which is conducted by NEPAD's African Peer Review Mechanism (APRM).[23] In 2005, there were 24 countries representing 75 percent of Africa's population that had agreed to the APRM.[24] It remains to be seen, however, the degree to which peer pressure legitimized by the APRM will change damaging governance. The review board member states do not have an immaculate governance record, to put it gently, and there has been criticism that civil society groups have not been sufficiently included in the process. Moreover, half of the countries in Africa have not agreed to the APRM.

The AU and Promotion of Economic Integration

The African Union and its predecessor, the Organization of African Unity (OAU), have long promoted continental economic integration and done so paradoxically, with precision on the one hand—specific steps to take toward economic integration—and misjudgment on the other because the specific steps are not rooted in the economic or political realities on the ground. How so? The AEC calls for continental integration based on five specific subregional trade groupings, each from a different subregion of Africa, serving as stepping stones to the hoped-for establishment of an integrated AEC in 2025. This structure, inherited from the 1980 Lagos Plan of Action and reauthorized by the 1994 Abuja Treaty, calls for the Arab Maghreb Union (AMU) to represent North Africa, ECOWAS to represent West Africa, ECCAS to represent Central Africa, COMESA to represent Eastern Africa, and the SADC to represent Southern Africa. See table 2.1 for REC membership. Yet there are numerous cross-cutting memberships among the groupings, there are countries excluded from them, and there are significant subregional competitors to these regional economic cooperation (REC) agencies.[25] For instance, in West Africa, ECOWAS has a subgrouping within it, WAEMU (also known as UEMOA in French), which has led to considerable tension between the two RTAs. The differences among the various sets of competing subregional trade groupings are not superficial, but instead can be tied to significantly different and contending conceptions of integration and divergent interests regarding integration. As one observer put it, "Part of the tensions between the various sub-regional integration agencies derives from differences in the approach to integration, the degree, scope and speed of liberalization, and the ultimate objective of the integration process."[26] More confusion and difficulty is added because it is not always clear which trade grouping has what authority in a given subregion.[27]

To get to the integrated AEC envisioned by the AU, the subregions will have to become more effective FTAs, customs unions, common markets, and then monetary unions. This will prove difficult; customs unions and common markets are quite rare, and successful ones rarer still. There are currently a number of examples of successful monetary integration in Africa, but these do not necessarily complement the AU's AEC plans and, in fact, may complicate them further. Monetary integration, like trade integration, creates winners and losers. Those with stronger financial systems and better financial reputations will be hesitant to risk their hard-earned credibility to enter into a monetary union with less "responsible" states—those with less stable political systems, tenuous hard currency sources, and records of illiberal fiscal or monetary policy.

Thus, most observers are very skeptical that the AEC will lead to true integration and believe the AEC to be highly unrealistic. According to one expert, the AEC is under the AU secretary general's control and remains "fundamentally a figment of the imagination of the organization."[28] Nevertheless, the AEC continues to resonate with many in Africa and continues to be prominent on the AU's agenda.

There are some ongoing steps suggesting the possibility of inter-REC integration: COMESA, EAC, and SADC leaders met in the Tripartite Summit and agreed to work toward a single free trade agreement within six months.[29]

Table 2.1. Proposed African Economic Community's Regional Economic Cooperation (REC) Agencies

Acronym	RTA Name	Subregion Represented	Members		
AMU	Arab Maghreb Union	North Africa	Algeria Libya	Mauritania Morocco	Tunisia
COMESA	Common Market for Eastern and Southern Africa	East Africa	Burundi Comoros Congo, DR Djibouti Egypt Eritrea Ethiopia	Kenya Libya Madagascar Malawi Mauritius Rwanda	Seychelles Sudan Swaziland Uganda Zambia Zimbabwe
ECCAS/CEEAC	Economic Community of Central African States	Central Africa	Angola Burundi Cameroon C.A.R.	Chad São Tomé and Principe Congo, DR Congo, Rep. of	Eq. Guinea Gabon Rwanda
ECOWAS	Economic Community of West African States	West Africa	Benin Burkina Faso Cape Verde Côte d'Ivoire Gambia	Ghana Guinea Guinea-Bissau Liberia Mali	Niger Nigeria Senegal Sierra Leone Togo
SADC	Southern African Development Community	Southern Africa	Angola Botswana Congo, DR Lesotho	Madagascar Malawi Mauritius Mozambique Namibia	South Africa Swaziland Tanzania Zambia Zimbabwe

The 26 countries—nearly half of the countries in Africa—hope to eventually form a customs union. Some hailed this as a major step toward establishing a United States of Africa, but the history of "paper RTAs" suggests it prudent to wait for the RTA's details to be established and implemented before hailing it as a major breakthrough.[30] The EAC is not officially a REC, although the treaty calling for the AEC allows for more RECs to be created. More significantly, there are numerous wars within and between many of the 26 African states in the Tripartite's region. In fact, some of the 26 nations are in significant danger of breaking up into separate states. When asked whether it was time to partition Somalia as a way to end nearly two decades of fighting, AU Commission chairman Jean Ping said, "We can't go in that direction, otherwise we'll light the whole continent on fire."[31] Setting aside the merits of Somali partition, the viability of many African states remains in question. The forces pulling many African countries apart may or may not prove stronger than those integrating Africa, but it is clear the various factions fighting across and within many of Africa's borders are indifferent toward the inconsistencies between their goals and those of continental unification.

Central African Economic and Monetary Community (CAEMC/CEMAC)

The Central African Economic and Monetary Community (CAEMC), also known by its French acronym CEMAC, is one of the two CFA franc zone regions. CEMAC/CAEMC's forerunner, the UDEAC, or the Central African Economic and Customs Union (the *Union Douanière et Économique de l'Afrique Centrale*), was established in 1964 by five French-speaking African states—Cameroon, the Central African Republic, Chad, Republic of Congo (Brazzaville), and Gabon—and began operations in 1966. UDEAC had replaced the Equatorial Customs Unions (*l'Union Douanière Équatoriale*), which had been created in 1959.[32] Equatorial Guinea joined UDEAC in 1992, becoming its only Spanish-speaking member.[33] See box 2.3 for a list of CEMAC members.

BOX 2.3. CAEMC/CEMAC MEMBERSHIP

Cameroon	Congo, Republic of (Brazzaville)
Central African Republic	Equatorial Guinea
Chad	Gabon

Source: World Bank, *2005 World Development Indicators*, section 6, Global Links, Table 6.5, "Regional Trade Blocs," http://www.worldbank.org/data/wdi2005/index.html; Masson and Pattillo, *Monetary Geography of Africa*.

In 1972, UDEAC members created the BEAC (*Banque des états de l'Afrique Centrale*), and in 1990 a regional banking supervision commission, COBAC (*Commission Bancaire de l'Afrique Centrale*), was established. In 1992, members agreed to a convention establishing harmonization of their banking regulation.[34]

There are grand plans for CAEMC/CEMAC institutions—including a parliament—but as of 2004, half of the CEMAC/CAEMC members had not ratified the CAEMC/CEMAC's 1994 treaty.[35] There has been, however, a CEMAC peacekeeping mission in the Central African Republic since 2002, including 380 troops.[36]

CEMAC/CAEMC's forerunner, UDEAC, cofounded the ECCAS/CEEAC, the Economic Community of Central African States (*Communauté Économique des États d'Afrique Centrale*) with the Economic Community of the Great Lakes States (CEPGL) and with São Tomé and Principe. The EC-CAS/CEEAC, however, remains an entity on paper more than in reality.[37]

CFA Franc Zones[38]

The West and Central Africa CFA franc zones are currency unions with roots dating to the 1940s; France introduced the CFA franc (originally from *Colonies Françaises d'Afrique*) currency in 1945 and pegged it to the franc in 1948.[39] After a number of institutional developments associated with decolonization, the CFA franc zone emerged in 1964 with institutions that would, with some alterations, last for decades. The CFA franc zone's goal was to form a monetary union among countries whose currencies were linked to the French franc.[40] In reality, the CFA franc zone comprises two regional monetary unions (one each in West and Central Africa) and the Comoros, each with distinctive CFA currencies and with France guaranteeing the convertibility of each of the three CFA franc zone currencies into euros (previously into francs) at specified exchange rates. The two regional monetary unions in the CFA franc zone are the Economic and Monetary Community for Central Africa (CAEMC/CEMAC) and the West Africa Economic and Monetary Union (WAEMU/UEMOA).[41] Each of the two has its own central banks—the BEAC (*Banque des états de l'Afrique Centrale*) for CAEMC/CEMAC and the BCEAO (*Banque Centrale des états de l'Afrique de l'ouest*) for WAEMU/UEMOA—and each, in addition to issuing its own version of the CFA franc, pools its members' foreign exchange reserves, which must equal at least 20 percent of the banks' short-term deposits.[42] The CFA franc currencies are, for West Africa, the franc of the *Communauté Financière Africaine* and, for Central Africa, the franc of the *Coopération Financière en Afrique Centrale* (and the Comoros currency).[43]

All of France's sub-Saharan colonies joined the CFA franc zone upon independence except Guinea and Mali, which sought to distance themselves from capitalism and promote self-reliance. Mali rejoined the CFA franc zone in 1984.[44] See box 2.4 for a list of CFA franc zone members. Madagascar and Mauritania had been members but quit the CFA franc zone when new treaties between CFA members and France were needed following some institutional adaptations to the CFA franc zone's two regional central banks in 1972 and 1973. Madagascar quit to form a planned economy, and Mauritania quit because of differences with its regional neighbors, including ethnic conflicts.[45]

BOX 2.4. TOTAL CFA FRANC ZONE MEMBERSHIP

(Combining East African region, West African region, and the Comoros)

Benin	Equatorial Guinea
Burkina Faso	Gabon
Cameroon	Guinea-Bissau
Central African Republic	Mali
Chad	Niger
Comoros	Senegal
Congo, Republic of	Togo
Cote d'Ivoire	

The CFA franc zone has experienced lower inflation than found elsewhere in Africa, but it is unclear whether the CFA franc zone countries experienced increased economic growth relative to the rest of Africa.[46] Can lower inflation in the CFA franc zone be attributed to the CFA franc zone itself, and should monetary union be something that other developing nations should attempt in order to gain financial stability? According to one recent study, it is difficult to tell because France's convertibility guarantee—the guarantee to exchange CFA francs for euros—is also a credibility guarantee. Credibility is a critical component in any foreign exchange regime, and most African countries do not have the possibility of guaranteed convertibility and thus credibility by a developed country.[47]

Might the CFA franc zone expand? It is possible, but there is a considerable hurdle: French and EU willingness to support convertibility of an expansion. Currently, the French government guarantees convertibility of the CFA franc. If the Franc zone were to increase in size, France would need to get approval from EU members to extend its guaranteed convertibility to the expanded Franc zone.[48] The larger the CFA franc zone, ceteris paribus, the larger France's financial risk from extending convertibility.

In the 1980s, currency overvaluation was increasingly a problem for the CFA franc zone economies. The link to the franc made their currencies more highly valued than would have otherwise been the case, and this put downward pressure on the region's exports. This was made worse after the European Monetary System (EMS) came under strain and the EMS's fluctuation band widened. Thus the CFA franc zone economies took some difficult medicine in 1994: devaluation. Both France and the CFA franc zone members resisted devaluation, but economic crisis eventually led France and then CFA franc zone members to accept devaluation.[49] They also decided that they needed greater economic coordination to go along with their monetary integration, and they created the above-mentioned WAEMU and CAEMC. The devaluation made imports from outside the region more expensive but also served as a catalyst for increased exports. The CFA franc zone economies' growth rates increased substantially after the devaluation.[50]

The West African portion of the CFA franc zone hopes to form a West African Monetary Zone (WAMZ) to then join with the West African CFA zone, the WAEMU/UEMOA, to form a single currency for ECOWAS.[51]

Community of Sahel Saharan States (CEN-SAD), Also Known as COMESSA or CSSS

The CEN-SAD, created in 1998, is headquartered in Libya, and the organization has 28 members, as shown in box 2.5.[52] It envisions itself as a free trade

---

BOX 2.5. CEN-SAD MEMBERSHIP

Benin	Ghana	Nigeria
Burkina Faso	Guinea	São Tomé and Principe
C.A.R.	Guinea-Bissau	Senegal
Chad	Kenya	Sierra Leone
Comoros	Liberia	Somalia
Côte d'Ivoire	Libya	Sudan
Djibouti	Mali	Togo
Egypt	Mauritania	Tunisia
Eritrea	Morocco	
Gambia	Niger	

Source: CEN-SAD website, http://www.cen-sad.org.

agreement with harmonization of some policies. As the Arab Maghreb Union (AMU) has become dormant, interest in the CEN-SAD has increased.

COMESA—Common Market for Eastern and Southern Africa, Including COMESA-FTA

COMESA, the Common Market for Eastern and Southern Africa, was established in 1981 with the goal of free trade, a customs union, a common market, and, eventually, a common currency.[53] It has established a free trade area for 11 of its 19 members and hoped to begin a customs union in 2008.[54] See box 2.6 for a list of COMESA and COMESA-FTA members. At its founding it was known as the Preferential Trade Area for Eastern and Southern Africa (PTA) and consisted of eight members: Comoros, Djibouti, Ethiopia, Malawi, Mauritius, Somalia, Uganda, and Zambia.[55] The PTA, which began lowering tariffs in 1984, was one of the regional organizations that the African Union's forerunner, the Organization of African Unity (OAU), chose as a building block for its proposed African Economic Community (AEC) and in 1993 became COMESA.[56] Nine COMESA members launched the COMESA-FTA in October 2000.[57] These countries removed tariffs on intra-COMESA trade, which is a COMESA-FTA

BOX 2.6. COMESA MEMBERSHIP

Burundi	*Malawi*
Comoros	*Mauritius*
Congo (Dem. Rep.)	*Rwanda*
Djibouti	Seychelles
Egypt	*Sudan*
Eritrea	Swaziland
Ethiopia	Uganda
Kenya	*Zambia*
Libya*	*Zimbabwe*
Madagascar	

Source: "COMESA in Figures" from the COMESA Secretariat, http://about.comesa.int/attachments/060_COMESA%20In%20Figures.pdf (November 2, 2008).

Notes: COMESA-FTA members are in *italics*.

* Libya was approved to be a member in June 2005, and in August 2006 it officially entered COMESA. *Xinhua News Service*, December 6, 2005; "Libya Becomes Full COMESA Member," *Coastweek* (Kenya), September 22–28, 2006. Despite this, Libya is not listed in the WTO's "Madagascar Trade Policy Review" in April 2008.

requirement, while other COMESA members had only partially lowered their tariffs on intra-COMESA trade (Comoros, Eritrea, Uganda, Burundi, and Rwanda), and others had not lowered tariffs on intra-COMESA trade (Democratic Republic of Congo, Ethiopia, Namibia, the Seychelles, and Swaziland).[58] Namibia and Swaziland are also members of the Southern African Customs Union (SACU) and may therefore have to withdraw from COMESA to prevent their serving as a conduit for transshipments of COMESA exports into those fellow SACU countries that are not in COMESA (Botswana, Lesotho, and South Africa).

COMESA's Depth of Integration

The variation of trade openness COMESA members grant one another varies greatly, depending upon their status in the COMESA-FTA and, for those not in the COMESA FTA, upon the degree to which they have achieved tariff reductions in the COMESA's Preferential Trade Agreement. Goods trade among COMESA-FTA members is duty free. COMESA-FTA members will grant tariff reductions reciprocal to those achieved by COMESA's non-COMESA-FTA members, with a minimum tariff reduction of 60 percent. Those that have not met the tariff reduction minimum of 60 percent will get no preferential treatment for their exports to those that have achieved the 60 percent minimum tariff reduction (and, therefore, also to COMESA-FTA members).[59]

When the COMESA-FTA was created in 2000, COMESA had hoped to establish a common external tariff (CET) by 2004, but the goal of a customs union had to be pushed back to 2008 and then to June 2009.[60] The agreed-upon CET rates are zero for raw materials and capital goods, 10 percent for intermediate goods, and 25 percent for finished goods, but the COMESA-FTA's members' domestic classification schemes for what constitutes each of these three categories had not been harmonized as of 2008.[61] This and other nontariff barrier issues suggested that achieving a functioning CET by the end of 2008 might not be practicable.[62] Nontariff barriers have long been a roadblock to freer intra-COMESA trade (as well as external-COMESA trade) and have posed problems in establishing the CET.[63]

COMESA is moving toward greater integration on a number of other fronts. It has established an institution to promote common "national treatment" for foreign investment. The COMESA Common Investment Area (CCIA) was created in 1998, with the Regional Investment Agency (RIA) created in 2006 to implement it. The CCIA is expected to be fully operating by 2010 and offer national treatment by 2015.[64]

Relations among Southern African Regional Groupings and Impact on COMESA Membership

COMESA and SADC had been considering a merger, and the SADC even went so far as to vote for a merger in 1992. COMESA was eager for a merger, but the SADC was hesitant. Thus the two remained competitors. South Africa joined the SADC, and, given South Africa's towering relative economic size in the region, the SADC gained much credibility.[65]

That joint membership is awkward is reinforced by the COMESA secretariat's being in Lusaka, Zambia, which is also an SADC member state.[66] Why do some countries continue to have joint membership? Three potential answers: (1) they are not committed to either agreement; (2) some are concerned with South African dominance in the SADC and so are in COMESA to potentially counter this dominance; and (3) political reasons, such as the desire of Zimbabwe's Robert Mugabe not to be overshadowed by South Africa's leaders.[67] Since South African economic dominance in the region is not going to be challenged in the foreseeable future, one scholar on southern African political economy argues that COMESA is likely to be "used as a forum for anti–South African rhetoric."[68]

Four SADC countries have withdrawn from COMESA: Angola, Lesotho, Mozambique, and Tanzania, although most reportedly did not pull out because of the rivalry. Tanzania's decision to pull out in 2000 came from a combination of Tanzanian industry pressure and concern about a loss of government revenue from tariffs on goods from COMESA members.[69] Instead, the government began working on bilateral preferential agreements with individual COMESA members. This does not sit well with the COMESA secretariat, and it has called for Tanzania to return to COMESA. A business association in Tanzania has also called on the government to return to COMESA and has reportedly offered to help the government pay COMESA membership fees. Other Tanzania businesses, however, fear the increased foreign competition that renewed COMESA membership would bring.[70]

Mozambique pulled out of COMESA to save on fees required to pay its share of the COMESA secretariat and because COMESA did not match Mozambique's economic focus—Mozambique trades more with SADC members than it did with COMESA members, and Mozambique did not intend to enter the COMESA. Additionally, much of Mozambique's trade is already preferential because Mozambique is so poor.[71] Angola pulled out of COMESA—technically suspending its COMESA membership—because of its SADC membership.[72]

In 2000, COMESA signed a Trade and Investment Framework (TIFA) with the US which formalizes discussion between the two about trade and investment.[73] It is often a first step in reaching a bilateral investment or trade agreement.

Common Monetary Area—CMA

The Common Monetary Area (CMA) is made up of four out of the five Southern African Customs Union (SACU) members—Lesotho, Namibia, South Africa, and Swaziland are members, but Botswana is not—and is dominated by the South African rand. It operates effectively, but the three smaller members have no monetary policy autonomy in exchange for greater monetary stability and liquidity. (See the Southern African Customs Union [SACU] section in this chapter for more.)

East African Community (EAC) (Formerly East African Cooperation)

The treaty re-creating the East African Community, which included Kenya, Tanzania, and Uganda was signed in 1999, and the EAC was relaunched in July 2000.[74] Burundi and Rwanda then joined in 2007. The first EAC officially collapsed in 1977 from economic and political disagreements. It had come under pressure from member states' ideological differences—Tanzania moved toward socialism while Kenya and Uganda did not—combined with the war in Uganda to oust Ugandan dictator Idi Amin.[75] Some also believe that the concentration of manufacturing production in Kenya, which was heightened from the EAC's trade integration, contributed significantly to the EAC's premature end.[76] In 1993 the East African Cooperation was formed. This was a far less ambitious agreement that served as a forerunner to the reestablished East African Community.[77]

The East African Cooperation viewed itself as a more rapidly integrating subset of COMESA, but in 2000 Tanzania withdrew from COMESA.[78] This is problematic for the EAC because it now has four of its members in COMESA and one, Tanzania, out of COMESA while at the same time being a customs union that should, in principle, have a common external tariff (CET) for all external trade. Trade from non-EAC members with membership in COMESA will have to be charged COMESA tariff rates under COMESA rules or Tanzania will, by definition, be violating the principle of a CET. But the gulf between principle and reality can be far indeed. If Tanzania goes ahead and charges higher import tariffs on COMESA imports (from non-EAC COMESA members), in violation of the CET principle, companies in COMESA countries could theoretically use Kenya or Uganda to get COMESA tariff rates and then ship to Tanzania at EAC rates.

These technical problems aside, the EAC's relaunch included ambitious goals. EAC nations pledged to first form the East African Customs Union with a common external tariff (CET) and eventually a common market. Other goals were further in the distance: an East African central bank, monetary union, and, reportedly, political federation.[79]

The three original EAC members have experience with monetary integration from the colonial period as members of the British pound-based East African

Currency Board, which initially consisted of Kenya, Uganda, and Tanganyika and later included Zanzibar (which combined with Tanganyika to form Tanzania), Aden, Somalia, and Ethiopia. The three original EAC countries considered establishing a monetary union, but negotiations ended unsuccessfully in 1966.[80] The EAC includes a Court of Justice, the East African Legislative Assembly, and a secretariat in Arusha, Tanzania. The EAC initially believed the customs union would be launched in 2002, but negotiations lasted six years—until March 2004—and the customs union did not come into force until January 1, 2005.[81] Internal tariffs remained on Kenyan industrial exports to its two less-industrialized EAC partners, Tanzania and Uganda, for five years.[82] In 2010, the full customs union was successfully phased in, but there have been immediate complaints about implementation problems at the border.[83]

As this suggests, the EAC has run into some significant implementation problems, even as it moves toward deeper integration. Discord in the EAC emerged in September 2005, with Kenya accusing Uganda of violating the customs union agreement only eight months after it went into effect. Tanzania has been upset with Kenya's abolishing tariffs on pharmaceuticals imported from outside the EAC because, Tanzania believes, it will harm EAC drug companies.[84] Even fully implemented, there are numerous exceptions to the CET.[85] Given some of the contention above and delays, some consider the hoped-for target date for monetary union of 2012 to be overly ambitious.[86]

Economic Community of Central African States (ECCAS), or *Communauté Économique des États d'Afrique Centrale* (CEEAC)

ECCAS, the Economic Community of Central African States, or, in French, CEEAC, the *Communauté Économique des États d'Afrique Centrale*, was jointly formed by the Central African Customs and Economic Union (CACEU/ UDEAC)—which has itself changed into the Central African Economic and Monetary Community (CAEMC/CEMAC)—and the Economic Community of the Great Lakes States (CEPGL) and São Tomé and Principe.[87] See box 2.7 for membership details. ECCAS/CEEAC was established in 1983 and was in force in 1985, but has been inactive since 1992. Despite this, ECCAS/CEEAC remains one the RECs that the African Union envisions as its building blocks to constructing the African Economic Union. The member states of EC-CAS/CEEAC, however, are certainly not moving toward integration, and the ECCAS/CEEAC is an entity only on paper.[88] It was paralyzed by a dearth of funding—members were not paying their membership dues—and by its members' divergent stands on the war in the Democratic Republic of Congo (Kinshasa). Angola joined in January 1999 after a long stint as an observer.[89] An attempt was made in 1998 to "relaunch" the organization, and other institutions have been planned within the organization, but ECCAS/CEEAC remains an institution in name more than in fact.

BOX 2.7. ECCAS/CEEAC MEMBERSHIP

Angola	Congo, Rep. of
Burundi	Equatorial Guinea
Cameroon	Gabon
C.A.R.	Rwanda
Chad	São Tomé and Principe
Congo, Dem. Rep.	

Source: ECCAS/CEEAC, http://www.ceeac-eccas.org/images/map2.jpg; *World Development Indicators, 2005*, World Bank, section 6, Global Links, table 6.5, "Regional Trade Blocs," http://www.worldbank.org/data/wdi2005/index.html.

Economic Community of the Countries of the Great Lakes (CEPGL)

The Economic Community of the Countries of the Great Lakes, also known by its French acronym, CEPGL (*Communauté Économique des Pays des Grands Lacs*)—consists of Burundi, Rwanda, and Democratic Republic of Congo (Kinshasa). It became dysfunctional with the 1994 genocide in Rwanda and effectively fell apart in 1998 due to the subsequent war between Rwanda and fellow CEPGL member, the Democratic Republic of Congo (Kinshasa). Rwanda invaded in order to destroy the Democratic Forces for the Liberation of Rwanda (FDLR). This group includes many extremist Hutus responsible for the Rwandan genocide (primarily) of Tutsis. The Hutus fled into Congo when the then Tutsi rebels, led by Paul Kagame, now Rwandan president, drove the extremist Hutu government from power. He had reportedly backed Congolese Tutsi rebel leader Laurent Nkunda, who had renewed fighting with the Congolese government of Joseph Kabila, but following warming relations with President Kabila and a split among Nkunda's forces, stopped backing Nkunda and then arrested him.[90] An effort was made to relaunch the CEPGL in 2004, but the region remains far too fragile and insecure.[91] Continued warfare in Eastern Congo and tension between Rwanda and Congo remain enormous barriers for the CEPGL to promote any integration in the foreseeable future.

ECOWAS—Economic Community of West African States

Overview

ECOWAS, the Economic Community of West African States, is one of the five RECs on which the AU hopes to build the African Economic Community. The 15-member ECOWAS was created in 1975. See box 2.8 for details on ECOWAS membership. In 1993 ECOWAS's founding treaty was revised to deepen economic integration, calling for a CET in 2000 and monetary union by 2004.[92] ECOWAS did adopt a common external tariff, but it was delayed and only partially went into force in October 2005.[93] The term *partially* applies because two years after its 2005 adoption, the timetable for implementing the CET was still under negotiation.[94] One significant barrier to ECOWAS's CET being implemented is that individual countries lose sole control over tariff revenue.[95] They would still get revenue on tariffs from out-of-region imports, but the level of the tariff could not be changed unless the other CET members agreed, and the revenue is typically pooled and distributed by formula. Moreover, tariff revenue is far more important in funding governments in developing countries because they lack the capacity to effectively implement more administratively burdensome forms of taxation such as income taxes. ECOWAS has not liberalized in other ways: it has yet to harmonize NTBs or establish a program to liberalize free trade in services.[96] ECOWAS aspires to monetary union, but presently this remains only an aspiration. Indeed, there are some deep divisions that prevent ECOWAS from integrating more deeply, despite supranational institutions to carry out deeper integration.

BOX 2.8. ECOWAS MEMBERSHIP

Benin	Liberia
Burkina Faso	Mali
Cape Verde	Niger
Côte d'Ivoire	Nigeria
Gambia	Senegal
Ghana	Sierra Leone
Guinea	Togo
Guinea-Bissau	

Source: OECD, "Regionalism and the Multilateral Trading System," 2003.
Note: Mauritania was a member until 2002. Reportedly it quit over ECOWAS's plans to start a common currency, although others have noted that ethnic conflict has distanced Mauritania from its neighbors. ECOWAS Secretariat and "Mauritania to Quit Ecowas," BBC, December 26, 1999, http://news.bbc.co.uk/2/hi/africa/578966.stm. The decision to quit was made in 1999; it quit in 2002. Ethnic conflict reference in Masson and Pattillo, *Monetary Geography of Africa.*

Falling Short of Monetary Union

ECOWAS's efforts toward this monetary union have been carried out by the ECOWAS Monetary Co-operation Programme (EMCP). Established in 1987, the EMCP was supposed to create a single monetary zone and, by 2000, monetary union, complete with a central bank and shared currency. As is often the case, monetary integration ambition and reality did not correspond. Due to a slow program, ECOWAS moved to a two-track approach. One track consisted of most French-speaking members of ECOWAS, who were already part of a monetary union, the WAEMU/UEMOA. The second track would consist of ECOWAS's non-WAEMU members, who were to create the (second) West African Monetary Zone (WAMZ) by 2003, which would later join with the WAEMU to form the ECOWAS Monetary Zone.[97]

But in 2002, the WAMZ members assessed their progress toward meeting convergence criteria and decided that the January 1, 2003, date for a common currency, the ECO, and a common central bank, the West African Central Bank (WACB), was unrealistic. They pushed the date back to July 1, 2005.[98] As the IMF noted shortly after the missed 2003 deadline, "Member countries of the West African Monetary Zone have a long way to go before achieving convergence among themselves, let alone with the WAEMU countries, making the goal of establishing a single monetary union in West Africa very ambitious and not likely to be viable at this point."[99] As the 2005 deadline approached, the WAMZ members again realized their goal was unrealistic and extended the date until 2009. As the 2009 deadline approached, ECOWAS again pushed the date back to 2015.[100] Monetary union would require WAMZ members to have fully convertible currencies and comply fully with the ECOWAS customs union.[101] They have a long way to go. Only one country, Gambia, met all of the convergence criteria in the three years prior to the missed 2009 deadline.[102] Further inspiration will be required to achieve their monetary aspirations.

Depth of Integration

As noted above, ECOWAS is a customs union with a CET that hopes to become a monetary union. While it struggles on its path to monetary union, ECOWAS does have a high level of institutionalization in many aspects of its members' relations. Supranational policymaking in monetary affairs has been slow to materialize, but there are supranational elements to ECOWAS that operate more smoothly.[103]

ECOWAS has a functioning high court, the Community Court of Justice, which is authorized to issue binding rulings. It has overturned a Niger court ruling that a former slave, Hadijatou Mani, was guilty of bigamy after escaping her "husband," actually her master who had purchased her for $400 when she was 13, and marrying a man of her choosing. The ECOWAS ruling included damages for Mani.[104] Other examples of institutionalization include ECOWAS's issuing passports, although each nation sets its own rules about the permissibility of carrying and recognizing the passports.[105] ECOWAS has been oriented toward security issues far more than is typical in RTAs, and as will be examined below, has authorized and sent peacekeepers into its member nations' territories.

ECOWAS has been oriented toward security issues far more than is typical in RTAs. In fact, by establishing ECOMOG, the ECOWAS Monitoring Group, ECOWAS became the first RTA to establish a multinational peacekeeping force.[106] ECOWAS adopted defense-related protocols in the late 1970s and early 1980s that authorize ECOWAS to intervene in "internal armed conflict with any Member State engineered and supported actively from outside likely to endanger the security and peace in the entire Community."[107] When the AU authorizes peacekeepers, it uses troops from its subregional groupings such as ECOWAS, and ECOWAS troops have been quite active in peacekeeping. In 2003, ECOWAS sent Nigerian-led peacekeepers into Liberia to stop fighting between President Charles Taylor and rebels.[108] Previously it had sent troops to Liberia (1990–1998), Guinea-Bissau (1999), Sierra Leone (1997–1999), and Côte d'Ivoire (2002).[109]

Barriers to ECOWAS Integration

As this suggests, significant divisions in ECOWAS hinder integration. These divisions include those between English and French speakers, widespread poverty, political insecurity, which is both driven by and exacerbates national and ethnic divisions, and smaller countries' fears that regional power Nigeria will come to dominate them.[110]

Anglophone-Francophone Barriers to Monetary Integration

Nine of the 15 ECOWAS members are French speaking, while six are primarily English speaking. The attempt to merge the two subregional monetary unions (one as of yet not created) is hindered by the well-functioning monetary union, the CFA, whose western contingent consists of WAEMU, whose members are all ECOWAS members. The division between the primarily English-speaking members of ECOWAS and the primarily French-speaking members of the WAEMU/UEMOA has blocked further movement toward full monetary integration.[111]

Economic Barriers to Integration: Economic Survival

While the Anglophone-Francophone division in ECOWAS's subregions clearly hinders ECOWAS's effectiveness, there are more immediate problems in the region. One of the most significant is economic survival for some. Niger is facing a significant food crisis that has been made worse by its neighbors' policies; ECOWAS members Nigeria, Burkina Faso, and Mali all restricted grain exports to Niger in 2005—in violation of trade agreements between Niger and fellow ECOWAS members—a move that heightened Niger's food crisis.[112] Trade restrictions among ECOWAS members are not unique to the food crisis. In 2005 Nigeria restricted numerous imports from Ghana and other African countries. Some of these restrictions—on textiles and apparel—were nominally done to stop counterfeiting, but exporters are not convinced.[113] Certainly trade in counterfeit goods is problematic in West Africa, as it is elsewhere.

Insecurity in the ECOWAS Region

There has been a notable lack of security in many ECOWAS countries. Recent history seems filled with coup after coup in West Africa and governments fighting rebels over the control of government and natural resources such as diamond mines. Liberia, which experienced nearly one and a half decades of civil war, and Sierra Leone got most of the headlines due to some terrible atrocities, but sadly, there were other unstable states in the area. Côte d'Ivoire had been among the more stable countries and one of the better economies in the region, but it too succumbed to civil war. Guinea-Bissau had a coup in 2003. So too did Guinea in December 2008. ECOWAS responded by suspending its membership until civilian government was restored. Guinean officials will be banned from attending ECOWAS meetings until Guinea's military government, which took power in a coup shortly after the death of longtime dictatorial president Lasana Conte, agrees to a return to an interim civilian government and elections, as called for in the Guinean constitution.[114] This instability is obviously costly in human lives, but it is also economically devastating, and not just to the countries directly involved. Mali is landlocked, and the fighting in the Côte d'Ivoire cut off its best link to a port, thus raising the costs of both its imports and exports.[115]

Intergovernmental Authority on Development (IGAD)

The seven-member IGAD (see box 2.9 for membership), with a secretariat in Djibouti, is the successor organization of the Intergovernmental Authority on Drought and Development (IGADD). Its forerunner, IGADD, was created in 1986 by six countries in the Horn of Africa—Djibouti, Ethiopia, Kenya, Somalia, Sudan, and Uganda—to coordinate development. Eritrea joined in 1993 after winning its independence.[116] It had little success in coordinating agricultural and environmental programs, and IGADD changed into the IGAD in part to become an RTA.[117] Its efforts to form an RTA have been overshadowed by war and instability within and between IGAD members. Ethiopia and Eritrea have fought bitterly over a territorial dispute, and Ethiopian troops went into Somalia in 2006 to drive out the Eritrean-backed Union of Islamic Courts that had been driving the Transitional Federal Government, the official interim Somali government, out of much of southern Somalia. Sudan's long-running civil war between the Arab-dominated north, which controlled the government, and the "African"-dominated south finally ended, only to see fighting intensify in Sudan's Darfur region. Uganda, one of the more stable IGAD countries in the past two decades, continues to struggle with the bizarre and brutal insurgency of the Lord's Resistance Army. Kenya, which had been the most stable of IGAD countries and moving toward democracy, exploded in ethnic violence in early 2008 in the aftermath of the 2007 elections. IGAD has therefore had to place security issues above economic issues.

BOX 2.9. IGAD MEMBERSHIP

Djibouti	Somalia
Eritrea	Sudan
Ethiopia	Uganda
Kenya	

Fortunately, IGAD has had some successes in diplomacy among its members; it has been heavily involved in the peace process in Sudan and Somalia and, since 2002, monitors conflicts through the Conflict Early Warning and Response Mechanism (CERWARN).[118] CERWARN does more than simply monitor conflicts; it acts preemptively to prevent them with activities such as antiviolence educational campaigns and the branding of livestock, which prevents cross-border cattle rustling.[119] CERWARN monitors three "clusters" of high-violence areas in the IGAD region, but not some of the highest-violence areas such as Sudan's Darfur region.[120]

Despite this continued focus on security issues, IGAD has restructured itself toward economic issues. This was done in part to attract foreign partners, and these foreign partners helped guide its restructuring.[121] IGAD's leader,

Executive Secretary Mahboub Maalim, claimed IGAD would become an FTA in 2009. It did not happen, and such claims about an IGAD FTA in the forseeable future seem doubtful given the continued violence and instability.[122]

Indian Ocean Commission (IOC)

The Indian Ocean Commission was established in 1982 between four Indian Ocean countries—Comoros, Madagascar, Mauritius, and the Seychelles— and Réunion, an overseas department of France. Its primary activities are related to the environment, promoting tourism and tuna fishing.[123] It has not been considered particularly effective, and some have called for it to be abolished and others for it to be a subgrouping of COMESA. It certainly has been overshadowed by both the larger COMESA and SADC, which offer an overwhelmingly larger market. The IOC has been funded substantially by the European Union, which also commissioned a study that called for the IOC to focus on three areas: economic integration; coastal and marine natural resources; and cultural identity and training.[124]

Indian Ocean Rim Association for Regional Cooperation (IOR-ARC)

The Indian Ocean Rim Association for Regional Cooperation (IOR-ARC) began in 1997 and is intended to have broader membership and a broader agenda than the IOC. That agenda includes trade, tourism, investment, and science and technology. [125] See box. 2.10 for a list of the 18 current IOR-ARC members (there had been 19 before the Seychelles quit the organization in 2003 because of financial difficulties).[126]

BOX 2.10. INDIAN OCEAN RIM ASSOCIATION FOR REGIONAL COOPERATION (IOR-ARC) MEMBERSHIP

Australia	Mozambique
Bangladesh	Oman
India	Singapore
Indonesia	South Africa
Iran	Sri Lanka
Kenya	Tanzania
Madagascar	Thailand
Malaysia	UAE
Mauritius	Yemen

Source: "Indian Ocean Rim Association,"Australian Dept. of Foreign Affairs.

Mano River Union (MRU)

The three Manu River Union members—Guinea, Liberia, and Sierra Leone—established a CET in 1977, but civil war and the resulting instability in the 1990s paralyzed the MRU.[127] One Africanist scholar notes, "It shares similar aims with other regional groups, but the MRU is possibly the least meaningful of all of them."[128]

Permanent Inter-State Committee for Drought Control in the Sahel (CILSS) (*Comité Permanent Inter États de lutte contre la Sécheresse dans le Sahel*)

The Permanent Inter-State Committee for Drought Control in the Sahel, better known by its French acronym, CILSS, was established in 1973 to combat desertification in the Sahel and increase food security through cooperation.[129] In practice, this means a coordinated effort to get foreign aid to help cope with reoccurring droughts and associated desertification. The nine-member CILSS (see box 2.11) is not moving toward forming an RTA.

BOX 2.11. CILSS MEMBERSHIP

Burkina Faso	Mali
Cape Verde	Mauritania
Chad	Niger
Gambia	Senegal
Guinea-Bissau	

Source: CILSS, http://www.cilss.bf/.

Regional Integration Facilitation Forum (RIFF)—Formerly the Cross-Border Initiative (CBI)

The Regional Integration Facilitation Forum (RIFF)—known as the Cross-Border Initiative (CBI) until 2000—is a "framework of harmonized policies" that stresses lower barriers to trade, investment, and labor for its 14 member states in Eastern Africa, Southern Africa, and the Indian Ocean.[130] See box 2.12 for RIFF membership details. The RIFF—established in 1993—is open to the members of COMESA, the IOC, and the SADC, and it is sponsored jointly by the International Monetary Fund (IMF), the World Bank, the EU, and the African Development Bank (AfDB).[131] The RIFF is somewhat unique in that it promotes "integration by emergence" instead of through formal treaty obligation. The RIFF uses variable geometry integration, which allows member states to go at their own speed in adopting economic liberalization, but at the same time seeks policy harmonization through agreed-upon targets. These two elements are, theoretically, at odds with each other, but the RIFF hopes peer pressure and the demonstration effect of liberalization's success in RIFF members will lead to harmonization. The RIFF process has established policy parameters that serve as goals for a particular issue area. An example of this is the Road Map for Tariff Reform.[132] This program established a goal of having simpler tariff structures (no more than three rates above zero tariffs) and having a maximum tariff rate of no more than 20–25 percent.[133]

BOX 2.12. REGIONAL INTEGRATION FACILITATION FORUM (RIFF) MEMBERSHIP (FORMERLY THE CROSS-BORDER INITIATIVE)

Burundi	Rwanda
Comoros	Seychelles
Kenya	Swaziland
Madagascar	Tanzania
Malawi	Uganda
Mauritius	Zambia
Namibia	Zimbabwe

Source: World Development Indicators, World Bank, 2005.
Note: Mozambique has requested membership.

The RIFF does not have a secretariat because the RIFF intentionally sought to avoid creating new institutions. The RIFF has facilitated the formation of groups of experts on specific economic reform issues—called technical working groups—which consist of both government personnel and private-sector representatives within each country.[134] To RIFF's proponents the inclusion of the private sector in the technical working groups has helped the RIFF be successful in increasing policy awareness between the governments and business community and in generating support for economic liberalism.

Given some of RIFF's cosponsors—namely, the IMF and World Bank—it should not be surprising that it promotes economic liberalization. Importantly, this economic liberalization includes economic liberalism toward countries outside of the RIFF. Specifically, the RIFF framework seeks low tariff barriers to non-RIFF countries. Some are critical of the RIFF, particularly before its transformation when it was known as the CBI, precisely because of this fact; the CBI was seen as being at cross-purposes with the strategies of the regional groupings from which the CBI drew its membership: COMESA, IOC, and the SADC. These critics viewed the CBI as weakening the RTAs' ability to develop somewhat protected from globalization and to face globalization as a larger unit, not as an individual country. These critics would rather see the region's RTAs be able to keep their members more insulated from, not exposed to, developed countries' economies. Furthermore, CBI critics argue that it is a framework imposed from abroad, not an indigenous, that is to say African, initiative. In response to such criticism, the CBI emphasized that it is merely a vehicle for COMESA members that wish to integrate and liberalize more rapidly than the other COMESA members.[135] This view is extended to SADC and IOC members of the RIFF because many observers note that the CBI/RIFF became more supportive of the agendas of all three RTAs from which it draws its members when it became the RIFF in 2000.[136] Questions remain about the RIFF's role relative to these RTAs, but there is more agreement that there are too many regional groupings in Southern Africa (and elsewhere in Africa) with overlapping and confusing memberships that can make economic activity and therefore development more difficult.

Southern African Customs Union (SACU)

The Southern African Customs Union (SACU), established in 1910, is the oldest customs union in the world. Its roots go back even further, predating the 1910 establishment of the Union of South Africa.[137] The Customs Union Agreement of 1910 provided for customs revenues for the High Commission Territories (HCTs) of Basutoland (later Lesotho), Bechuanaland (later Botswana), and Swaziland, but only on imports from outside the SACU, not from South African–originating trade. Thus South Africans reaped tax revenue benefits from SACU at the expense of the HCTs until the policy was changed in the 1969 South African Customs Union Agreement, which came into force in 1970.[138] Namibia joined in 1990.[139]

Barriers to agricultural trade remain, but other goods move freely among SACU members,[140] and the labor market is also quite integrated.[141] SACU's trade integration does not extend to trade in services, investment, and intellectual property rights (IPRs). But four of the five SACU members have integrated deeply in monetary relations: they share a single currency as legal tender, the South African rand. Botswana is the lone SACU member that is not in the Common Monetary Area (CMA), with Lesotho, Namibia, South Africa, and Swaziland being in both the SACU and CMA. (See also the section earlier in this chapter about the Common Monetary Area.) All five members are also members of the SADC.

Southern African Development Community (SADC)

The Southern African Development Community (SADC), headquartered in Gaborone, Botswana, is a 14-member organization, with 13 having formed a free trade agreement, the SADC Protocol on Trade.[142] See box 2.13 for membership details. The SADC itself was established in the Treaty of Windhoek, signed in 1992 and going into effect in 1993, which calls for SADC members to enter into protocols for deeper cooperation in numerous areas. In 1996 the SADC Protocol on Trade was signed by 11 SADC members, and it entered into force in 2000.[143] Angola joined the SADC Trade Protocol in 2003, with Madagascar joining in 2006.[144] The Democratic Republic of Congo remains the sole SADC member to have not signed the SADC Trade Protocol.

BOX 2.13. SADC MEMBERSHIP

Angola	Mozambique
Botswana	Namibia
Congo, Dem. Rep.	South Africa
Lesotho	Swaziland
Madagascar	Tanzania
Malawi	Zambia
Mauritius	Zimbabwe

Source: SADC, http://www.sadc.int/index.php?action=a1001&page_id=about_corp_profile.

Note: Congo Dem. Rep. has not ratified the SADC Protocol of Trade.

SADC Roots

The SADC's roots are unique and predate the 1992 establishing treaty, the Treaty of Windhoek. The SADC evolved from the Southern African Development Coordination Conference (SADCC), which was created in 1980 by nine states: Angola, Botswana, Lesotho, Malawi, Mozambique, Swaziland, Tanzania, Zambia, and Zimbabwe.[145] The SADC/SADCC uniqueness is that it developed first as a political organization, with its political goal to assist the frontline states—Angola, Botswana, Mozambique, Tanzania, and Zambia—to stand united against the apartheid minority white regime in South Africa.[146] Because South Africa dominated the Southern African economy, the SADCC obviously had to address many economic matters, but this was secondary to the larger goal of changing the South African regime.[147] The primary economic goal for the SADCC was to increase regional cooperation and development in order to reduce the members' dependence upon South Africa; market integration was a future goal.[148]

Despite the assistance the SADCC was receiving from Western countries, establishing the SADCC was brash: the SADCC founders specifically denied South Africa membership and also served as a direct challenge to South African foreign policy and to domestic policies that supported minority white rule: apartheid. The South African government regularly destabilized its neighboring countries—including military incursions—to pressure them into denying the main South African opposition to apartheid, the African National Congress (ANC), safe haven and to prevent communist governments from winning in the region's civil wars. The SADCC campaigned to get the international community to impose sanctions on South Africa. South African president F. W. de Klerk, who came to power in 1989, moved to end apartheid. This led the SADCC in 1992 to change its goal toward market integration. In 1994, the same year that South Africa held its first free, fair, and open elections that led Nelson Mandela and the African National Congress (ANC) to govern South Africa, it joined the SADC.[149]

The SADC faced a tough road toward integration: the countries' economies were not very diversified, the region's infrastructure remained inadequate, and some SADC members—Angola and Mozambique—were devastated by many years of war.[150] Why the change? Many argue that the SADC was an external construct.[151] Western countries paid for nearly all of the development projects undertaken by the SADC and its forerunner, the SADCC.[152] In fact, for approximately four years, British nationals ran the secretariat.

SADC Development Status

The SADC is dominated economically by South Africa. In 1999 South Africa accounted for approximately 71 percent of the SADC's GDP.[153] Many SADC members are desperately poor. Seven SADC countries are categorized as least-developed countries (LDCs), according to the 2001 UNDP Human Development Report: Angola, Democratic Republic of Congo (Kinshasa), Lesotho, Malawi, Mozambique, Tanzania, and Zambia.[154] In fact, even within South Africa itself, poverty is widespread. The region has been hit hard socially and economically by HIV/AIDS. Some SADC members struggle financially and politically. In particular, Zimbabwe has teetered on the edge of bankruptcy for years as its economy collapses from the controversial policies of its president, Robert Mugabe. By contrast, Botswana, Mauritius, and South Africa have the SADC's strongest economies.

The SADC's Trajectory and Depth of Integration

The SADC's distant goal is monetary union in 2016, with intermediate goals of becoming a customs union in 2010 and a common market in 2015.[155] The SADC's more immediate goal is to implement the free trade area that it launched in 2000.[156] Implementation is scheduled to be completed by 2012 for all members except Mozambique, which is scheduled to complete implementation by 2015.[157] SADC Trade Protocol members' liberalization granted one another extended to approximately 41 percent of tariff lines upon entry into force and will rise to 99.7 percent of tariff lines when fully implemented in 2015.[158] Measured by the value of trade, 36 percent of trade was liberalized upon entry into force and 91 percent of the value of trade within the SADC's Trade Protocol will be liberalized by full implementation in 2015.

The SADC's rules of origin (RoO) are, like many RTAs, complex. There are no RoO that apply across all products covered in the SADC Trade Protocol. Most products with non-SADC inputs receive SADC tariff treatment if there is production sufficient to change its tariff classification (CTC) in the Harmonized System (HS).[159] Additionally, specific production steps must be taken within the SADC for some products and the total non-SADC inputs total no more than 30 percent to 65 percent, depending on the product, to receive SADC trade benefits.[160]

Eleven of the 13 SADC Trade Protocol members (all except Madagascar and Swaziland) have also agreed to eliminate technical barriers to trade (TBT) such as sanitary and phytosanitary measures (SPS).[161] The elimination of NTBs such as this will be a crucial demonstration of the SADC's desire for liberalized integration. There are provisions for intellectual property rights (IPRs) that are consistent with the WTO's TRIPS. In other words, unlike many US bilateral RTAs, the SADC Trade Protocol is not "TRIPS-plus." The SADC's dispute resolution mechanism is also similar to the WTO's.[162]

Despite this picture of progress toward integration, most analysts suggest that the SADC members are not fully committed toward market integration as of now and cite membership in conflicting RTAs in the region as evidence. Whether the SADC Trade Protocol members meet their tariff liberalization schedules and eliminate NTBs will also determine that commitment.

Sahel and West African Club (SWAC)

The Sahel and West African Club (SWAC) describes itself as an informal forum. It was created in 1976 to encourage coordinated and sustained aid programs in the Sahel region and West Africa.[163] It is "responsible to" the OECD and has a secretariat in Paris.[164] Programs are approved by a strategy and policy group, which comprises donors and West African civil society groups. See box 2.14 for details on the SWAC membership.

BOX 2.14. SWAC MEMBERSHIP

Benin	Guinea
Burkina Faso	Liberia
Cameroon	Mali
Cape Verde	Mauritania
Chad	Niger
Côte d'Ivoire	Nigeria
Gambia	Senegal
Ghana	Sierra Leone
Guinea-Bissau	Togo

Source: OECD, "Sahel and West Africa Club," http://www.oecd.org/document/62/ 0,3343,en_38233741_38242551_38257982_1_1_1_1,00.html.

West African Economic and Monetary Union—WAEMU/UEMOA

The West African Economic and Monetary Union (WAEMU), or *Union Économique et Monétaire de l'ouest Africaine* (UEMOA), formerly known as the West African Monetary Union (WAMA/UMOA), is the Western African portion of the CFA franc zone. The WAEMU/UEMOA was founded January 10, 1994, after the CFA franc was devalued, replacing the West Africa Economic Union (WAEU/CEAO).[165] WAEMU members (see box 2.15 for details) have sought to liberalize internally so that trade integration might catch up to currency integration. Trade liberalization's pace has been gradual, according to the WTO secretariat. In 2000, the WAEMU began its CET, which operates with harmonized tariff and statistical classifications and common customs valuation procedures.[166] The WAEMU coordinates economic policies in a number of key economic sectors—agriculture, energy, and industry—and has agreed on a common competition policy but has been unable to agree on a common investment policy.[167] See the discussion of the CFA franc zone earlier in this chapter for more.

BOX 2.15. WAEMU/UEMOA MEMBERSHIP

Benin	Mali
Burkina Faso	Niger
Côte d'Ivoire	Senegal
Guinea-Bissau	Togo

Source: Crawford and Fiorentino, "Changing Landscape of RTAs"; WTO Regional Trade Agreements, http://www.wto.org/english/tratop_e/region_e/region_e.htm.

3

The Americas

In 1990 President George H. W. Bush (the elder Bush) boldly called for free trade from "Anchorage to Tierra del Fuego." Thus the idea and political momentum for what would become the Free Trade Area of the Americas (FTAA) began. Why the call for hemispheric free trade? There were two primary reasons: a change in economic models across the Americas and what would later be called "competitive liberalization" whereby countries are motivated to enter into RTAs with the US to match preferential access to the US market granted to competitors.

By the 1990s, the dominant economic model in much of Latin America, import substitution industrialization (ISI), had run aground. ISI helped many Latin American countries industrialize, but the protectionism that initially allowed so-called infant industries to be established also sheltered industries from competition to the point that they did not keep up with productivity gains elsewhere in subsequent decades. ISI's shortcomings were made more acute by the debt crisis of the 1980s, thus many countries in the region began to liberalize their economies.[1] Free trade can be seen as a natural extension of liberalizing one's domestic market. But there was another force that also changed the economic strategy of many Latin American and Caribbean (LAC) countries in the 1990s: competitive liberalization. Competitive liberalization flowed from NAFTA and, with President Bill Clinton's upgrading of the Asia Pacific Cooperation Forum (APEC) in 1993, making it central to his trade strategy in the Pacific Rim, Latin America's non-NAFTA and non-APEC countries feared being excluded from the world's largest market.[2] Relative exclusion from the US market would make these LAC countries less attractive for foreign investment than their rivals that have relatively better preferential access.[3] To accentuate this point, a surge of investment flowed into Mexico in anticipation of NAFTA as the agreement was still being negotiated. Caribbean countries already had preferential access to the US market through the Caribbean Basin Initiative (CBI), but that access was not as good as Mexico's would be under NAFTA. There were US programs designed to minimize the degree to which NAFTA would diminish the gap between Mexico's access to the US and that given to other LAC countries. For instance, President Bush (the elder) announced the Enterprise for the Americas Initiative (EAI) just after NAFTA negotiations were announced.[4] After NAFTA passed in 1993, the CBI nations pushed for CBI parity, which would grant NAFTA-like access for apparel exports to the US; but CBI parity faced deep political resistance in the US and did not materialize. In 1992, the US initiated the Andean Trade Preference Act (ATPA), which extended CBI-like benefits to Andean nations.[5] It was clear to many LAC countries that these measures were insufficient; the measures were often more piecemeal than a regular FTA and were not permanent. Moreover, not every country in the region qualified for these programs. Thus, NAFTA, combined with APEC's increased importance, shifted the dynamics underlying integration in the Western Hemisphere dramatically toward accepting regional integration with the US.

Despite an environment more supportive of hemispheric trade integration in the 1990s, there were significant differences between the US and South American visions of integration in the Americas. These divergent visions and tension that flow from them remain today. In fact, there are substantial tensions over integration within South America itself, between MERCOSUR and Andean nations and between centrist and more radical critics of the economic liberalization pushed for by the US. In some cases this reflects differences in ideology, as one can readily gather from Hugo Chávez's repeated criticism of the US. At other times, it reflects differences between countries' existing trade relationships with the US—can access be unilaterally dissolved by the US?—and whether a country has viable alternatives to embracing the US. Some countries have reciprocal trade agreements with the US, such as NAFTA and CAFTA, granting them guaranteed access to the US market. Others have nonreciprocal and partial-scope preferential trade agreements, such as the Andean Trade Preference Act (ATPA) for Andean countries, the Caribbean Basin Initiative (CBI) for the Caribbean and Central American countries, and the multilateral GSP program, which all provide access to the US market but can be removed unilaterally and apply only to some products and product volumes. Nonreciprocal and partial-scope preferential trade agreements offer no shelter against the US using trade remedies such as antidumping duties (AD) and countervailing duties (CVD). This was made quite apparent when President Bush temporarily raised tariffs against steel imports in 2002 but exempted countries that had RTAs with the US.[6] Variation in the degree to which economies are dependent upon the US market led to alternative visions of regional integration in South America. Some countries are less dependent upon the US market because they have alternative strategies that may not be viable for others. Venezuela has oil; most other LAC countries do not. Brazil has a larger industrial sector and larger overall domestic market than other LAC countries, giving it more to lose to US competition and allowing it a greater range of possible negotiated trade agreements with other sizable markets, such as the EU.

SOUTH AMERICAN RTAs

There are two subregional trade groupings in South America: MERCOSUR and the Andean Community of Nations (CAN). See figure 3.1, "South American Spaghetti Venn Diagram," for membership details of these and other RTAs in the Americas. Of these two, MERCOSUR's economic weight is substantially greater. Only a handful of countries in South America do not belong to one of these two groupings: Chile and some smaller countries along the Caribbean—Guyana, Suriname, and the French dependency, French Guyana. The two main blocs, MERCOSUR and CAN, have agreed to form a free trade agreement. Chile is an associate member of MERCOSUR, while the other three independent South American countries—Guyana and Suriname—remain outside of these blocs, as does French Guyana. All the independent South American countries have joined together in the Union of South American Nations (UNASUR), but currently UNASUR promotes political integration more than economic integration.[7] There are some serious security problems that interfere with political integration in South America. Tension between Colombia and some of its neighbors over harboring, or at least housing, FARC camps has been an ongoing source of political acrimony.[8] In March 2008 this acrimony threatened to escalate into war. Colombia attacked FARC camps in Ecuadorian territory. The Colombian military claimed to find computers that provided evidence of Venezuelan president Hugo Chávez's having given financial support to the FARC. In response to this violation of Ecuadorian sovereignty, Venezuela and Ecuador severed diplomatic ties with Colombia and mobilized troops along their respective Colombian borders. The war scare ended through diplomacy, but the episode demonstrated lingering tensions that make the UNASUR's vision of political integration unlikely in the current environment.

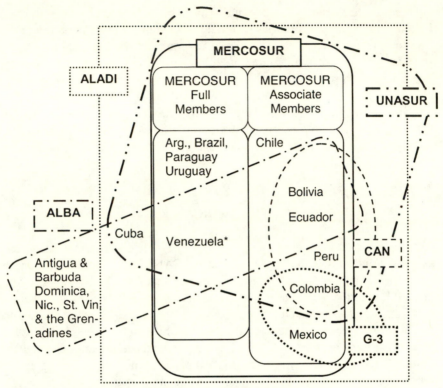

Figure 3.1.   South American Spaghetti Venn Diagram
Key: See list of abbreviations.
*Venezuela withdrew from CAN and the G-3 in 2006 and will, pending ratification, enter MERCOSUR as a full member.

The FTAA could also integrate the economies of South America with the rest of the hemisphere, but it has reached a stalemate that is not likely to be broken until the Doha Development Agenda talks are completed. The FTAA remains stalled over both wider economic strategic differences—Brazil and others are hesitant to integrate fully with the US until South America is itself more integrated, thus strengthening the South American negotiating position relative to the dominant US economy—and more narrow economic concerns. The US, for instance, is hesitant to open its agricultural markets, especially for some sensitive crops such as sugar and oranges, and many South American countries are hesitant to open their markets in industrial goods or to support the investment and intellectual property rights provision the US wants.

CONTEXT OF SOUTH AMERICAN RTAS: SOUTH AMERICAN IPE—STATISM, ECONOMIC LIBERALISM, AND ITS CRITICS

There has been a backlash against the economic liberalism promoted in the 1980s and 1990s that so notably changed decades of South America's economic nationalism. The state's significant role in Latin American economies took many forms, but generally governments attempted to promote their domestic industries by restricting industrial imports through high tariffs or other trade barriers. Captive domestic markets helped domestic industries succeed across much of Latin America and fostered economic growth and development. Once established, however, most domestic producers never fully weaned themselves off state support and a protected market, and gaps between them and foreign companies—in productivity, quality, and innovation—showed the limitations of this model. As economic growth slowed, other problems brought sea changes to the statist economic model. The debt crisis of the 1980s meant that many Latin American countries had to open their economies in order to attract desperately needed investment. Mexico, for instance, which had not been a GATT member, lowered trade barriers and joined the GATT in 1986. By the early 1990s, Mexico had entered into negotiations for a free trade agreement with the US and Canada, had tamed its historically high inflation, and was attracting significant foreign investment. Many other Latin American economies followed similar economically liberal trajectories in the hope of trade, investment, and economic growth. Brazil also was able to tame its high inflation. It did so by linking its currency to the US dollar. This successfully brought stability to Brazil's currency to such a degree that the finance minister given credit for the policy, Fernando Henrique Cardoso, became the next Brazilian president. This demonstrates economic liberalism's ascendancy all the more, given Cardoso's past. He had been an academic strongly associated with dependency theory, a set of theories that generally argues that economic liberalism was to blame for Latin American underdevelopment.[9]

While many of the economically liberal policies did lower inflation and attract foreign investment, there were complaints that turned into a backlash. Income inequalities grew; economic growth was not the same as economic development, argued critics. Some notable successes from the liberalization efforts became high-profile debacles. Mexico's currency dropped through the floor in 1994–1995, and Brazil was forced to break the link between the real and the dollar amid a currency crisis. Both economies recovered from these setbacks, but what faith in liberalism there had been was tempered.

Others, such as Venezuela's president Hugo Chávez—went beyond doubting liberalism. For a long time Chávez had been one of the most vocal anti–economic liberals in South America, but his following increased as economic liberalism came under greater criticism in the region and as his ability to spend oil revenues in support of his worldviews grew. High oil prices have helped Venezuela's ability to preferentially sell oil and therefore extend his influence. In 2005, six Caribbean and Central American countries agreed to purchase oil using Venezuela's preferential financing. This includes Cuba, which has sent doctors to Venezuela to treat poor patients for free. Argentina has paid for Venezuelan oil with cattle exports to Venezuela.[10] In 2008, the Petrocaribe initiative offered 185,000 barrels of oil per day to 15 Caribbean and Central American countries. The oil, half of which goes go Cuba, is offered on easy terms: Venezuela offers 25-year loans at 1 percent interest rates.[11]

His attraction is not merely cheap oil. There is populism to his economic strategy, known as *Chavismo*. *Chavismo* is Chávez's ideology, policies, and style, all reminiscent of his friend, Cuba's Fidel Castro. In some ways Chávez is "Castro-lite." They share a bombastic style, and Chávez is clearly a leftist, but he is not communist. He speaks of helping the poor using government but also seeks full membership in a capitalist FTA, MERCOSUR. Private property remains legal in Venezuela, but he is targeting 700 plants for expropriation, and he is considering forming a national mining company. He has increased spending on health care and education for the poor, but foreign investment is dropping.[12] Thus, money from Venezuela's state-owned oil company, *Petróleos de Venezuela* (PDVSA), is key to implementing Chávez's "Bolivarian" revolution, as he calls it.

Chávez is ambiguously and decreasingly democratic—he was elected after a failed coup attempt but has consolidated power and thus diminished democracy in Venezuela, while Castro is virulently antidemocratic. Chávez is rhetorically anti-American, as is Castro, but operationally Chávez is more ambiguously anti-American. He lambastes the US and speaks out loudly and repeatedly to stop the FTAA, but the oil exports continue to flow to the US, and other economic ties between the two have not been curtailed.

His attacks on the FTAA moved from oratorical to operational when he proposed an alternative to the FTAA and when he began programs to sell oil at below-market rates to many countries in the region. His alternative integration scheme is the "Bolivarian Alternative for the Americas." Initially, Fidel Castro was the only leader to have officially endorsed it, but since then other countries have joined. The initiative's goals are broad—to reduce poverty—and have yet to be fleshed out as specific policies. Access to below-market-rate oil is the primary inducement in the initiative.[13] As noted above, Chávez has initiated the Petrocaribe initiative to preferentially sell oil to Caribbean countries. He has also established the Petrosur alliance with Argentina and

Brazil for joint oil exploration and development, and he is reportedly considering another similar alliance with Bolivia, Colombia, and Ecuador.[14]

No matter what becomes of his regional integration ambitions, Chávez clearly enjoys being the thorn in the side of the US: Citgo, owned by Venezuela's state-owned oil company, *Petróleos de Venezuela* (PDVSA), started selling home heating oil with a 40 percent discount to low-income households in Massachusetts and New York in 2005.[15]

CARIBBEAN RTAs

Since Caribbean nations typically have small populations and economies, globalization's challenges loom even larger for them, and they also find themselves short on power in international trade negotiations. Efforts to stem their economic vulnerability and to increase their clout in international trade negotiations have propelled Caribbean economic integration. A truly integrated Caribbean would certainly amplify the voices of the member states.

The primary regional institutions are CARICOM and the Association of Caribbean States (ACS). See figure 3.2, "Caribbean Spaghetti Venn Diagram," for an overview of the overlapping Caribbean RTAs' membership. The ACS is a wider and broader institution whose primary purpose is to foster cooperation, while CARICOM consists mostly of English-speaking Caribbean states and focuses on integration. CARICOM states have had a free trade agreement and customs union for some time, and in January 2006, six CARICOM states entered into a single market. That the ACS focuses on cooperation while CARICOM focuses on integration is not surprising, given the different scope of their membership. The ACS consists of 25 full members with three associate members that represent approximately 237 million people, while CARICOM has 15 members that represent approximately 13 million people, most of whom have closer historical and cultural ties with one another than found in the ACS.[16]

Another grouping is in the East Caribbean subregion among the seven states of the Organization of Eastern Caribbean States (OECS). The OECS, formed in 1981, includes deeper integration than is typically found in regional integration initiatives in the form of a common currency and central bank.

CONTEXT OF CARIBBEAN RTAs:
CARIBBEAN IPE—DIVERSITY,
VULNERABILITY, AND SECURITY

The island nations of the Caribbean are diverse ethnically, linguistically, and in their colonial legacies. Great Britain, France, and Spain were the dominant

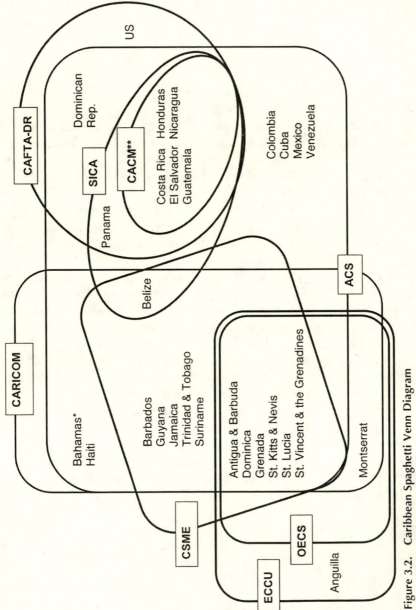

CARICOM

CAFTA-DR

US

CSME

Bahamas*
Haiti

Barbados
Guyana
Jamaica
Trinidad & Tobago
Suriname

Belize

Panama

Dominican
Rep.

SICA

CACM**

Costa Rica   Honduras
El Salvador Nicaragua
Guatemala

Colombia
Cuba
Mexico
Venezuela

OECS

ECCU

Antigua & Barbuda
Dominica
Grenada
St. Kitts & Nevis
St. Lucia
St. Vincent & the Grenadines

Montserrat

Anguilla

ACS

Figure 3.2.   Caribbean Spaghetti Venn Diagram
Key: See list of abbreviations.
* The Bahamas is a member of the Community but not the Common Market.
** Belize and Panama have joined the CACM's political body.

colonial powers in the region and have each left their legacy on it, but other colonial powers also influenced the region, such as the Netherlands and the US. Indeed, one difference among Caribbean states is their current sovereignty status. Some—such as Puerto Rico and the Netherlands Antilles—remain dependent and thus part of their colonial country, while many others have only recently become independent, such as Dominica in 1978. Some have been independent for a long time, such as Haiti, independent since 1804.[17]

There is also a great deal of economic diversity in the Caribbean. Some of the region's countries and dependencies have per capita incomes near or even above the EU average.[18] Typically this is achieved through tourism, offshore banking, and ship registrations. But more of the region's countries and dependencies are poor, and some, such as Haiti, are desperately so. Overreliance on a handful of commodities is also typical in the region, with bananas typically being the dominant export. The islands tend to have small populations—many Caribbean countries have fewer than 100,000 people—but some in the region stand out as comparatively large, having populations above or approaching 10 million, such as Cuba, the Dominican Republic, and Haiti.[19] Despite the small populations, many countries are small islands and thus have population pressures that often strain resources in the region.

Traditional security issues—matters of international war and peace—are not as significant in the Caribbean today as they are in most of the world, nor are they as important in the Caribbean as they once were. Animosity and conflict between Cuba and the US could worsen at any time, but armed conflict is not considered likely. The US military has been used in the Dominican Republic in 1965, Grenada in 1983, Panama in 1989, and Haiti in 1994. The US was involved in many of the Central American civil wars that peaked in the 1990s. Haiti remains the most significant security problem in the region, but most of the concerns are humanitarian. Haiti often serves as a prime example of a failed state, and it remains one of the poorest countries in the world. It remains unstable despite the efforts of peacekeepers and much aid. Haiti and the Dominican Republic—who share the island of Hispaniola—have an uneasy relationship with each other. The Dominican Republic fears a flood of Haitians seeking stability and employment; there are already approximately one million Haitians in the Dominican Republic. Haiti accuses the Dominican Republic of abusing Haitian immigrants.[20] Today the region's security is threatened by nontraditional issues such as drug trafficking and violent crime more than by traditional security threats.

One commonality across the region is the feeling of vulnerability. The vulnerability goes beyond hurricanes and global warming to more mundane economic vulnerabilities shared by the Caribbean's economies. The most significant vulnerability is their dependence upon tourism and too narrow a range of export goods. There are vulnerabilities from changes in the global economy. For instance, some of the more developed economies in the region have come under pressure to change their financial services laws to minimize the degree to which they are used to launder drug trafficking profits and to serve as tax havens. The OECD initiative against tax havens—the Forum on Harmful Tax Practices—applied pressure on Caribbean financial services to increase transparency or face sanctions from OECD countries.[21] Over half of the territories and countries on the OECD's 2000 list of tax havens were in the Caribbean; all Caribbean territories and countries on the list have since changed policies and are no longer considered "uncooperative" tax havens.[22] The region is also vulnerable to changes in unilateral preferential trade agreements with both the EU and the US.

The Caribbean's preferential access to the EU market comes from the Africa, Caribbean, Pacific-EU Partnership Agreement. Since the agreement allows Caribbean exports into the EU at preferential rates, it discriminates against other countries that also want to export into the EU. The ACP-EU Partnership had long received an exception from WTO provisions because it discriminated against non-ACP countries' exports. That exception to WTO provisions ran out in 2008; thus the region has had to renegotiate the agreement to make it WTO-compatible.[23] The Caribbean banana producers' preferential access to the EU market has been under attack since a 2001 WTO ruling against the EU's banana import regime, with the end to the ACP-EU Partnership being yet another blow. The EU has attempted to continue banana preferences for ACP countries, but in a different manner and to a lesser degree, but WTO dispute resolution panels continue to reject EU proposals. A recent and significant EU proposal that was rejected would have taken effect on January 1, 2006, and would have allowed a quota of duty-free access for ACP bananas and a single tariff for non-ACP banana exporters (lower than the previous non-ACP-banana tariff that had already been rejected).[24] In short, the Caribbean's ACP preferences in the EU market have been in jeopardy and cannot be counted on in the future.

Many Caribbean countries have preferential access to the US market through the Caribbean Basin Initiative (CBI), and it too is in a multiple-step process of ending. The CBI, first implemented in 1984, gives preferential access for many goods exported to the US. After NAFTA made CBI access to the US relatively less preferential than NAFTA access, CBI nations began to push for CBI parity that would grant roughly NAFTA levels of preferential access to the US for apparel exports. This, however, ran into deep political resistance in the US. CBI access to the US market was enhanced in 2000 with the United States Caribbean Basin Trade Partnership Act. This program gives

NAFTA-like access to the US for those CBI nations that are preparing to join NAFTA or a similar FTA, but it was set to expire in 2008. This deadline was pushed back to September 30, 2010.[25] Thus, the Caribbean has a massive reason to enter into a free trade accord with the US. The US hoped this would be the FTAA, but the FTAA's future has been clouded by stalled negotiations.

Given their unique position in the global economy—small and vulnerable—Caribbean nations have been calling out for different rules for small and developing economies in the world trading system. See box 3.1 for a synopsis of the development challenges facing small states. As one regional trade minister put it, "In a world of giants, the only space we have is where people understand that there are differences and there must be different rules."[26] This perceived need for greater clout has been a powerful incentive for Caribbean countries to coordinate and integrate. They hope to amplify their voice and thus increase their chances for economic survival and, for some, prosperity.

BOX 3.1. SPECIAL DEVELOPMENT CHALLENGES FACED BY SMALL STATES

- Remoteness and isolation
- Openness (greater susceptibility to international economic developments)
- Susceptibility to natural disasters and environmental change
- Limited economic diversification
- Poverty
- Limited administrative capacity in the public and private sectors

These six challenges lead to greater income volatility and lower access to external capital markets.

Source: "Small States: Meeting Challenges in the Global Economy," Report of the Commonwealth Secretariat/World Bank Joint Task Force on Small States, April 2000, http://www.worldbank.org/smallstates/ and http://www.thecommonwealth.org, ii–iii.

Caribbean Security Anachronism: US-Cuban Relations

The US conspicuously excludes Cuba from its calls for hemispheric free trade; this is not surprising, given its longstanding embargo on trade with Cuba. It was first instituted under President Kennedy in 1961 as a way to punish the newly established Castro regime.[27] In 2008, eight US presidents later, Castro announced his resignation, but his political system and the embargo remain. During most of this period, the embargo had been quite stable. US policy toward Cuba was not about to change significantly during the Cold

War, and so the longtime virulently anti-Castro Cuban-American voters in Florida—a large swing state in presidential elections—remained themselves swing voters and politically active. But with the end of the Soviet Union and therefore Soviet financial help, Cuba struggled economically and started to change its policies. Out of desperation it began to open to foreign investment, which came mostly from the European Union and Canada. Some in the US began to argue it was time to engage with Castro's Cuba in order to reward its increased openness and to moderate Castro.

Instead US policy became tougher after two US civilian aircraft were shot down in 1996 over international waters. Two Republican members of Congress, Senator Jesse Helms and Representative Dan Burton, sponsored a bill that extended the US embargo to companies and individuals in third countries. The Cuban Liberty and Democratic Solidarity Act, better known as Helms-Burton, was signed by President Bill Clinton but was not implemented because other countries were incensed and threatened to retaliate against the US if the bill were implemented. Under Helms-Burton, US companies could sue—in US courts—any foreign company or individual that profited from business involving property in Cuba that had been owned by US companies before the revolution and that had been nationalized without compensation. US dominance of pre-Castro Cuba was so extensive that this would essentially mean that any company in the world that did a significant amount of business in Cuba could be taken to court in the US. Implementing this law was stopped by mutual agreement between the US and its allies after US allies took legal action in a number of jurisdictions: Canada and Mexico filed a suit with NAFTA's dispute resolution mechanism, arguing that Helms-Burton violated NAFTA; the EU brought a case to the WTO arguing that Helms-Burton violated WTO provisions; and Canada and the EU both passed legislation allowing companies to sue any US company that had won a Helms-Burton lawsuit.[28] The negotiated settlement meant that countries had to list their companies that invested in Cuba if the investment used any of the formerly US-owned, nationalized property. In exchange, the US would not implement Helms-Burton.

As the disastrous Helms-Burton episode demonstrated, the rest of the world was going to do business with Cuba, no matter what the US wanted. US companies felt they were being punished by the embargo more than Castro. They could watch their foreign competitors export to Cuba, or they could try to change US law. In 2000, Congress eased the trade ban with the Trade Sanctions Reform and Export Enhancement Act, signed into law by President Bill Clinton. This law allowed the sale of agricultural products to Cuba, and Cuban purchases of US agricultural products—which had been zero—rose so that by 2004 Cuba was the 25th-largest US agricultural importer. This trade is highly regulated; it requires a license from the US Treasury Department, and it requires payment in cash instead of using US-backed financing arrangements that are common with agricultural exports to developing nations.[29] The George W. Bush administration (the younger Bush) tightened some of the regulations regarding trade and travel with Cuba, but US agricultural exports are still legal under those tight regulations.

Before Helms-Burton, the rest of the world viewed the US embargo on Cuba with curiosity and some disdain. With Helms-Burton, this curiosity and disdain turned to hostility. With Helms-Burton's implementation halted, the view is back to curiosity with some disdain. In 2005, the UN General Assembly voted 191–4–1 to urge the US to end the embargo.[30] This nonbinding vote—reminiscent of many previous votes—was symbolic of the status quo of US-Cuban relations.

CONTEXT OF CENTRAL AMERICAN RTAs:
CENTRAL AMERICAN IPE—HISTORY AND SECURITY

History of Central American Integration

There is a shared history of on-again, off-again integration in much of Central America. Five Central American states—Costa Rica, El Salvador, Guatemala, Honduras, and Nicaragua—all declared their independence from Spain shortly after Mexico did in 1821. Under Spanish colonial rule, the five had administratively linked (with portions of Mexico) in the Audencia of Guatemala, with Guatemala City as the administrative capital. The declarations of independence were not only from Spanish rule but also from Guatemala City's rule.[31] The five Central American nations considered federation with Mexico, but political upheaval there led to the five instead establishing the Federal Republic of Central America, with a national government and five state governments. The Central American Federation, as it was often called, lasted from 1825 to 1838.[32] The states in the newly formed federation, however, refused to fund the federal government in Guatemala, leading to a civil war from 1826 to 1829. The federation was reorganized, but then, like Mexico itself, was torn by liberal-conservative divisions, and the union ended in 1838. There were numerous attempts to reconstitute the union during much of the 1800s and beyond. Indeed, the US proposed a union at the Central American Conference of 1922–1923 in Washington, DC. Given the history of heavy-handed US policies in the region, the proposal was not popular.[33] It was not until 1960 that four Central American states—El Salvador, Guatemala, Honduras, and Nicaragua—signed the General Treaty of Central American Integration. The treaty, which established the Central American Common

Market, went into effect with Costa Rica joining shortly thereafter.[34] The integration brought by the CACM would soon be shattered, first by the so-called Soccer War between El Salvador and Honduras in 1969 and then by ideological civil wars of the 1970s and 1980s. The CACM was brought back to life in the 1990s with Central American peace, and the CACM members integrated more deeply into a customs union in 2003. States in the region also joined the Association of Caribbean States, a loose organization with broad membership, and Costa Rica, El Salvador, Guatemala, Honduras, and Nicaragua—along with the Dominican Republic—entered into the Central American Free Trade Agreement (CAFTA) with the United States.

Central American Security Integration?

Seven Central American countries are considering forming a joint military battalion to better respond to shared security concerns such as drug trafficking, organized crime, and natural disasters. Defense officials from Belize, Costa Rica, El Salvador, Guatemala, Honduras, Nicaragua, and Panama met with then US secretary of defense Donald Rumsfeld at a conference on security relations in Key Biscayne, Florida, in 2005. Some question the wisdom of increasing the role of Central American militaries because many of the region's militaries have such deplorable human rights records. Proponents of the proposed 700-soldier battalion argue that the region's growing gang-related violence—combined with long-standing problems such as drug trafficking and the need for coordinated disaster relief—suggest such a force is needed.[35] The limits to security cooperation are strong given the very different approach taken by Costa Rica compared to many of its neighbors. Costa Rica has no traditional military; its 1949 constitution abolished the military and established the much-revered civil guard.

RTAs IN THE AMERICAS

Andean Community of Nations (CAN), Including the Andean Free Trade Area (Formerly the Andean Group or Andean Pact)

The Andean Community of Nations (CAN), known as the Andean Group until 1997, was established by Bolivia, Colombia, Ecuador, Peru, and Chile in 1969. Venezuela joined in 1973 only to withdraw in 2006, and Chile withdrew in 1976.[36] Thus the CAN is left with four members: Bolivia, Colombia, Ecuador, and Peru.

The initial goal was an Andean customs union and then a Latin America common market, but integration stalled in the 1970s. The debt crisis in the 1980s further stalled integration.[37] In the 1990s, integration was substantially revived, and the Andean Community is one of the most institutionalized regional agreements among developing countries.[38]

In 1991 CAN members agreed to establish a free trade area to be effective in 1992 and called for the establishment of a common external tariff. The free trade zone was achieved in 1993, and the CET entered into force in 1995 for three CAN members: Colombia, Ecuador, and Venezuela.[39] The CET has four tiers—5 percent for raw materials, 10 percent or 15 percent for semimanufactured goods, and 20 percent for finished goods—with a nominal average rate of 13.6 percent.[40] CAN members Bolivia and Peru have not followed the CET—Bolivia has kept its two-tier system, and Peru, which had pulled out of the CAN in 1992, rejoined but is not yet participating in the CET.[41]

In the early 1990s, Peru became estranged from its fellow CAN members over the need to harmonize specific macroeconomic policies. In 1992 CAN members approved Peru's suspension from a number of CAN's trade provisions: Peru did not move to fully reduce tariffs for CAN members, did not join the CET, and did not harmonize its macroeconomic policies. Peru did, however, enter into bilateral FTAs with CAN members to institutionalize the existing trade relations. In other words, Peru resisted deeper integration but wished to preserve the integration it already had with CAN members.[42] Peru was readmitted in 1994, although it remained on the sidelines of CAN integration until a 1997 agreement phased in Peru's participation in the CAN's free trade area, the Andean Free Trade Area. Peru's full inclusion in CAN's free trade area was completed on December 31, 2005.[43]

Bolivia has been the scene of political upheaval in recent years. Presidents have been driven from office and massive protests against globalization have become a staple of Bolivian political life. A significant left-right divide exists and was exacerbated by the underclass indigenous population and corruption of the European-Bolivian dominated government. The election of President Evo Morales—Bolivia's first indigenous president, who used the protests to come to power and is an ally of leftist Venezuelan president Hugo Chávez—could signal a change in Bolivia's regional trade priorities.[44] Under Morales, Bolivia has joined ALBA, but it remains in CAN, and Morales faces resistance to his rules at home; wealthy coastal regions seek greater autonomy from the national government.

One security-related barrier to CAN's economic integration has been removed: tension and periodic war between CAN members Peru and Ecuador over contested territory. In 1998, after six decades of animosity and three wars—most recently in 1995—the two countries signed a treaty ending the dispute.[45] Elsewhere in the CAN region, security concerns focus on guerrillas and drug traffickers (which are sometimes one and the same). The CAN's dispute resolution mechanism—which utilizes the Andean Court of Justice—has been used on "limited occasions," and the general secretariat also has authority to adjudicate disputes.[46]

Andean Trade Preferences Act, ATPA, or as Amended, ATPDEA—Andean Trade Promotion and Drug Eradication Act

The Andean Trade Preferences Act (ATPA) was established in 1991 and amended in 2002 as the Andean Trade Promotion and Drug Eradication Act (ATPDEA). It offers unilateral preferential access to the US market for the four Andean nations—Bolivia, Colombia, Ecuador, and Peru—and is thus not a free trade agreement.[47] It was scheduled to expire in 2008 but has had its provisions extended.

Association of Caribbean States, or ACS

The Association of Caribbean States' (ACS) 25 members are comprised of the 15 CARICOM states, other Central American countries, the Dominican Republic, Cuba, and, as associate members, dependent territories in the region.[48] See box 3.2 for additional ACS membership details. The Association of Caribbean States is a looser organization than CARICOM and one that stresses cooperation instead of integration. The ACS does address trade issues but is not actively moving toward economic integration. The ACS stresses the promotion of tourism and responding to natural disasters, and it has a secretariat in Port of Spain, Trinidad and Tobago.[49] The treaty establishing the ACS was signed in 1994, and the ACS heads of state first met in 1995.[50]

BOX 3.2. ACS MEMBERSHIP

Antigua and Barbuda	Haiti
Bahamas	Honduras
Barbados	Mexico
Belize	Jamaica
Colombia	Nicaragua
Costa Rica	Panama
Cuba	St. Kitts and Nevis
Dominica	St. Lucia
Dominican Republic	St. Vincent and the Grenadines
El Salvador	Suriname
Grenada	Trinidad and Tobago
Guatemala	Venezuela
Guyana	

Source: ACS Secretariat, http://www.aes-aec.org/; World Bank, *2005 World Development Indicators.* In addition to these 25 full members, there are associate members: two Dutch dependencies (Aruba and Netherlands Antilles), three French dependencies (French Guiana, Guadeloupe, and Martinique), and one British dependency (Turks and Caicos Islands).

Bolivarian Alliance for the Americas (ALBA), or *Alianza Bolivariana para las Américas* (Formerly Bolivarian Alternative for the Americas, or *Alternativa Bolivariana para las Américas*)

The Bolivarian Alliance for the Americas (formerly the Bolivarian Alternative for the Americas), or, as it is more commonly known, ALBA (its Spanish acronym for *Alianza Bolivariana para las Américas*, formerly *Alternativa Bolivariana para las Américas*) was founded in 2004 by Venezuela and Cuba.[51] In 2006 Bolivia joined, followed by Nicaragua in 2007, Dominica and, temporarily, Honduras in 2008, and Antigua and Barbuda, Ecuador and Saint Vincent, and the Grenadines in 2009.[52] See box 3.3 for ALBA membership details. Honduras joined ALBA in 2008 under president Manual Zelaya, but he was overthrown in June 2009 after attempting to extend his rule to a second term, also a contravention of the Honduran constitution. Coup supporters installed Robert Micheletti as interim president, and Honduras pulled out of ALBA during his controversial tenure. While the Honduran constitutional crisis appears to have abated following the controversial November 2009 election of president Porfirio Lobo, a Zelaya opponent, Honduras's rejection of ALBA continues.[53] While three CARICOM members—Antigua and Barbuda, Dominica, and Saint Vincent and the Grenadines—have joined ALBA, other CARICOM members are hesitant, and some, like oil producer Trinidad and Tobago, are strongly against joining.

ALBA aspires to be an RTA; more specifically, ALBA seeks to be a socialist alternative free trade agreement to the US-promoted FTAA. It can be thought of as Venezuelan president Hugo Chávez's practical international application of his unique version of socialism, which has thus far consisted primarily of rhetoric—nationalist and structuralist critiques of capitalism—with selected noncapitalist programs such as the exchange of Cuban doctors for Venezuelan oil and offering oil at below-market costs through Petrocaribe.[54] Venezuela also induces ALBA membership with foreign aid. Reportedly, in

---

BOX 3.3. ALBA MEMBERS AND MEMBERSHIP DATES

Antigua and Barbuda	2009
Bolivia	2006
Cuba	2004
Dominica	2008
Eduador	2009
Nicaragua	2007
Saint Vincent and the Grenadines	2009
Venezuela	2004

Note: Honduras joined in 2008 but withdrew in 2010.

exchange for joining ALBA, Venezuela offered to purchase Honduran bonds for $100 million, with proceeds directed toward housing for the poor. Venezuela also gives more direct aid, such as $30 million offered for Honduran farming, tractors, and low-energy lightbulbs and in-kind aid such as literacy teachers and doctors.[55] Like Chávez's domestic programs, the price of oil is an essential component of ALBA's attractiveness. The higher the oil prices, the more money Chávez has for promoting ALBA through aid and Petrocaribe and the more aid and Petrocaribe's subsidized oil are needed.

The question for ALBA's future economic importance is whether the rhetoric translates into specific provisions that are adhered to and whether membership widens. Both need to be sufficient to create a true alternative to US-style RTAs. In addition to trade provisions, ALBA hopes to create a common currency, the sucre. In January 2010 it came into use for some government-to-government transactions in ALBA. A common currency poses problems for ALBA's Caribbean members who already share a common currency, the Eastern Caribbean dollar, with other Caribbean countries, and membership in both would be impossible.[56]

Liberals are skeptical that a meaningful ALBA can be created and sustained short of exceptionally high oil prices. There is simply not a possibility of ALBA forming a true alternative to the giant US market, nor do the social programs that come with ALBA survive long in the face of what liberals consider to be inevitable inefficiencies. Nationalists too are skeptical: while ALBA might be useful for its members to receive some benefits from Venezuela and to serve as a reminder for the US to keep its Latin American allies happy, Venezuela's larger role is not universally welcomed in the region. Venezuelan-Mexican diplomatic rows and then the more serious matter of Venezuela's alleged support for the Colombian FARC guerrillas serve as dramatic examples. Broader and quieter discontent was seen when Venezuela was unable to win regional support for a position on the UN Security Council despite significant lobbying. With Chávez in power, ALBA will not be going away either; he relishes his role as leader of anti-US rhetoric and provocateur. ALBA is increasingly a stage for that role.

Caribbean Basin Initiative, or CBI, Including the US-Caribbean Basin Trade Partnership Act of 2000 (CBTPA)

The term *CBI* is often used to identify both the original CBI, established in 1983 through the Caribbean Basin Economic Recovery Act (CBERA), and the amended version established in 2000 through the US-Caribbean Basin Trade Partnership Act. The CBI allows preferential access to the US market for some products for nearly 20 countries. See box 3.4 for membership de-

---

**BOX 3.4. CARIBBEAN BASIN
INITIATIVE (CBI) MEMBERSHIP**

Antigua and Barbuda	Haiti
Aruba	Jamaica
Bahamas	Montserrat
Barbados	Netherlands Antilles
Belize	St. Kitts and Nevis
British Virgin Islands	St. Lucia
Dominica	St. Vincent and the Grenadines
Grenada	Trinidad and Tobago
Guyana	

Note: The following countries had been CBI members, but FTAs with the US supersede CBI membership: Costa Rica, Dominican Republic, El Salvador, Guatemala, Honduras, Nicaragua, and Panama.

---

tails. Membership is dwindling because CBI's preferential access ends when countries join FTAs with the US, like the CAFTA-DR FTA. Its scheduled expiration of September 2008 was extended to September 2010.[57]

CARICOM—Caribbean Community and Common Market, Including the Caribbean Single Market and Economy (CSME)

The 15-member CARICOM is a customs union—an RTA with tariff-free internal trade and a common external tariff. The Caribbean Common Market was established in 1973. All but one of the CARICOM members—the Bahamas—are also members of the Caribbean Community.[58] Twelve of its members have formally begun a single market, which, when fully implemented by 2015 as planned, allows for the free flow of goods, services, capital and, labor. See table 3.1 for additional CARICOM membership details.

The English-speaking Caribbean, also known as the Commonwealth Caribbean—consisting of 12 independent states and six territories—forms the basis for CARICOM. The English-speaking Caribbean has a long history of cooperation through regional integration, first as British colonies in the West Indies Federation, then in the Caribbean Free Trade Association (CARIFTA), initiated in 1968, which became the CARICOM in 1973.[59] CARICOM expanded to include two non-English-speaking states: Suriname in 1994 and Haiti in 1997. In January 2006, six of its members joined the Caribbean Single Market and Economy (CSME), with six more expected to

Table 3.1. CARICOM Membership, Associate Membership, and CSME Membership

		CARICOM *Associate Members*
Antigua and Barbuda	*Jamaica*	Anguilla
Bahamas*	Montserrat	Bermuda
Barbados	*St. Kitts and Nevis*	British Virgin Islands
Belize	*St. Lucia*	Cayman Islands
Dominica	*St. Vincent and the Grenadines*	Turks and Caicos Islands
Grenada	*Suriname*	
Guyana	*Trinidad and Tobago*	
Haiti		

Source: CARICOM Secretariat website, http://www.caricom.org/ (March 15, 2010).
Note: Members of the CARICOM's Caribbean Single Market and Economy (CSME) are in *italics.*
*The Bahamas is a member of the community but not the common market.

follow shortly. CARICOM members have considered political integration but are currently not ready to move in that direction.[60]

CARICOM members Guyana, Jamaica, Suriname, and Trinidad and Tobago are designated as more-developed countries. All other member states other than the Bahamas are designated as less-developed countries (LDCs).[61] The CARICOM secretariat is in Georgetown, Guyana.

Caribbean Single Market and Economy (CSME)

The single market that began in January 2006 for six CARICOM members will allow the free flow of goods, services, capital, and skilled workers within its membership when fully phased in by 2015. Some CSME members have signaled they would like to delay implementation and will discuss "more reasonable targets for implementation" at the July 2010 annual CARICOM heads of government meeting.[62] The six inaugural CSME members—Barbados, Belize, Guyana, Jamaica, Suriname, and Trinidad and Tobago—were expected to be joined by six more members from the Eastern Caribbean—Antigua and Barbuda, Dominica, Grenada, St. Kitts and Nevis, St. Lucia and St. Vincent, and the Grenadines—by March 2006. The OECS members missed that deadline but did manage to enter the CSME in July 2006. Much of the OECS members' foot dragging on the issue had to do with fear of being inundated by migrants from more populous CARICOM countries and by the desire for compensation from CARICOM's larger members for the costs of implementing the CSME. The CARICOM Development Fund, which became the price CARICOM had to pay for OECS inclusion in the CSME, was launched in July 2008.[63] The states in the Organization of East Caribbean States (OECS) were hesitant to join the CSME because their economies are smaller and already face significant trade deficits with the rest of CARICOM. Haiti and the Bahamas have declined to enter the single market, and Montserrat, a British dependency, also intends to join once it receives permission from Great Britain. That the Bahamas and Haiti are not planning on entering the CSME is not surprising. While the Bahamas is a CARICOM member, it is not a member of CARICOM's common market. The Bahamas feels its economic interests would be harmed by higher agricultural barriers that would come with participation in CARICOM's common market. Haiti is too preoccupied with its own internal political struggles to participate effectively.[64] The CSME includes the right of skilled CARICOM nations' workers to live and work in other CARICOM states. The category of skilled workers currently includes "university graduates, media workers, musicians, artists, and sports persons."[65] There are concerns among CARICOM members that the CSME will lead to a flood of migrants coming to wealthier states.

CARICOM's External Relations

CARICOM's 15 members also form a significant portion of the 25-member Association of Caribbean States, which is a looser organization than CARICOM and which stresses cooperation instead of integration.

CARICOM has also established the Caribbean Regional Negotiating Machinery (CRNM) to coordinate its external negotiations. The CRNM was created in 1997 with the realization that preferential access CARICOM's members had through their former colonial powers would be ending. The CRNM coordinates CARICOM's bilateral, regional, and multilateral trade negotiations.[66] It has also formed the Caribbean forum to coordinate negotiations between the EU and the Caribbean ACP states.[67]

Cariforum

Cariforum, meaning Caribbean forum, was established in 1992 as a forum for the Caribbean states involved in the Africa, Caribbean, Pacific-European Union Partnership Agreement (ACP-EU Partnership Agreement), popularly known as the ACP. In 1992 Cariforum included the CARICOM members at that time and then non-CARICOM members Suriname, Haiti, and the Dominican Republic. Suriname and Haiti have since joined CARICOM and, in 2001, the Dominican Republic signed an FTA with CARICOM.[68]

Central American Free Trade Agreement (CAFTA), Also Known as CAFTA-DR, or Central America Free Trade Agreement-Dominican Republic

The Central American Free Trade Agreement (CAFTA) was signed in May 2004 between Costa Rica, El Salvador, Guatemala, Honduras, and

Nicaragua. In August 2004, the Dominican Republic joined (thus CAFTA-DR, which will hereafter be referred to as CAFTA). CAFTA was hotly controversial in the US Congress. The US sugar industry, in particular, was dead set against the agreement, and the agreement's passage was highly contested despite the minimal number of changes to the US trade law that CAFTA would bring.[69] The US was already quite open to trade from the CAFTA countries, except in sensitive agricultural areas, in which it conceded little ground in the CAFTA negotiations. Nevertheless, the US sugar industry did not want to set the precedent that the US sugar markets could be opened in trade agreements to help other sectors gain more open markets abroad. Its bigger fears were that a significant CAFTA opening might lead to a larger opening in the FTAA or WTO negotiations. In addition to specific sectoral concerns, many Democrats were concerned with CAFTA's insufficient labor and environmental provisions. These provisions require that member countries enforce their existing laws on worker rights and environmental protection, but there is no mechanism in CAFTA through which trade sanctions can be imposed on violators.[70]

Thus CAFTA faced a close vote in the US House of Representatives, passing by just two votes despite a Republican majority. President George W. Bush (the younger) signed the Central American Free Trade Agreement (CAFTA) into law in August 2005.[71] It was scheduled to go into effect on January 1, 2006, but this was delayed. Delayed ratification in Costa Rica—where the agreement was less popular—and slow passage of implementing legislation in other Central American CAFTA partners slowed CAFTA-wide implementation. Ratification in Guatemala did not encourage Costa Rica to hurry; Guatemala's ratification came with significant protesting and rioting.

Some wonder why the agreement was controversial when it did not significantly change the status quo. CAFTA members already had preferential access to the US market through the Caribbean Basin Initiative (CBI). More than 80 percent of the region's exports to the United States were duty free before CAFTA.[72] These programs were set to expire in 2008, and CAFTA makes preferential access to the US market permanent, with few other significant changes. The question remains, why the controversy? There are two answers. First, many view the status quo as the problem. After the terrible conflicts that harmed the region economically in the 1980s, the 1990s saw peace and economic growth breaking out; but economic growth did little to alleviate the region's intense poverty.[73] There was little change in access to the US in areas in which CAFTA members consider it most important. Those economic sectors in which the US market was closed to Central American exports before CAFTA—such as sugar—are little changed from CAFTA. Secondly, there are specific CAFTA provisions that were controversial: more stringent intellectual property rights, especially relating to medicine, the opening of the Central American service sector, and the prospect of Central American farmers competing with US-subsidized farmers.

The controversial IPR provisions in CAFTA include extending patents beyond the 20-year patent period for administrative delays during the patenting process, granting data exclusivity—the right to *not* release medicine test data (which delays generic drug production)—and allowing the patenting of plants.[74] There are also provisions that prohibit generic drug makers from marketing their medicines in the CAFTA countries.[75]

But Central America had little choice in the matter. Global textile and apparel quotas ended on January 1, 2005, and thus more economical textile and apparel producers such as China were expected to increase exports to the US at the expense of Central American exporters. This is one of the region's most important industries. Preexisting preferential access programs such as the CBI were going to expire in 2008. This would exacerbate the region's woes, unless, of course, a free trade agreement with the US cemented preferential access.

The region's economies were already quite intertwined: the US is the region's most important trading and investment partner. The role of the US dollar was also significant for Central American economies. Two countries in the region—El Salvador and Panama, which have negotiated FTAs with the US—already have engaged in unilateral monetary union through dollarization. Moreover, non-US intraregional trade is likely to increase because CAFTA will eliminate many of the NTBs that hinder trade among the non-US CAFTA members.[76]

CAFTA includes a Trade Capacity Building Committee, which is intended to assist the CAFTA nations in adapting to the administrative and economic changes that CAFTA will bring.[77]

Central American Integration System (SICA), or *Sistema de la Integración Centroamericana*

The Central American Integration System, better known by its Spanish acronym, SICA, was established in 1991 by the five Central American Common Market (CACM) countries and Panama with the signing of the Protocol of Tegucigalpa. See box 3.5 for membership details. It went into force in 1993. The CACM created the SICA as a framework to coordinate economic and political integration in Central America. A secretariat was established in Guatemala City.[78] See also "Central American Common Market (CACM)," below.

BOX 3.5. SICA MEMBERSHIP AND ASSOCIATE MEMBERSHIP

SICA Members   **SICA Associate Member**
Belize   Dominican Republic
Costa Rica
El Salvador
Guatemala
Honduras
Nicaragua
Panama

Source: SICA Secretariat, http://www.sica.int/sica/aviso_legal_en.aspx?IdEnt=401&Id
m=2&IdmStyle=2.

Central American Common Market (CACM)

The CACM consists of Costa Rica, El Salvador, Guatemala, Honduras, and Nicaragua, with Belize and Panama members of the CACM's political body, the SICA.[79] Established by a 1960 treaty between El Salvador, Guatemala, Honduras, and Nicaragua that went into force in 1961, Costa Rica joined in 1963, and Panama became an observer for some issues within the CACM.[80] For the first ten years, integration was considered successful, but security, political, and economic problems, the latter in the form of the debt crisis, overwhelmed CACM members and effectively ended it.[81] War between El Salvador and Honduras in 1969 obviously stalled the CACM's integration. So too did the sharp ideological battles and civil wars in the 1970s and 1980s, which included the Nicaraguan Revolution and civil wars in El Salvador and Guatemala (although Guatemala's had been long-standing).[82] After peace returned to devastated Central America in the early 1990s, the CACM was revived. In 1991 CACM members signed an agreement creating the Central American Integration System (*Sistema de la Integración Centroamericana*), or SICA, which went into effect in 1993. SICA's role is "to serve as a governing body for the integration process" by coordinating two other CACM institutions, SIECA and BCIE.[83] SIECA is the Secretariat of the General Treaty on Central American Economic Integration (*Secretaría Permanente del Tratado General de Integración Económica Centroamericana*), with headquarters in Guatemala City. The BCIE— the Central American Bank for Economic Integration (*Banco Centroamericano de Integración Económica*)—has headquarters in Tegucigalpa, Honduras, and provides loans to CACM states for infrastructure projects.[84]

In 1993 the CACM members signed a free trade agreement for most products and included provisions for capital liberalization and for the free movement of people.[85] The CACM's goal was to form a customs union by 2003.[86] According to the Inter-American Development Bank, most intraregional trade is tariff free, the main exceptions being sugar, coffee, and a few other agricultural products.[87] On average, there is a tariff level of about 7.5 percent. The CACM has established a CET with a four-tier tariff schedule of 0, 4, 10, and 15 percent, with some exceptions in some sectors and for some countries. As of 2002, about 80 percent of the common external tariff had been implemented, and as of 2005, 90 percent.[88]

Central American Group of Four

The Central American Group of Four—El Salvador, Guatemala, Honduras, and Nicaragua—are the four CACM members that have moved the most rapidly to integrate.[89] Costa Rica has been more hesitant to embrace free trade with the other CACM members.

FTAA—Free Trade Area of the Americas

The 34-member FTAA includes all the Western Hemisphere's independent countries except Cuba, which is excluded, at US insistence, on antidemocratic grounds. See box 3.6 for a list of FTAA countries. The FTAA has been faltering for some time. Its grander ambitions—one overarching trade agreement for virtually all of the Americas—had already been scaled back into a

---

BOX 3.6. FREE TRADE AREA
OF AMERICAS (FTAA) MEMBERSHIP

Antigua and Barbuda	Guyana
Argentina	Haiti
Bahamas	Honduras
Barbados	Jamaica
Belize	Mexico
Bolivia	Nicaragua
Brazil	Panama
Canada	Paraguay
Chile	Peru
Colombia	St. Kitts and Nevis
Costa Rica	St. Lucia
Dominica	St. Vincent and the Grenadines
Dominican Republic	Suriname
Ecuador	Trinidad and Tobago
El Salvador	United States
Grenada	Venezuela
Guatemala	

two-track FTAA, with a basic FTAA for all members and a more ambitious FTAA for those who wanted a deeper (i.e., the originally intended) level of integration. The negotiations over this so-called FTA-lite or FTAA à la carte were supposed to be concluded by January 2005 but ended unsuccessfully and have not been rescheduled, despite US prodding.[90]

Many of the 34 FTAA countries hoped to relaunch talks at the Summit of the Americas in Mar del Plata, Argentina, in November 2005. FTAA supporters, such as the US and Mexico, hoped to renew the FTAA's faltering momentum by achieving an agreement to negotiate. Some detractors also had high hopes: to end the FTAA. Other detractors were more circumspect and sought to change the FTAA, not end it. These detractors were (and remain) hesitant to join the FTAA unless the US accepts greater openness for itself and demands less openness for the rest of the Americas than it is currently willing to accept. Specifically, they want greater US openness in agriculture, including a reduction in agricultural subsidies, and they want the US to back away from their demands that Latin American countries accept investor-friendly rules on government procurement and more stringent "WTO-plus" intellectual property rights.

One summation of the FTAA's status after the Mar del Plata Summit was typical: "At the first Summit of the Americas, in Miami in 1994, all the region's governments signed up to a common vision of democracy and free trade. That consensus was starting to fray by the third summit, in Quebec in 2001; now at Mar del Plata, the fourth, it has unraveled."[91] From listening to Venezuelan president Hugo Chávez—who came to kill the FTAA and who declared it dead—or from viewing the massive, sometimes violent, and consistently anti-American protests in the street, one could easily think the FTAA was dead. Rancor between then Mexican president Vicente Fox, an FTAA supporter, and President Chávez turned personal, with Chávez criticizing Mexico's relationship with the US by calling Fox a "puppy dog of the empire." This sniping led both countries to withdraw their diplomats from each other's territory.[92] While Mexico's new president Felipe Calderón Hinojosa and Chávez do not share this personal animosity, they do not agree about hemispheric trade integration.

The FTAA is indeed gravely ill compared with how it was originally envisioned, but the prognosis is complex. After the Mar del Plata Summit, there are two factions regarding the FTAA's future. The US-led faction, now numbering 29 of the 34 FTAA countries, seeks to restart the FTAA and finish the FTAA negotiations. Mexican president Fox had been the most vocal of this hurry-up faction, calling for an "FTAA of the willing." The other group consists of four hesitant countries—Argentina, Brazil, Paraguay, and Uruguay—and one hostile country—Venezuela. Venezuelan president Chávez calls the FTAA "an annexation plan," and told an anti-FTAA rally that he sought to bury the FTAA at the summit. Venezuela seeks to end the FTAA, while the other four holdouts seek to alter its terms. As the Brazilian foreign minister said, "'We are here neither to bury FTAA nor to resuscitate it' but to see 'what are the advantages.'"[93] Oil revenue helps explain why Venezuela can turn away from better access to the world's largest market; the US will always be willing to import Venezuelan oil.[94] Other FTAA-hesitant countries cannot withstand shunning the US while their competitors gain better access to the US market through subregional or bilateral agreements such as NAFTA, CAFTA, or bilateral trade agreements. But neither can their economies survive a full embrace with the economic giant. They want to change the terms of the FTAA toward their interests. To that end, Bush made a special visit to Brazil's president Luíz Inácio Lula da Silva ("Lula") after the Argentine summit. This reflects both Brazil's dominant role in MERCOSUR and its role as a swing vote in the FTAA. Lula—who was a populist leftist as a presidential candidate—has turned into a more pragmatic centrist in his economic policies as president. That he has not rejected the FTAA but instead has called for changes in it has enhanced his image as pragmatic and increased Brazil's importance in determining the FTAA's future. As of 2009, there are no FTAA negotiations planned. Movement on the FTAA is further stalled because of the pending Doha talks, where similar issues in the multilateral setting are under negotiation.

Group of Three (G-3)

Now misnamed, the Group of Three (G-3) is an FTA that entered into force in 1995 between Colombia, Venezuela, and Mexico but now includes only Colombia and Mexico.[95] For most of its history, two of the G-3—Colombia and Venezuela—were members of the Andean Community of Nations (CAN), while Mexico was instead a NAFTA member. In 2006, however, Venezuela pulled out of both the G-3 and the CAN. Security and political differences among the three countries proved to be too wide a gap: Colombia accuses Venezuelan president Hugo Chávez of giving safe haven and money to guerrillas fighting the Colombian government, and Chávez and then Mexican president Vicente Fox publicly traded harsh words at the Summit of the Americas in 2005 with continued barbs in the media afterwards.

The G-3 does remain in force for Colombia and Mexico. There is little institutional framework to the G-3, which covers investment, services, intellectual property rights, government procurement, and, since 2005, the automotive sector.[96] Most trade between the remaining two G-3 nations is duty free, with agriculture being the primary exception. Colombia and Mexico continue to refine the G-3, which could be overtaken by larger trade agreements such as the FTAA.

Latin American Free Trade Association (LAFTA)

Now defunct, LAFTA, also known by its Spanish acronym, ALALC, was the forerunner to the Latin American Integration Association (LAIA), or ALADI. See the following discussion of the Latin American Integration Association.

Latin American Integration Association (LAIA), Also Known as *ALADI—Asociación Latinoamericana de Integración*
(Formerly the Latin American Free Trade Area [LAFTA])

The Latin American Integration Association (LAIA), better known by its Spanish acronym ALADI, was established by eleven states with the 1980 Treaty of Montevideo. In 1999 Cuba became ALADI's 12th member.[97] See box 3.7 for membership details. As of 2002, ALADI, with a secretariat in Montevideo, Uruguay, had 40 partial-scope agreements involving two or more countries in force under its auspices.[98] ALADI replaced the collapsed LAFTA, which had been established in 1960 and had sought to establish a South American common market. But 20 years after LAFTA's creation, only 14 percent of member-country trade was covered by LAFTA rules. LAFTA was an attempt to increase the economic scale of ISI programs, but since ISI programs are inherently protectionist, LAFTA success at integration was going to be limited from the beginning, and hence the shift toward establishing ALADI.[99]

BOX 3.7. LATIN AMERICAN INTEGRATION ASSOCIATION (LAIA)/ALADI MEMBERSHIP

Argentina	Ecuador
Bolivia	Mexico
Brazil	Paraguay
Chile	Peru
Colombia	Uruguay
Cuba	Venezuela

Source: ALADI, http://www.aladi.org/nsfaladi/arquitec.nsf/VSITIOWEBi/aviso_ jur%EDdicol; World Bank, *2005 World Development Indicators.*

As was LAFTA's goal, ALADI seeks to eventually establish a South American common market.[100] Also like LAFTA, ALADI is not in a hurry. It does not include timetables for trade barrier reductions; instead it encourages bilateral preferential trade agreements among those ALADI members that want them.[101] ALADI does recognize the principle of differential treatment for its poorer members such as Bolivia, Ecuador, and Paraguay, and ALADI allows flexibility for its members to lower barriers at different speeds, a significant contrast to the less-flexible LAFTA that ALADI replaced. ALADI hopes to one day multilateralize these varied bilateral and subregional agreements, but some view this as difficult given the disparate membership, economic interests, and contending trade agreements. To these critics, ALADI is generally seen as having failed at being a catalyst for regional free trade. Some, however, see MERCOSUR as an outgrowth of ALADI, and thus ALADI is seen as having been more successful at creating South American integration than it is usually credited as having been.

MERCOSUR, *Mercado Común del Sur* (Spanish), or Common Market of the South, Also Known as *MERCOSUL for Mercado Comun do Sul* (Portuguese)

MERCOSUR—somewhere between a customs union and a common market—was established by Argentina, Brazil, Paraguay, and Uruguay in 1991 by the Treaty of Asunción, as modified by the 1994 Protocol of Ouro Preto. See box 3.8 for additional MERCOSUR membership details. Its common external tariff (CET) came into effect on January 1, 1995. MERCOSUR's primary institutional structures include the Council for the Common Market (comprising MERCOSUR members' ministers of foreign affairs and finance), the Common Market Group, MERCOSUR's executive body, which can issue mandatory resolutions, and its dispute resolution body, which includes an arbitration court, the Permanent Review Court.[102]

BOX 3.8. MERCOSUR MEMBERSHIP

Full Members	Associate Members
Argentina	Bolivia
Brazil	Chile
Paraguay	Colombia
Uruguay	Ecuador
Venezuela*	Mexico
	Peru

* Full membership awaits MERCOSUR ratification.

Venezuela has agreed to join MERCOSUR, but its accession awaits ratification in Paraguay. Venezuela's entry into MERCOSUR is not guaranteed, and the road so far has been bumpy. Argentina and Uruguay ratified Venezuela's accession in 2006, shortly after Venezuela applied for full membership. Brazil, MERCOSUR's dominant economy, hesitated. It took until December 2009 for Brazil's legislature to approve of Venezuela's entry, leaving Paraguay as the holdout. While Paraguayan president Fernando Lugo, a Chávez supporter, supports Venezuela's entry into MERCOSUR, Congress, especially the opposition-controlled Senate, remains opposed. The Chávez soap opera's MERCOSUR episode continues. If Venezuela does enter MERCOSUR, it will certainly be entertaining.[103]

MERCOSUR is a departure from the historical precedent of South American RTAs that exist more as platitudes on paper than as a real impetus to lower economic barriers. Not everyone agrees, and certainly MERCOSUR has had its share of problems. Paraguay's vice president Luis Alberto Castiglioni complained that (Paraguay's) "MERCOSUR partners 'proclaim integration but work very slowly toward achieving it.'"[104] MERCOSUR's fealty toward its own rules was challenged by the financial crises that struck in the 1990s and early 2000s and is again being challenged by disgruntled smaller members and a potentially divisive enlargement to include Venezuela that may exacerbate differences over MERCOSUR's primary role.

MERCOSUR's four full members—Argentina, Brazil, Paraguay, and Uruguay—have successfully brought down many of the economic barriers that existed between them. To many, Venezuela's nearly approved inclusion in MERCOSUR challenges MERCOSUR's stated commitment to relatively promarket capitalism and toward democracy and may move MERCOSUR in the direction of being a political rather than economic bloc. MERCOSUR's original members have moved in the direction of economic liberalism in the 1980s and 1990s, with a slight shift toward economic nationalism in the later 1990s and into the 2000s. Venezuela has moved in the direction of economic structuralism to some degree. MERCOSUR's varied economic strategies may cause division. Venezuela itself faces some problems from its inclusion in MERCOSUR; Venezuelan businesses are reportedly quite concerned that its full membership will lead to a massive increase in Brazilian imports.[105]

MERCOSUR's Integration Depth

By 1994 MERCOSUR had established free trade among its members, although there were some significant exceptions.[106] MERCOSUR adopted a common external tariff (CET) in January 1995, thus achieving its goal of being a customs union. Again, this has been partial because of national exemptions.[107] It had hopes of becoming a common market—this would allow not just free trade, but the free flow of labor and capital—but these more ambitious plans faced setbacks from economic turmoil in MERCOSUR's two most important members, Argentina and Brazil. For instance, because of Argentina's economic free fall, it was granted exemptions to the CET until December 2002.[108] Common regional provisions covering trade in services, safeguards, antidumping, and dispute settlement have been approved but only partially implemented.[109] In December 2005, the MERCOSUR's dispute resolution tribunal was established.[110] It has been a bumpy ride, and MERCOSUR's integration still falls short of some of its stated goals, but MERCOSUR integration has been deeper than is typical in South America.

MERCOSUR Widening

MERCOSUR also has associate members with which it has free trade agreements: Bolivia, Chile, Mexico, Peru, and, until its recent change in status, Venezuela. MERCOSUR's dominant member, Brazil, has long sought broader integration with South America in order to have greater leverage relative to the US in negotiations on the Free Trade Area of the Americas (FTAA), and associated status can serve as a first step toward South American integration. In 1996 it completed a free trade agreement with Chile and then, later in 1996, with Bolivia. Argentina was keen for MERCOSUR's FTA with Chile because it helps give Argentine exports greater access to Pacific ports, provides a counterweight to the MERCOSUR's giant, Brazil, and helps heals old wounds: Argentina and Chile had nearly gone to war one decade earlier.[111] Bolivia's FTA with MERCOSUR requires that Bolivia be granted an exemption from the Andean Community of Nations (CAN). MERCOSUR countries are an important export market for Bolivia, but the reverse is not true; Bolivia is a small market for MERCOSUR. Instead, MERCOSUR views Bolivia's inclusion as constituting a step toward South American integration.[112]

Mexico may join as a full member. Mexico has been an associate member, and former Mexican president Vicente Fox stated that he sought full membership. Mexico and Venezuela were given associate member status at MERCOSUR's 2004 presidential summit in Buenos Aires, Argentina. Mexico has entered into multiple partial-scope trade agreements with MERCOSUR members under the LAIA framework, which has lowered tariffs in some sectors. Brazil and Mexico have agreed to continue negotiations toward establishing a free trade agreement.[113]

MERCOSUR: Deeper Integration Still?

That MERCOSUR has integrated as much as it has is surprising to some, particularly in light of 150 years of Brazilian-Argentine rivalry and South America's record of failed integration attempts.

Argentina and Brazil—by far the overwhelming powers in MERCOSUR—have had difficult economic and political relations. Brazil made a high-profile attempt to achieve a permanent seat on the UN Security Council in recent years, and Argentina conspicuously did not support Brazil's attempt.[114] Both countries have had difficult currency histories, to put it mildly, and this has deeply strained their economic relationship. But in the 1980s both countries emerged from military dictatorships and began democratic rule. Both also moved away from their statecentric ISI economic development models, and they sought a way to develop their economies and their clout.[115] MERCOSUR served both purposes, and relations between the two are better than during most of their history.

MERCOSUR would like to deepen further. It emulates, with only mixed success, another common market, the European Union. One significant difference between MERCOSUR and the EU is that MERCOSUR has not included formal institutions to coordinate macroeconomic policy.[116] The EU member nations institutionalized their exchange rate relations in order to narrow the differences in their macroeconomic policies and therefore minimize the degree to which currency fluctuations influenced other aspects of their internal economic relationship. Indeed, currency fluctuations became a significant problem for MERCOSUR countries and for MERCOSUR's ongoing survival. Argentina's economic problems in 2001 and 2002 reverberated outward within MERCOSUR: in 2002, Uruguay's GDP fell by 11 percent.[117] Both the Argentine and Brazilian currency storms passed, but MERCOSUR has other difficulties.

MERCOSUR: Internal Tensions

It is common in any international relationship between asymmetrical powers for the smaller nation to feel that it gets less than its share of making decisions. Occasionally, the griping goes the other way. Recent announcements that two paper plants would be built in Uruguay on the Argentine border led the Argentine government to protest that these plants would harm Argentina's environment and that Uruguay made these decisions without consulting Argentina. Uruguay, whose capital, Montevideo, houses MERCOSUR's secretariat, is not bound by MERCOSUR to enter into a joint decision-making process on the issue, but the lack of consultation certainly caused tension in the relationship. A nonbinding binational panel will examine the issue, but anti-MERCOSUR feelings have remained strong in Uruguay over the issue.[118]

The smaller MERCOSUR partners have complaints about Brazilian dominance of MERCOSUR and of their economies. Many Paraguayans, for instance, fear their culture is becoming dominated by Brazil's. As a Paraguayan senator said, "Our sovereignty is threatened by Brazil, not by the United States."[119] Paraguayans complain that exports to Brazil are often slowed by bureaucratic hurdles and that some significant trade decisions are made by Brazil without sufficient consultation by or consideration of other MERCOSUR members.[120] Paraguayan president Nicanor Duarte Frutos said that unless MERCOSUR reformed, Paraguay might "apply the principle of euthanasia and let it go. . . . If there are no options for our economy to improve, to diversify our markets to allow us to be competitive, any of us could unplug the oxygen apparatus that is keeping MERCOSUR alive." He accuses Brazil and Argentina of "selfishness and even hypocrisy" in their protectionism, combined with criticism of US and EU protectionism.[121]

The growing security relationship between Paraguay and the US has Paraguay's MERCOSUR partners concerned. Former US secretary of defense Donald Rumsfeld visited Paraguay in August 2005 to discuss military cooperation with Paraguay (military exercises along the Bolivian border). This alarmed Bolivia because Bolivia and Paraguay fought a war there from 1923 to 1935. Brazil was not happy, either: Brazil's foreign minister suggested that Paraguay must make a choice "between MERCOSUR and other possible partners."[122]

One goal of the Paraguayan complaints against MERCOSUR may be winning permission from other MERCOSUR members for Paraguay to negotiate bilateral agreements with other countries, such as the US. Paraguayan vice president Luis Alberto Castiglioni has called for Paraguay to get a waiver from MERCOSUR so that it can negotiate trade agreements with other countries without all MERCOSUR members going along.[123]

NAFTA—North American Free Trade Agreement

The North American Free Trade Agreement, with its side accords on labor and the environment, was signed in 1993 and went into effect on January 1, 1994. It was enormously controversial in the US, despite the fact that it led to few changes in the US trade regime. It served as a catalyst for other regional trade negotiations to be launched in other regions in order to avoid falling behind in the RTA "arms race." It also served as a blueprint for provisions in subsequent RTAs. For instance, there are NAFTA-style rules of origin in numerous other RTAs.

NAFTA's forerunners for the two more-developed NAFTA partners were the 1965 US-Canadian Auto Pact and the 1988 US-Canadian Free Trade Agreement, and for the US and Mexico, the maquiladora program that led to many US companies assembling final products in Mexico from US inputs.

Brief NAFTA Negotiations Chronology

The battle over NAFTA began with the George H. W. Bush (the elder) administration seeking fast-track negotiating authority in March of 1991. After gaining fast-track approval, the main text of NAFTA was negotiated in 1991 and 1992. It was initialed by leaders of the three nations in August 1992 and signed in December 1992. Newly elected president Bill Clinton called for supplemental negotiations on the environment and worker rights, which began in March 1993 and were completed in August 1993. After a heated ratification vote in the US Congress during autumn 1993 (and far less heated ratification votes in Canada and Mexico), the agreement went into force on January 1, 1994.

NAFTA's Implementation and Recent Issues

NAFTA goes beyond its forerunners in both scope and depth. Well before NAFTA was fully implemented in January 2008, tariffs on most goods were removed. Over 90 percent of goods were tariff free in 2002, according to the Inter-American Development Bank.[124] Despite this, there have been some significant difficulties in carrying out some of NAFTA's provisions. The US has been hesitant to allow Mexican truckers access to the US market due to widely held safety fears. The US and Canada fought in court over Canadian softwood trade practices (and the US response to them) in numerous jurisdictions, with NAFTA's Chapter 19 mechanism and the World Trade Organization's Dispute Settlement Body (DSB) being the most prominent. The US had charged that Canada was receiving the equivalent of a subsidy because the Canadian government undercharged producers for harvesting lumber on public lands. The US placed punitive duties on Canadian softwood lumber exports to the US. Dispute resolution cases tended to rule for Canada but did allow some continued duties and did little to stem growing animosity. The US and Canada ultimately agreed to settle the matter in a bilateral agreement, the 2006 Softwood Lumber Agreement, in which most of the duties already charged would be given back to Canadian producers and the US would not impose duties, but the Canadian government would impose export taxes of 5–15 percent if the price of lumber went too low.[125]

NAFTA's Environmental and Labor Accords: Unique
Institutions Highlight Greater Importance of "New" Trade Issues

In order to get NAFTA through the shoals of Congress, the Clinton administration agreed to negotiate side accords on the environment and labor. These were the North American Agreement on Environmental Cooperation (NAAEC) and the North American Agreement on Labor Cooperation (NAALC), better known as the supplemental (or side) agreements on the environment and labor, which established, respectively, the Commission for Environmental Cooperation (CEC) and the Commission for Labor Cooperation (CLC).

In NAFTA's environmental and worker rights provisions, the United States and Mexico agreed to sanctions if they were found in violation of their own environmental or labor laws. The Canadian negotiators refused to subject Canada to such sanctions, keeping with their stated goal to insulate themselves from further capriciousness of the US government.[126] Instead, Canada agreed that its own court system would levy fines based on the recommendation of the trilateral commissions.[127] Reports from the talks contended that the US ultimately went along with this concession for Canada because the fears of lax environmental and labor law implementation were directed at Mexico, not Canada.[128]

NAFTA's Environmental and Labor Institutions' Dispute Resolution
Mechanisms: Structure to Address Globalization's Woes or Façade?

The side accords on the environment and labor in NAFTA are unique in that they create a dispute resolution mechanism for environmental and labor practices within a free trade agreement. They were intended to address two of the most contentious elements of the globalization debate: environmental degradation and labor rights abuses. Many contend weak environmental and labor laws, or at least weak enforcement, lead MNCs to invest in poor countries so that they can more easily pollute and exploit cheap labor. The argument that these practices—called competition in laxity in economics terminology—are detrimental to developing countries is quite familiar. Critics also contend they harm wealthy countries by sending jobs elsewhere and placing downward pressure on environmental and safety standards, wages, and worker rights. Thus the environment and labor have become politically important elements of trade politics.

Some hailed NAFTA's side accords on the environment and labor as major advances at taking these rough edges off of globalization. For the first time, whether a country follows its own environmental and labor laws is a matter of adjudication to other countries in a free trade agreement, even if those practices are not explicitly considered a barrier to trade in the main text of the agreement. Others contend that they are merely a façade to give the appearance of a more just globalization and therefore make trade agreements more politically palatable. They represent only a gesture because they are largely toothless and are not given the same weight as regular trade disputes in NAFTA's main dispute resolution mechanism. To evaluate these claims, a closer examination of the provision and institutions that administer the environmental and labor side accords is warranted

Disputes arising regarding a nation's not enforcing its own environmental or labor laws are to be sent to the relevant commission: the Commission for Environmental Cooperation (CEC) or the Commission for Labor Cooperation (CLC).[129] To send a dispute to either of the commissions, two of the three NAFTA nations must believe that there have been "persistent" abuses. There must be a pattern of abuse, not merely one incident.

The commissions are organized with a council of ministers at the top of the hierarchy, consisting of the top officials from each nation in the given issue area. The US representative to the labor council is the secretary of labor, for instance. Each council has a secretariat for administrative support, with the CEC's secretariat in Montréal and the CLC's in Dallas.[130] There are also citizen advisory boards and various groups of experts, described below.

Complaints, officially called submissions, are sent to the respective secretariat, although disputes about worker rights are sent first to the national administrative offices (NAOs) of each country.[131] If a given NAO wishes to pursue a complaint about labor violations in another country, the NAOs then try to resolve the dispute with each other. After a complaint is lodged, the secretariat establishes the facts surrounding the case. In doing so, the secretariat does *not* have the authority to inspect sites nor to issue subpoenas. It relies upon public documents and documents voluntarily submitted.[132] This factual record becomes public only if two of the three nations agree. The factual record is not intended to make suggestions for remedying the complaint. The disputants consult, and if there is no resolution after 60 days, the complaining party can convene the respective council. At this point, the council may call for outside expert advice. In the case of worker rights violations, the body is the Evaluation Committee of Experts (ECE), which comprises one nongovernmental member from each nation.[133] If there is still no resolution at the council level, the council may form an arbitration panel from a previously agreed-upon roster of experts. This is not an automatic step. Two of the three NAFTA nations must agree to form the arbitration panel.

The arbitration panel makes an initial report within 120 days and a final report within another 60 days. If the arbitration panel finds against a party, the parties might agree on a remedy. If the parties cannot agree, the panel responds to the offending party's remedy plan, called an action plan, by either accepting it or devising its own action plan.

If the final action plan is not implemented, the arbitration panel determines the fine, capped by the agreement at approximately $20 million. It is not the violating company that pays the fine, but rather the government. In Canada, a domestic court enforces the implementation of the action plan and can fine the government. Trade sanctions apply only in the most egregious cases: when fines remain unpaid. The trade sanctions apply only to US-Mexico trade. Trade sanctions are not to exceed the amount of the fine and consist of temporarily retracting NAFTA benefits.

The agreement does set up a formal mechanism for groups or individuals to submit a complaint but does not allow them to start the investigative process. Only the national governments have this power, prompting many environmental and virtually all labor groups to remain skeptical. Moreover, any complaint by a public citizen or group will be made public only if two of the three nations agree. The Commission for Environmental Cooperation does have a joint public advisory committee (JPAC) with five nongovernmental members from each of the NAFTA nations to provide advice. The JPAC does not automatically get all information regarding a case, however. It does not get information about whether to consider a submission to the CEC unless two of the three nations on the CEC council allow it.[134] The CEC also has the US National Advisory Committee (NAC), which advises the council.[135] This ensures that nongovernmental actors' voices will be officially heard. Whether they are listened to is, of course, another matter. As the JPAC itself put it, "The capacity of the CEC to attract and engage the public must be improved."[136]

The Commission on Labor Cooperation does not have a citizen advisory mechanism.[137] Instead, the NAOs are supposed to serve as the point of contact for public input on NAFTA-related labor issues. The US Labor Department formed a public advisory committee that advises the US NAO.[138]

There are other problems with the supplemental agreements, according to environmental and labor activists. Fines and trade sanctions for failure to adhere to a nation's labor laws can be levied for labor infractions only in certain areas: occupational health and safety, child labor, and minimum wages. Other labor abuses can be the subject of review by independent experts, but not fines or sanctions. Labor issues in this category include migrant workers, forced labor, employment discrimination, equal pay for men and women, and compensation in cases of work accidents or occupational diseases.[139] A third category of labor violations cannot even be the subject of official independent expert review. Labor issues in this category include the right to strike, the right to bargain collectively, and the right to freely associate and organize.[140] That the latter issues remain the furthest from international scrutiny should not come as a surprise to analysts of Mexican politics. These issues cut to the core of the power of the primary Mexican labor union, actually a grouping of unions, the Confederation of Mexican Workers (CTM). CTM has very close ties to the PRI, the ruling party as NAFTA was negotiated. In return for delivering many votes and labor stability for the PRI, the CTM is granted the authority to control much of the labor organizing that takes place in Mexico. Without the possibility of fines or trade sanctions for many types of labor violations, many argue that the labor agreement lacks teeth.

Similarly, the CEC does not have the authority to address failures to comply with a nation's own environmental laws in certain areas: commercial harvest or exploitation of natural resources.[141] This serves as another loophole with which to avoid NAFTA's pledge to have member nations follow their own environmental laws.

In short, no one argues that these environmental and labor institutions and mechanisms have a great deal of power. This does not mean that they have been unimportant. They have been used to publicize their respective issues and serve as loci for information sharing on their topics. Most importantly, they set the precedent that environmental and labor practices are more central to trade and trade politics than ardent economic liberals are willing to concede.

Post-NAFTA Institutional Developments

In March 2005, the three NAFTA members began the Security and Prosperity Partnership of North America (SPP). The SPP is a new framework to expand cooperation beyond trade integration. It incorporates preexisting programs with new initiatives. The SPP will focus on a wide array of issues such as fostering easier border travel and shipping through shared data and enhanced border infrastructure, increasing economic liberalization, and monitoring the environment.[142] There are numerous critics of NAFTA's impact on travel across the border. Customs officials are overloaded with the increased volume of trade. This, combined with high levels of business and personal travel and increased fears about border security, means that the logistics of crossing the border have become a barrier to integration.

NAFTA and Mexico's Problems

NAFTA was seen as a significant step toward economic liberalization for the formerly statist Mexican economy. Dramatic reforms had been put into motion by Carlos Salinas de Gortari that seemed to have finally conquered

Mexico's endemic inflation and helped Mexico recover from the economic shocks of the 1980s. NAFTA was to be his crowning achievement that would also cement his reforms in the form of a treaty—much more difficult to reverse than merely presidential decrees or national laws. But Salinas's legacy was much more controversial: on the very day that NAFTA entered into force, Zapatista rebels in southern Mexico began a guerrilla movement against NAFTA and for greater rights for the indigenous peasants in the region. Moreover, the Mexican peso collapsed early in the presidency of Salinas's successor, Ernesto Zedillo, and numerous scandals from the Salinas years surfaced. His ruling party, the PRI, had its candidate assassinated. Many thought that the early NAFTA years would signal Mexico's entry into the first world of economic development, but instead they showed how far Mexico had to go.

NAFTA's economic legacy has also been controversial in the US. Trade between the US and Mexico has gone up substantially in both directions, but this has happened during difficult times for many industries in both Mexico and the US in the face of growing Chinese production. See the discussion that follows for more on NAFTA's economic legacy.

Assessing NAFTA's Economic Legacy[143]

The "patient"—the Mexican economy—was not thriving as many thought it should, so its own leaders and those from the world's strongest economy prescribed an exercise regimen of economic openness. For a time, the exercise seemed to be working. The patient's vigor increased (substantial economic growth), and many signs suggested full recovery was possible (high foreign investment). The patient then committed to the exercise regimen more fully by joining NAFTA, thus locking in many of the reforms. Mexico then suffered the economic equivalent of a heart attack (the peso collapse, or so-called Tequila Crisis of 1994–1995). The patient seems to have recovered from the heart attack, but it has been a difficult and painful recovery. Did the patient have the heart attack because of the exercise regimen, or did the exercise help it recover from the heart attack more easily? Mexico had suffered two economic heart attacks in the 1980s—high debt inspired peso collapses—so to place blame on NAFTA for recent financial problems is unfair. Clearly, NAFTA has not helped Mexico, nor the US, nor Canada as much as proponents thought it would. Nor has it been as damaging as critics feared it would be. In fact, this was inevitable because both its proponents and opponents oversold their cases in the debate to pass NAFTA.

Nevertheless, the question of the NAFTA effect is important to other patients. Mexico's experiences in NAFTA give those developing nations considering greater economic openness with developed nations reasons to think that the exercise of openness is beneficial, but that exercise regimens need to be created with great care to avoid injuries. Mexico has also been faulted for not making many other reforms during the past 10 years. For instance, tax collection is very low, thus the government's ability to fund many basic services remains low. Corruption remains high, even as Mexico becomes more democratic. In other words, while the Mexican economy was on its exercise regimen, it continued eating junk food. Given this, should one place blame on the openness that NAFTA fostered?

As this suggests, NAFTA's record is mixed and difficult to untangle from the economic crisis that hit Mexico in late 1994, the year that NAFTA went into effect. What is the record on specific measures? Exports to and from each of the NAFTA countries did go up, at least partially because of NAFTA. There were very few changes in the US-Canadian economic relationship from NAFTA simply because the two countries were already quite integrated through the Canada-United States FTA (CUSFTA). Foreign investment in Mexico did go up substantially after 1994. Economic growth in the NAFTA region as a whole has been strong during NAFTA's ten years, despite the post-technology boom going bust in the US.[144]

Some US manufacturing jobs surely went to Mexico's maquiladora production along the US-Mexican border—assembly production using US inputs—and the US did lose manufacturing during this period, but NAFTA's impact on overall US job loss is small, according to most economists. Why? First, the US economy was already open to imports from Mexico before NAFTA. Second, the US increased exports to Mexico, thus creating jobs, including manufacturing jobs, to compensate in the aggregate for many lost jobs. Third, the US economy is losing manufacturing jobs more broadly. In fact, in recent years Mexico has lost many maquiladora jobs to Chinese production. According to the Mexican government, 500 of Mexico's 3,700 maquiladoras have closed. To blame NAFTA for many lost US manufacturing jobs is misplaced.[145]

NAFTA's influence on agricultural sectors, especially in Mexico, is a more straightforward case. Some segments of Mexican agriculture, like avocados, have done well exporting to the US. But in Mexico's most socially important agricultural sector, NAFTA has been terrible. US corn producers have increased their exports to Mexico considerably since NAFTA's inception, and this has harmed many poor Mexican corn farmers. Mexican corn farmers were already struggling before NAFTA and were leaving the farm in large numbers, but NAFTA certainly quickened the exit. The Mexican government has also been faulted for not doing enough to either help them continue farming through better infrastructure and more credit, or ease their transition into some other crop or industry. One lesson for other developing nations is clear, according to a much-cited Carnegie study of NAFTA: developing nations cannot compete directly with highly mechanized and massively subsidized agriculture. The study calls for "shock absorbers" such as slower tariff reductions and special safeguards to slow and mitigate the effects of subsidized agriculture.[146]

Organisation of Eastern Caribbean States (OECS)

The seven-member Organisation of Eastern Caribbean States (OECS), with a secretariat in St. Lucia, was established in 1981.[147] Already a monetary union, OECS members have decided to integrate more deeply in the form of the Eastern Caribbean Economic Union. This will entail a full customs union and harmonized economic policies and would include some elements of supranational political institutions (indeed, some already exist), or put another way, elements of political union.[148] See box 3.9 for additional OECS membership details.

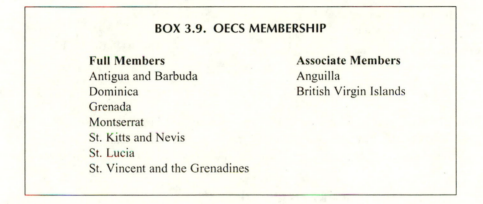

BOX 3.9. OECS MEMBERSHIP

Full Members	Associate Members
Antigua and Barbuda	Anguilla
Dominica	British Virgin Islands
Grenada	
Montserrat	
St. Kitts and Nevis	
St. Lucia	
St. Vincent and the Grenadines	

The OECS's roots are in the 1958 West Indies Federation, a grouping of British colonies that were preparing for independence.[149] The West Indies Federation included all the English-speaking Caribbean except the Bahamas, Belize, and Guyana. Disagreements over the distribution of power and finances led the two largest members—Jamaica and Trinidad and Tobago—to opt for immediate independence and pull out of the federation in 1962. Barbados followed in 1966, leaving seven small federation members in the Eastern Caribbean. Britain created a new category of territorial relations—associated statehood—in order to allow them independence except for defense and foreign affairs.[150] The West Indies Federation faced its decline using two caretaker institutions to coordinate Eastern Caribbean states' interactions—the West Indies Associated States Council of Ministers (WISE) in 1966 and the East Caribbean Common Market (ECE) in 1968. These were in effect until the 1981 establishment of the OECS with the Treaty of Basseterre.[151]

Eastern Caribbean Currency Union (ECCU) and
the Eastern Caribbean Central Bank (ECCB)

Eight Eastern Caribbean States make up the Eastern Caribbean Currency Union (ECCU), which is a monetary union. See box 3.10 for an ECCU membership list. These include the seven members of the OECS and Anguilla, which is a British overseas territory (and is therefore an associate OECS member). The eight ECCU members share a common currency, the East Caribbean dollar, which is pegged to the US dollar. They also share a central bank, the Eastern Caribbean Central Bank (ECCB).[152]

BOX 3.10. ECCU MEMBERSHIP

Anguilla	Montserrat
Antigua and Barbuda	St. Kitts and Nevis
Dominica	St. Lucia
Grenada	St. Vincent and the Grenadines

Rio Group

The Rio Group, established in 1986, is a forum for Latin American and Caribbean countries to discuss matters of common interest. Its focus is primarily political, but members also discuss trade and economic development matters.[153]

Union of South American Nations (UNASUR)

The Union of South American Nations (UNASUR), known initially as the South American Community of Nations (SCN) or *Comunidad sudamericana de naciones* (CSN), had its founding summit in Cuzco, Peru, in December 2004. The UNASUR consists of economic integration between the Andean Community of Nations (CAN) and MERCOSUR and political integration also including Chile, Suriname, and Guyana. See box 3.11 for more on UNASUR membership. The UNASUR's goals are ambitious—to create an EU-style organization for South America with a common currency and coordinated economic policy—and meeting them will require a great deal more unity than the countries in the region have historically exhibited. Since deep divisions remain on key economic issues, the South American countries decided to focus on political integration more than economic integration. This is a reversal of the EU's own developmental pattern, in which economic cooperation helped foster political unity.[154]

BOX 3.11. UNION OF SOUTH AMERICAN
NATIONS (UNASUR) MEMBERSHIP

Argentina	Guyana
Bolivia	Paraguay
Brazil	Peru
Chile	Suriname
Colombia	Uruguay
Ecuador	Venezuela

Source: "A Dream with Many Hurdles," BBC, December 9, 2004, http://news.bbc
.co.uk/2/hi/business/4082027.stm.

The economic divisions in South America are significant. MERCOSUR member nations are substantially more developed than the Andean region nations, and the Andean region is more skeptical of capitalism than are MERCOSUR members. One should not overstate MERCOSUR's commitment to economic liberalism because most governments and citizens in MERCOSUR have substantial doubts about economic liberalism. The Andean region, however, is significantly more skeptical, and its ideological divides between left and right are currently more substantial and conflictual. Setting aside their somewhat divergent approaches to economic development, trade between Andean and MERCOSUR countries is dramatically lower than trade within the blocs. From this standpoint alone, the countries in the region are not ripe for integration.

The institutional resources being applied to the endeavor are scant. The founding Cusco Declaration on the South American Community of Nations specifically calls for using "existing institutions," thus avoiding "new financial expenses."[155] Moreover, this particular lack of commitment is on the political track, which is expected by many to be smoother than the economic track. In fact, political unity will be no small task given the frosty relations between some UNASUR members. Four countries—Argentina, Ecuador, Paraguay, and Uruguay—did not send their top leaders to the founding summit. Worse still, Chile and Bolivia have a border dispute and do not have diplomatic relations.[156] Former Chilean president Ricardo Lagos called his inability to improve relations with Bolivia a "great failure" of his administration.[157] Chile's relations with much of South America are somewhat distant. Chile had been a member of the CAN, but it withdrew. Other relationships in South America are not warm. Colombia has accused Venezuela of allowing safe haven for guerrillas fighting the Colombian government and, more

recently, of funding them. Venezuelan president Hugo Chávez accuses Colombian intelligence agencies of plotting a coup against him.[158] Colombia has
sent its troops into Ecuador's territory in an attack on guerrillas given safe
haven there, leading Venezuela to mobilize its troops in sympathy (or in a
calculated indignant provocation, according to critics).

However, the South American level of conflict is low in comparison to the
European experience in the first half of the 1900s. In the aftermath of World
Wars I and II, who would have predicted that France and Germany would
ever become the engines for economic and political integration and—half a
century after horrific war—that they would hold an amicable joint session of
parliament? In the case of the EU, the US spurred European integration first
through the Marshall Plan—which required European cooperation to receive
reconstruction money—and later through European fears that they were
falling behind a more economically dynamic US. South America is coming
together in order to avoid being crushed in trade negotiations with, and ultimately dominated by, the larger US economy. Many view the UNASUR as
an attempt to increase leverage with the US in the FTAA trade negotiations.

There has been no obvious march toward integration such as that which
characterized the EU process, once initiated. The negotiating path to reach an
agreement between the CAN and MERCOSUR was a long one. In the 1990s
the two discussed an agreement but disagreed on a number of integration
issues: the number of products that would be exempted from liberalization
(CAN wanted many, MERCOSUR wanted few), the degree to which the
CAN would receive special provisions for its lower level of development,
how stringent a rule of origin would be (CAN wanted a comparatively non-
restrictive rule of origin compared to MERCOSUR's rule of origin), and the
degree to which agriculture would be initially exempted.[159] In 1998, the two
subregional RTAs agreed to negotiate and implement an FTA with each other
by 2000.[160] The gap between the two remained too wide, and the two sides
missed the deadline. But with Brazil and other MERCOSUR countries eager
to integrate in order to better negotiate with the US in the FTAA and other
settings, MERCOSUR decided to be more flexible in order to reach an agreement. MERCOSUR made the bulk of the trade concessions. Ninety percent of
Andean exports to MERCOSUR are slated to be duty free within two years of
the agreement, while it will take ten years for MERCOSUR exports to have
this access to the Andean market.[161]

To encourage greater economic development and integration, the UNASUR
has created an infrastructure initiative—the Initiative for the Integration of
Regional Infrastructure of South America (IIRSA)—which is planning 31 infrastructure projects to be completed by 2010.[162] Funding will come from other
non-UNASUR institutions such as the Inter-American Development Bank.[163]

4

Asia

Asian RTAs have a number of distinctive aspects. First, they tend to be less formalized and less institutionalized than RTAs in other regions. Second, they tend to follow economic integration more than lead it, again compared with RTAs elsewhere. For instance, within ASEAN, production and trade patterns created integration that was noticeably ahead of ASEAN's efforts to codify integration through an RTA. Third, monetary cooperation is, at least in some prominent cases, more obvious than trade cooperation. For instance, the Chiang Mai initiative includes greater monetary cooperation between ASEAN nations and Japan than have the efforts to form an RTA between ASEAN and Japan of various configurations. Fourth, the region's largest traders are divided over their vision for RTAs in the region. China and Japan do not agree with each other on a number of RTA-related issues. For instance, should the US be included in a regionwide RTA? Japan thinks so; China does not. China is hesitant to include Australia and India. China, in fact, would prefer to cut Japan out of subregional RTAs. The contrast to European integration—where French and German desire for integration with each other and with the rest of Europe is one of the central factors that has propelled the EU forward—is stark indeed. It is as if Germany wanted European integration only if France were excluded, and France sought it only if Germany were excluded. The result would limit European integration. So it goes for Asian hemispheric-wide integration.

Thus, there has been much jockeying over the future shape of hemispheric RTAs as subregional RTAs have continued apace. The most important of these is the 10-member ASEAN and its increasing network of RTAs and potential RTAs such as the ASEAN plus three (China, Japan, and South Korea), which is still a work in progress. APEC (the Asian Pacific Economic Cooperation Forum) had been a contender for being a leading Asia-wide

RTA when then president Bill Clinton upgraded its importance, and APEC subsequently agreed to move toward deeper trade integration. The details, however, were vague, and APEC lost momentum.[1] See figure 4.1 for details on Asian RTA memberships.

South Asian RTAs have been slowed by the elephant in the living room: Indian and Pakistani acrimony. South Asian RTAs include some in which India and Pakistan are both members, but these will never truly integrate when the two most significant countries are not on speaking terms and, indeed, have nearly gone to war. What are the chances of a successful marriage if restraining orders have been issued? Indeed, given the very real wars between India and Pakistan, now both nuclear-armed, a restraining order is actually an improvement in relations compared with hair-trigger brinksmanship.

CONTEXT OF EAST ASIAN RTAS: EAST ASIAN IPE (OF TIGERS, CUBS, DRAGONS, AND RISING SUNS)

Asia has been and remains the most economically dynamic region in the world. Japan, the Asian tigers (Hong Kong, Singapore, South Korea, and Taiwan), the Asian cubs (Indonesia, Malaysia, the Philippines, and Thailand), and more recently China have each been the most rapidly developing during their ascendant eras. India hopes to join this list of historic outperformers. Despite strong growth, all of these nations and their neighbors face significant economic challenges, and security relations continue to be a source of tension in the region.

Japan

Post–World War II Japan's development seemed to make Japan an economic superpower. With a distinctly economic nationalist development model, popularly called "Japan Inc.," the government played a prominent role in economic development by directing capital toward domestic producers and minimizing domestic competition in order to focus resources on longer-term global competition. The government's role was sufficiently crucial that one eminent Japan scholar dubbed the government's role the "developmental state."[2] Domestic protectionism is seen by economic liberals as hindering innovation, but in Japan protectionism combined with policies and outlook produced a system that promoted Japanese companies' success and innovation in global competition. Japanese productivity in industries such as automobile manufacturing, electronics, computers, computer chips, and robotics surged from the 1960s through the 1990s. Japan's economic miracle

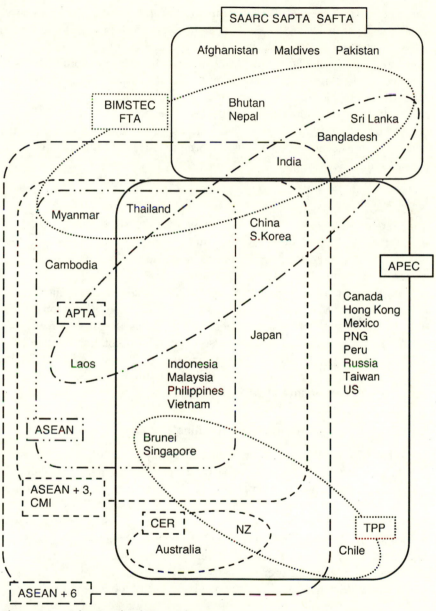

SAARC SAPTA SAFTA

Afghanistan   Maldives   Pakistan

BIMSTEC
FTA

Bhutan
Nepal   Sri Lanka
Bangladesh

India

Myanmar   Thailand

China
S.Korea

Cambodia

APEC

Canada
Hong Kong
Mexico
PNG
Peru
Russia
Taiwan
US

APTA

Japan

Laos

Indonesia
Malaysia
Philippines
Vietnam

ASEAN

Brunei
Singapore

ASEAN + 3,
CMI

CER   NZ   TPP

Australia   Chile

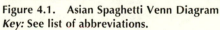

ASEAN + 6

Figure 4.1.   Asian Spaghetti Venn Diagram
Key: See list of abbreviations.

had created what seemed like an economic superpower, but the speculative bubble in Japan burst in 1990 and Japan has yet to fully return to its former status as economically infallible. It remains an economic giant with world-class productivity in its manufacturing sector but much lower productivity in agriculture and much of its service sector, such as construction and retail. The Japan Inc. model has changed dramatically, but it is still more economically nationalist than the model followed by many developed countries. It continues to face a massive economic challenge domestically, to get its economy firmly and consistently growing, and internationally, from the faster growing giant, China.

China's Rise

Superlatives flow easily when describing China's economic success: the world's largest population, fastest-growing economy over the past two decades, largest exporter of many goods, and also largest importer and consumer of many products. The OECD estimates that China's exports could surpass those of the US and Germany by 2010, making China the world's largest exporter.[3] Many Asian countries view China's rise in the global economy like Walmart's entry into a local market. Local businesses fear being put out of business by the chain but also hope to be suppliers to such a large and fast-growing company. So when China began seeking RTAs with Asian countries, there was a scramble to be included in the RTAs, have alternative RTAs with China, or have alternative RTAs with China's partners.

Japan and RTAs: Japan's Response to China's Rise

Japan had historically pursued an economic policy of multilateralism, counting on its close relationship with the US to provide both security—the US continues to station troops in Japan—and prosperity. Prosperity came through close financial and trade ties to the US; the US has served as Japan's primary market for its exports. Japan, along with the US, long dominated Asia economically. Japanese investment fueled much of the growth of the Asian tigers, and the yen is an important currency in the region. But with China's rise as a major manufacturer of nearly everything, major investor in many Asian economies, massive importer of many Asian goods, and increasingly as an RTA partner for Asian countries on both a bilateral and subregional level, Japan became concerned it was losing influence and market share in the region and needed to cement its ties with Asian countries. In short, it needed to embrace RTAs. It also seeks to keep the US integrated into any pan-Asian or pan-Pacific RTAs that might emerge.

Broader Chinese-Japanese Relations

There is still a great deal of tension between Japan and its neighbors over their memories of World War II. Many people in the region believe that Japan has not adequately atoned for its World War II sins; they resent Japan's reluctance to fully apologize and even to internally discuss its World War II role. This perceived reticence extends to Japan's aggression as a cause of the war and to more specific atrocities during the war. Ongoing territorial disputes with Japan over various islands and Japanese government officials visiting Tokyo's Yasukuni Shrine—a memorial to Japan's war dead, whose buried include a number of Japanese war criminals—lead to continued resentment in the region. At the 2005 APEC summit in Pusan, South Korea, South Korean and Chinese leaders publicly criticized Japan, and China refused a bilateral summit with Japan at the APEC talks, although South Korea and Japan did meet in bilateral talks at the APEC summit. China and South Korea then cancelled foreign ministers' meetings that were to be held on the sidelines of the ASEAN summit in Malaysia in December 2005.[4] Many believe that a Willy Brandt-like sorrowful apology would go far toward easing the tension, but South Korean president Roh Moo Hyun called specifically for action, not apologies. The territorial disputes make a deeply heartfelt apology more difficult because nationalists in all countries call for their leaders to uphold national dignity.[5] There seems to be some warming in the relationship between China and Japan. The two are negotiating an agreement to jointly develop a natural gas deposit that both countries claim to be theirs. Whether negotiations are ultimately successful, the negotiations themselves and the more amicable tone used by government officials suggest a pragmatic warming between the two Asian economic giants.

Other East Asian Security Issues

There are other security issues in East Asia that are significant impediments to integration and that influence relations on a host of issues. Chief among these security issues is the continued division of the Korean Peninsula and, more specifically, North Korea's continued belligerence, which includes a police state that spews external verbal assaults, engages in counterfeiting, and has substantial conventional weaponry, missile technology, and a growing nuclear weapons capability. Other security issues include China-Taiwan and territorial disputes between South Korea and Japan, China and Japan, and numerous countries over the Spratly and Paracel Islands and, more importantly, economic rights in the seas surrounding them.

CONTEXT OF SOUTHEAST ASIAN RTAS: SOUTHEAST ASIAN IPE

Malaysia and Singapore

The Federation of Malaya—forerunner to today's Malaysia—became independent from Great Britain in 1957. The Federation of Malaya included Malaya but excluded Singapore. Both Malaya and Singapore viewed each other with some suspicion. Singapore had a majority of ethnic Chinese while Malays, called *bumiputera* (sons of the soil), were the majority in Malaya. Ethnic Chinese in Malaya dominated economics, and thus the Malay government policies favored the ethnic Malay over the Chinese. Despite these misgivings, the two were united—along with Sabah and Sarawak—as the Federation of Malaysia in 1963. This union was short-lived. In 1965, under the leadership of Lee Kuan Yew, Singapore became independent, with the remaining elements staying together as Malaysia.[6] Singapore, with an important harbor, started successfully courting foreign investment and began its rapid economic development.

Malaysia

Malaysia also was successful at economic development under Prime Minister Mahathir Mohamad's long and paternalistic rule, although at a slower pace than Singapore. Dr. Mahathir, as he is commonly called, developed Malaysia with a stable workforce and economic environment. It became one of the Asian cubs—the group of rapidly developing Asian countries following the Asian tigers. After the 1997 financial crisis, Malaysia's approach was different from that of its neighbors. Malaysia put on capital controls and moved to insulate itself from capital markets. Economic liberals predicted disaster, but Malaysia stabilized and recovered better than many of its peers. Dr. Mahathir did not allow full democracy to flourish and remains influential even after his retirement.

Malaysia and Thailand

Malaysia currently has some tension with its neighbor Thailand. The primary issue between them is the treatment of Muslims in southern Thailand and the status of 131 Muslim Thais that crossed into Malaysia in August 2004 to seek refuge. Southern Thailand has seen an increase in violence between the government and local Muslims since the January 2004 bombings and subsequent Thai government crackdown. Thailand is overwhelmingly Buddhist, but its southern regions are predominately Muslim—and ethnic Malays—thus when 80 Muslim men and boys died in police custody in Thailand, Malaysia, a majority Muslim country, was concerned. Malaysia does not want to let the 131 Thai Muslims go back to Thailand until their rights are guaranteed. This, combined with Malaysian criticism of Thailand, has led to an anti-Malaysian backlash in Thailand. But Malaysia and Thailand's relationship has been defined more by cooperation than hostility, and so the tiff may be healed and thus stop damaging their relationship.[7]

Indonesia

Amazingly diverse Indonesia was a Dutch colony that won independence after the Indonesia Revolution, 1945–1949.[8] In 1966, after years of growing turmoil, a strongman, Suharto, seized power from Indonesia's founding father, Sukarno. Suharto ruled for over thirty years by putting down calls for autonomy that came from Indonesia's various regions and with repression against leftist movements. Suharto's authoritarian rule brought stability, industrialization, and economic growth. This growth, however, partially masked economic inequality and massive corruption. Ultimately Suharto's rule would end with the economic turmoil brought on by the 1997–1998 Asian currency crisis. This crisis ended the long run of economic growth that had been a façade hiding the full extent of Indonesia's corruption and its economic vulnerability. By 1998 Suharto had given power to his vice president, and Indonesia has since had two increasingly fair elections, which have led to the peaceful transition away from military rule. Indonesia has taken significant strides toward being a democracy, but that has also made some regions call for greater autonomy, thus raising the specter of political violence. Another increasing problem for Indonesia was terrorism associated with Islamic militants. There has long been violence associated with Islamic areas seeking independence, but after 2001, there were a series of terrorist bombings aimed at Western interests in Indonesia.

Timore-Leste (East Timor)

Indonesia faced increased calls for independence with the successful movement to create East Timor, since renamed Timore-Leste. Portugal granted then East Timor independence in 1975, but Indonesia invaded in 1976 and brutally put down the independence movement. In 1999, after massive international pressure, Indonesia allowed a UN-sponsored referendum on independence. The East Timorese voted for independence, which led to violent retribution on the independence-minded population. This brought more international pressure on Indonesia to allow East Timor to gain its independence, which finally came in 2002.[9]

Australia

Australia's relationship with its neighbors seems to be undergoing a dramatic change. For a long time Australia regarded itself as an outpost of European heritage in Asia, rather than an Asian country. But as Great Britain's role in the world economy decreased and that of various Asian nations increased, it became clearer that Australia's economic future would be tied more directly to Asia. Australia had some negative images to overcome, and it has done so to a remarkable degree: Australia has become a hugely attractive study-abroad destination for Asian students, and immigration to Australia from Asia has increased. Moreover, it managed to get itself invited to the East Asian Summit. The summit failed to produce an agreement—in part over how closely Australia, New Zealand, and India should be included in any future East Asian community that might emerge—but Australia's inclusion speaks to its increasing Asian ties.

CONTEXT OF SOUTH ASIAN RTAs: SOUTH ASIAN IPE—CAN GEOPOLITICS BE OVERCOME?

South Asia certainly has a big kid on the block: India, a nuclear power with more than a billion people and a rapidly growing economy, also has cultural ties to many countries in the region. Ties with India therefore dominate the foreign relations of many nations in the region. But India is checked by fellow nuclear club member Pakistan, with whom India has fought numerous wars and continues to dispute the Kashmir region. Pakistan is clearly the weaker of the two. It is much smaller and at times is self-absorbed with simply staying together as a country. The India-Pakistan dispute has been moderated in recent years but continues to hinder more extensive subregional integration. India's influence is not without competition; China is also in the neighborhood and has a territorial dispute with India, and the US has long had interests in the region.

Economic growth during the post–World War II period was notoriously slow in India. Some derisively referred to the Hindu rate of growth, suggesting cultural impediments to growth. The answer was more pedestrian: excessive regulation. India was among the most regulated economies in the world during much of the post–World War II era. The "British raj" (rule) had been replaced by the "license raj," and only when India faced financial ruin in the early 1990s did it begin to seriously liberalize its economy. India has been rewarded by significant economic growth.[10] It has sought greater South Asian integration and has also sought to integrate with the dynamic Southeast Asian area by calling for an RTA with the Association of South East Asian Nations (ASEAN).

RTAs IN ASIA

Association of Southeast Asian Nations (ASEAN)

ASEAN was formed in 1967 with five countries: Indonesia, Malaysia, the Philippines, Singapore, and Thailand. Brunei joined in 1984 and in the 1990s sought to expand to represent all of South Asia and therefore included Vietnam, then Myanmar (Burma) and Laos, and finally Cambodia (see box 4.1).[11] Members are typically categorized today by their level of development, with the first six being the most developed and the newer four being substantially poorer. ASEAN carries considerable weight: ASEAN's 10 member countries have a combined population of almost one-half billion, and their combined GDP rivals China's.[12]

BOX 4.1. ASEAN MEMBERSHIP

Brunei	Myanmar
Cambodia	*Philippines*
Indonesia	*Singapore*
Laos	*Thailand*
Malaysia	Vietnam

Source: WTO, http://wto.org/.
Note: Original ASEAN members are in *italics*.

Designed initially as a forum for consultations to soothe frayed nerves over regional tensions, such as Indonesian hostilities toward Malaysia and Singapore from 1963 to 1966, ASEAN's role expanded during the Indochina refugee crisis of 1975–1978, when it began to represent the region externally and take on a policy leadership role.[13] The Asian financial crisis of 1997 showed that ASEAN was not able to play the role many felt was needed in the face of an economic crisis, and ASEAN moved toward economic integration through internal free trade, through free trade with other economies, and through monetary cooperation. Regional tensions within ASEAN have not fully abated. Cambodian and Thai troops have intermittently skirmished at a disputed temple, with soldiers on both sides killed. The temple was officially awarded to Cambodia, but territory surrounding it remains a matter of dispute.[14]

ASEAN's founding principle of noninterference in member nations' internal affairs has come under increasing pressure, thanks to the actions of one of its members, Myanmar (Burma, controversially renamed by the ruling military junta). Certainly the internal affairs of ASEAN members and potential ASEAN members had not always been completely ignored; Cambodia's membership, for instance, was postponed because of a coup d'état. Nevertheless, Myanmar's actions against human rights and democracy and intransigence toward foreign calls for reforms have led ASEAN to rethink nonintervention.

In the 1980s, the repression by Myanmar's military dictatorship worsened. In 1988, months of peaceful protests led by students and monks threatened the military's rule, and the protests were ended with a significant crackdown and the establishment of an Orwellian-named ruling military board: the State Law and Order Restoration Council (SLORC). International pressure mounted on Myanmar following the crackdown. The US, Japan, and many European countries halted aid to Myanmar and began trade boycotts.

SLORC then made a number of unexpected moves: it banned the one legal party—the Burma Socialist Programme Party—and then called for multiparty elections. Aung San Suu Kyi—the daughter of Burmese independence hero General Aung San—had returned to Myanmar in 1988 to take care of her ill mother. She helped organize the 1988 protests and then led a party, the National League for Democracy (NLD), in the 1990 elections, although she was barred from running. The NLD won 82 percent of the vote, trouncing the military-backed party. Suu Kyi was not allowed to form a government; instead she was put under house arrest, and SLORC's repressive rule continued.[15] She was awarded the Nobel Peace Prize in 1991 and has become a global hero. She has remained under one form of captivity or another nearly every moment since.

ASEAN's approach to Myanmar has been "constructive engagement." Myanmar's 1997 entry into ASEAN was meant to minimize its isolation and encourage good behavior, but Myanmar has remained an embarrassment to ASEAN. As the democratic tide that had swept much of Asia in the 1980s and 1990s consolidated in many countries in the region, Myanmar seemed increasingly like an anomaly.[16] Renaming SLORC as the State Peace and Development Council (SPDC) in 1997 did not placate critics.[17]

Myanmar was scheduled to host the rotating ASEAN presidency in 2005, but it declined the position under a great deal of pressure from the international community. ASEAN remains hesitant to punish Myanmar other than to note its disapproval of the military and the organization through which it governs Myanmar, the SPDC. There has been a change in ASEAN's tone and attitude toward Myanmar. ASEAN is well known for not criticizing its own members, but that is changing. Malaysian foreign minister Syed Hamid Albar said, "We respect the position of Myanmar as a member of ASEAN, but at the same time, I don't think any single country in ASEAN does not feel impatient, or does not feel uncomfortable, because it does create problems and difficulties for us. . . . Myanmar itself must be able to show us movement in respect of the roadmap [to democracy] as well as the position of Aung San Suu Kyi."[18] Myanmar, however, continues to treat its citizens terribly. In 2007 government incompetence and xenophobia was cited as the reason the government kept out aid after a cyclone killed tens of thousands. Later in 2007, monks were the subject of a crackdown after the "saffron" revolution—peaceful prodemocracy protests—with many killed, arrested, or driven out of the country. Myanmar's junta seems impervious to the ASEAN approach.

ASEAN Free Trade Area (AFTA) and the ASEAN Economic Community (AEC)

ASEAN members agreed to an ASEAN-wide FTA in 1992 that went into force in 2002 for the original ASEAN members with phased-in entry for ASEAN's newer and poorer members: 2004 for Vietnam, 2006 for Laos and Myanmar, and 2008 for Cambodia.[19] Thus, AFTA allows variable speed, based on development level. It also allows flexibility in what items will be excluded from schedules of tariff reduction.[20] AFTA's tariff provisions were not expected to dramatically affect trade flows among its members because tariff levels among members were already quite low.[21] In 1995, ASEAN established the ASEAN Framework Agreement of Services (AFAS), which ensures that ASEAN free trade includes services. The intent of AFAS is to establish "GATS-plus" levels of integration, but as of yet its members do not live up to that level of integration. Here too ASEAN has offered flexibility for countries to offer service sectors for integration on a unilateral basis. This flexibility has meant little liberalization beyond the WTO's GATS.[22]

In 2003 ASEAN members pledged to establish the ASEAN Economic Community (AEC), which will include "full liberalization of trade in goods, services and investment by 2020." ASEAN members have since agreed to move "Vision 2020" up to 2015. To get there, ASEAN has created the ASEAN Economic Community Blueprint (AECB), which spells out what steps will be taken over the course of a series of four two-year periods ending in 2015. The 2003 Protocol for Elimination of Import Duties sped up the reduction of tariffs, and now applied tariffs are between 0 and 5 percent for the more-developed ASEAN-6. They plan on reaching 0 percent tariffs by 2010, with the poorer ASEAN-4 reaching 0 percent by 2015.[23] At the 14th ASEAN summit in February 2009, ASEAN members agreed to another agreement on free trade in goods, the ASEAN Trade in Goods Agreement (ATIGA), designed to place all ASEAN goods-related measures in one treaty.[24]

ASEAN External Trade Relations

ASEAN has considerable economic weight in both consumption and exports. AFTA was once the sole RTA in all of East Asia but now finds much
company and competition. In fact, it is joining with that competition to form
new RTAs.[25] ASEAN has signed a "tariff-cutting agreement" with China
and started talks for similar deals with India, Japan, Australia, New Zealand,
and Korea.[26] This resulted in the signing of the ASEAN-Australia-New Zealand FTA (AANZFTA) at the 14th ASEAN summit in February 2009. The
AANZFTA covers both goods and services, with chapters on investment,
intellectual property rights, and dispute settlement. It will enter into force
60 days after Australia, New Zealand, and four ASEAN members ratify it.[27]
ASEAN is also considering an FTA with the EU.[28]

ASEAN is now the home of the East Asian Summit meetings among the
ASEAN + 6 countries. Some had hoped that the East Asian Summit would
create an East Asian Community (EAC), but there were disagreements over
whether this should include all ASEAN + 6 countries or only the ASEAN
+ 3 countries. Countries only managed to have future EAS meetings in the
shadow of ASEAN meetings. See the discussion of the ASEAN + 3 FTA/
ASEAN + 6 FTA and the East Asian Summit, below.

ASEAN + 3 Free Trade Area and ASEAN + 6 Free Trade Area

The ASEAN + 3 FTA proposed by China is, as of yet, only a proposal. It calls
for an RTA between ASEAN China, Japan, and South Korea. Japan had been
a reluctant RTA participant but felt excluded by China's increasing interest in
RTAs—China proposed an RTA with ASEAN in 2000, signed an RTA with
ASEAN on goods in 2004, which took effect on January 1, 2010, and signed
another RTA on services in 2007.[29] In 2006 Japan proposed adding India,
Australia, and New Zealand.[30] India had already been under consideration as
an addition to the ASEAN + 3 FTA.[31] In addition to this trade integration,
ASEAN + 3 countries have been moving toward monetary cooperation and
monetary integration through the Chiang Mai Initiative. (See "Chiang Mai
Initiative [CMI]," later in this chapter.)

APEC—Asian Pacific Economic Cooperation Forum

The 21-member APEC members now represent approximately 57 percent
of the world economy and 47 percent of world trade. See box 4.2 for
APEC membership details. It therefore generates considerable attention

despite its current description as moribund.[32] APEC began in 1989 and had been just a forum to politely discuss issues of common interest. But that changed in 1993 when President Clinton signaled his intent that APEC be something more. The US had been forging NAFTA, and the European Community had recently transformed into the European Union, so Asian countries were more interested in a Pacific trade grouping than they had been in the past. The character of APEC changed. In 1994, at its meeting in Bogor, Indonesia, it established the Bogor goals of free and open trade in the region by 2010 for its developed members and by 2020 for its developing members.[33]

BOX 4.2. APEC MEMBERSHIP

Australia	Papua New Guinea
Brunei	Peru
Canada	Philippines
Chile	Russia
China	Singapore
Hong Kong	South Korea
Indonesia	Taiwan (officially Chinese Taipei)
Japan	Thailand
Malaysia	United States
Mexico	Vietnam
New Zealand	

Source: APEC website, http://www.apec.org/.

APEC's integration is based on nonbinding commitments and the results show it; few steps have been taken toward implementing the Bogor goals. Many economic liberals have praised APEC for its "open regionalism," but others lament its meandering steps toward integration.

The November 2005 APEC summit in Pusan, South Korea, saw an extension of previous APEC summits in which security concerns—North Korean nuclear ambitions and Avian flu—are higher on the agenda than economic integration. The upcoming WTO ministerial meeting in Hong Kong was also of greater interest than further APEC integration. This attests to the importance of these issues and to the drift that has entered into APEC integration.[34]

Asia-Pacific Trade Agreement (APTA),
Formerly the Bangkok Agreement

The Asia-Pacific Trade Agreement (APTA), formerly known as the Bangkok Agreement, consists of six states in the region (see table 4.1) that have agreed to mutually lower tariffs with one another on an agreed-upon set of goods. APTA does not cover services, investment, intellectual property rights, or nontariff barriers, although APTA members are considering provisions covering lower barriers in services, investment, and intellectual property rights. The agreement—signed in Bangkok in 1975—was created under the auspices of the forerunner of the United Nations Economic and Social Commission for Asia and the Pacific (UNESCAP) and UNCTAD.[35] Since there is no secretariat, UNESCAP's trade and investment division performs the agreement's secretariat duties. Seven countries signed the Bangkok Agreement—known as the First Agreement on Trade Negotiations among Developing Member Countries of ESCAP—with five countries ratifying it. The seven original signatories were Bangladesh, India, Laos, South Korea, Sri Lanka, the Philippines, and Thailand, with all but the latter two ratifying the agreement.[36] China joined in 2001. Papua New Guinea (PNG) acceded to the agreement in 1993 but did not ratify it. In 1998 Pakistan began accession to the APTA and continues to be in the accession process. Membership is open to any developing nation in the UNESCAP region, which includes South and Southeast Asia. China's inclusion in APTA has raised its profile, and more countries have expressed interest in joining. Numerous countries—such as Indonesia, Iran, Malaysia, Nepal, the Philippines, and Thailand—were observers during some of the negotiations for revisions to the Bangkok Agreement. The second and third Bangkok Agreements were completed in 1990 and 2005, respectively. Accession requires the support of two-thirds of APTA's members. If any member state objects to a country's accession, the agreement will not apply between the two countries.[37]

Table 4.1. Asia-Pacific Trade Agreement (APTA) Membership (Bangkok Agreement)

Bangladesh	1975
China	2001
India	1975
Laos	1975
South Korea	1975
Sri Lanka*	1975

Note: Papua New Guinea (PNG) acceded in 1993 but has not ratified. Pakistan has been in the accession process since 1998 but is not a member. Trade and Investment Division of UNESCAP, "Facts about the Bangkok Agreement (Asia-Pacific Trade Agreement)," June 2005.
* Not a participating member because there have been no customs notifications of tariff concessions granted.

Bay of Bengal Initiative for Multi-Sectoral Technical and Economic Cooperation Free Trade Agreement (BIMSTEC-FTA), Also Known as the Bangladesh, India, Myanmar, Sri Lanka, Thailand-Economic Cooperation FTA

BIMST-EC, or more commonly BIMSTEC, is the acronym for the first five member countries in the organization: Bangladesh, India, Myanmar, Sri Lanka, Thailand-Economic Cooperation and its other name, the Bay of Bengal Initiative for Multi-Sectoral Technical and Economic Cooperation. It was created in 1997 on Thailand's initiative by four of these five countries—Bangladesh, India, Sri Lanka, and Thailand—and was known as BIMST-EC. Myanmar joined in December 1997 and had its name included in the organization's title. In February 2004, Bhutan and Nepal became members (see box 4.3), but there was not a name change because bigger changes were afoot. The very next day, all BIMSTEC members except Bangladesh signed the framework agreement to negotiate the FTA. In July 2004 negotiations formally began, and Bangladesh agreed to participate.[38] Thus, BIMSTEC, which had long focused on economic cooperation rather than trade integration, began its long journey, which it hopes will lead to a free trade agreement, the BIMSTEC-FTA, to be called the Bay of Bengal Initiative for Multi-Sectoral Technical and Economic Cooperation.[39]

BOX 4.3. BIMSTEC MEMBERSHIP

Bangladesh	Nepal
Bhutan	Sri Lanka
India	Thailand
Myanmar (Burma)	

Source: BIMSTEC, http://www.bimstec.org/.

India is the largest weight in the BIMSTEC. The Indian government considers BIMSTEC a bridge between the SAARC and ASEAN as BIMSTEC has members from each of these two organizations.[40] Some observers consider a BIMSTEC FTA to be an alternative to the SAARC's FTA, the South Asian Free Trade Area (SAFTA), for India because the BIMSTEC-FTA does not include Pakistan and thus could move forward if Indian-Pakistani hostility stalls SAFTA.[41] Trade among BIMSTEC members is low, as is the case for trade among SAARC members. BIMSTEC members hope an FTA will change that.

The negotiations for a BIMSTEC FTA began in July 2004 and were planned to be completed on goods by December 2005 for implementation in July 2006. As is often the case, the ambitions for negotiations were not matched by the ability to reach agreement. In November 2008, Indian prime minister Manmohan Singh called for the "early" conclusion of the BIMSTEC FTA in goods, two and a half years later than hoped for, before the more difficult investment and services negotiations conclude.[42] In June 2009, BIMSTEC members had agreed upon rules of origin but were still not finished negotiating the tariff reduction schedules, and in a December 2009 ministeral meeting, BIMSTEC noted more negotiations were needed.[43] Negotiations on trade in services and on investment began in December 2005 and were to be scheduled to be completed by the end of 2007, but this date was not met because the goods FTA has been more difficult than anticipated.[44]

The agreement allows for different phase-in schedules, depending upon a member's level of development and the sensitivity level of the product. There will be a "fast track" liberalization schedule for the least-sensitive products and a normal liberalization schedule for less-sensitive products. Each of these schedules will be differentiated by whether the BIMSTEC FTA member is a least-developed country (LDC) or developing economy. The LDC members—Bangladesh, Bhutan, Myanmar, and Nepal—will have longer phase-in periods for trade with developing members. BIMSTEC FTA LDCs were to reduce tariffs to between 0 and 5 percent on qualifying fast-track goods from one another by June 30, 2009 and from the developing BIMSTEC members—India, Sri Lanka, and Thailand—by June 30, 2011, but tariff reduction schedules remain a matter for negotiation in 2010. The developing BIMSTEC members' fast-track schedule was July 1, 2006, and June 30, 2009, for each other's and LDCs' imports, respectively. A second phase, for normal liberalization on somewhat more sensitive products, had developing BIMSTEC members reducing tariffs on LDC members' products by June 30, 2010 and on one another's imports by June 30, 2012. In contrast, the LDC BIMSTEC were to lower tariffs in phase 2 by 2015 for trade with one another and 2017 on trade from developing BIMSTEC members.[45] Still at issue is which items will qualify for fast-track versus normal liberalization or be excluded entirely. A central disagreement in the negotiations has been the list of sensitive items that would be excluded from either round of tariff reductions.[46] Thailand has called for a cap on each country's "negative list"—the list of items to be excluded from liberalization—to be twice as short as the cap called for by all other BIMSTEC-FTA members.[47] India too has complained, but more narrowly; it complained that Bangladesh's listed items are concentrated in sectors that make up over half of India's exports to Bangladesh.[48]

Chiang Mai Initiative (CMI)

The Chiang Mai Initiative is a loose grouping of a set of bilateral monetary cooperation treaties between ASEAN + 3 members (the ten ASEAN members plus China, Japan, and South Korea) and is at the same time a process of moving toward more institutionalized monetary cooperation. The impetus for the Chang Mai Initiative—named for the Thai city in which members originally met in 2000—came from the Asian financial crisis of 1997–1998. The Asian crisis saw massive currency drops as investors sought to get out of what had been booming markets. Southeast Asian leaders were disappointed that Asia had no institutional mechanism to deal with the crisis and instead had to turn to the International Monetary Fund (IMF), the US, and Japan for emergency liquidity, the equivalent of desperately needing blood donations from faraway hospitals. The liquidity came, but the anxiety that came due to this dependence upon extraregional actors left the region feeling vulnerable.

There was talk of creating an Asian Monetary Fund, but instead a set of bilateral swap arrangements (BSAs) were created. Countries facing liquidity crises could turn to one another for capital as set out in numerous bilateral treaties, collectively known as the CMI. Activating a bilateral swap during a crisis is not automatic—the lending country must also agree—but will be much quicker than arranging financing from the IMF or the US and increases the amount of capital a country could have access to in the event of a crisis. The CMI is not a challenge to the IMF; in fact, the two are formally linked. To get access to most of the bilateral swap capital, a country must agree to an IMF program (which will set conditions for fiscal responsibility). Currently, 20 percent of the swap amount in a CMI BSA can be accessed without an IMF program in place.[49] This IMF link is designed to ensure the discipline and thus credibility that the IMF confers due to its typically stringent program requirements. This reassures likely creditor nations, especially Japan, that credit extended during a crisis will be repaid. In addition to the BSAs, the CMI has initiated a regional surveillance mechanism—the Economic Review and Policy Dialogue—designed to warn countries that are nearing financial crises. This too seeks to reassure likely creditors. The 13 CMI countries are discussing whether a more traditionally governed regional bank should be created, but there are many issues to work out, including voting rights and conditions for loan dispersal.[50] The effectiveness of the CMI is unknown. It has not been turned to in a crisis. Some may take this as evidence of success—that the CMI confers sufficient credibility so that it need not be used. But there is more to suggest that instead, it is not seen to be as effective or credible as other sources of liquidity in a crisis, such as the US or IMF.

East Asian Summit (EAS) and the Road Not Taken
to the East Asian Community (EAC)

Leaders at ASEAN's 2004 summit in Laos decided to organize the East
Asian Summit (EAS). Because the EAS was intended to be an impetus for
the creation of a new Asian RTA—probably to be called the East Asian
Community—the list of countries included and excluded from the EAS
would be critical.

The call for a new Asian RTA was not a new idea, and one had not been
created largely over disagreements about its composition. Should it include
Japan, which previously had preferred the WTO to either bilateral or multilateral RTAs? Should it be extended to South Asia? Should it include developed
nations in the region, such as Australia and New Zealand, that are geographically but not culturally Asian? Most significantly, should it include the US,
which would likely come to dominate any organization created? In April
2005, ASEAN foreign ministers agreed to include India in the EAS—along
with China, Japan, and South Korea.[51] After significant lobbying, Australia
and New Zealand were also included; Russia attended as an observer. Conspicuously, the US was not included despite Japanese pressure for the EAS
to include the US.[52]

The Road to the EAS

Getting to the first East Asian Summit was controversial. The former Malaysian prime minister had long advocated an Asian regional organization of
significant weight that specifically excluded the US. His early 1990s proposal
for the East Asian Economic Caucus, the EAEC, also excluded Australia and
New Zealand and was thus dubbed a "caucus without Caucasians." More
ominously, US secretary of state James Baker argued it would "draw a line
down the Pacific," and Japan and South Korea ultimately did not support establishing the EAEC.[53] At that time, both countries were hesitant to enter into
any regional trade groupings, let alone one that excluded the US, for a number of reasons. First, they were concerned with alienating their largest trading
partner: the US. Second, they were concerned that regional trade groupings
would diminish energy and political capital needed for the Uruguay Round
negotiations that were taking place at the time. Third, multilateral agreements
were not likely to cut deeply into Japanese and South Korean agriculture, the
most protected and sensitive economic sector for both countries. Many potential FTA partners would expect preferential access to Japanese and South
Korean agriculture markets, the very last sector to which they wanted to grant
access. This limited the value of regional agreements to them at the time, but

the political and economic calculus has changed significantly, making the 2005 EAS possible.

Since the failure of the EAEC, Japan and South Korea have abandoned their no-RTAs policy and entered into a number of them, and they are negotiating many more. What changed? Three main factors for Japan and South Korea's changed RTA policy stand out: RTAs proliferating elsewhere, especially in the Americas, the Asian financial crisis of 1997, and China's rise and increasing regional economic leadership. These reasons apply to the increasingly favorable view other Asian countries had toward forming RTAs in general and, for many, toward having the 2005 EAS in particular.

Many observers point to the increase in FTAs outside Asia that excluded these and other Asian countries. Specifically, NAFTA and the FTAA were catalysts for Asia to establish its own FTAs, further nudged by the European Community's march toward the becoming the European Union. Japan initially was against NAFTA passing in the US, but Japanese leaders eventually changed their minds because they saw the forces of protectionism fighting against NAFTA and thought that Japan could become the next target if protectionist political forces won the NAFTA battle. Nevertheless, establishing NAFTA was a powerful incentive for Japan to enter into FTAs of its own. Another was the FTAA, which, in the mid- to late 1990s, seemed to be heading toward regional trade on a massive scale and again excluded Asia. A further impetus was given when the primary US trade policy official, US trade representative Robert Zoellick, announced the US policy of "competitive liberalization," in which the US would negotiate FTAs granting countries preferential access to the US market in exchange for liberalization to Washington's liking (strong intellectual property rights, little if any preferential access for agriculture) in order to pressure other countries into making similar deals with Washington. This would slowly spread liberalization and would, he argued, create more support for the stalled DDA negotiations. As the former Singaporean prime minister Goh Chok Tong said about the EAS, "We have little choice but to construct a new architecture for East Asia. If East Asia does not coalesce, it will lose out to the Americans and Europe."[54]

The Asian financial crisis changed the opinion of many in Asia toward greater Asian integration. Many in the region believed the US and IMF responses to the crisis were inadequate; thus the crisis demonstrated the need for greater coordination in Asian financial affairs and an institution controlled by Asian countries themselves to react to future Asian financial crises. Finally, China's rise and aggressive promotion into regional trade agreements was a challenge to regional economic leadership that Japan in particular could not let go unanswered. Thus Japan jumped on the FTA bandwagon.

Japan, however, remains less inclined to form an Asian FTA that excludes the US than others in the region. Japan is more opposed to an EAS-style FTA—without the US—than other countries in the region. For instance, South Korea remained quiet about US exclusion at the EAS. Singapore, typically pro-US and in a bilateral FTA with the US, acquiesced. The Filipino Gloria Macapagal-Arroyo—who had close personal ties to President Bush—also supported the exclusion of the US.

Japan may yet agree to a pan-Asian FTA without the US, but it remains very hesitant. Why? If it is in a regional grouping with China, Japan believes its weight relative to China will be stronger if the US is included. Japanese interests, especially security interests, are far more similar to those of the US than those of China. In short, both Japan and the US are alarmed by China's growing military presence in the region, and both are more concerned about North Korean nuclear weapons than is China. This is compounded by the continued Chinese-Japanese animosity over Japan's whitewashed version of its role in World War II and by continued territorial disputes between the two. These security differences between Japan and China threaten to damage the substantial and growing commercial relationship between the two, despite considerable diplomatic efforts.

Others in the region obviously disagree: the EAS met without the US and almost met without Australia and New Zealand. Even though he is retired, former Malaysian prime minister Dr. Mahathir Mohamad remains influential in the EAS. On the eve of the EAS, he said that Australia and New Zealand are neither "East, nor are they Asia." And he called the East Asian Summit an "East Asia Australasian summit."[55] China did not want these countries to attend, nor did they want the US or India.

Other Asian countries' preferences about the attendance list at the East Asian Summit and therefore, ultimately, of any organization created by it, depended largely upon two factors: the countries' desire to include or exclude the US and the countries' perception of their influence in the EAS relative to their influence in current regional institutions. For instance, Indonesia was hesitant to have an EAS because it feared China and Japan's inclusion would significantly weaken its power in ASEAN. Moreover—similar to Brazil's strategy in the Americas relative to the US—Indonesia would rather see ASEAN strengthened prior to negotiating with the bigger outside powers; ASEAN could thus negotiate from a stronger position than the one in which it currently finds itself.[56]

India stated it would be interested in joining an EAS pan-Asian free trade agreement and would reportedly be interested in such an entity's also including security issues. India and China's relationship has gotten much better in recent years. They have settled some border disputes and have decided to focus on economic cooperation more than the security issues, where there are still considerable differences between the two giants. Nevertheless, China would prefer that any EAS-inspired FTA exclude India (and exclude Australia and New Zealand), and it would like to stick to economic issues, not issues that hit upon more touchy questions regarding domestic governance, such as human rights. India's inclusion in the EAS was supported by Singapore and Japan, which would like to balance China's influence in any EAS-inspired FTA that might emerge.[57]

What is still unknown about any organization that comes from the EAS is the number of countries involved, how deeply they will integrate, if at all, and if integrated, the different levels of membership. One observer noted, "What you're seeing now is a gathering of a group of countries that are testing out what types of relationship they are most comfortable with . . . over the next 10 years, you're going to get a whole lot of new acronyms—coming up with brand new groupings. Or you're going to get old acronyms—like ASEAN—being completely redefined from what they were before."[58] Or perhaps the same dynamics that created current institutions with their current roles will prevail.

South Asian Association for Regional Cooperation (SAARC), Including the SAARC Preferential Trading Arrangement (SAPTA) and the South Asian Free Trade Area (SAFTA)

If one wants an example in which security relations dominate economic considerations in cooperation and integration, the South Asian Association for Regional Cooperation (SAARC), created in 1985, would be an excellent example. The security relations that matter the most for the organization are those between India and Pakistan. Their acrimonious relationship—including four wars between 1947 and 1999, countless border skirmishes, and terrorism from groups that are thought to train in Pakistan—has dramatically limited the integration potential for the organization. SAARC member nations realize that SAARC has not led to a great deal of integration or economic change. As Indian prime minister Manmohan Singh said, SAARC is "marginalized at the periphery" of the "emerging Asian resurgence."[59] SAARC members' trade with one another is only 5 percent of their total trade with the world.[60] SAARC's initial attempt at increasing integration was through the 1993 SAARC Preferential Trading Arrangement (SAPTA), which did reduce tariffs on some goods but was clearly not going to spur integration like a more comprehensive RTA would.

SAARC's supporters argue that the low level of integration achieved thus far need not be the case and hope cooperation on nonsecurity issues in SAARC could build trust-enabling broader cooperation. In fact, it is precisely this effort that has breathed some new life into SAARC. So too has the realization that to have greater weight in international trade negotiations,

SAARC members will have to be more economically integrated. Toward that end, at the 12th SAARC summit in January 2004, SAARC members agreed to lower tariffs on their free trade agreement, the South Asian Free Trade Area (SAFTA), starting on January 1, 2006.[61] The tariff reductions, which will be phased in by 2016, are set to be significant, but their impact has been minimized because SAFTA members created a list of sensitive goods to be exempt.[62] Another hurdle in the negotiations that seems to have been overcome concerned the loss of government revenues from the lowering of tariffs. Because some SAFTA member nations are so poor, tariff reductions would lead to a significant loss of government revenue; poorer SAFTA countries want some compensation for lost revenues.[63] Why is the loss of tariffs revenue a more significant problem for poorer-country governments? Poorer countries find it more difficult to collect income and value added taxes because they have less administrative capacity and because the informal sector represents a larger percentage of the economy than in industrial economies. A committee of experts from all SAFTA countries will determine the level of compensation under formulae in the Mechanism for Revenue Loss Compensation.[64] SAARC members do not have a track record of moving dramatically toward freer trade in either SAPTA or SAFTA. In the late 1990s, the date for free trade was in the early 2000s, with each successive SAARC summit envisioning freer trade at later and later dates. This does not instill confidence that SAFTA will lead to the level of liberalization envisioned by some of its promoters.

SAARC and SAFTA will now include Afghanistan as well (see box 4.4); SAARC members voted approval for its accession at their 13th annual summit in November 2005 in Dhaka, Bangladesh.[65] Afghanistan, one of the poorest countries in the world, faces the aftermath of decades of instability, war, and economic isolation (aside from its poppy exports). It is not alone in this legacy. Nepal and Sri Lanka both face recently ended civil wars. Sri Lanka's was long-standing, while Nepal's began in 1996, worsened significantly in 2001, and ended in 2006 with a peace accord.

BOX 4.4. SAARC AND SAFTA MEMBERSHIP

Afghanistan	Maldives
Bangladesh	Nepal
Bhutan	Pakistan
India	Sri Lanka

Source: SAARC, www.saarc-sec.org.

The India-Pakistan relationship is not the only relationship that impinges upon integration. Bangladesh and India's relations have been strained by accusations that Bangladesh gives safe haven to insurgents who fight Indian rule. Nepal and Pakistan both pushed to have China included as an observer at SAARC, and Pakistan has indicated it will push for full membership for China. Why? China's presence would counterbalance India's dominance of SAARC.[66] India and China fought a border war in 1962, and India is home to the Dalai Lama and many other Tibetan Buddhists who fled Tibet in the face of Chinese repression. Relations between China and India have grown warmer in recent years, but not so warm that India wants China in SAARC; India has grown accustomed to dominating SAARC and frowns upon arrangements that would dilute its dominance.[67] Japan, a significant donor to SAARC countries, also became an observer in 2005.[68]

Trans-Pacific Strategic Economic Partnership Agreement (TPP) (Formerly the P-4)

The Trans-Pacific Strategic Economic Partnership Agreement (TPP) had been the Pacific-4 (P-4), so named for its trans-Pacific membership, which consisted of Brunei, Chile, New Zealand, and Singapore. Negotiations on the P-4 began in 2002 and concluded in 2005, and the agreement went into force in 2006. In 2008, the US and the P-4 announced they would begin negotiations in March 2009.[69] The TPP is an FTA in goods, not services. It is, however, negotiating extending the FTA into both investment and services. In addition to the US, Australia and Peru announced they will negotiate their entry into the TPP, and Vietnam is reportedly considering joining the talks.[70]

5

Europe

European regional integration is dominated by the European Union (EU), the most successful model of interstate regional economic and political integration. The EU increased its membership dramatically in 2004 from 15 to 25 states and in 2007 expanded to 27. Many other countries would like to get in, but it is an exclusive club, with only a handful of countries officially negotiating EU accession and another handful negotiating about potential negotiations. Sixteen of the 27 have adopted a stable and successful common currency, the euro. The EU aspires to form a common foreign policy but struggles in this endeavor. It also struggled in its attempt to update its governance through the Lisbon Treaty, also called the EU reform treaty. A previous effort, the EU Charter, had been rejected in referenda in France and the Netherlands, causing EU members to renegotiate the charter. They created the Lisbon Treaty and were taken aback when Irish voters rejected it in a referendum. Ireland pledged to put it up for another vote and it did pass, thanks in part to the economic crisis that hit Ireland so hard. Ireland was happy indeed to be in the EU and the EU's eurozone, especially when it compared its situation to that of even harder-hit non EU member Iceland. Irish voters did pass the Lisbon Treaty.[1]

The EU is not the only regional integration effort in the region. Other important regional groupings include the European Free Trade Association (EFTA), whose membership has been dwindling as it members join the EU, and the European Economic Area (EEA), a free trade area between the EU and three of the EFTA countries—Iceland, Liechtenstein, and Norway (EFTA member Switzerland opted out)—encompassing 28 countries, roughly 500 million people, and nearly 20 percent of world trade.[2] See figure 5.1.

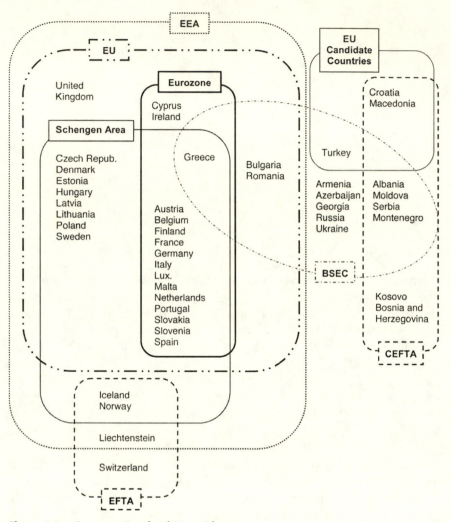

Figure 5.1.   European Spaghetti Venn Diagram
Key: See list of abbreviations.

CONTEXT OF EUROPEAN RTAS:
WHY EUROPEAN INTEGRATION?

That contemporary integration should be attempted in Europe is not surprising because its history includes numerous episodes of integration, such as the Roman Empire and Charlemagne's Frankish Empire. Some integration efforts were more successful than others, and their legacies are mixtures of greatness, oppression and, ultimately, failure. But more importantly, at least for contemporary integration, they established periods that intensified the cross-pollination of languages and cultures in Europe and, in some instances, led to the sharing of common languages and cultures. Typically, if unity lasted beyond the warfare often associated with integration, commerce intensified, thus further increasing commonalities within the diverse European continent.

But when one considers the history of warfare in this period, it is a marvel that Europe would be home to successful integration of any kind; the most destructive wars in history—World Wars I and II—came from European nation-states' nationalism, competition, suspicion, and misjudgment. These wars stand out primarily in their destructiveness and scale, but they are part of a long European tradition. How, then, did they give rise to European integration?

Rather than hindering integration, it was precisely the bloodiness and destructiveness of the world wars that inspired contemporary European integration by making it a more attractive option. Inspiration and attraction are not enough to explain Europe's turn toward integration; if they were enough, integration would have followed World War I. Other factors made integration possible: the Cold War's division of Europe united noncommunist Europe behind a common enemy—the Soviet Union—while the dominant nation-state in the noncommunist world, the US, both allowed and, to a degree, required integration. The US *allowed* integration by providing a security guarantee to noncommunist Europe ("Western" Europe hereafter). Western European states did not have to fear one another militarily because the US would not allow them to seriously compete in this arena, thus making integration a possibility. Moreover, the US hegemon *required* European integration—initially at least—by tying Marshall Plan aid to Western European nations' ability to cooperate in setting levels of aid for one another. The US also served as an economic catalyst for integration by helping Europe recover from World War II; US dollars poured into capital-hungry Western Europe to help the region rebuild, and the US served as Europe's most important foreign market.

The post–World War II European economic miracles—first rebuilding and then moving to high-tech economic development—became among the most powerful elements in the EU's growing gravitational pull. Western European prosperity and the other elements in the EU's gravitational pull—freedom and stability—combined with Soviet leader Gorbachev's permissiveness toward the satellite states within its orbit, motivated East Germans to defy their government en masse in 1989, culminating in the opening of the Berlin Wall and ultimately the end of the Cold War itself. For the former communist states of Central and Eastern Europe, including some former republics of the Soviet Union, the EU's gravitational pull of prosperity, freedom, and stability offered another substantial benefit: it got them further from Russia's gravitational pull. During communist times they were within the Soviet Union's security umbrella, and they also underwent economic integration through the Council for Mutual Economic Assistance, better known as Comecon. After communism, they had spent too many years within the Russian orbit to trust that newly noncommunist Russia would remain innocuous and non-expansionist. They began seeking entry into the EU soon after establishing autonomy from Soviet dominance, and in 2004 the first round of former communist states successfully joined the EU, with others officially in line to negotiate EU entry and still others having announced their desire to join.

The eagerness of former communist states to join the EU makes the juxtaposition of contemporary Europe with its cataclysmic past sharper. If bombed-out cities and concentration camps were the symbols of European conflict in 1945, French and German leaders François Mitterrand and Helmut Kohl literally and metaphorically holding hands in 1984 and the French and German parliaments meeting in Versailles in 2003 serve as the symbols of how far European integration has moved since 1945.[3] That France and Germany, enemies in so many European wars, would embrace each other and European integration so publicly attests to the sea change in thinking in EU states.

Of course, one should be careful not to overstate the EU's considerable success; it is telling that public pronouncements of EU unity are needed. Leaders do not publicly celebrate the daily rising of the sun because there is no question that it will rise. Public shows of unity in Europe have been needed of late. Despite recent achievements—such as the adoption of the euro as a common currency for 16 of 27 EU members (including 13 of 15 pre-2004 members) and the 2004 and 2007 expansions of the EU from 15 to 25 and 27 members, respectively—the EU has hit a number of difficulties. Long-standing problems such as slow economic growth and high unemployment have never fully abated, while other problems are newer, such as the rejection of the EU Charter by founding EU states France and the Netherlands, forcing renegotiation and culminating in the Lisbon Treaty, which was initially rejected by Ireland before passing in a second vote, the growing tension between Islamic minorities and the majority populations in many EU states, and, finally, the global economic crisis of 2008–2009 that has led some EU countries to put up internal barriers and has led others to intense economic crises.

Just as the EU's considerable successes should not be overstated, neither should its problems. Negotiations over EU membership or governance, as is the case everywhere, involve occasional brinksmanship. This is not new, but it is easily forgotten. Brinksmanship in the EU's past did not mean the end of the EU, nor even the issue over which there was brinksmanship. France singlehandedly kept Great Britain out of the EU for years in the 1960s, but this brinksmanship is (mostly) forgotten now. Negotiations also include the negotiators having to convince the people, groups, and parties they represent that the negotiated outcome is worthwhile. Sometimes they are unable to do this successfully, and even when possible, it is often contentious.

RTAs IN EUROPE

Black Sea Economic Cooperation (BSEC)

The Black Sea Economic Cooperation (BSEC) organization was formed in 1992 by the Istanbul Summit Declaration of BSEC. BSEC seeks to promote economic cooperation among the states of the Black Sea region (not all of which are littoral states) and, as a longer-term goal, it seeks the creation of the BSEC FTA. To get there, it has already established a trade and development bank. BSEC members, however, have not implemented many of the agreements that have been negotiated already, casting doubt on future plans. This should not be surprising when one considers that BSEC members have quite different economic levels of development and sometimes clashing political interests.[4] See box 5.1. Armenia and Azerbaijan are a dramatic example; they still have not settled the status of the contested Nagorno-Karabakh region that led to war between the two neighbors in the 1980s and 1990s. A less-dramatic example is that some BSEC members are (or are on their way to becoming) EU members, while Russia is concerned with the EU's growing influence in the region.

BOX 5.1. BSEC MEMBERSHIP

Albania	Moldova
Armenia	Romania
Azerbaijan	Russia
Bulgaria	Serbia and Montenegro
Georgia	Turkey
Greece	Ukraine

Central Europe Free Trade Area (CEFTA), Including CEFTA 2006

The new Central European Free Trade Agreement (CEFTA) is a comprehensive free trade agreement consisting of eight Southeastern European members—Albania, Bosnia and Herzegovina, Croatia, Kosovo, Macedonia, Moldova, Montenegro, and Serbia (box 5.2). The modern incarnation of CEFTA is often called CEFTA 2006 to distinguish it from its predecessor, established in 1994, that had consisted of four Central European transition countries: the Czech Republic, Hungary, Poland, and Slovakia. They were later joined by Bulgaria, Romania, and Moldova. The four original CEFTA countries left in order to join the EU as part of the EU's 2004 "big bang" expansion. Bulgaria and Romania left to join the EU in 2007, leaving only Moldova, but CEFTA 2006 had already been signed and the Southeastern European countries joined the more comprehensive CEFTA 2006, which went into force in 2007.[5] In short, the remaining CEFTA members consist of Albania, Moldova, and former republics of Yugoslavia. It is telling that the CEFTA 2006 secretariat is in Brussels: the EU remains central to CEFTA members' economic, trade, and security strategies; all CEFTA members except Moldova hope for EU entry in the foreseeable future. CEFTA members would like to follow in the footsteps of their absent founders and join the EU.

BOX 5.2. CEFTA MEMBERSHIP

Albania	Macedonia
Bosnia and Herzegovina	Moldova
Croatia	Montenegro
Kosovo	Serbia

Source: CEFTA Secretariat, http://www.cefta2006.com/.

European Economic Area (EEA)

Created in 1994, the European Economic Area is an FTA between the 27-member EU and three of the four EFTA members: Iceland, Liechtenstein, and Norway (with EFTA member Switzerland opting out of the EEA); thus the EEA has 30 members. Its economic weight is enormous, and it has achieved deep integration, including free trade in goods, services, capital, and labor. In many respects, the non-EU EEA members are brought within the EU, but with slightly more autonomy and, of course, no say in the making of EU policy. EEA integration is sufficiently close that the EU extended financial aid to Iceland during the global banking crisis and subsequent recession that hit Iceland particularly hard. EEA integration is also sufficient that it has disallowed antidumping actions except in the case of agriculture and the fishing industry.[6]

European Free Trade Association (EFTA)

Established in 1960 by European countries seeking shallower integration than the EEC (now the EU) was providing, EFTA's membership has dwindled as members have successively joined the EU. In 1994, the European Economic Area went into effect, which created an FTA between the EU and three of the four EFTA members: Iceland, Liechtenstein, and Norway, with only EFTA member Switzerland opting out of the EEA. The EFTA services agreement went into force in 2002, extending the EFTA's coverage to both goods and services. The EFTA members have open labor markets for one another and the right to establish residence (assuming sufficient financial means).[7] The EFTA may shrink again as Iceland negotiates entry into the EU.

European Union (EU)

Overview of European Union Integration

The European Union is the most studied integration effort in history because it has been the most ambitious and successful integration project in history. When one considers its width, depth, institutionalization, and prosperity, the EU towers over other regional agreements. More impressive still has been the EU's role in Europe's remarkable march from its chaotic history toward stability. Yet for all this audacity and success—peace, cooperation, and affluence among states that have experienced so much war and conflict—the EU remains internally divided and parochial in many regards. Despite the EU's affluence, the EU economies face deep structural problems that it has been unable to resolve and, some argue, have been exacerbated by its penchant for regulations and layers of bureaucracy. Moreover, many have different views of what an ideal EU should look like. These debates echo earlier disagreements about whether the EU should be a supranational organization—with institutions that have autonomy from and influence over national governments in some issue areas—or an intergovernmental organization with institutions that carry out the national wishes of the EU members where there is agreement, but with autonomy and influence over events strongly restricted by those members.[8] This debate has not ended; indeed, the EU has both supranational and intergovernmental elements, and this dichotomy is unlikely to end in the foreseeable future.

Development of the EU

From today's vantage point, the EU's development toward deeper integration, like the eroding of canyon walls, seems steady, but this can be misleading. While erosion involves the steady work of water and gravity slowly
wearing away softer rocks, canyons are also shaped by more turbulent developments such as floods that scour canyons differently and more rapidly than
during more gentle times. Thus the EU has been shaped by the most turbulent
of developments—World War II, the Cold War, the fall of the Berlin Wall,
and the end of communism—and the more mundane but essential elements
such as prosperity and stability.

As noted above, the EU's institutional development was driven by the
legacy of World War II and the emerging Cold War. A more united Europe's
interdependence would foster peace through prosperity and by tying historically oversized Germany into a European institutional framework. A more
united and prosperous Western Europe would inoculate it from communism
and eventually form a counterweight to the Soviet Union.

The EU's institutional lineage began with the European Coal and Steel
Community (ECSC), created by a 1951 treaty that went into force in 1952.
See table 5.1 for the EU's major treaties and box 5.3 for major steps in
the EU's development. The ECSC was supranational over a limited set of
issues—the ECSC's high authority had power to set policy among its original
six members: France, Italy, West Germany, and the Benelux countries of Belgium, the Netherlands, and Luxembourg.[9] The prime architect of the EU, Jean
Monnet—civil servant, diplomat, and first president of the ECSC—intended
that this supranational character extend to other European integration institutions such as the European Defence Community, which failed to win ratification in France, and to the less supranational European Economic Community
(EEC) established in 1958 by the 1957 Treaty of Rome.[10] The EEC had a
fundamental tension between its supranational-leaning EEC Commission and
the intergovernmental Council of Ministers. Initially, the EEC Commission
operated in a relatively supranational fashion, but by the early 1960s it found
itself—and the question of the EEC's status relative to its member states—at
the center of an EEC crisis when French president Charles de Gaulle attempted to assert his intergovernmental vision of European integration.[11] A
number of French attempts to create a more intergovernmental EEC failed
in the early 1960s. The Commission continued to operate in a supranational
fashion, and France forced the issue to a conclusion by employing its "empty
chair" policy in 1965 and 1966: it simply refused to attend Council of Ministers meetings, thus preventing any change in EEC rules that might weaken
a member country's ability to veto EEC policies. Majority voting for some
decision making—officially called qualified majority voting (QMV)—was to
be phased in as part of the Treaty of Rome; France wanted nothing to do with

Table 5.1.   EU Treaties

Treaty Name	Year Signed	Major Accomplishment
Treaty of Paris	1951	Established the European Coal and Steel Community (ECSC)
Treaty of Rome,* a.k.a. the Treaty Establishing the European Community (EEC)	1957	Established the European Economic Community (EEC), also known as the Common Market. Later called simply the European Community (EC).
Single European Act	1986	Created a timetable to establish a true common market. Also strengthened parliament and allows for QMV on some issues in the Council of Ministers.
Maastricht treaty, a.k.a. the Treaty on the European Union (TEU)	1992	Creates the EU. Maastricht also called for a common currency and two new pillars of activity: foreign policy and justice/home affairs.
Amsterdam Treaty	1997	Agreement to prepare the EU for future enlargement. Extends the use of QMV in the Council of Ministers. The EU is given more power over immigration and border controls, although countries choose national control on this issue.
Nice Treaty	2001	Agreement to prepare the EU for future enlargement. Extends the use of QMV in the Council of Ministers.
Lisbon Treaty	2007	This was a negotiated replacement for the French- and Dutch-rejected EU Charter or constitution. Its passage was also difficult, with two referenda needed to obtain a yes vote in Ireland. The Lisbon Treaty, like the rejected constitution, attempts to streamline EU governance. It increases the powers of the European Parliament, changes voting in the Council, creates an EU "foreign minister," and reduces the number of EU commissioners.

Source: Adapted from Elizabeth Bomberg and Alexander Stubb, eds., *The European Union: How Does It Work?* (Oxford University Press, 2004), 5 and 15; Dick Leonard, ed., *Economist Guide to the European Union* (Bloomberg Press, 2002); "The Treaty of Lisbon," Euractive.com, April 27, 2007, http://www .euractiv.com.
*There was another 1957 Treaty of Rome that established the European Atomic Energy Community (Euratom).

it. This crisis ended with the Luxembourg compromise, which allowed the veto to be employed on "very important interests" when qualified majority voting was called for. In essence, France was able to prevent a substantially supranational EEC from emerging. True, there were and would be supranational elements to the EU, but France had assured that these supranational elements would be deeply constrained by the member governments.

BOX 5.3. CHRONOLOGY OF EU DEVELOPMENTS

Year	Event
1945–1947	Europe—ravaged by World War II and increasingly divided by the coming Cold War—considers how to ensure peace and prosperity as it rebuilds.
1947	US establishes the Marshall Plan to rebuild Europe.
1948	Organization for European Economic Cooperation (OEEC)—later called the OECD—is set up to distribute US Marshall Plan aid.
1948	Benelux Union, a customs union between Belgium, the Netherlands, and Luxembourg, comes into force. The Benelux Union will provide half of the original six EU members.
1949	The North Atlantic Treaty Organization (NATO) is established, helping to ensure a US security guarantee for Western Europe.
1950	Schuman Plan—named after French official Robert Schuman—is proposed for the creation of a supranational organization to regulate European coal and steel production.
1951	European Coal and Steel Community (ECSC) Treaty signed.
1952	ECSC goes into effect.
1952	European Defence Community Treaty signed.
1954	European Defence Community fails to be ratified in France.
1957	Treaty of Rome signed, which will create the European Economic Community (EEC). Euratom treaty also signed in Rome.
1958	European Economic Community (EEC) established and with it, the EEC Commission.
1960	Alternative to the EEC, the European Free Trade Association (EFTA) is agreed upon.
1961	EFTA enters into force.
1962	Common Agriculture Policy (CAP) regulations adopted by the Council of Ministers.
1963	Franco-West German Treaty signed pledging friendship and coordination of policy in a number of policy areas—including defense.
1963	France rejects Great Britain's application to join the EEC. Two years later it is again rejected.
1964	Common Agricultural Program (CAP) is operative.
1965–1966	French president Charles de Gaulle employs his "empty chair" policy in battle over decision making on the Council of Ministers, in essence a battle between supranationalism and intergovernmentalism.
1966	Luxembourg compromise ends the stalemate over Council of Ministers powers. It allows veto to be used on "very important

interests" and is a victory for those seeking an intergovernmental EC over those seeking a supranational EC.

1967	The ECSC, EEC, and Euratom officially form the European Communities (EC).
1968	Customs Union established: tariffs and quotas removed and a common external tariff (CET) established. This was completed 18 months ahead of schedule.
1973	Denmark, Great Britain, Ireland enter the EC. Norway had been accepted also, but EC membership was rejected in a Norwegian referendum in 1972.
1979	European Monetary System (EMS) is operating.
1981	Greece joins the EC.
1985	Single European Act to achieve true internal market is agreed upon.
1986	Portugal and Spain join the EC.
1987	Single European Act (SEA) enters into force.
1991	Maastricht European Council agrees on treaty to establish the EU with a common currency by 1999.
1992	European currency crisis. Great Britain and Italy must pull out of the exchange rate mechanism (ERM). Exchange rate bands for ERM are widened.
1993	European Single Market program is "achieved." Internal common market supposed to be created, but barriers remain.
1993	Maastricht treaty goes into force, and the EC officially becomes the EU. (Technically, the EU is comprised of the EC as well as the second and third pillars, which are common security and foreign policy, justice, and home affairs.)
1994	European Economic Area (EEA) agreement comes into force, creating an FTA with the EU and most EFTA nations.
1995	Austria, Finland, and Sweden become EU members.
1995	Schengen Pact, which lowers internal EU border controls for seven EU countries, goes into effect.
1995	Treaty establishing Europol is signed.
1998	European Central Bank established, replacing the European Monetary Institute.
1999	Euro is launched in eleven EU countries.
1999	Commissioner Jacques Santer resigns under pressure from the European Parliament amid accusations of mismanagement of the Commission.
2001	Greece joins the eurozone, bringing eurozone membership to 12.
2002	The euro permanently replaces local currencies in eurozone countries.

2004	"Big bang" expansion moves EU borders eastward and southward as the EU increases from 15 to 25 members.
2004	EU charter, also called the EU constitution, is signed after years of negotiations. It calls for reforms intended to make EU governance in a larger EU smoother.
2005	French and Dutch voters reject the proposed EU charter.
2007	Bulgaria and Romania join the EU, bringing membership to 27.
2007	Slovenia joins the eurozone, bringing eurozone membership to 13.
2007	Lisbon Treaty signed, replacing the rejected EU charter/constitution and including most of the proposals.
2008	Cyprus and Malta join the eurozone, bringing membership to 15. They become the first of the 2004 "big bang" EU entrants to join the eurozone.
2008	Irish voters reject the Lisbon Treaty, bringing its ratification into doubt.
2009	Slovakia joins the eurozone, bringing membership to 16.
2009	Iceland applies for EU membership after being hit hard by the 2008–2009 financial crisis.
2009	Irish voters ratify the Lisbon Treaty. The Czech Republic and Poland also ratify the Lisbon Treaty, which goes into force December 1.
2009	Eurozone member Greece on the verge of bankruptcy.

Source: Derek W. Urwin, *The Community of Europe: A History of European Integration Since 1945* (London and New York: Longman, 1991), 101–15; Dick Leonard, *Economist Guide to the European Union* (Bloomberg Press, 2002), 6; Delegation of the European Commission to the USA, http://www.eurunion.org/; European Commission, http://ec.europa.eu/index_en.htm; Elizabeth Bomberg, John Peterson, and Alexander Stubb, eds., *The European Union: How Does It Work?* (Oxford University Press, 2003).

With the empty chair crisis passing and with de Gaulle out of power in the late 1960s, British membership, and that of Denmark and Ireland, became possible. They joined in 1973. The EU continued to move toward both deeper and wider integration. Deeper integration came with the establishment of the European Monetary System (EMS), which became operational in 1979. Under the EMS, members' currency values were coordinated relative to one another. Wider integration came again when Greece joined in 1981, followed by Portugal and Spain in 1986.

The EU took two more significant steps toward deeper integration with the Single Union Act (SEA), agreed upon in 1985 and entered into force in

1987, and the Maastricht treaty, negotiated in 1991. The SEA was designed to achieve what the EC was supposed to have already achieved: an internal common market. Also driving the SEA was fear that the EC was not sufficiently keeping up with US and Japanese technological and economic dynamism and was instead suffering from "Eurosclerosis," an economic disease consisting of high unemployment and slow economic growth driven by excessive regulation. Thus there are elements of both economic liberalism and economic nationalism to the SEA. Economic liberalism in the SEA was in the form of reduced internal barriers and the internal competition and efficiencies this would bring, while economic nationalism in the SEA came from fears of relative economic decline compared to the rising Japanese and US economies. While the SEA goals were officially achieved in 1993, the reality is that the EU, which became the EU's official name in 1993, is still not a single market in many areas, especially services.

The EU also agreed to significantly deeper integration with the Maastricht treaty, negotiated in 1991. The Maastricht treaty called for the establishment of a common currency by 1999 and also created an EU with three pillars: the Economic Community is pillar 1 with, at least theoretically, supranational decision making. Pillar 2 consists of common foreign and security policy, with primarily intergovernmental decision making, and pillar 3 is justice and home affairs (cross-border policing), with primarily intergovernmental decision making. One observer argues the Maastricht treaty "undoubtedly represented the most important development in the EC's history since the signing of the Treaty of Rome."[12] The Maastricht treaty's goal was achieved: the European Central Bank became operational in 1998, and the common currency was successfully established in 1999 for 11 of the 15 EU members and for 12 of the 15 as soon as Greece qualified for eurozone membership. The eurozone, now with 16 members, involves very deep integration; members give up autonomy in setting their monetary policy.

The EU did not stop becoming wider either before or after these events: accession waves came in 1995, 2004, and 2007. Austria, Finland, and Sweden joined in 1995, bringing the EU's membership to 15, followed by the more dramatic 2004 "big bang" expansion, increasing EU membership to 25. The "big bang" expansion included many former communist states and brought the EU all the way to the Russian border. In 2007 Bulgaria and Romania acceded, bringing EU membership to 27 and extending EU borders to the Black Sea.

In addition to the "big bang" expansion, 2004 also saw the signing of the EU Charter, sometimes referred to as the EU "constitution." It was to streamline decision making in the enlarged EU but was of greater symbolic importance than substantive importance. In 2005, after being ratified in a number of EU member countries, the new constitution was rejected in France and a few weeks later in the Netherlands. The EU, which had been barreling toward both deeper and wider integration, had not convinced majorities of two of its founding members that the constitution was a good idea. The vote was not simply about the constitution itself, nor even the EU. Some voters used the referenda to voice their opposition against their governments and others to protest the growing globalization that made them feel insecure. Nevertheless, the constitution was rejected. Many proclaimed this to be the most significant crisis in EU history, but this was hyperbole. An organization that was born of the rubble of World War II, grew in the shadow of the Cold War, and survived the internal paralysis of the empty chair crisis is not so easily damaged. In 2007 after further negotiations, the Lisbon Treaty was signed. It is not a constitution but contains nearly the same governance reforms. It too has had a rocky ratification process. After most EU member states had approved it, Irish voters rejected it in a referendum in 2008. In late 2009 they revoted, and it passed. Any perceived increase in supranationalism didn't look so bad with the global economic crisis hitting Ireland worse than most EU countries and with the EU unquestionably helping Ireland weather the crisis. With the financial gales threatening Ireland, EU institutions that had recently seemed to be harmful suddenly seemed like sensible structural necessities.

EU Institutions

The EU is the most institutionalized of all RTAs, and its decision-making procedures and overall governance are among the most difficult to understand. The European Commission—essentially the executive of the EU—provides the most succinct description: "The EU is governed by five main institutions: the Commission proposes, the Parliament advises and shares with the Council of Ministers the power to legislate, the Council takes the final decision, the Court of Justice rules and the Court of Auditors ensures transparency."[13] See table 5.2.

This description is simple and clear, but some might contend it is too simple and too clear—to the point of missing how the EU actually operates. Determining the primary EU institutions is clear enough, but explaining their role in the EU policymaking process is not easy because, despite the description above, the reality is exceptionally complex and, according to critics, less than transparent. This lack of transparency has led to the so-called democratic deficit: the charge that EU policymaking lacks clear lines of authority and therefore of accountability. Those who charge that there is a democratic deficit in the EU also maintain that all too often, various EU regulations are promulgated without the public's understanding their origins or purpose and without sufficient public input.

Table 5.2. Primary EU Institutions' Functions and Structure

Institution and Location	Primary Functions and Organization
European Council*—Headquarters located in Brussels, but *European Council summits,* usually referred to as *EU summits* or just *summits,* are held in the country that holds the presidency of the *Council of Ministers,* a.k.a. the *Council of the European Union* (see directly below).	Sets overall EU strategy and direction. Resolves issues that are at an impasse in the *Council of Ministers.* Represents individual EU member countries. Formally it was not officially part of the European Community governing system, despite having been necessary to governing the EU. The Lisbon Treaty makes it formally part of the EU.
Council of Ministers, a.k.a. *Council of the European Union, EU Council,** or simply, *the council*—General secretariat in Brussels, meetings primarily in Brussels but also in Luxembourg)	Makes legislation, sometimes jointly with the European parliament. Represents individual EU member countries. The council typically meets by issue area, so each member nation sends an appropriate minister to each "configuration" of the council. The president of the council represents the council to other EU bodies and helps set the council agenda during his two-and-one-half-year tenure.
European Commission—Typically referred to as simply *the Commission*—Brussels and Luxembourg	The Commission proposes legislation and actually drafts the legislation (although making legislation is more in the hands of the Council of Ministers and parliament). The Commission also administers legislation by formulating regulations giving greater detail to EU legislation. The Commission also monitors compliance with the EU provisions. Represents the EU as a whole, not individual governments. The president of the Commission (the EU commissioner) represents the EU in settings outside of the EU. The Commission president and the EU commissioners are chosen every five years by consensus of the member states. Parliament must ratify the entire Commission.

(continued)

Table 5.2. (continued)

Institution and Location	Primary Functions and Organization
European Parliament—Regular sessions in Strasbourg, France, secretariat in Luxembourg, but most active in Brussels, where legislators meet with Council of Ministers and with *the Commission.*	Represents EU citizens. Shares legislative duties with the Council of Ministers. Can amend legislation and has the power of veto in some issue areas such as enlarging the EU. Organized by parties that cut across national boundaries.
European Court of Justice (ECJ)—Luxembourg	Adjudicates. With the Maastricht treaty, it is able to impose fines on members for some issues. Can fine member states that ignore its rulings. Currently, allows individuals to petition against EU institutions. Judges are appointed by member states for six-year terms that may be renewed.
Court of Auditors—Luxembourg	Oversees EU spending to ensure that it is free of fraud.
European Central Bank—Frankfurt	Sets monetary policy for the euro. ECB run by the governing board, which consists of six executive board members and 16 national central bankers of the eurozone members.

Source: European Union, "Introducing the European Union," Delegation of the European Commission to the USA, http://www.eurunion.org/ (March 24, 2006); "Introduction to EU Institutions 2004," BBC Online; UK EU Presidency 2005, http://www.eu2005.gov; Elizabeth Bomberg and Alexander Stubb, eds., *The European Union: How Does It Work?* (Oxford University Press, 2004). "Treaty of Lisbon," EU Commission, http://eur-lex.europa.eu/JOHtml.do?uri=OJ:C:2007:306:SOM:EN:HTML. Information on the Council of Europe can be found at its website, http://www.coe.int/DEFAULTEN.ASP.

* The Council of Europe, best known for the establishment of the European Convention on Human Rights and the European Court of Human Rights, has a broader membership than the EU and is neither an EU institution nor an RTA.

EU citizens do elect their representatives to the European Parliament, but it is not the primary lawmaking body in the EU. It shares that power with the Council of Ministers, whose legislative authority clearly exceeds that of the Parliament. It does not help that the European Parliament has three homes: Strasbourg, France, is its regular home for plenary sessions (meetings in full), but this sometimes takes place in Brussels, Belgium, where committee meeting may also be held. Parliament's administrative offices—the general secretariat—are in Luxembourg.[14] Moreover, the lines of authority vary, depending upon the issue area. Most significantly, the quotation at the beginning of this section makes no mention of the European Council summits, which are meetings of the heads of state of member EU countries. These summits set the general direction the EU will take but also serve to address more specific issues that have been unresolved by the Council of Ministers. Finally, the way decisions are carried out varies as well. On some issues, the commission itself is responsible for carrying out EU policies. On others, the national governments are responsible. Disputes over implementation are sometimes resolved in the courts but may also be resolved at the EU summits or in subsequent treaty negotiations.

EU Governance Reform: The EU Charter to the Lisbon Treaty

In May 2004, EU membership jumped from 15 to 25, and EU borders moved dramatically eastward. In June 2004, the EU finally reached agreement on the long-sought EU Charter. The EU was on the move both wider and deeper, or so it seemed. The deeper integration of the charter needed approval in all 25 EU countries to come into force. After approval in 10 countries, the charter lost in public referenda in France and the Netherlands in May and June 2005, respectively, placing significant doubt on the charter's future. The choices facing the EU over the charter were unclear; it could not go into effect without all EU members ratifying it, but negotiations were already lengthy and contentious. Why the need for EU governance reform, and why has it been so controversial?

EU governance is a study in confusion, with EU members making some decisions independently, others as an intergovernmental organization, and others with the EU acting as a supranational institution. EU institutions have overlapping power, and there is no one policymaking process—it varies by issue area. One might think that the European Parliament (EP), directly elected through EU-wide elections, would be the most powerful, but the EP is weak. This confusion adds up to the EU's "democratic deficit," and the EU Charter was intended to address these concerns. The 300-page document called for a more united Europe with a foreign minister to represent the EU as a whole, a bill of rights, called the Charter of Fundamental Rights, and a stronger EU Parliament. The charter was highly symbolic of the EU's continued commitment to integration, and thus the charter's failure in two founding countries demonstrates the EU's contentious and confusing relationship with its member states and the EU population.[15] Two years after the charter's rejection, the EU successfully renegotiated governance reform, signing the Lisbon Treaty in 2007.[16] It was easily ratified in most EU member states but rejected in its first referendum in Ireland, passing in a second referendum in 2009 and entering into force on December 1, 2009.

The Lisbon Treaty is remarkably similar to the EU Charter in its governance reform measures. It has dropped some of the EU Charter's symbolic elements, such as an EU anthem and calling the treaty a constitution. It has dropped the name of the EU's bill of rights, the Charter of Fundamental Rights, but has retained the actual rights (with an opt-out for Great Britain and Poland).[17] As this suggests, the Lisbon Treaty also includes a greater number of opt-outs than found in the EU Charter. Like the charter, it attempts to increase efficiency and transparency. In short, the Lisbon Treaty attempts to remedy the EU's "democratic deficit."

Institutional Reforms in the Lisbon Treaty. Like the rejected charter, the Lisbon Treaty increases the powers of the European Parliament so there are more decisions involving "codecision" whereby both the parliament and the EU Council create legislation.[18] Over time the European Parliament's powers have increased, from consultation (the EP could offer only advice), to cooperation (the EP could amend legislation), to assent (the EP could accept or reject some measure), to codecision (jointly making legislation). The European Parliament does not and will not have universal codecision, but the Lisbon Treaty continues its expansion into more issues. Before the Lisbon Treaty, nearly half of all EU laws involved codecision (with most of the rest falling under cooperation).[19] With the Lisbon Treaty this will increase yet again.

Despite the increase in the European Parliament's power, the EU Council will remain the more significant body. Substantive voting on the EU Council is either by unanimous vote or qualified majority voting (QMV), depending upon the issue area (with simple majority voting on some procedural matters). Most EU Council votes on pillar 1 items—those involved with economic integration—will be with QMV, with votes on pillar 2 (foreign policy) and pillar 3 (police and judicial cooperation relating to crime) remaining primarily unanimous.

QMV—where a threshold of states representing a threshold of the EU's population—is the EU's solution to problems facing legislative bodies in federal systems where states or provinces have significantly different population levels. If the Council of Ministers' voting rules were simply one country, one vote, less-populous countries would have excessive power: Luxembourg or Malta's population—under a half-million people each—would each have the same weight as Germany's 82 million people.[20] If the Council of Ministers were to give full weight to population, more-populous countries could easily impose their will on less-populous countries. The four most populous EU members—Germany, France, Great Britain, and Italy—account for approximately 55 percent of the EU's 491.5 million people.[21] Clearly, any voting scheme weighted too strongly toward population would find the majority of EU countries without a significant voice. Thus a country is given a number of votes somewhat proportional to population. Less-populous states get more votes per population but remain dwarfed by the more-populous states. Before the Lisbon Treaty reforms are phased in, QMV requires a majority of EU members to vote for a measure, representing a majority of the population and at least 255 (73.9 percent) of the total 345 Council of Minister votes.[22] Under the Lisbon Treaty, this would become somewhat simplified, although admittedly there would be a great deal of complication remaining: 55 percent of member states (15 of the current 27 members) representing 65 percent of the EU's population are required for passage. If 15 members vote to pass a measure, it may or may not pass, depending upon which countries voted for it.

Prior to the Lisbon Treaty, the presidency of the council rotated among EU members every six months. Nominally, the main task was to organize the EU summit, but in reality, the country with the presidency also helped set the overall EU agenda. This changed with the Lisbon Treaty. Instead of the six-month rotating presidency, criticized as too short by many, the council will elect a council president by QMV who will serve a two-and-one-half-year term, renewable once. The council president's formal powers will be few, and therefore, in a relatively united council with a skilled council president, the position will be substantially important, but potentially far less important in a more divided council or in less-skilled hands.[23] The first president of the council is Herman Van Rompuy. It remains to be seen what the relationship will be between the EU member governments and the president of the council generally and in the case of Van Rompuy. There will also be lower-level six-month rotation by country for specific issue areas within the council, officially called Council Configurations.[24]

The Lisbon Treaty, also like the charter, creates one person responsible for EU-wide foreign policy, the High Representative of the EU for Foreign Affairs and Security Policy, merging what is currently two positions in the EU (EU Council's High Representative and the Commissioner for External Relations). Like the current EU Council's High Representative, the new EU foreign minister will speak for the EU on diplomatic and security policy—inasmuch as EU governments agree upon what that voice should say—and like the Commissioner for External Relations will oversee the significant EU foreign affairs budget. Under the charter, this position would be called the EU Foreign Minister, but because this sounded too much like the function of a single nation-state, Great Britain insisted on the name change.[25]

Changes will come to the EU's executive arm, the EU Commission. Traditionally, each country receives a commissioner's position; this is the equivalent of a ministry position (or cabinet-level secretary in the US). This may have been sensible with a smaller EU, but with 25 and then 27 EU members, it has become increasingly unwieldy. The Lisbon Treaty will dispose of this one country, one minister rule and instead cap the number of ministers at two-thirds of EU membership, and countries will send commissioners on a rotating basis.[26]

The EU Enlargement Process

Accession to the EU is not easy. Aspiring entrants—acceding members—must meet the Copenhagen criteria: (1) democratic governance, including institutional stability and the protection of human rights; (2) a functioning market economy and the ability to compete within the EU market; and (3) accepting the goals of EU membership and the ability to meet the obligations of EU membership.[27] In practice, this means successful applicants must have a good human rights record—including a fair justice system, good treatment of minority populations, and the abolition of the death penalty—and must harmonize a wide array of their domestic laws to meet EU standards.[28] Entry has huge payoffs to states. Ireland and Spain are examples in which EU entry notably helped economic growth. Investment went up notably for each after EU membership, and EU money to alleviate poverty and subsidies for farmers also facilitated prosperity. The benefits to the 10 "big bang" entrants—the 2004 entrants—began before their EU entry was official. Foreign direct investment went up in anticipation of EU entry as companies sought lower wages than could be found in the EU 15, duty-free entry into the massive EU market, and the stability offered by pending EU membership. Additionally, the EU provided much-needed funds for economic development projects such as infrastructure. See figure 5.2 for EU membership waves and current acceding candidates.

Accession is difficult for the EU itself, and it would never have fully recovered from its 2004 growing pains without reforms. Voting rules that were becoming unwieldy for 15 countries could be paralyzing for 25 or 27 countries; therefore, the EU's expansion led to calls for constitutional changes to the EU. This proved more difficult than expected, and some in the EU did

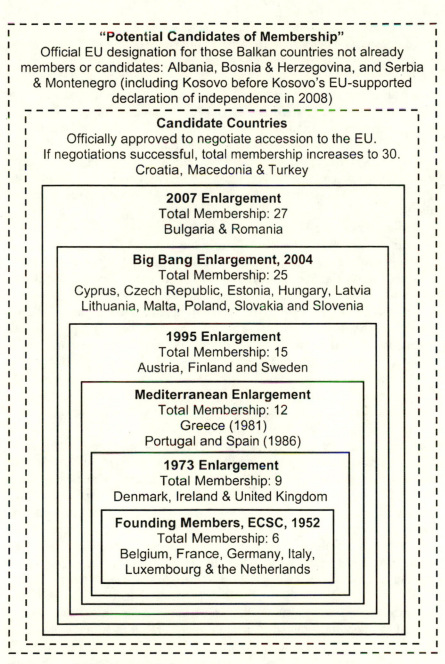

"Potential Candidates of Membership"
Official EU designation for those Balkan countries not already members or candidates: Albania, Bosnia & Herzegovina, and Serbia & Montenegro (including Kosovo before Kosovo's EU-supported declaration of independence in 2008)

Candidate Countries
Officially approved to negotiate accession to the EU.
If negotiations successful, total membership increases to 30.
Croatia, Macedonia & Turkey

2007 Enlargement
Total Membership: 27
Bulgaria & Romania

Big Bang Enlargement, 2004
Total Membership: 25
Cyprus, Czech Republic, Estonia, Hungary, Latvia
Lithuania, Malta, Poland, Slovakia and Slovenia

1995 Enlargement
Total Membership: 15
Austria, Finland and Sweden

Mediterranean Enlargement
Total Membership: 12
Greece (1981)
Portugal and Spain (1986)

1973 Enlargement
Total Membership: 9
Denmark, Ireland & United Kingdom

Founding Members, ECSC, 1952
Total Membership: 6
Belgium, France, Germany, Italy,
Luxembourg & the Netherlands

Figure 5.2.   EU Enlargement Onion
Key: See list of abbreviations.

not want to commit to any further expansion until voting procedures and other constitutional issues were worked out. The 2004 "big bang" expansion has also changed the calculus for the EU budget. Before the "big bang" 10 entered the EU, most of the EU budget went to agriculture through the CAP. Since the new entrants' economies had higher dependence on agriculture than found in the EU15 countries, the CAP had to be reduced. As the EU struggled with consensus on creating its seven-year budget (2007–2013), some EU members wanted expansion put on hold until agreement on the budget. For example, in December 2005, France resisted formally granting Macedonia candidate status until the budget uncertainties were resolved.[29] In part, this reflects France's concerns that the CAP will come under greater pressure as the EU expands.

As of 2009, three countries have official candidate status with the EU: Croatia, Macedonia, and Turkey. Croatia was put on hold for a time because it was not fully cooperating with the International Criminal Tribunal for the former Yugoslavia. Specifically, Croatia was asked to arrest General Ante Gotovina, suspected of wars crimes against Serbs.[30] After the EU suspended accession talks, Croatia turned over the general, much to the chagrin of Croatian nationalists, who view him as a hero. Croatia's membership is not guaranteed; a bilateral dispute between it and EU member Slovenia that stalled Croatia's entry for a time has been resolved but could possibly resurface later in the accession process.

It appears there will be another official candidate country soon: Iceland. EFTA and EEA-member Iceland had long flirted with EU membership and seemingly had decided against it, partially out of the desire to have continued control over its fisheries. After all, Iceland had privileged access to EU markets through the EEA and could continue to manage its own fisheries without interference from the EU bureaucracy. Iceland's calculation about its relationship with the EU changed radically with the financial crisis that hit Iceland exceptionally hard in 2008. Iceland had moved aggressively into finance with much success, courting many British, Dutch, and other foreign customers. But with the mortgage crisis Icelandic financial institutions became dangerously exposed to the credit crisis, and banks began to fail. So too did Iceland's finances. Iceland had to turn to the International Monetary Fund and the EU to stabilize its finances. Iceland had previously viewed EU membership as a claustrophobic reduction in autonomy; it suddenly appeared as a soothing embrace that could give comfort against the downsides of globalization. In July 2009, Iceland formally applied for EU membership. In February 2010 the EU Commission gave a positive review of Iceland's capacity to meet the Copenhagen criteria: the political criteria of stable and democratic institutions guaranteeing minority rights, the economic criteria of having a market economy, and the more ambiguous criteria of having the ability to meet membership obligations—that is, to align Icelandic standards with EU standards relating to political, economic, and monetary union. Iceland is poised to officially become a candidate country once the European Council votes its approval. Iceland will then be able to begin accession negotiations.[31] Aligning thousands of laws to those of the EU is no small task, but it will be made easier by Iceland's already close relationship with the EU through the EEA. There are other political hurdles: other EU countries will have to approve of the terms of Iceland's entry, and Iceland itself will have to approve. This is not a foregone conclusion as Icelandic public opinion on joining the EU is divided.

EU Expansion and Turkey. With the 2004 and 2007 expansions the EU became more diverse in terms of language, culture, and level of economic development. That diversity would increase again dramatically if accession negotiations with Turkey are successful. If acceded, Turkey would be the first country in the EU whose territory is not primarily European; Turkey has one foot in Europe and the other across the Bosporus Strait in Asia. Turkey would be a significant increase to the EU population; its population would be second only to Germany in the EU. This would require larger changes to EU voting arrangements than other enlargements. Turkey is also poor, at least by EU standards. Turkey's combination of size and poverty certainly set it apart from other EU enlargements, but these issues are surmountable. More controversial are the cultural differences between Turkey and the rest of the EU.

Many of the complaints above, though real, mask a deeper question over Turkish accession: whether Turkey is "sufficiently" European to be in the EU. It would be the first Islamic country in the EU, and Turkey's democracy is only a recent development. Indeed, Turkey's commitment to liberalizing its political system has been uneven.

Turkish accession is certainly a challenge to both EU and Turkish identity, and as such carries enormous symbolism. This symbolism has been dramatically amplified by events in recent years. In November 2003 two bombings by groups tied to al Qaeda hit British targets in Istanbul, demonstrating the Islamic world's division over Turkey's relations with Western nations. In the EU, tension had been mounting for years between the majority population and Muslim citizens and immigrants when a number of incidents made the tension explosive, sometimes literally: the murder of Dutch filmmaker Theo Van Goh in November 2004 by an angry Muslim who had been offended by a Van Goh documentary that depicted Islam as misogynist; the October and November 2005 riots in France over the French government's ban on wearing religious symbols in public schools; the Islamic terrorist bombings on March 11, 2004, "3/11" in Madrid, and on July 7, 2005 "7/7" in London; and the furor that erupted in 2006 in the Islamic world over Danish cartoons with negative depictions of the Prophet Muhammad.[32]

Turkey's potential EU entry has led to soul searching in both Turkey and the EU. EU member states view their societies as open and tolerant but find this claim increasingly difficult to maintain when they express hesitation at integrating with a moderate and secular Islamic country. Meanwhile, Turkey has had to examine its identity. Modern Turkey was founded on Mustafa Kemal Ataturk's militant secularism, but the country is an overwhelmingly Islamic nation with Islamic political parties. To some Turks, EU membership is too Western. Just before the EU vote on Turkish negotiations, the Ankara governor's office ordered a ban on a gay rights association. The intent, apparently, was to *help* the anti-Turkish-accession forces within the EU because the ban would be a violation of the European Convention on Human Rights and presumably make Turkish entry more difficult for the EU to accept. The ban was reversed 10 days after the EU vote, which gave approval for Turkey's accession negotiations.[33] The EU vote to allow Turkey to officially begin accession negotiations was close even at the last moment. There were Austrian objections to Turkish entry just before the vote. Turkey prevailed in the vote and was officially approved to begin accession negotiations, but the mood in Turkey had been soured by the ordeal.

Turkey's *potential* inclusion in the EU influenced the ratification votes in some countries of the EU Charter, the rejected forerunner to the Lisbon Treaty. In France, for instance, where the EU Charter was rejected, some 450,000 French-Armenians urged a no vote to pressure Turkey to publicly accept responsibility for the Turkish massacre of Armenians in 1915–1917. Tension over whether to call this episode genocide, as the Armenian government and the Armenian diaspora have called for, or to call it a massacre, as EU governments describe it, or to call it a civil war, as the Turkish government insists, was heightened with the 90th anniversary of the start of the mass killings. It is possible that if Turkey apologizes for the mass killings—and does so with gravity and tact—it would be a step toward exorcising this ghost of its history. At the same time, the EU's self-image and its image, especially in the Islamic world, will certainly be influenced by its handling of Turkey's potential EU entry, despite that image being shaped so strongly and, to the majority populations of EU states, so confusingly, by the furor surrounding the Danish cartoons.

The Eurozone

On January 1, 2002, the 12 EU nations that had then adopted the euro took another step toward deeper integration with elimination of their national currencies. The euro was now legal tender, and the eurozone's national currencies were officially gone. The euro had been born on January 1, 1999, but would have to settle for baby steps for three years: electronic transactions.

On January 1, 2002, the euro was finished with its baby steps and had grown up sufficiently to be on its own. It had been a long gestation. In 1979 the EU created the Exchange Rate Mechanism (ERM), which created convergence of EU currencies in a band.[34] The ERM members' currencies would be allowed to fluctuate within a band—described as the snake in the grass, slithering between the floor and ceiling of the band. This would produce convergence yet also allow flexibility. The next trimester in the euro's gestation began with the signing of the Maastricht treaty in 1991, in which EU members pledged to the European Monetary Union (EMU), which was to include a single currency. The EMU was challenged shortly thereafter with morning sickness. In 1992 speculators bet European currencies would lose value and be forced out of the band. They bet correctly. After spending millions of dollars of their hard currency reserves, EMU member governments were forced to widen or abandon the bands. Like morning sickness, this was miserable, but it passed without long-term damage to the baby. Ratification of the Maastricht treaty helped the recovery. So too did good nutrition in the form of fiscal discipline, the so-called Maastricht criteria that limit government budget deficits and debt requirements. Thus, the euro was successfully born on time.

Not all member states were able to take part, nor did all want to. Three of the 15 pre-2004 EU members continue to remain outside the eurozone: Denmark, Great Britain, and Sweden. Greece initially remained outside of the eurozone because it did not qualify for the eurozone's budget deficit and debt requirements, but it was able to later join the eurozone. See table 5.3 for a list of eurozone members and year of euro adoption. Why is there some hesitation and difficulty in joining the eurozone?

There are costs to joining any monetary union and some additional costs specific to joining the eurozone. The primary cost to joining any monetary union is lost autonomy to set monetary policy as needed for national economic conditions. Monetary policy will be set for the eurozone as a whole, and if a given economy is out of sync with eurozone monetary policy needs, it will not get the monetary policy it needs. For instance, if most of the eurozone is growing slowly, stepping on the monetary gas will be the likely policy, but this could be harmful to faster-growing countries in the eurozone that might need monetary brakes. And there are costs specific to the euro: eurozone members have pledged to meet government budget deficit and debt requirements. This requirement is designed to ensure that member governments' fiscal policies do not undermine the strength of the currency. More specifically, the requirements helped inflation-averse Germany risk its hard-earned monetary credibility by mixing its deutschmark with the currencies of more profligate governments, such as the Italian lira. These requirements entailed cuts in government budgets, which led to protest in some countries, but nothing sufficiently widespread to pose a serious challenge to the larger eurozone economies from launching the euro.

Table 5.3.   Eurozone Membership and Year of Adoption

Austria	1999
Belgium	1999
Cyprus	2008
Finland	1999
France	1999
Germany	1999
Greece	2001
Ireland	1999
Italy	1999
Luxembourg	1999
Malta	2008
Netherlands	1999
Portugal	1999
Slovakia	2009
Slovenia	2007
Spain	1999

Source: European Central Bank, http://www.ecb.eu/ecb/orga/escb/html/index.en.html (April 14, 2008) and updated by the author.
Note: The 1999 euro was in electronic form only; the change to the physical euro took place in 2002. Greece's 2001 adoption was electronic only; its cash adoption was in 2002. In subsequent adoptions electronic and cash adoption was simultaneous.

But there also is much to be gained from adopting the euro. For many of the eurozone countries, the euro held out the promise having a more stable currency. There are other benefits as well: a common currency would facilitate business transactions of all sorts in the eurozone and make financial services integration easier. The euro also held out the possibility of one day challenging the dollar as the world's most important currency. In the meantime, it was hoped the euro would create a larger bond market in Europe and facilitate growth of financial services. These gains, however, seemed to be secondary to the political reason for a common currency: it propelled the EU toward deeper economic and political integration. A single currency is a strong symbolic commitment to integration as well as a concrete way to increase actual interdependence. A single currency also requires greater shared policymaking—in the form of the European Central Bank (ECB)—than ever before. Thus for those in the eurozone, the euro has served as a powerful cement for deeper integration. There are lingering questions about the euro and eurozone that will have to be addressed in the future. Does the euro's cementing of deeper integration create a barrier between those EU members in and out of the eurozone? Could the management of the eurozone be better, and, specifically, should the ECB be given more latitude to promote economic growth?

Potential Eurozone Adopters. Two EU members have opt-outs from joining the eurozone: Denmark and Great Britain. All other EU members are expected to join. The newer EU countries would certainly like to join the eurozone, especially after experiencing the pain of the 2008–2009 financial crisis. Unfortunately for them, the crisis made eurozone membership more desirable, but also more difficult to obtain. As potential eurozone adopters come under financial pressure, investors may be less willing to hold their currency. Thus the value of their currencies comes under pressure, making it more difficult to maintain the value of their currencies within the plus or minus 15 percent band required by the Exchange Rate Mechanism-II. Besides the added difficulty staying within the ERM-II currency fluctuation range, other convergence criteria—limits on the size of yearly government deficits (3 percent of GDP), accumulated debt (60 percent of GDP), inflation convergence (at least one year with an average inflation rate within 1.5 percent of that of the three eurozone members with the lowest inflation), interest rate convergence (within 2 percent above that of the lowest three eurozone members), and two years of staying in the ERM-II—became more difficult to achieve.[35] The EU's non-euro members' status in moving toward euro adoption varies greatly and is outlined in table 5.4. Those in the ERM-II, currently only the Baltic states Estonia, Latvia, and Lithuania, are the most ready to join. Among these three, Estonia is likely to be the next to join.[36]

The urgency to have their economic houses in order is somewhat greater for eurozone hopefuls than the eurozone's original members because new adoptees will change from their old currencies to the euro in a "big bang"

Table 5.4.   Non-Eurozone EU Members' Euro Adoption Status

Country	Exchange Rate Mechanism-II (ERM-II) Status	Target Date for Euro Adoption
Bulgaria	Not in ERM-II	No target date
Czech Republic	Not in ERM-II	No target date
Denmark	Eurozone opt out	Not applicable
Estonia	ERM-II since 2004	No target date
Latvia	ERM-II since 2005	No target date
Lithuania	ERM-II since 2004	No target date
Hungary	Not in ERM-II	No target date
Poland	Not in ERM-II	No target date
Romania	Not in ERM-II	2014
Sweden	Not in ERM-II	No target date
United Kingdom	Eurozone opt out	Not applicable

Source: ECB website, updated May 4, 2009 (accessed March 18, 2010), http://ec.europa.eu/economy_finance/ euro/countries/index_en.htm.

fashion; as soon as they join the eurozone, euro paper notes and coins will be legal tender, compared with a three-year transition for the initial eurozone members. Moreover, they will also have a shorter time period—two weeks— in which there will be dual circulation (when the old currencies and the euro are both legal tender).[37]

The EU's Common Agricultural Policy (CAP)

Among the most expensive of the EU's policies, and certainly its most controversial economic policy for the rest of the world, has been the Common Agricultural Policy (CAP). First established in 1964, initially the CAP paid above-market prices for farmers' crops, and the EU would subsidize the export of this excess production. Not only did this lead to excess production, it lowered global agricultural prices and, as the CAP grew to enormous proportions, became the largest budget item in the EU, accounting for more than two-thirds of the EU budget. Agricultural producers elsewhere were not happy to compete with twice-subsidized agriculture from Europe. Some in the EU were not happy with the CAP because it ate up so much of the budget and because it alienated key EU trading partners. Countries such as Germany and the United Kingdom that are more reliant on industrial rather than agricultural exports began to see CAP as a threat to open markets abroad for their industrial exports. The world held up the CAP as an example of rich country unfairness in trade and tied CAP reform to advancement in trade negotiations.

The CAP was partially reformed in 2003 when the payment mechanism to farmers was altered so as to be less market distorting. Rather than pay above-market prices for production and subsidize exports—which encourage overproduction and depress worldwide agricultural prices—the CAP began to subsidize farmers' income. This eliminated the incentive to overproduce in order to maximize the government subsidies under the old CAP.[38] The CAP still encourages excess agricultural production and still is expensive, eating up some 40 percent of the EU's budget.[39]

Schengen Area

Twenty-two EU countries and two non-EU countries—Iceland and Norway—share European responsibilities for border security and have abolished internal border controls through the Schengen Area.[40] Once in a Schengen Area country, one is able to travel freely without further border checks. Five EU countries are not convinced that this is a good idea— Bulgaria, Cyprus, Ireland, Romania, and the United Kingdom—or need further border governance reforms before they are able to implement the EU's Schengen Area border regulations. In 1985, five EU countries agreed to create the Schengen Area, and it was implemented by seven EU countries in 1995. It has steadily expanded to its current membership of 24.

Since the Schengen Area extends EU border policies to member countries, it means Schengen Area members share a common border database and follow common procedures for visas, customs, and many other facets of border governance.[41] Meeting EU standards for border control is a difficult feat for new EU members, and thus the EU established the Schengen Facility to help the EU's 2004 entrants—poorer than pre-2004 EU members—to meet Schengen Area requirements.[42]

Not all of the Schengen Area's neighbors are happy about the Schengen Area; in some cases, travelers from countries outside the Schengen Area may find entry into the Schengen Area more onerous and costly.[43]

6

Russia and the Former Soviet Republics

Most of the RTAs in the former Soviet Union are defined by the members' relationship with the most powerful nation-state in the region: Russia. RTAs with countries more willing to have close ties with Russia (or without an alternative) such as the Eurasian Economic Community (EEC) can be contrasted with those in which some members are trying to distance themselves from Russia (such as GUUAM—the Georgia, Ukraine, Uzbekistan, Azerbaijan, and Moldova Organization). For those countries wanting to distance themselves from Russia, trade ties are more apt to be cultivated with the EU or China, but as of yet, these are less-likely options for RTA formation. The primary RTA in the former Soviet Union was intended to be the successor to the Soviet Union itself, the Commonwealth of Independent States (CIS). But with many former Soviet republics wishing distance from Russia, the CIS would never function as intended, and a number of overlapping and sometimes competing RTAs emerged, such as the Central Asian Cooperation Organization (CACO), the GUUAM, EEC, and others. See the discussion on the CIS below, the section "The Road to CIS Spaghetti," and figure 6.1 for more. There is also one grouping in the region of growing importance that has emerged outside of the CIS itself, the Shanghai Cooperation Organization (SCO). Initially focusing mostly on security issues, the SCO includes former Soviet Central Asian countries with both Russia and China. It increasingly has taken up economic issues, but as of yet, it is not an RTA.

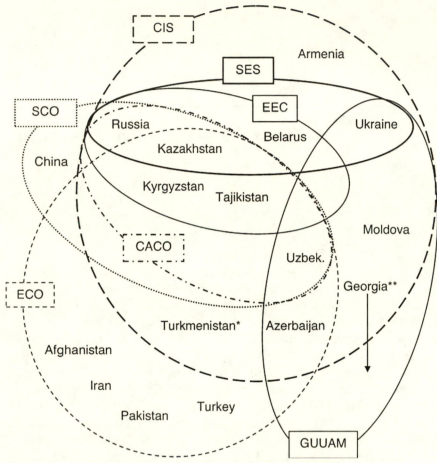

Figure 6.1.   Central Asian/Ex-Soviet Union Spaghetti Venn Diagram
Key: See list of abbreviations.
* Turkmenistan is only an observer in the CIS but does follow the CIS FTA.
** Georgia has been a CIS member but withdrew in August 2009.

CONTEXT OF RTAs IN THE FORMER SOVIET UNION REGION: IPE OF INCOMPLETE AND VARIED TRANSITIONS

The 15 former republics of the Soviet Union (USSR) have seen incredible change in the past two decades. In 1991 they became independent upon the breakup of the USSR and faced economic and political changes without precedent: moving from a socialist, or command, economy to capitalism while simultaneously moving from communist dictatorship toward democracy. Some moved rapidly toward the twin goals of capitalism and democracy, while others barely moved at all. A commonality, however, was that this was socially wrenching for all of the former republics. The USSR's history included 70 years of repressive governance and large-scale industrialization. The industrialization was massively inefficient, and the gap between the USSR and its socialist spheres of influence in Central Europe on the one hand and prosperous capitalist countries of Western Europe on the other hand grew more obvious. The USSR's leader, Mikhail Gorbachev, initiated reforms intended to modernize the sluggish superpower, but he ultimately unleashed forces that would pull the Soviet Union apart. Russia, the dominant republic in the Soviet Union, went into economic free fall as it transitioned to capitalism amid the political conflict of moving toward, but not quite achieving, democracy. By the late 1990s, Russia's economy and political system had both substantially stabilized, and Russia emerged as a regional power.

Russia

Russia's transitions of its economic and political systems were difficult and incomplete. The incomplete transition to democracy included violence between the conservative forces of the Communist Party and the new ruling elite that included some reformers under Russian president Boris Yeltsin. Yeltsin consolidated power by waging political battle with the conservatives, which in 1993 led to some real shooting. After clashing with the conservative-controlled parliament, President Yeltsin suspended parliament and called for new elections. The conservatives refused to leave parliament, and after a standoff, Yeltsin ordered the army to attack. A new constitution and election created a democracy with a strong presidency—too strong to qualify as a democracy, according to many.

Battles, both political and real, took place outside of Moscow's power struggles. Chechnya, an Islamic republic in the Caucasus region of southern Russia, sought independence from Russia. In 1994 Yeltsin moved to quell the separatist movement, and Russia became mired in the Chechen wars. The first was widely unpopular in Russia and ended in stalemate. The second, fueled by Chechen terrorist attacks elsewhere in Russia, was popular in Russia, and Russia's scorched-earth tactics flattened Chechnya's cities and drove separatists into the mountains and other regions. Russia's military presence is now strong there, but reconciliation has been absent, and Chechen-Russian relations remain a potential flashpoint.

Yeltsin's economic reforms fared little better. Russia's economy contracted dramatically in the first years of the transition, and Russia faced high inflation. Yeltsin's primary economic achievement was halting this contraction and inflation. His primary economic failure was the corrupt privatization of the Russian economy. Capitalism became equated with corruption and gangsterism in the minds of average Russians, whose pensions shrank. In the late 1990s, Russia faced insolvency as it could no longer pay its debts, and there was a currency crisis. Russia finally stabilized with greater tax enforcement—tax evasion had become endemic—and, more importantly, greater energy exports. President Yeltsin handed over power abruptly to President Vladimir Putin, who presided over massive energy exports that helped Russia's finances. Russia's economy remains problematic, notwithstanding the energy boom, and life remains difficult for average Russians.

The other former republics of the USSR also faced trauma in their transitions, some emerging with far more economic and political reform than others. The Baltics—Estonia, Latvia, and Lithuania—moved quickly to consolidate their independence and were quick to make it clear they would be orienting to the West, not the East in political and economic matters. They made joining the EU one of their top priorities and in May 2004 were among the 10 new EU entrants. For Armenia, Azerbaijan, Belarus, Georgia, Moldova, Ukraine, and the five "Stans," the "rewards" of the transitions have been few.

Armenia and Azerbaijan

Armenia and Azerbaijan began fighting over the Nagorno-Karabakh region in the late 1980s, before the Soviet Union broke up. Approximately 20,000 to 30,000 were killed in the fighting, which still occasionally flares despite a 1994 ceasefire, which might better be called a stalemate. The region is inside what is nominally Azerbaijan, but Armenia won the fighting and controls the region with a buffer zone that connects it to Armenia proper. Refugees do not yet dare to go home until the stalemate ends. Armenia has paid heavily in economic terms for the fighting: the landlocked country's borders with Azerbaijan and Turkey are closed. Many Armenians—probably 25 percent of the population—have left the country.[1] Armenia and Turkey have discussed reestablishing diplomatic ties, and Turkey has considered opening its border with Armenia—closed since 1993 to punish Armenia for fighting in the Nagorno-Karabakh—but better relations will require that the two come to some agreement about the darkest chapter in their shared history: the mass killings of Armenians by the Ottoman Turkish Empire in 1915–1917. Armenia calls the systematic killing of 1.5 million Armenians "genocide" while Turkey argues there were fewer killed—300,000—and that the killings were not systematic, but the result of fighting between Armenians and Turks that killed as many Turks as Armenians.[2]

Azerbaijan has a long history of oil production, which sparked renewed interest from foreign investors after the breakup of the Soviet Union, despite the fighting with Armenia. Oil also attracts the governments of other countries to become more interested, and Russia, the US, and others seek to ensure they have a hand in Azeri oil exports. In May 2005, oil finally began to flow from Azerbaijan through a Georgian pipeline to a Turkish port. Azerbaijan is not a democracy, and the most recent change in power was when the president Ilham Aliyev, then prime minister, took over after his father's death. His father, President Heydar Aliyev, had governed Azerbaijan from 1993 until his 2003 death and had a poor human rights record. This has continued under President Ilham Aliyev.[3]

Belarus

Belarus is considered to be among the least reformed of the former Soviet republics in both economics and politics. Belarusian president Alexander Lukashenko has ruled ruthlessly and shows little interest in either capitalism or democracy. The state still controls some 80 percent of the economy, which has continued to stagnate. President Lukashenko's political repression—which includes missing opposition leaders and a stifled press—has led both the US and EU to impose travel restrictions on Belarusian leaders. Belarus cracked down anew after democracy movements in other former Soviet republics, such as Ukraine's Orange Revolution. His desire for political union with Russia usually gets warm words but little else from Russia.[4]

Georgia

Georgia has faced a number of separatist movements—in Abkhazia and South Ossetia—that Russia has sometimes used as leverage over the Georgian government. The longtime government of former Soviet foreign minister Eduard Shevardnadze was not able to effectively quell the insurgencies, nor was it able to reverse Georgia's economic and lawless slide. A democracy movement ousted Shevardnadze in 2003, and in January 2004 a reformer, Mikhail Saakashvili, became president. He has enjoyed greater legitimacy than Shevardnadze but still faces widespread corruption, poverty, and the tensions over the separatist movements flared into war with Russia in the summer of 2008. Russia has now recognized the separatist regions as sovereign countries.[5]

Moldova

Moldova and has faced an armed separatist movement in its Trans-Dniester region, which declared independence in 1990 shortly before the Soviet Union dissolved. The region feared Moldova's linguistic, cultural, and historical ties with Romania might lead to reunification. Fighting killed over 700 people, and a 1992 ceasefire, enforced by Russian peacekeeping troops, holds, but negotiations have stalled. The Trans-Dniester region is more industrialized than the rest of Moldova and is currently considered lawless.[6] Moldova is connected to Southeastern Europe through the Central European Free Trade Agreement (CEFTA).

Ukraine

When the Soviet Union dissolved in 1991, there were significant tensions between Ukraine and Russia over military bases on the Black Sea. Ukraine's transition has been rocky. Economically, Ukraine has struggled and has faced high levels of crime and corruption, much like Russia itself. Its political system had reformed on paper, but in reality President Leonid Kuchma and the state security apparatus ensured that little changed. Kuchma, first elected in 1994, ruled during a period of continued economic hardship and political corruption. Inspired by the Georgian democracy movement, opposition to Kuchma's rule grew into the Orange Revolution of 2004. The reform candidate—Viktor Yushchenko—narrowly lost to the old-guard candidate backed by Kuchma in November 2004 elections that were widely considered flawed. After 10 days of protest in Kiev calling for a new election, the military and security apparatus remarkably did not crack down; the Orange Revolution had its way, and new elections were called. The reformer, Viktor Yushchenko, won and became president in January 2005.[7]

President Yushchenko called for EU membership and closer ties to the West, although he used diplomatic language to avoid alienating Russia. Russia—which backed the old-guard candidate—clearly felt it had been given a bloody nose by the West—which had backed the reformers and called for new elections. In any case, Ukrainian efforts to avoid alienating Russia did not work: Russia and Ukraine bickered over natural gas prices in December 2005, and in January 2006 Russia unilaterally hiked its natural gas export prices fourfold—to market levels—for exports to Ukraine, in violation of previous contracts. In retaliation, Ukraine hiked the transit fees for Russian natural gas passing through pipelines in Ukraine on its way to other export markets. These fees were also put at market levels and, as with the unilateral gas price increase, were in violation of previous contracts. Russia backed down when customers in the EU shouted their displeasure at having their gas supplies threatened or diminished. Many observers viewed the Russian price hike as punishing Ukraine for its greater independence under Yushchenko; this is a message Russia hoped would also be noticed in other former Soviet republics. The battle continued in the winter of 2008–2009 and again resulted in reduced gas supplies to much of the EU. Many customers lost gas supplies during a deep cold snap. The cold snap subsided, Russia and Ukraine reached an agreement to begin gas supplies again, but the cold snap in their relations continues.

Central Asian Former Soviet Republics: The "Stans"

The five Central Asian ex-Soviet republics—Kazakhstan, Kyrgyzstan, Tajikistan, Turkmenistan, and Uzbekistan—have struggled since independence. They remain economically and militarily dependent upon Russia to varying degrees and are therefore concerned with Russian influence in the region. Russia is their most important economic partner, and Russian troops can provide stability in the face of militant Islamic movements, although some argue that concerns over the latter are typically used as a pretext for human rights abuses.

The Central Asian former Soviet republics are landlocked, which brings isolation made worse by mountains and deserts. *Stan* means "land of"; the rest of each country's name is formed by the dominant language and ethnic group in the country: Kazakh, Kyrgyz, Tajik, Turkmen, and Uzbek. The Stans' populations are a mix of these and other Central Asian ethnicities with Slavic ethnicities such as Russians and Ukrainians that came to settle and develop the region during communist rule. The states in the region vary by the degree to which they are homogeneous and "settled" (well-established agriculture with densely settled cities) as compared to heterogeneous and less settled (nomadic and less densely settled cities). Uzbekistan is the most homogeneous (or is at least among the least Slavic) and settled, while Kazakhstan is the least homogeneous and settled. Kazakhstan "is a Soviet creation," with approximately as many Slavs as Kazakhs and with the Kazakhs having a nomadic and thus less-settled heritage.[8] Islam is the region's religious heritage, but because of Soviet atheism, many in the region are Islamic more by heritage than identity. The degree and nature of Islamic influence is, of course, open to change, as the leaders in the area are aware.

International Political Economy of the Stans

The Central Asian former republics of the USSR find themselves in somewhat different economic and political situations, depending upon the structure of their economy and natural resource distribution, international strategic factors, and domestic social and political factors. One difference among them is the degree to which they have economically reformed. Kyrgyzstan and Kazakhstan have implemented the most economically liberal reforms in the region, with Uzbekistan and Turkmenistan less reformed (and Tajikistan simply recovering from civil war). A central divide among the region's states is the degree to which they have significant energy resources and infrastructure to exploit these resources. Turkmenistan and Kazakhstan have ample energy resources, with Tajikistan and Kyrgyzstan having the least and Uzbekistan falling in the middle. But even those with energy resources to use and export have high levels of poverty.[9] Cotton production is an essential component of many of the region's economies, but this has also played a significant role in depleting the Aral Sea, which has shrunk dramatically. Nuclear contamination remains a concern in many of the region's countries.[10]

After 9/11, the US viewed the Stans differently: suddenly, they had the potential to become either terrorist collaborators, bystanders, or allies in the coming war in Afghanistan—primarily as potential launchpads. The US was able to have bases in two of the republics—Kyrgyzstan and Uzbekistan—which it used to prosecute the war in Afghanistan. Uzbekistan had allowed the US bases in part to help with the destruction of an Afghanistan-based Islamic movement that sought to overthrow the government of Uzbek president Islam Karimov, the Islamic Movement of Uzbekistan (IMU). Besides fighting the IMU, Karimov was interested in balancing Russian influence with that of the US.[11]

The US remained largely quiet about the human rights situation in Uzbekistan until a government massacre in Andijon, Uzbekistan, in May 2005. Uzbek president Islam Karimov has been accused of ordering the use of force to clear the streets of Andijon of peaceful protesters, which resulted in 700–1,000 deaths. He has since refused to allow an outside investigation into the killings, resulting in widespread international criticism. This has included criticism from the US and the EU. Russia and China did not criticize the crackdown. Uzbekistan has begun to use closer ties to Russia and the Shanghai Cooperation Organization (SCO) to distance itself from the newly critical US and EU. In July 2005, the SCO issued a statement calling for the withdrawal of US troops from Central Asia, and the Uzbek government directly told the US that the base would no longer be available to it. The EU has placed travel restrictions on 12 Uzbek officials. Kyrgyzstan, which is also a member of the SCO, told the US in October 2005 that its Kyrgyzstan bases will remain open.[12] Kyrgyzstan's relations with the US became warmer in 2005 when the Tulip Revolution protests drove out dictatorial president Askar Akayev, who had ruled since 1991, clearing the way for former prime minister Kurmanbek Bakiev to win presidential elections, possibly moving Kyrgyzstan in the direction of democracy.[13]

Kazakhstan. Kazakhstan is geographically the largest of the Central Asian ex-Soviet republics. It has been led by President Nursultan Nazarbayev since 1989, two years before independence.[14] It has fared better economically than its neighbors because of significant oil and natural gas reserves, which have attracted significant foreign investment. Kazakhstan also has significant natural resources for mining.[15]

Kyrgyzstan. Kyrgyzstan does not have the natural resource wealth—such as oil and gas—found in many of its neighboring countries.[16] It is also small and thus has decided to open more to the rest of the world in order to develop. It has adopted more economically liberal reforms than most or all of the others in the region and has been a WTO member since 1998.[17]

As noted above, protests led to the ouster of a longtime dictator and the election of Kurmanbek Bakiev as president. Kyrgyzstan was considered to be less repressive than its neighbors before the Tulip Revolution, but the leadership change was nevertheless an enormous opening for democracy. Unfortunately, the democratic gains there have eroded again as President Bakiev has been consolidating his power.[18] The US Manas Air Base was in Kyrgyzstan, but so too was a Russian base only 30 kilometers away.[19] This clearly made Russia nervous. The Kyrgyzstani president ended the US base there after receiving over $2.1 billion in Russian aid.[20]

Tajikistan. Tajikistan went through a civil war from 1992 to 1997 and has had Russian troops stationed there to promote stability.[21] As part of the settlement, President Emomali Rahmonov includes the Islamic opposition in his government, which has given Tajikistan a reputation for open government, at least compared with many of its peers. President Rahmonov—who has ruled since he won a 1994 election that was not considered free, fair, and open—won a referendum in 2003 giving him the authority to run for two more seven-year terms.[22] Tajikistan does not have the energy reserves found in many of its neighbors and faces severe poverty, including a famine in 2001.[23] Tajikistan is the poorest of the ex-Soviet republics.

Turkmenistan. Turkmenistan has large natural gas reserves but has been unable to successfully bring much of them to export due, in part, to the need for greater pipeline capacity.[24] Turkmenistan is more ethnically homogeneous than the other Central Asian former Soviet republics.[25] Governance in Turkmenistan has been both repressive and strange. President Saparmyrat Niyazov led Turkmenistan beginning in 1985, first as head of the Turkmen Communist Party and then as president since its independence in 1991, until his death in 2006.[26] His rule included a personality cult, including the naming of months after family members, much of which has been reversed under the rule of his predecessor, President Kurbanguly Berdymukhamedov.

Uzbekistan. Uzbekistan is the most populous and homogeneous of the Central Asian former Soviet republics. Its human rights record has been bad and has gotten worse with the massacre of peaceful protesters in Andijan in May 2005.[27] Uzbekistan has less-extensive oil and gas reserves than many of its neighbors and has not attracted energy investment like Kazakhstan has. It has therefore been slower to increase production.[28] It tends to be suspicious of integration with outsiders because it fears inexpensive imports.[29] It, like Turkmenistan, needs greater pipeline capacity for gas exports.

RTAs IN THE FORMER SOVIET UNION

The Russia Belarus Union

Belarus and Russia have the closest integration of any of the CIS states. Small Belarus was Russia's second-largest trading partner in 2003 (after Germany). The two countries have been integrating their economic and political systems since the end of the Soviet Union in 1991. In 1993 they agreed to economic union, a free trade agreement was signed in 1995, and the customs checks between the two countries were removed. In 1999 they signed the Treaty on the Formation of a Union State, which is supposed to establish a joint monetary system, but Russia will not allow the Belarusian Central Bank to have the authority to print rubles, thus the anticipated January 1, 2005, beginning to the monetary union passed without monetary union. When Russian president Vladimir Putin came to power in late 1999, the relationship began to stress security matters more than it had under President Boris Yeltsin's, and the two countries have merged a number of weapons companies. Belarus wants to form a common army for the two, but Russia has resisted this because of cost. Belarus has stated that it will accept Russian missiles on its soil, depending upon the status of a potential US antimissile system in the EU. Energy has cemented the relationship in the past—Belarus purchased Russian energy at prices well below market levels—but Russia since doubled the prices for Belarus.[30] Loyalty only got Belarus so much.

Central Asian Cooperation Organization (CACO), Formerly the Central Asian Economic Union (CAEC)

The forerunner to the Central Asian Cooperation Organization (CACO) was the Central Asian Economic Union (CAEC), created in 1994 by Kazakhstan, Kyrgyzstan, and Uzbekistan. Tajikistan joined in 1998, and the CAEC became the CACO in 2002. In 2004 Russia joined and Afghanistan became an observer (see table 6.1).[31] The CAEC's goals were economic—to create a single economic space, otherwise known as a single, or common, market—

Table 6.1. CACO Membership

CACO Members	
Kazakhstan	1994
Kyrgyzstan	1994
Russia	2004
Tajikistan	1998
Uzbekistan	1994

CACO Observers
Afghanistan
Georgia
Turkey
Ukraine

but with the change in 2002 to the CACO, the group's goals became some-what wider, including cooperation in non-economic spheres. With Russia's 2004 entry, security and stability have become the primary focus. The CAEC did implement some tax harmonization, but most proposals were proposals and nothing more; implementation was rare. The CACO members have called for a single market and, in 15 years, the establishment of an FTA.[32] In October 2006, the CACO agreed to merge with the Eurasian Economic Community (EEC). All of the CACO members except Uzbekistan are also EEC members, and all EEC members except Belarus are also CACO members.[33] Notably absent from this Central Asian institution is Afghanistan, which is also a Central Asian state.[34] Without stability in Afghanistan, other Central Asian states will face additional challenges in the form of refugees, separatist training grounds, drug trafficking, and other maladies that flow from dysfunctional states.

Commonwealth of the Independent States (CIS) and the CIS Free Trade Agreement

The Commonwealth of Independent States (CIS) was created in 1991 by most of the former republics of the Soviet Union (USSR) following the USSR's 1991 breakup. All former republics except the three Baltic states—Estonia, Latvia, and Lithuania—joined, giving the CIS its typical post-Soviet Union membership: 12 of the 15 ex-republics of the Soviet Union. Membership has gotten more complex. Turkmenistan has downgraded its membership to associate member, arguing full membership stood against its policy of neutrality. In the aftermath of the war between Georgia and Russia in the summer of 2008, Georgia announced it would pull out of the CIS, effective August 2009. Thus membership stood as 11 full members and one associate member until August 2009, after which there were 10 full members and one associate member. See box 6.1.

BOX 6.1. CIS MEMBERSHIP

Armenia	Moldova
Azerbaijan	Russia
Belarus	Tajikistan
Georgia	Turkmenistan*
(member until August 2009)	(associate CIS member)
Kazakhstan	Ukraine
Kyrgyzstan	Uzbekistan

*Turkmenistan does abide by the CIS FTA rules despite not being a CIS FTA member.

Initial goals for the CIS were always more than just economic; the CIS is viewed by many as a vehicle for Russia to dominate the former Soviet republics. The CIS's economic goals were to establish an FTA, a customs union, a common market for goods, and a monetary union. The more ambitious economic steps were not to be. In fact, one scholar has called the CIS "functionally dead."[35] What prevented the CIS's grander plans? In short, fear of Russian domination has the primary brake on CIS integration. Similarly, others—such as Ukraine—are hesitant because they would prefer warmer relations with the EU and even EU membership. In any case, instead of CIS-wide economic integration, to which the CIS still aspires, the CIS members dove into the spaghetti bowl of RTAs and created an overlapping patchwork of regional integration groupings. The three listed by the United Nations Economic Commission for Europe as the most relevant and significant to the CIS's initial economic integration desires are the Russian-Belarus Union, the Single Economic Space (SES), and the Eurasian Economic Community (EEC). To this should be added the Central Asian Cooperation Organization (CACO), which is planning to merge with the EEC. The CIS secretariat is in Minsk, Belarus.[36] The CIS also established a CIS FTA, intended as an intermediary step until deeper levels of integration can be met.

The Road to CIS Spaghetti

In 1993 nine CIS members agreed to create an economic union, joined later by Georgia and Turkmenistan, leaving Ukraine as the only CIS member not fully in the CIS economic union, although it was an associate member.[37] The economic union existed on paper, not in reality, and thus led some in the CIS to integrate on their own in a customs union.[38] In 2000, the Eurasian Economic Community (EEC) was formed out of previous agreements between Russia, Belarus, Kazakhstan, and Kyrgyzstan, with Tajikistan joining in the customs union.[39] It has had difficulty implementing what it has agreed upon, and there is plenty it doesn't agree upon. In 2003, Belarus, Kazakhstan, Russia, and Ukraine agreed to form a Single Economic Space (SES), a variable-speed RTA whose members have quite different visions about the depth of integration. One of these issues stems from fears of Russian dominance of the region's RTAs. Thus Georgia, Ukraine, Azerbaijan, and Moldova created an informal bloc, later joined by Uzbekistan, called the GUUAM Organization (Georgia, Ukraine, Uzbekistan, Azerbaijan, and Moldova Organization), which conspicuously excluded Russia and would thus serve as a counterweight to the CIS.[40]

In October 2005, the Central Asia Cooperation Organization (CACO) and the Eurasian Economic Community (EEC) agreed to merge. This will help eliminate duplicated duties and paperwork. The CACO, which includes Kazakhstan, Kyrgyzstan, Russia, Tajikistan, and Uzbekistan, will merge with the EEC, whose members include Belarus, Kazakhstan, Kyrgyzstan, Russia, and Tajikistan. Belarus is the only EEC member that is not already a CACO member. Uzbekistan is the only CACO member that is not in the EEC. A merger with the SES in the future is a possibility.[41]

The primary issue within the CIS has been each republic's relationship with Russia, the most economically, militarily, and culturally dominant of the ex-Soviet republics. The level of autonomy each of the republics has had relative to Russia varies significantly. Russia has certainly been hesitant to grant autonomy to its former junior-partner Soviet republics. Russia regards the ex-Soviet republics as the "near abroad" and as inherently within the Russian sphere of influence, as the above reference to Russian support for Georgian insurgents suggests.

Turkmenistan, with large natural gas deposits, and Azerbaijan, with large oil reserves, have somewhat greater economic autonomy relative to Russia than most of the former Soviet republics.[42]

There are territorial disputes among some of the CIS members. Two of the largest CIS members, Ukraine and Russia, both coveted access to the Black Sea and Soviet naval facilities there. The issue has been resolved, but Ukraine remains wary of Russia. Russia has become suspicious of Ukraine after the Orange Revolution, in which the old-guard, Russian-backed candidate ultimately lost the election to the reformist Viktor Yushchenko. Armenia and Azerbaijan fought a war over the disputed Nagorno-Karabakh region that is geographically within Azerbaijan. (Most of the fighting has ended, but the matter is not yet settled. Armenia won the fighting and maintains control of the Nagorno-Karabakh and a corridor to connect it with Armenia proper.) Numerous insurgencies have taken root in the ex-Soviet republics. Among the most intractable is within Russia itself. Chechnya, a predominantly Islamic republic in Russia's Caucasus region, has been left destroyed from years of fighting between separatists and the Russian government. Refugees, violence, and instability from Chechnya have migrated to other Russian republics in the Caucasus while Chechnya faces a stalemate, despite Russian government pronouncements of progress.

Russia and four other CIS members—Armenia, Georgia, Tajikistan, and Uzbekistan—formed a joint defense system, which is to say, the latter four accepted Russian defense. Georgia wanted to diminish Russia's influence in Georgia. It sought an end to Russian support for two breakaway regions that sought autonomy from Georgia. Russia had long supported Abkhazia and South Ossetia with money, arms, and political support, but tensions between Russia and Georgia escalated. Russia was wary of Georgia because Georgia is where the reformist pro-Western democracy "color" revolutions of the early 2000s began. A Western-educated Georgian candidate, Mikhail Saakashvili, beat the more pro-Russian candidate and promoted reform. Although Saakashvili was initially quick to avoid alienating Russian president Vladimir Putin, relations deteriorated. As they did so, Saakashvili became more vocally anti-Russian and pro-Western while Russia solidified its support for the breakaway regions. The example of an anti-Russian pro-Western reform movement had already spread, and Russia clearly did not want this to be rewarded. In the summer of 2008, this escalated into war, as Georgia tried to take back South Ossetia from separatists. Russian troops moved into portions of Georgia beyond South Ossetia and Abkhazia. South Ossetia and Abkhazia declared their independence from Georgia and were recognized by one country: Russia. In October 2008, Russian troops pulled out of the "buffer zones" in Georgia outside the breakaway regions, but Russian troops remain stationed in South Ossetia and Abkhazia as both sides argued over who started the war.

Belarus—arguably one of the most badly governed countries in Europe—has often sought to be closer to Russia and looks back on the USSR with greater fondness than do the other ex-Soviet republics. In 1996 the two signed a treaty to coordinate defense policymaking, eliminate trade barriers, and unite their currencies, but actual progress has been slow.[43] Belarus has been rethinking its closeness with Russia now that it too pays higher prices for Russian natural gas, but it has thus far remained loyal.

The CIS has its Economic Court of the CIS for dispute resolution among its members, but it is not considered effective. In fact, as of October 2006, exactly zero cases had been brought before it, despite there being plenty of economic disputes between CIS members, including a trade war between Ukraine and Russia and numerous trade spats between Georgia and Russia. More economically significant were the disputes between Ukraine and Russia over natural gas prices that led to the pipeline's temporary closure, much to the consternation of natural gas consumers in the EU.[44]

Eurasian Economic Community (EEC), Also Known as the EAEC

The Eurasian Economic Community grew out of a 1995 agreement to form the CIS Customs Union, which ended up being a customs union between only Russia, Belarus, and Kazakhstan. In 1996, Kyrgyzstan joined, making the customs union the "union of four," and in 1998 Tajikistan joined, making it the "union of five" before becoming the Eurasian Economic Community in October 2000.[45] Uzbekistan, joining in 2006, was the newest member, but it pulled out of the EEC in October 2008.[46] See box 6.2.

BOX 6.2. EURASIAN ECONOMIC COMMUNITY (EEC) MEMBERSHIP

Members	Observers
Belarus	Ukraine
Kazakhstan	Moldova
Kyrgyzstan	
Russian Federation	
Tajikistan	

The EEC has the goal of becoming a common market and is currently supposed to be a customs union.[47] As with any organization, the gap between what is agreed upon and what is implemented can be wide. The EEC has agreed on many issues, with implementation pending indefinitely, but has disagreed on some issues: members failed to agree upon a common external tariff (CET) and an antidumping agreement.[48]

The EEC's governance is dominated by Russia through weighted voting. It has 40 percent of the votes, with 20 percent each for Belarus and Kazakhstan and 10 percent each for Kyrgyzstan and Tajikistan. Because a two-thirds vote is required for "major policy issues," Russia can veto any significant measure it dislikes.[49] As this indicates, integration in the EEC has been a process of moving toward Russian policies. For instance, harmonizing tariffs, a step toward a CET, has meant moving toward Russian tariffs.[50] Kazakhstan and Kyrgyzstan have not accepted this, and with Kyrgyzstan having entered the WTO, it is bound by its tariffs that are lower than Russia's. Thus if a CET were to be established and be consistent with WTO rules, Russia would have to adopt the lower Kyrgyz tariffs.[51] This is not likely.

In October 2006, the EEC members announced that they would be merging with the Central Asian Cooperation Organization (CACO). All the EEC members except Belarus were already CACO members.[52]

Economic Cooperation Organization (ECO)

The ECO was founded by three countries, Iran, Pakistan, and Turkey, in 1985, based on the Regional Cooperation for Development (RCD) organization and a funding treaty, the 1977 Treaty of Izmir. After the Soviet Union dissolved in 1991, the ECO took in six former Soviet republics and Afghanistan, raising its membership to 10. See box 6.3 for more ECO membership details. In 1996, with the revised Treaty of Izmir, the ECO pledged to lower barriers to trade, but the ECO also has the broader goals of promoting social, cultural, and scientific cooperation among its members. In July 2003 its members agreed to form an ECO Trade Agreement (ECOTA), which would be a PTA that sets maximum tariffs of 15 percent on at least 80 percent of goods and a reduction of nontariff barriers among members. ECOTA awaits agreement.[53]

BOX 6.3. ECONOMIC COOPERATION ORGANIZATION (ECO) MEMBERSHIP

Afghanistan	Pakistan
Azerbaijan	Tajikistan
Iran	Turkey
Kazakhstan	Turkmenistan
Kyrgyzstan	Uzbekistan

The GUUAM Organization (The Georgia, Ukraine, Uzbekistan, Azerbaijan, and Moldova Organization)

In 1997, the original four GUUAM members—Georgia, Ukraine, Azerbaijan, and Moldova—agreed to create the organization as a regional forum. In 1999, Uzbekistan joined. See box 6.4. In 2002 the GUUAM changed from a regional forum—just a "talk shop"—into a regional organization. In 2000 an FTA among GUUAM members was proposed, and in 2002, member states agreed to work toward a GUUAM FTA, but little has been done about it since. Uzbekistan reportedly almost withdrew from the grouping.

GUUAM conspicuously excludes Russia. Indeed, the rationale for establishing GUUAM was for it to act as a counterbalance to the Russian-dominated CIS.[54] As if to remove any doubts about GUUAM members' wish for distance from Russian influence, GUUAM's first meeting was held in Washington, DC.[55]

BOX 6.4. GUUAM ORGANIZATION MEMBERSHIP

Azerbaijan   Ukraine
Georgia   Uzbekistan
Moldova

Source: GUUAM, http://www.guuam.org.

Shanghai Cooperation Organization (SCO)

The Shanghai Cooperation Organization (SCO) is an organization in flux. The organization—originally called the Shanghai Five—formed after the end of the Cold War and focused on border issues. In 2001, it added Uzbekistan as a member and became the Shanghai Cooperation Organization. Thus today its members include China, Russia, and four of the five Central Asian former Soviet republics—Kazakhstan, Kyrgyzstan, Tajikistan, and Uzbekistan—with Turkmenistan conspicuously remaining a nonmember. Iran would like to be a member, but other SCO members are not so sure and have been politely noncommittal. Iran, along with India, Mongolia, and Pakistan are observers in the SCO, but it is unclear whether any will become full members.[56] See box 6.5.

BOX 6.5. SHANGHAI COOPERATION ORGANIZATION (SCO) MEMBERSHIP

Members   **Observers**
China   India
Kazakhstan   Iran
Kyrgyzstan   Mongolia
Russia   Pakistan
Tajikistan
Uzbekistan

The organization's focus has steadily grown and now serves as a political discussion forum to foster regional economic cooperation and as a way to balance the growing US presence in the region. After 9/11, the US established military bases in the region, which prompted both China and Russia to use the SCO to limit US power in the region. In July 2005, the SCO issued a statement calling for the withdrawal of US troops from Central Asia, although one SCO member, Kyrgyzstan, reassured the US in October 2005 that its base in Kyrgyzstan will remain open.[57] This reassurance turned to rejection in 2009. Kyrgyzstan announced it would close the US base shortly after receiving $2.1 billion in economic aid from Russia.[58]

China's primary economic interest in Central Asia is access to sources of energy. The growing Chinese economy is very thirsty and is concerned with finding additional energy supplies like those prevalent in Central Asia. China has other concerns about the region, such as its fears that militant Islam could spread into its own borders. It has experienced some violence relating to separatist Uighurs in Xinjiang Province, and since Uighurs also live in the "Stans," China wants no fanning of Uighur nationalism from abroad.

Russia has close and sometimes difficult ties with the former republics in the region. It maintains military bases in Kyrgyzstan and Tajikistan and extensive investment in the region's energy sector. It also is concerned with instability along its borders. Russia clearly views the SCO as a vehicle for controlling its former republics in the Soviet Union. As one scholar put it when describing intra-SCO dynamics, "China recognizes the right of Central Asian states to make their own decisions . . . Russia does not."[59] Russia also would like the SCO to serve as a basis for a natural gas cartel.

While the "Stans" clearly need both Russia and China, they remain distrustful of both, thus limiting the level of integration likely to develop.

Single Economic Space (SES)

The Single Economic Space (SES) is a subgrouping of four CIS members—Russia, Belarus, Kazakhstan, and Ukraine—that seek deeper economic integration than found in the CIS itself. They are seeking the establishment of the SES Free Trade Zone but need to sign, ratify, and implement many agreements for the SES Free Trade Zone to be established. Three of the members nearly agreed to establish a common currency. Russia, Belarus, and Kazakhstan agreed in principle to establish a common currency, but Russia and Belarus wanted it to be called the ruble, the name for the existing Russian currency, but Kazakhstan disagreed.[60] In September 2004, SES members agreed to a common value-added tax (VAT) that was to take effect on January 1, 2005.[61] The four reportedly discussed entering the WTO as one entity but found there was too much divergence in their visions for the SES. Russia and Kazakhstan reportedly wanted the SES to become a customs union—in part, at least, to facilitate WTO membership—while Ukraine was against this deeper level of integration.[62] Ukraine, at that time still under pro-Russian president Kuchma, sought a free trade area. Ukraine was interested in an SES-wide value added tax (VAT). Under VAT schemes, governments tax each step of the production process. Ukraine sought the VAT combined with a free trade area to shift an estimated $800 million in tax revenues from Russia to Ukraine associated with Russian energy exports.[63] This, of course, would be of limited interest in Russia.

Differences between Russia and Ukraine grew notably after the late 2004 Orange Revolution brought pro-Western and anti-Russian president Viktor Yushchenko to power. The Ukrainian opposition had been opposed to the SES because they felt it made EU membership less likely.[64] Thus it might seem odd that in May 2005 reformist Ukrainian president Vladimir Yushchenko announced that Ukraine is ready to move ahead with the SES and that "we welcome all SES-related initiatives that would ensure mutual ties in transit, customs, budget and fiscal relations."[65] Notice that this is far short of Russia's desired level of SES integration: in SES negotiations Russian president Vladimir Putin sought a CET, shared competition rules for the SES members, and a supranational regulatory body for pursuing SES policies.[66] The Russian vision for the SES would be a far cry from the current SES, which better fits Ukraine's SES vision. The current SES is a variable-speed RTA that allows each member state to determine the degree to which it will integrate. This can be used to foster integration where there is not consistent political will across a group of states, but it can also be used to avoid integration by states determined to do so.[67]

Russian and Ukrainian relations became more acrimonious in late 2005 over Russian gas exports to and through Ukraine, when Russia announced that it would cut off gas exports to Ukraine if Ukraine did not pay the demanded fourfold increase in prices. Ukraine refused and, as promised, Russia cut off Ukrainian gas exports. Ukraine demanded a higher payment for Russian gas passing through pipelines in Ukraine and took remaining Russian gas from its pipelines as payment. Gas supplies across much of Europe were threatened or interrupted before the two countries reached a settlement. But this turned out to be only the first round, as a similar dispute arose a few years later, with a similarly disruptive outcome. In both cases Russia and Ukraine negotiated a settlement, but the dispute shows that the two will not likely be integrating more deeply anytime soon.

The Middle East and North Africa

The regional integration that has spread so rapidly around the world has been noticeably less pronounced in the Middle East and North Africa. This has not been for lack of trying. Numerous regional trade integration initiatives have been proposed over the years, but few have been successfully negotiated, let alone implemented. There has been increased interest in recent years, and a number of states in the region have publicly committed to economic liberalization more generally—such as Saudi Arabia's successful accession to the WTO—which makes opening to one's neighbors less of a dramatic economic and political change. The GCC and a grouping of some Arab League countries have each been more successful of late in integration, and there is greater seriousness elsewhere in the region about concluding and implementing RTAs.

The six-nation Gulf Cooperation Council (GCC) established a customs union in 2003 and a common market in 2008. The GCC—comprising Bahrain, Kuwait, Oman, Qatar, Saudi Arabia, and the United Arab Emirates—planned a single currency by 2010. The GCC countries have already met the convergence criteria they set for themselves to facilitate monetary union, although the 2010 deadline seemed increasingly difficult to meet, and two GCC members—the UAE and Oman—announced they would not participate in the monetary union.[1] See figure 7.1 for MENA RTA membership details.

This recent track record of low economic integration seems to be changing with the Pan Arab Free Trade Area (PAFTA), which officially began on January 1, 2005, and with the deeper integration at the subregional level. Before examining the recent increase in integration, the historical record of low actual economic integration should be examined in some depth.

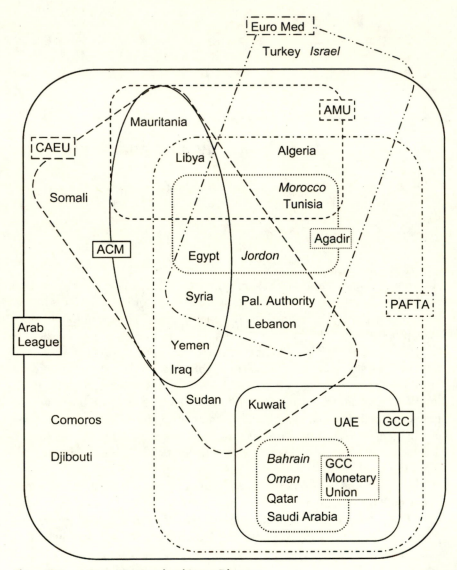

Figure 7.1. MENA RTA Spaghetti Venn Diagram
Key: **See list of abbreviations.**
Note: ***Italics*** **indicate bilateral FTA with the US.**

RTAs and countries outside of the region have shown an increased interest in forging trade agreements with existing Middle Eastern and North African RTAs or individual MENA countries.

The six-member GCC has started FTA negotiations with China.[2] Meanwhile, the EU's Euro-Mediterranean Partnership Agreements nudged Jordan,

Egypt, Morocco, and Tunisia toward an FTA (the Agadir Agreement). Not to be outdone in regionalism, the US has been promoting bilateral FTAs in the region with the goal of establishing the Middle East Free Trade Area (MEFTA) by 2013. Israel, Jordon, Morocco, Bahrain, and Oman each have bilateral FTAs with the US. The US had been negotiating bilateral FTAs with Qatar and the UAE, but both talks were halted and the US backed away from its consideration of a bilateral FTA with Egypt.[3] Thus MEFTA appears to be stalled.

EXPLAINING LOW LEVELS OF MENA INTEGRATION IN THE POST–WORLD WAR II PERIOD

The low level of regional integration is somewhat puzzling, at least in the Arab portions of the MENA, given the long-standing sense of pan-Arabism in the region and the 1945 establishment of the Arab League to foster, initially, regional cooperation and, later, economic integration. Pan-Arabism has used what many thought would be a sufficiently strong glue to bond the region together—the Arab language and Islam—but pan-Arabism's glue has been set with some significant solvents that weaken the bonds of integration: low levels of economic and political development, ethnic divisions, strong divisions between branches of Islam, and a lack of security in the region. Pan-Arabism led Egypt and Syria to briefly merge into the United Arab Republic (UAR) from 1958 until Syria's withdrawal in 1961 due to Egyptian dominance in the union. The unity of the broader Arab League was notably absent with Egypt's 1979 to 1989 suspension after the 1978 Camp David Accords, in which Egypt made peace with and recognized Israel. The Arab League's headquarters was moved from Cairo to Tunis, Tunisia, during Egypt's suspension.

Pan-Arabism has been far more focused on non-economic matters than economic integration. Why such a lack of success in economic integration in the region? There are a host of reasons for this.

The most significant reasons for a lack of Arab economic integration include (1) protectionism and a lack of liberalization within the regions' economies; (2) regional economies that do not complement one another well; (3) underdeveloped (nonpluralist) political systems; and (4) continued political and security divisions among and within the region's states.

1. High levels of protectionism and a profound lack of economic liberalization within the region's economies.

Historically, the region's desire for economic integration ran counter to another trend in the region: import substitution industrialization (ISI). ISI made wonderful political sense to newly independent countries the world over because it was a development strategy that highlighted independence from the colonial (and industrial) powers and, for a time, ISI seemed to be helping many developing nations industrialize. Arab countries were not exempt from the lure of ISI.[4] But ISI began to fail in many of the same places where it had been previously seen as successful. Despite ISI's problems, the tradition of strong state intervention in the economy had been established in the Arab world. Furthermore, many argue that strong state intervention in the economy fit with the political-economic culture of many Arab states. The political-economic structure in many Arab states includes "networks of families and individuals with parallel stakes in politics and business."[5] This is not a recipe for economic integration—global or regional—which can often upset the domestic status quo. Thus many governments in the region have retained a strong hand in the economy. Since it is often private companies that press for regional integration in other regions, in the Arab world they are less well developed, relative to state-run businesses and compared with other regions, and thus they are less influential in calling for regional integration.[6]

Many of the region's states are not as intertwined in the global trading system as other similarly developed nations because of high levels of protectionism. Average tariffs in the Arab world from 1995 to 1999 were nearly double those found in MERCOSUR, ASEAN, and NAFTA member economies.[7] Comparatively few of the region's economies are WTO members. As of 2002, 11 Arab countries were WTO members.[8] Saudi Arabia, one of the region's more important economies, was not a WTO member until 2005 despite high levels of oil and financial resources.[9]

High levels of trade protectionism are combined with lower restrictions on the movement of labor across borders, which means that workers often cross Arab borders more freely than do goods and services. This is an unusual pattern in regional integration; economic integration is typically greater in trade than in labor in most regions.[10] Intraregion investment levels are also low. The massive financial boom that came to many states in the region led primarily to investment outside of the region. To market believers, this is not surprising due to the high barriers against foreign investment that are pervasive in the region.

Last, a number of attitudes are widely held in the region that suggest a lack of openness for outsiders and thus, possibly, less support for economic liberalization and the concomitant interactions with those from other countries both inside and outside of one's region.[11]

   2. *Poor complementarity in the region's economies.*

Complementarity indexes, which measure the degree to which a given set of economies either mirror one another and therefore do not fit together well (a low score) or are opposite one another and therefore do fit together well, are low for Arab-to-Arab economies compared with scores for national economies in other countries.[12] This means that there will probably be fewer economic benefits from the freer trade that integration brings than in economies with higher complementarity scores. To put it starkly, two economies that specialize in banana production that have free trade between them will likely gain less than will two economies that have different endowments and specialties, such as one country that specializes in banana production and another that specializes in, say, corn production. However, there is some controversy over this analysis in the Middle East. If analysts exclude oil from the analysis, the complementarity index scores for the region increase markedly to levels similar in other regions.[13]

3. "Underdeveloped" (nonpluralist) political systems.

There are no Arab democracies. There are democracies in the Middle East and in the Islamic world, but none are Arab. Why might this limit economic integration? Capitalist economic integration requires a basic level of government openness that is remarkably absent in Arab countries. Arab states have been quite hierarchical with little independent civil society allowed to develop. Similarly, corruption is high, thus further lowering openness. Governing elites are not eager for the openness that integration might bring. Governance in Saudi Arabia is famously secretive. The ages of many of the leading royal family members—who are the Saudi state—are routinely reported inaccurately by the government. Trials and executions combined sometimes take one day.

4. Continued political and security divisions among and within the region's states.

The conflict with Israel has obviously added much conflict to the region, but there has been plenty of tension elsewhere in the region. Arabic is not the only culture and language in the region—Israel, Turkey, and Iran, for instance, are all part of the region, but none are predominantly Arab. Iran has a Shi'a Islam majority, while Sunnis are the majority in most Arab countries. Sunni and Shi'a Islam sometimes manage to peacefully coexist, but Iran's relationships with many Middle Eastern and North African countries have been strained by this schism.

There has been quite a lot of feuding between leaders of Arab states. Libyan leader Muammar el-Qaddafi has been accused by US and Saudi officials of having once set up a plot to assassinate then de facto Saudi leader Crown Prince Abdullah.[14] The Arab League's annual meeting is often characterized by discord. At the March 2005 Arab League event, some leaders did not attend, and some who did refused to be photographed together.[15] Unfortunately, this is not atypical. Egyptian President Hosni Mubarak refused to attend the 2009 Arab League summit in Qatar after Qatari media criticized Egypt's position on the Israeli bombing of the Gaza Strip in late 2008 and early 2009.[16] At the 2009 summit, Qaddafi continued the personal feud with soap opera drama by publicly calling now Saudi King Abdullah a liar and by walking out of the conference.[17] While Qaddafi's ongoing theatrics are indeed dramatic, other issues have led to greater discord in the Arab League such as when Egypt broke ranks with the rest of the Arab world and made peace with Israel, signing the 1978 Camp David Accords and becoming the first Arab state to recognize Israel's right to exist. The Arab League responded by expelling Egypt in 1979, despite the fact that the Arab League's headquarters were in Cairo, Egypt. AL headquarters were moved to Tunisia until Egypt was allowed back into the Arab League in 1989.

There are divisions over the price of oil. Not all states in the region are as well endowed in energy resources as are the better-known oil producers. Moreover, some large producers have small populations and therefore face less immediate financial pressures and can more easily afford to keep oil production down (and therefore prices high), but more populous oil producers may feel more immediate need for higher production because of larger populations.

The Gulf War divided much of the Arab world: Iraq invaded Kuwait and then deployed its military along the Saudi border until the US sent in troops. Which was the bigger threat to states in the region? An emboldened Iraq, which can use its military to threaten its neighbors, or an excuse for a larger US military presence in the region with the possible implosion of multiethnic Iraq? Middle Eastern countries were divided.

And then there are the region's many and divisive wars. Iraq and Iran fought an eight-year war that is often compared with World War I in brutality (and tactics). Syria occupied war-torn Lebanon for years and pulled out under strong pressure from Arab League members.

CONTEXT OF MENA RTAs:
IPE OF THE MENA

Just as there is more cultural, linguistic, religious, and ethnic diversity in the MENA than is commonly believed (see box 7.1), so too is there more economic diversity. Many MENA countries do not have sufficient oil reserves to make them economically developed, and so they struggle to develop. Even the Saudis struggle economically as population increases have strained their oil-funded welfare state, thus prompting them to attempt to diversify and become more industrialized. The region also includes incredible poverty in many countries. The region has also witnessed a great deal of instability since World War II, with Israel fighting its neighbors in full-fledged war upon its inception in 1948 and again in 1956, 1967, 1973, and 1982–1985 as well as the ongoing Israeli-Palestinian conflict that has played a central role in the other conflicts. But there is instability beyond relations with Israel, such as civil war in Lebanon from 1975 to 1990, the brutal 1980–1988 Iran-Iraq war, Iraq's 1990 invasion of Kuwait, threats against Saudi Arabia and the subsequent Gulf War of 1991, and the current Iraq war as some of the most prominent examples.

BOX 7.1. CULTURAL GEOGRAPHY OF MENA

It is easy but wrong to equate the Middle East and North Africa (MENA) with the Arabic world. Arabic is the primary language spoken in the MENA, and it is, of course, the language of Islam's holy book, the Koran (or Qur'an). Saudi Arabia is home to many of Islam's holiest sites and home to the hajj, or holy pilgrimage to Mecca.

Yet there are Arabic states outside of the geographic Middle East and Arabic states where Arabic is not the primary language. The Arabic world includes much of North Africa and some states on the Horn of Africa, such as Djibouti and Somalia. The Arabic region, then, is based primarily on identity, with language, religion, and proximity to the Arabian Peninsula as strong foundations of that identity. But the region includes non-Arab states also.

Israel stands out as non-Arab, despite a large Arab population within its borders (however defined) and as a beacon of democracy to its supporters and a usurper to its detractors.

Turkey, which straddles Europe and Asia, is predominantly Islamic but is Turkish in culture and language, not Arabic. Turkey has strong historical ties to the Arab world because of the Ottoman Empire that was a force for economic integration before its demise at the end of World War I.

Iran stands out as a center for Shi'a Islam and also differs from its Arabic neighbors in its Persian (Farsi) culture and language. North African countries are also Islamic, but with varied ethnic composition, such as the Berbers.

In addition to this linguistic, ethnic, and religious diversity across the MENA, there are profound differences between those who seek secular governance and those who seek Islamic governance, as witnessed by the division in Iraq over its future after the US invasion in March 2003, and in arguments over governmental and societal reforms across the MENA.

RTAs IN THE MIDDLE EAST AND NORTH AFRICA

Arab Maghreb Union (AMU) or Union du Maghreb Arabe (UMA)

The Arab Maghreb Union was established February 17, 1989, to promote cooperation and integration among the Arab states of northern Africa.[18] There was a "Maghreb Customs Union formed in the 1960s but it was for the most part not implemented."[19] In 1991, members agreed to an ambitious integration process: an FTA in 1992, a common market by 2000, and eventually a monetary union. But in 1993, member countries agreed to postpone integration.[20] There have been attempts to revive the AMU, but it remains dormant. Despite its current condition, the Arab Maghreb Union is one of the African Union's "pillars" for constructing the African Economic Community. This is not a very strong pillar to construct much of anything, let alone a continent-wide economic community. AMU members include Algeria, Libya, Mauritania, Morocco, and Tunisia.[21]

Arab League (AL), Also Known as the League of Arab States (LAS)

Established in 1945 by its seven original members—Egypt, Iraq, Jordon, Lebanon, Saudi Arabia, Syria, and Yemen—the Arab League's membership has expanded to 22 (see box 7.2). The Arab League is not a supranational organization like (some aspects of) the European Union. "It lacks the legal and political authority to override the sovereignty of its member states."[22] But to call it institutionally weak is to miss the primary purpose of the Arab League: a forum to enable Arab countries to meet. The degree to which the

---

BOX 7.2. ARAB LEAGUE (AL) MEMBERSHIP

Algeria	Morocco
Bahrain	Oman
Comoros	Palestinian Authority
Djibouti	Qatar
Egypt	Saudi Arabia
Iraq	Somalia
Jordan	Sudan
Kuwait	Syria
Lebanon	Tunisia
Libya	UAE
Mauritania	Yemen

Source: Arab League, http://www.arableagueonline.org/arableague/index_en.jsp.

AL has influence in the region and in the world is determined by the degree of unity among the AL members. This has been in short supply at the AL due to a greater degree of diversity among the AL's members than is typically understood.

The organization includes traditionally politically important countries such as Saudi Arabia and Egypt, but also North African countries. The AL includes both Sunni- and Shi'a-dominated countries, but because it is dominated by its more numerous Sunni members, it is viewed with some suspicion by many Shiites.[23] Some members are virulently anti-US while others, such as the Arabian Peninsula states—Kuwait, Saudi Arabia, the UAE, and Bahrain—supported, often quietly, the US buildup of troops prior to the 2003 Iraq war.[24] AL summits have had their share of drama. In 2004, Libya's Muammar el-Qaddafi stormed out of the summit during the opening session, and in 2003 he traded insults with Saudi Arabia's Crown Prince Abdullah.[25]

The most prominent current policy divides within the AL surround Syria's relationship with Lebanon—including implications that Syria was involved in the assassination of Lebanese prime minister Rafik Hariri in 2005—and Syria's links to Iran. Iran and Syria share the goal of supporting Shi'a Hezbollah, an anti-Israeli militia/terrorist group that commands wide support in Lebanon. Saudi Arabia is especially concerned with Iranian influence in the Middle East—it has some unrest among its own Shi'a minority, and Saudi Arabia took seriously Iran's pledge to export the Iranian Islamic Revolution (Saudi ears would hear "Shi'a Revolution") and thus views Syrian relations with Hezbollah negatively. The split with the Palestinian Authority (PA) between the more militant Hamas and the more centrist Fatah faction, the latter represented by PA president Mahmoud Abbas, is echoed within the AL, with Syria and Qatar supporting Hamas and Saudi Arabia and Egypt supporting Fatah in their respective perceptions of the December 2008–January 2009 offensive in the Hamas-dominated Gaza Strip.[26]

CAEU—Council of Arab Economic Unity and the Arab Common Market

Established in 1964 to implement the 1957 Arab Economic Unity Agreement (AEUA), the CAEU's primary achievement was the creation of the Arab Common Market in 1964. Initially four of the 11 AEUA members were in the Arab Common Market. This expanded to seven with the inclusion of Libya, Mauritania, and Yemen, but this leaves nearly half of the AEUA members choosing to stay out of the Arab Common Market (see box 7.3).[27]

**BOX 7.3. COUNCIL OF ARAB
ECONOMIC UNITY (CAEU) AND ARAB
COMMON MARKET MEMBERSHIP**

Egypt	Palestine
Iraq	Somalia
Jordan	Sudan
Kuwait	*Syria*
Libya	*Yemen*
Mauritania	

Source: CAEU, http://www.caeu.org.eg/; Jeffrey Frankel, *Regional Trading Blocs in the World Economic System* (Washington, DC: Institute for International Economics, 1997), 277; and World Bank, *2005 World Development Indicators.*
Note: Members of the Arab Common Market appear in *italics.*

Arab Cooperation Council (ACC)

An abandoned effort to promote cooperation and integration among some Arab Common Market members—Egypt, Iraq, Jordan, and Yemen—the ACC was established in 1989 with the eventual goal of forming a common market, but the short-lived ACC never became an effective organization.[28]

The Gulf Cooperation Council (GCC)

The Gulf Cooperation Council, whose official name is the Cooperation Council for the Arab States of the Gulf, consists of Bahrain, Kuwait, Oman, Qatar, Saudi Arabia, and the UAE. The GCC is the most integrated and institutionalized subregional development in the Middle East and North Africa, having established a customs union in 2003, a common market in 2008, and well on their way to a single currency among four of their members (scheduled for 2010).[29]

GCC members have nearly half of the world's oil reserves and the resources to easily meet the GCC's administrative and institutional needs associated with integration.[30] A more significant question is the degree to which GCC member states wish to integrate because integration, as it does everywhere, diminishes autonomy and challenges existing economic relationships. In recent years GCC members do seem determined to achieve greater integration (although not without setbacks), demonstrating that the GCC has come a long way from its roots.

The monetary union shows that GCC countries still show hesitation about diminished autonomy. Oman had dropped out of the monetary union in 2006 with little damage to the future single currency, as Oman's economic and financial weight is small. In 2009, however, the UAE, the second-largest economy in the GCC after Saudi Arabia, announced it would drop out of the single currency. Its rationale was that the proposed GCC central bank would be located in Saudi Arabia, leaving the UAE with no GCC institutions and, without the GCC central bank, a diminished ability to serve as a global financial hub, a clear goal of the UAE.[31]

The GCC began in May 1981 in reaction to the Islamic Revolution in Iran and the Iran-Iraq war. The primary concern was security in a tough neighborhood, but the GCC also moved toward economic integration in signing the United Economic Agreement on November 11, 1981.[32] This called for free trade among GCC members, which went into effect in 1993.[33] The agreement applied to agricultural and industrial goods but not oil. The 1993 FTA also allowed for the free movement of the factors of production: labor and investment. The GCC hoped to form a customs union by 1986 but could not implement the common external tariff in time and had to push back the date of the customs union.[34] In 2001, GCC members agreed to a customs union, which took effect on January 1, 2003. As of September 2005, the common external tariff (CET) for 85 percent of the tariff lines was either 5 or 0 percent, and the GCC sought to extend the CET to all goods. According to a Saudi Arabian official, customs tariffs have been removed on all goods for trade within GCC nations, and the GCC has "liberalized trade in services for roughly 100 sub-sectors of services," with plans for liberalization in other services subsectors.[35]

The Bahraini decision to seek an FTA with the US caused divisions within the GCC. Saudi Arabia argued that this would violate GCC provisions. However, in November 2004, Oman and the UAE announced their intentions to negotiate FTAs with the US, after which Qatar also began bilateral FTA talks with the US.[36]

Yemen has long sought GCC membership but has long been denied it. Its economy is much less developed than other GCC members and would be the only nonmonarchy in the GCC.[37]

Euro-Mediterranean Partnership, Also Known as Euro-Med, Including the Euro-Mediterranean Free Trade Area (EMFTA) and the Agadir Agreement

The Euro-Mediterranean Partnership, commonly called Euro-Med, is a process involving closer political and economic cooperation and free trade between the EU and 10 littoral Mediterranean states officially called "Partners of the

Southern Mediterranean." There could be an 11th Mediterranean partner state in the future; Libya has had observer status since 1999. The Euro-Med Partnership was launched at Barcelona in November 1995 and is thus also referred to as the Barcelona Process. One portion of the Euro-Mediterranean Partnership is the proposed Euro-Mediterranean Free-Trade Area (EMFTA) with a target date of 2010. The planned route to achieving this includes bilateral agreements between the EU and each of the Mediterranean partner states—called Euro-Mediterranean Association Agreements—and through regional free trade agreements among the Mediterranean partner states themselves, such as the Arab Maghreb Union (if revived and revised) between Morocco, Algeria, Tunisia, Mauritania, and Libya and the Agadir Agreement between Morocco, Tunisia, Egypt, and Jordan. The Association Agreements include provisions for phasing in freer trade and establishing the EMFTA. Turkey, a Mediterranean partner and an EU candidate country, has a closer economic relationship with the EU than the other Mediterranean partners; it has been in a customs union with the EU since 1996. As was the case with Cyprus and Malta, two former Mediterranean partners that became EU members, Turkish membership in the EU will supersede its Euro-Med agreements with the EU.

What shape will the EMFTA take if it is agreed upon and implemented? As envisioned by the EU, EMFTA includes free trade in manufactured goods and "the progressive liberalisation of trade in agricultural products."[38] In other words, Europe does not intend to open its agricultural markets soon, at least not in the EMFTA, and it is in precisely this sector that EMFTA's Mediterranean partners could achieve significant export gains.[39]

The EMFTA will include one set of rules of origin (RoO) for the entire region. A pan-Euro-Mediterranean protocol of the rules of origin was approved by trade ministers from the Euro-Med states in July 2003 and—if all goes according to EU plans—will be adopted in bilateral agreements between the EU and individual Euro-Med states and in agreements between the Mediterranean partner states themselves.

The EU funds development activities in the Euro-Med states through the MEDA program and through the European Investment Bank.[40]

The Euro-Mediterranean partners are also part of the European Neighbourhood Partnership, begun in 2004.[41] (See the list of all ENP countries in table 7.1.)

Agadir Agreement

The Agadir Declaration, signed in 2001 in Agadir, Morocco, led to the negotiation of a free trade agreement, called the Agadir Agreement, between Morocco, Tunisia, Egypt, and Jordan. It was signed in February 2004 with EU pledges for financial assistance to help the members with the changes stemming from the agreement and to help establish a secretariat.[42]

Table 7.1.   EU-MENA RTAs' Memberships (Agadir Agreement, Euro-Mediterranean Partnership, Euro-Mediterranean Free Trade Area [EMFTA], and European Neighbourhood Partnership Membership)

Agadir Agreement States
  Egypt
  Jordan
  Morocco
  Tunisia

Euro-Mediterranean Partnership Members
  Algeria
  Egypt
  Israel
  Jordan
  Lebanon
  Morocco
  Syria
  Tunisia
  Turkey
  West Bank and Gaza (Palestinian Authority)

Euro-Mediterranean Free Trade Area (EMFTA) Members
  Algeria
  Egypt
  EU
  Israel
  Jordan
  Lebanon
  Morocco
  Syria
  Tunisia
  Turkey
  West Bank and Gaza (Palestinian Authority)

European Neighbourhood Partnership Members
  Algeria
  Armenia
  Azerbaijan
  Belarus
  Egypt
  Georgia
  Israel
  Jordan
  Lebanon
  Libya
  Moldova
  Syria
  Tunisia
  Ukraine

Source: European Commission, "Commissioner Patten Attends Signature of Agadir Agreement," press release, February 24, 2004, IP/04/256, http://europa.eu.int/comm/external_relations/euromed/news/ip04_256.htm; European Commission, "The Euro-Mediterranean Partnership," undated, http://ec.europa.eu/external_relations/euromed/index_en.htm; European Commission, "European Neighbourhood Policy: Partners," undated, http://ec.europa.eu/world/enp/partners/index_en.htm (November 21, 2005).

Pan Arab Free Trade Agreement (PAFTA)

The Pan Arab Free Trade Area—previously called both the Arab Free Trade Area (AFTA) and the Greater Arab Free Trade Area (GAFTA)—has met with more success at economic integration than have previous attempts in the region. PAFTA got its start from the 1997 call by the AL's Economic and Social Council for the establishment of a Pan-Arab free trade area. PAFTA was different from previous attempts because initial implementation was spelled out and began shortly after the call to integrate. Implementation was to begin in 1998 and was to be completed by 2008 by averaging a 10 percent reduction in tariffs over the course of 10 years.[43] Implementation of PAFTA began as scheduled in 1998, when 14 of the AL's 22 members began to lower barriers with one another. The eight that were not in the program at that time consisted of Algeria and seven Arab least-developed countries (LDCs): the Comoros Islands, Djibouti, Mauritania, Palestine, Somalia, Sudan, and Yemen.[44] In 2001, the Economic and Social Council of the Arab League shortened the transition period by moving the date of full implementation from 2008 to January 1, 2005.[45] By the time of the PAFTA's inception in 2005, 17 of the AL's 22 members were PAFTA members. Of those eight AL members that were initially outside of PAFTA, Palestine, Sudan, and Yemen have since joined, and Algeria is in the process of joining. Four AL members remain outside of PAFTA: the Comoros Islands, Djibouti, Mauritania, and Somalia (see box 7.4).[46] PAFTA members now account for 90 percent of all Arab foreign trade and 95 percent of intra-Arab trade.[47]

BOX 7.4. PAN ARAB FREE TRADE AREA
(PAFTA) MEMBERSHIP

Bahrain	Qatar
Egypt	Saudi Arabia
Iraq	Sudan
Jordan	Syria
Kuwait	Tunisia
Lebanon	United Arab Emirates
Libya	West Bank and Gaza
Morocco	(a.k.a. Palestinian Authority)
Oman	Yemen

Source: WTO, "Trade Policy Review: Jordan," November 2008, WT/TPR/S/206, http://www.wto.org/english/tratop_e/tpr_e/tp306_e.htm, 16.

Some credit this FTA with greater implementation because the members have not waited for all AL members to join, but instead implemented an FTA of the willing.[48] The Union of Arab Chambers of Commerce has been asked to monitor the PAFTA with a report every six months.[49]

Despite more concrete integration than other Arab FTAs, the PAFTA remains a shallow FTA, with services excluded from the agreement and other areas of potential integration, such as the harmonization of standards, similarly excluded. In fact, there are some significant areas of trade in goods that are not fully integrated. For instance, many agricultural products are excluded from tariff-free treatment at harvest time. The 1997 agreement leading to the PAFTA does call for going beyond eliminating tariffs and includes guidelines to create dispute resolution mechanisms and to establish rules of origin.[50] In 2004, a framework agreement for the liberalization of trade in services among Arab countries was approved, and efforts were intensified to achieve unified Arab rules of origin.[51] Rules of origin in PAFTA require that 40 percent of the value added must be from within the region for goods to qualify for preferential tariff treatment, but the rules for implementing this have been described as too vague.[52] Nontariff barriers remain a significant hurdle to free trade between the PAFTA members.[53] PAFTA members hope to continue economic integration to create an FTA with greater depth. The history of such plans suggests that this is a possibility more than a probability, but PAFTA has led to more integration than most would have predicted before implementation of the FTA.

8

The Pacific Islands

Many RTAs involve members with asymmetrical economic size and power, but in the Pacific Islands region, this is far more likely to be the case. Any RTA between Australia and New Zealand and any Pacific Island nation will inherently be unequal. This necessarily causes some tension, yet Australia and New Zealand are the most significant markets in the region, and Pacific Island nations feel compelled to enter into RTAs with the Pacific Island region's developed pair.

The widest regional RTAs are those associated with the Pacific Islands Forum (PIF), an organization that hosts summits of Pacific Island nations. The PIF has created PACER, the Pacific Agreement on Closer Economic Relations, and for the least-developed PIF members PICTA, the Pacific Island Countries Trade Agreement. Also at the regional level is SPARTECA, the South Pacific Regional Trade and Economic Cooperation Agreement, which is a nonreciprocal preferential access agreement between the two developed Pacific Islands countries and 13 poorer countries in the region. There are also subregional groupings such as the Melanesian Spearhead Group Trade Agreement (MSG Trade Agreement) and the Australia-New Zealand Closer Economic Relations Trade Agreement (ANZCERTA), also known as the CER Agreement, which is one of the deepest RTAs in the world. See figure 8.1 for Pacific Islands RTA membership.

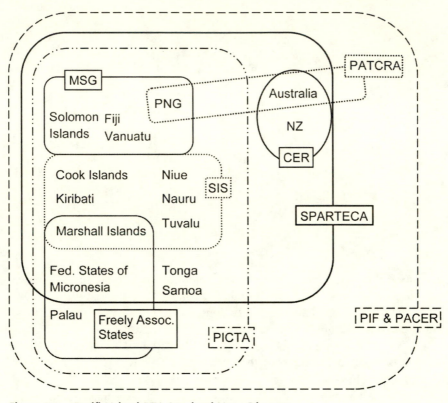

Figure 8.1. Pacific Island RTA Spaghetti Venn Diagram
Key: See list of abbreviations.

CONTEXT OF PACIFIC ISLANDS RTAs:
IPE OF THE PACIFIC ISLANDS REGION

The Pacific Islands face the same challenges that small island states of the Caribbean face, but the Pacific Islands are more physically isolated from one another and from global markets. (See box 3.1, "Special Development Challenges Faced by Small States.") Consequently, they are typically not able to sustain their economies without significant aid from elsewhere, usually outside the region. The economies of the region, especially the smaller and more resource-poor islands, have been described as MIRAB economies, those economies dependent upon MIgration, Remittances, Aid, and Bureaucracy.[1] Australia and New Zealand, the two big kids on a much dispersed block, are the primary sources of MIRAB support from within the region. Their dominance, more notable for Australia than New Zealand, was seen in 2003 when Pacific Island Forum (PIF) members chose a retired Australian diplomat, Greg Urwin, to be PIF's secretary general.[2] Other outside powers that are influential in the region are France and the United States as metropolitan powers to their various nonindependent territories in the region, the EU and Japan because of trade and aid, and China, whose influence is growing in the region as it counters Taiwan's policy of granting aid to reward those states that officially recognize it as the rightful government of China.

Six PIF members are in the WTO: Australia, New Zealand, and PIC nations Papua New Guinea, Fiji, the Solomon Islands, and most recently, Tonga.[3] Vanuatu has applied for WTO membership, but in 2002 Vanuatu put its accession on hold after it became hesitant about what WTO membership would entail.[4]

RTAs IN THE PACIFIC ISLANDS REGION

Australia-New Zealand Closer Economic Relations Trade Agreement (ANZCERTA), Also Known as the CER Agreement

The Closer Economic Relations Trade Agreement (CER Agreement) between Australia and New Zealand, which went into force in 1983, is now an FTA on both goods and services between these developed Pacific countries and involves so-called deep integration with considerable harmonization of numerous standards.[5] The CER agreement was preceded by a number of preferential trade agreements, the most important of which was the 1966 New Zealand Australia FTA. The CER began with a goods FTA in 1983 that was expanded in 1988 protocols to the CER Agreement, which included services and greater harmonization of quarantine procedures. Quarantine procedures—due to the unique flora and fauna of these island nations—are of greater importance than they might be to countries with fewer isolated and unique ecosystems. Subsequently, Australia and New Zealand increased regulatory harmonization. This now includes competition policy and various standards; harmonization is sufficient for the CER to specifically disallow any antidumping remedies.[6]

Compacts of Free Association with the US and US Pacific Territories

The Freely Associated States—Palau, the Federated States of Micronesia, and the Marshall Islands—have each entered into a Compact of Free Association with the US (see table 8.1). They are former territories of the US that have chosen to be sovereign nation-states but that retain close relations with the US and for which defense is maintained by the US. So these countries have self-governance even in foreign affairs, except for their defense responsibilities, which the US has assumed, as defined in the compact. While this status

Table 8.1.   Freely Associated States and US Pacific Territories

The Freely Associated States
   Palau
   Federated States of Micronesia
   Marshall Islands
US Pacific "Territories"*
   American Samoa
   Guam
   Northern Mariana Islands

*All the US Pacific territories listed above are "unincorporated" territories (as are Puerto Rico and the Virgin Islands), meaning that Congress has determined that only selected portions of the US Constitution apply and that governance is administered through the US Interior Department's Office of Insular Affairs (OIA). The Northern Mariana Islands (and Puerto Rico) are considered commonwealths, which means that they have a more "highly developed" relationship with the US, which includes a written mutual agreement. Furthermore, US territories may be organized or unorganized (organized refers to having an "organic act"—a body of laws enacted by Congress to govern the "insular" area, a generic term describing any non-state or nonfederal district that comes under US jurisdiction). Guam and the Virgin Islands are organized territories, while American Samoa is an unorganized territory. US Department of the Interior, Office of Insular Affairs, "Definitions of Insular Area Political Organizations," http://www.doi.gov/oia/Islandpages/political_types.htm, http://www.doi.gov/oia/, and http://www.doi.gov/oia/Firstpginfo/islandfactsheet.htm.

continues indefinitely, the economic aspects of each compact are renegotiated every 15 years. The first compact's economic provisions lasted 15 years and, after three interim years, another compact went into effect in 2004 that is scheduled to last until 2024. Under the current compacts, these countries may export duty free into the US, but rules of origin and other limitations constrain the extent of this duty-free access. For instance, there must be 35 percent local content, including the cost of the materials and "direct" costs of processing, for the goods to receive duty-free treatment in the US. Up to 15 percent of US-produced inputs may be included in this calculation. Some goods are governed by other agreements, such as textiles and apparel, and others are excluded from duty-free entry.[7]

Economic viability remains a significant issue for these Pacific nations; trade relations with the US and aid from the US Compact of Free Association are key elements to their survival. Other aid also is important: the US gives compensation to Marshall Islanders for illness and lost land from US nuclear bomb tests from the 1940s to the 1960s. The PIF has called on the US to increase this compensation.[8]

While the Freely Associated States are sovereign states, albeit ones that have chosen to have this sovereignty constrained in defense matters, there are numerous territories in the Pacific that have chosen to remain US territories: American Samoa, Guam, and the Northern Mariana Islands. US aid to its Pacific territories is important; they too receive money related to the Freely Associated States' Compact with the US: so-called Compact Impact funds compensate these territories for costs associated with immigrants from Freely Associated States.[9]

Trade from these US "territories," generically called "insular areas" by the US government, receives duty-free access to the US market, although it must meet rules of origin standards. These include that any imported inputs must be "substantially transformed" and no more than 70 percent of the product's value can be foreign to still receive duty-free entry into the US.[10]

There has been controversy about labor rights and low pay in some apparel factories in Saipan, the capital of the Northern Mariana Islands. The Northern Mariana Islands are a US territory, and textiles and apparel made there can be labeled "made in the USA," but US labor laws did not apply. Thus many apparel manufacturers set up shop there, importing primarily Asian workers, paying them well below the US minimum wage, and exporting their products as "US made." In the late 1990s, there were some 31 factories with about 15,000 guest immigrant workers.[11] This loophole in US wage and immigration laws closed in 2008 with the Consolidated Natural Resources Act.[12] Activists had already attempted to publicize and change these laws, but the bribery scandal involving lobbyist Jack Abramoff—who had worked to keep the loophole—served to further publicize the issue and concentrate the minds of wavering politicians who wanted to distance themselves from Abramoff as much as possible.

Melanesian Spearhead Group Trade Agreement (MSG Trade Agreement)

This preferential trade arrangement between Fiji, Papua New Guinea, the Solomon Islands, and Vanuatu was signed in 1993 between three of the four MSG Trade Agreement members, and in 1998 Fiji became a member.[13] The MSG Trade Agreement now provides preferential treatment for approximately 250 goods.[14] MSG Trade Agreement members that are also members of PICTA will have to ensure that any future trade liberalization through the MSG Trade Agreement is consistent with PICTA.[15] Fiji and Papua New Guinea (PNG) are the more powerful countries in the MSG Trade Agreement, and the smaller members sometimes feel their own interests have too often been overlooked in the agreement.[16]

PACER—Pacific Agreement on Closer Economic Relations

PACER is not a trade agreement, but a framework to develop trade relations among members of the Pacific Islands Forum. PACER was established in August 2001 and entered into force in October 2002. Under PACER, the Pacific Island Countries Trade Agreement (PICTA) was established. PICTA requires ratification of six of the member countries to come into effect.[17] See "Pacific Islands Forum (PIF), Formerly the South Pacific Forum" for more.

Pacific Islands Forum (PIF), Formerly the South Pacific Forum

This section includes Pacific Agreement on Closer Economic Relations (PACER), the Pacific Island Countries Trade Agreement (PICTA), and the Pacific Plan.

PIF Overview

The Pacific Islands Forum—called the South Pacific Forum until 2000—is the annual summit of the South Pacific countries' leaders. The forum, established in 1971, deals with a wide array of issues facing these small and isolated countries, including security issues and economic survival, and thus trade integration. The PIF has established the Pacific Agreement on Closer Economic Relations (PACER) and a free trade agreement among its developing and LCD members called the Pacific Island Countries Trade Agreement (PICTA) (see box 8.1). In October 2005, at its Heads of Government meeting in Papua New Guinea (PNG), the PIF officially endorsed the Pacific Plan. The Pacific Plan is not legally binding, but instead gives political support toward greater cooperation and integration in the region and spells out specific steps to be taken toward this end. Thus PIF members consider the Pacific Plan to be a road map toward implementing greater cooperation and integration on four pillars: economic growth, sustainable development, good governance, and security.[18] Additionally, the PIF adopted a new agreement establishing the PIF as an intergovernmental organization in international law. This will assist the PIF in being able to send a representative to speak for the entire PIF at various international organizations' meetings.[19]

BOX 8.1. PIF, PACER, PICTA, AND SIS MEMBERSHIPS

Australia	*Niue**
*Cook Islands**	*Palau*
Federated States of Micronesia	*Papua New Guinea*
Fiji	*Samoa*
*Kiribati**	*Solomon Islands*
*Marshall Islands**	*Tonga*
*Nauru**	*Tuvalu**
New Zealand	*Vanuatu*

Source: PIF Secretariat, http://www.forumsec.org/; and *Europa Directory of International Organizations*, 491.

Note: All PIF members are also in the Pacific Agreement on Closer Economic Relations (PACER). Pacific Agreement on Closer Economic Relations (PICTA) members are in *italics*, and * indicates the PIF subgroup of the small island states.

PIF Members' Relations

PIF members consist of the 14 Pacific Island countries (PIC) and Australia and New Zealand. The PIF's PIC members are poor and isolated, and the PIF's other two members, New Zealand and especially Australia, are the dominant powers in the region in terms of economic aid, trade, historical ties, and interest. They provide a great deal of financial aid, security assistance, and technical expertise to the PICs. They also provoke some resentment in the PICs; the PICs want to be as independent as possible from the two regional powers, yet at the same time they need help to develop and survive globalization's challenges. The PICs have also turned to the two developed PIF countries, especially Australia, to help with security problems in the Solomon Islands and Papua New Guinea.[20] Australian-led peacekeeping troops were sent to the Solomon Islands in July 2003 to quell fighting between two militant ethnic groups and end the general lawlessness that lingered beyond a 2001 peace agreement that was thought to have reestablished security. The peacekeepers were sent with the blessing of the PIF and of the Solomon Islands government.[21] A New Zealand–led peacekeeping group was sent to PNG's Bougainville Island in 1997 and 1998 to oversee a ceasefire between separatists and the PNG government. Australian-led peacekeepers then took over in 1998.[22] In 2004, Australia sent police to PNG but left after the PNG Supreme Court ruled their presence unconstitutional.[23] Other PIF countries also sent troops for the various peacekeeping missions in the Solomon Islands and PNG. Australia has a greater interest in ensuring that the PICs not become failed states in which terrorism, drug trafficking, and money laundering could easily be fostered, but it also knows that its influence is sensitive to many PICs.

Fijian domestic politics has caused a rift within the PIF. There was a coup d'état in Fiji in 2006 that ended with military leader Frank Bainimarama leading the country. He has shown little desire to hold an election, and PIF members have applied pressure for elections, especially Australia and New Zealand. They refused to grant visas to Fiji's leaders, their families, and any member of Fiji's military. After one Fijian official's son was denied a visa to study in New Zealand, Fiji expelled New Zealand's ambassador, and New Zealand responded by expelling Fiji's ambassador.[24] Three Australian newspaper publishers have been expelled from Fiji in retaliation for negative coverage regarding the coup and military governance.[25] In January 2009, the PIF called for elections by the end of 2009 in order for Fiji to avoid facing PIF sanctions.[26] Clearly, all is not pacific in the Pacific.

There are significant expatriate communities from the PICs in both Australia and New Zealand, and this has been a source of some tension. The PICs want better treatment of their expatriate communities and greater labor mobility to make it easier for their citizens to work in Australia and New Zealand. Australia and New Zealand are hesitant to grant greater access.[27]

While the differences between the two developed countries and the PIC islands in the PIF can be quite sharp, there are also some significant differences
among the 14 PIC members themselves. All 14 are categorized as small island developing states (SIDS) by the UN, and five of these—Kiribati, Samoa,
Solomon Islands, Tuvalu, and Vanuatu—are further categorized as least-
developed countries (LDCs).[28] Fiji and PNG are significantly more powerful
than other PIC members, no matter their status as developing or least developed, and the smaller PIC members feel somewhat disenchanted with their
lack of influence in the PIF. In 1990 five of the smaller islands—Kiribati, the
Cook Islands, Nauru, Niue, and Tuvalu—formed the Smaller Island States
subgrouping. They were joined by the Marshall Islands in 1997. The SIS
members seek to address their concerns of having poor natural resources, no
skilled workforce, and little involvement in world markets.[29] A small island
states (SIS) meeting consisting of three SIS members, Kiribati, the Marshall
Islands, and Nauru met before the 2005 annual PIF Heads of Government
meeting to strategize in order to better highlight their needs in the broader
PIF.[30] There are also ongoing trade spats between some PIF members: Fiji
has separate trade disputes with Vanuatu and PNG.[31]

Recently one PIF member—Nauru—has been teetering on the edge of fiscal collapse and is receiving help from the PIF in its recovery. Independent
since 1968, it sued Australia for phosphate mining royalties and eventually
received payment, but it faced additional economic hardships when it was
listed as uncooperative in fighting money laundering. In 2001 it agreed to
hold asylum seekers that were caught trying to enter Australia. In exchange it
received money from Australia, but this did not stave off Nauru's defaulting
on loan payments in 2004. In 2004 Australia sent officials to help put Nauru's
finances in order. The PIF adopted the Pacific Regional Assistance to Nauru
initiative, which funds an official from Samoa to assist Nauru's officials.[32]

PIF Membership History

The seven original members of PIF were Australia, the Cook Islands,
Fiji, Nauru, New Zealand, Tonga, and Western Samoa. By 1995, nine more
joined, bringing the group to its current size of 16 members. In 1998 the
PIF established criteria observer status for Pacific Territories: "A Pacific
Island territory on a clear path to achieving self-government or independence
may be eligible for observer status at the Forum." In 1999 New Caledonia
became the first French Pacific territory to become an observer. Since then,
East Timor, officially known as Timore-Leste, also became an observer, followed by French Polynesia and Tokelau[33] in 2004 and 2005, respectively.[34]
In October 2005, the PIF formally created a category of associate member,

which is designed to give nonindependent territories—such as American Samoa, Guam, and French Polynesia—formal, albeit partial, entry into the PIF. Associate members are granted greater participation in PIF activities but remain excluded from the PIF's highest decision-making body, the Heads of Government meeting.[35]

PIF Governance

The PIF has a secretariat in Suva, Fiji. Australia and New Zealand fund most of the secretariat (37 percent each), with other PIF members paying the remainder.[36] The PIF Heads of Government meeting is held in a host country that rotates annually. This meeting is preceded by the Forum Officials Committee (FOC) meeting, which reports to the Heads of Government meeting, and since 1989 is followed by the Post-Forum Dialogue, with representatives from some of the world's mid-sized and larger powers.

Primary PIF Integration and Cooperation Initiatives: PACER and PICTA

The Pacific Islands Forum established a framework to develop trade relations among its members. This framework, the Pacific Agreement on Closer Economic Relations (PACER), was established in August 2001 and entered into force in October 2002.[37] The primary benefit to the PIC in PACER is Australia and New Zealand's assistance with trade facilitation through their expertise and financial aid. The Regional Trade Facilitation Programme (RTFP) includes those PACER provisions that include trade facilitation. The RTFP, through other agencies, will implement PACER trade facilitation by educating businesses about standard customs practices and health and safety standards.[38]

PACER also served as a framework agreement for the Pacific Island Countries Trade Agreement (PICTA), established by the 14 PIC nations, excluding Australia and New Zealand. PACER does call for FTA negotiations between the 14 PICTA members and Australia and New Zealand to begin eight years after PICTA comes into force. Australia and New Zealand's joining PICTA is not considered likely because PICTA would have to be notified to the WTO, and it may not meet WTO standards for an acceptable FTA. PICTA negotiations began in 1999, and the agreement went into force in April 2003. As of August 2003, there were nine PICTA members that ratified the agreement: Cook Islands, Fiji, Kiribati, Nauru, Niue, Papua New Guinea, Samoa, Solomon Islands, and Tonga.[39]

Why did the PIC countries seek PICTA? Economies of scale and the desire to help attract investment drove PICTA members toward an FTA, much like FTAs elsewhere. PICTA members hope that a market of some six million with zero tariffs on many goods will be more attractive than the minuscule market size of the smaller members. In the Pacific, however, there are greater barriers to overcome to gain these benefits: PICTA members have low levels of trade with one another—interisland trade is 3 percent of overall trade—and their transportation links are tenuous and expensive. Another reason for PICTA is that its members view it as a stepping stone toward a greater level of interaction with the global economy. The increased scale and practice with openness to other countries will be a training ground for PIC businesses and governments.[40]

PICTA Provisions.   Tariffs of developing PICs will be reduced to zero by 2010 and by 2012 for small island states (SIS).[41] However, there will be a list of exempted exports that will follow these tariff reduction schedules. This negative list will be eliminated by 2016.[42] Quotas will be eliminated immediately. PICTA does not cover trade in services, investment, or labor, although the PICTA does state as its eventual goal that it should one day become a single market. There is a dispute resolution mechanism that includes consultations (i.e., talking), mediation (talking with the assistance of a mediator), and, if necessary, legally binding arbitration. If a PICTA member ignores the arbitration ruling, then the other member or members may rescind the granting of PICTA preferences to that member.[43] The PICTA does also allow some safeguards: PICTA preferences can be removed for the "protection of developing industries." This is intended to apply only to new industries.

PATCRA—Papua New Guinea Australia Trade and Commercial Relations Agreement

This is a bilateral FTA between the regionally dominant Australia and less-developed Papua New Guinea that has been in force since 1977. It covers goods and some services, and it does have investment measures.[44]

SPARTECA (South Pacific Regional Trade and Economic Cooperation Agreement)

SPARTECA, as the South Pacific Regional Trade and Economic Cooperation Agreement is more typically known, is a nonreciprocal agreement that dates to 1980 between developed Australia and New Zealand and 13 developing and less-developed Pacific countries (see box 8.2). It gives duty-free entry into Australia and New Zealand for most products from its members if they meet SPARTECA rules of origin, which require 50 percent local content. SPARTECA's PIC members want changes to the rules of origin, an issue that will be discussed in the context of the PACER agreement.[45]

BOX 8.2. SPARTECA MEMBERSHIP

Australia	Niue
Cook Islands	Papua New Guinea
Fiji	Solomon Islands
Kiribati	Tonga
Marshall Islands	Tuvalu
Micronesia	Vanuatu
Nauru	Western Samoa
New Zealand	

Source: WTO, http://www.wto.org.

9

Conclusion

As the spaghetti bowl of RTAs continues to be stirred, some clear patterns emerge, and lessons about RTAs, trade, and globalization can be discerned. Distinct patterns of RTAs emerge by region and are reviewed here, followed by a review of broader RTA patterns and their implications according to the three IPE perspectives outlined earlier in the book: economic liberalization, economic nationalism, and globalization skeptics, including economic structuralists/radicals and green critics of globalization.

RTAs: FAÇADE OR REAL STRUCTURES?

Patterns of RTAs in various geographic locations reflect the political, economic realities as much as or more than they shape them. Regions with deep security divides are not likely to have highly developed RTAs. Regions with weak rule of law domestically are less likely to enter into meaningful RTAs inasmuch as meaningful RTAs require the rule of law. Indeed, many RTAs are empty, providing only the façade of integration in international summits, headlines, or perhaps RTA preambles, with little real integration support to give them functioning structure. Façade RTAs have few concrete provisions to ensure specific market access, and their member states pass weak domestic legislation that insufficiently enables RTA implementation. Façade RTAs have weak dispute resolution mechanisms should there be a dispute, or they have seemingly sufficient dispute resolution provisions but might rely on notoriously corrupt domestic judicial systems.

RTAs: DYNAMIC, NOT STATIC

These façade RTAs can be compared to dead-letter law—laws on the books that are forgotten or, worse yet, remembered but ignored. Most dead-letter RTAs will remain that way, but occasionally a new context will bring an otherwise moribund RTA to life. This can come from changes in leadership with different ideology or interests, from changes in economic fortunes, such as a financial crisis that necessitates greater export earnings or growing inefficiency that makes attracting foreign investment of greater importance, or from changes in the international setting, such as a newly evolved security threat. Indeed, there are examples of such changes breathing life into RTAs that were empty. The Asia Pacific Economic Corporation Forum (APEC) was only an international forum for discussion before President Clinton publicly called for it to be a primary vehicle for trade integration in the Pacific Rim. The East African Community (EAC), which had been broken apart by war and ideological divides, has become meaningful again as its members have found relative peace and diminished ideological differences. It has become sufficiently consequential to attract new members, and as it continues to deepen, it should attract more. Numerous countries have sought to upgrade or begin RTAs in reaction to other RTAs so as not to be relatively disadvantaged. Central American countries were motivated to create the Central American Free Trade Agreement (CAFTA) in order to achieve parity with Mexico's relatively better access to the US market granted in the North American Free Trade Agreement (NAFTA). Their own RTAs granting preferential access to the US market were made relatively less preferential and more politically tenuous with NAFTA's passage. NAFTA hurried the demise of some RTAs and hastened the formation of others.

REGIONAL PATTERNS OF RTAs

African RTAs

African RTAs are highly varied, with many being empty RTAs, existing on paper but not in reality, and many others including deep monetary integration. Many African RTAs have deeper monetary integration than trade integration. There are grand plans for an Africa-wide RTA built on both functional and deep subregional RTAs as well as the all-but-dead subregional RTAs. African RTAs also have unusually high levels of cross-cutting memberships, even by global spaghetti-bowl RTA standards. This, coupled with poor infrastructure and highly inefficient and corrupt border crossings, further harm African integration efforts.

Asian RTAs

Asian RTAs are characterized by informality, although this is decreasingly true as Asian RTAs are becoming more institutionalized. In much of Asia, actual globalization is ahead of RTA integration. As with Africa, monetary integration in Asia is sometimes more advanced than formal trade integration. One reason for this unique pattern is the divergence of interests of the region's largest traders, especially China and Japan. Japan had resisted RTAs, preferring multilateralism, which would therefore include its closest economic, security, and political ally, the US. Japan, however, saw rising China promote RTAs in the region and felt compelled to change its RTA-averse strategy. With Asia's largest traders ambivalent for so long, ASEAN has been the most important Asian RTA and is now the RTA around which hemisphere-wide RTA efforts are orbiting. It is now pulling in the region's largest traders—China, Japan, and South Korea—and may facilitate even wider Asian trade integration.

American RTAs

Two primary RTAs, NAFTA in North America and MERCOSUR in South America, dominate their respective parts of the Americas but have yet to agree on hemisphere-wide integration in the Free Trade Area of the Americas (FTAA) due to divergent interests and, to a lesser degree, ideological differences. MERCOSUR's own divides have prevented it from fully maintaining its commitments, but it remains the most consequential RTA in South America. Venezuela's likely inclusion in MERCOSUR, with Hugo Chávez's unique ideology, intervention in the market, and abrasive style, will test MERCOSUR's ability to remain cohesive and to serve as an anchor for South American–wide integration.

There are other highly integrated portions of the Americas: the Caribbean Community and Common Market (CARICOM) and the Central American Common Market (CACM) are significant in their subregions.

European RTAs

The EU is the most successful and most integrated of all RTAs anywhere. It is the widest and deepest RTA and has spread stability and prosperity to wider and wider portions of Europe. Nevertheless, its governance is a multi-layered Rube Goldberg machine whose considerable institutional success is just short of miraculous. Its unique and confusing governance is clearly the result of much compromise, proving that the aphorism about committees and camels—that a horse is a camel made by a committee—also applies to RTA negotiations. Some view the EU's success as so historically unique that it might as well be a mirage, not a role model to be emulated. There is no doubt whatsoever that other RTAs are attempting to emulate it. The EU also has a host of RTAs with other countries and with other RTAs, so the EU shapes global trade and globalization well beyond its borders.

Ex–Soviet Union RTAs

RTAs in the former Soviet Union, excepting those in the Baltic states, now EU members, tend to foster integration more on paper than in reality. They are clouded by the member states' relationship with the dominant regional power—Russia—balanced by relations or potential relations with China, the EU, or the US, depending upon the subregion and countries in question. Russia's reforms toward economic liberalization and away from communism turned more nationalist during the Putin years, as numerous inchoate democratic reforms were reversed. Russia, newly confident from increased energy revenues, also reasserted itself regionally in both economic and security relations. A resurgent, assertive, and illiberal Russia has raised the stakes on RTAs in the region.

Middle East and North Africa RTAs

MENA RTAs reflect the region's lack of globalization, excessive reliance on energy exports, and sharp security and political differences. RTAs in the region have tended to be weak. They proclaim much integration in public pronouncements but don't deliver it in reality. Instead, they reflect insular economies whose rulers are focused more on autonomy than on globalization, and they reflect deep security differences among member states. But important subregional RTAs are emerging to challenge this pattern. The most important of these is the Gulf Cooperation Council (GCC), whose members are moving toward much deeper integration, including a common currency.

Pacific Islands RTAs

RTAs in the Pacific reflect the vulnerability of most of the region's economies and the underlying power of the region's big kids on the block, Australia and New Zealand. Other outside powers, such as the US and France, remain important due to their colonial ties and continued leading role in globalization, with China a rising influence. Pacific Island nations attempt to pool their resources and find a common voice in a very loud globalization auditorium.

Bilateral and Cross-Cutting RTAs

The explosion of bilateral RTAs and cross-regional RTAs is vigorously stirring the spaghetti bowl, adding complexity to an already complex picture. True, larger traders' arrays of bilateral RTAs follow patterns and thus bring some continuity to the spaghetti bowl. For instance, EU bilateral agreements tend to use the same type of spaghetti noodle—rules of origin in all EU bilateral agreements are similar—and the US array of bilateral RTAs uses a different spaghetti noodle—rules of origin tend to be variations of those found in NAFTA. But large traders are not the only players in the explosion of bilateral RTAs. Indeed, many RTAs are set up between RTAs in different regions, countries in numerous regions, the smallest of traders, and every possible combination of countries.

RTAs, GLOBALIZATION, AND INTERNATIONAL POLITICAL ECONOMY THEORIES

RTAs, Economic Liberalism, and Economic Nationalism

After having examined the spaghetti bowl of RTAs more closely, and having seen their incredible variation, it is worth revisiting the debate among economic liberals whether RTAs are stumbling blocks to free trade or building blocks for it. In short, do RTAs increase or decrease economic liberalization? It is hard to make the case that RTAs are collectively economically "rational"—the term used in its economics context, that is to say, efficiency maximizing. Even while a given RTA may lower trade and investment barriers substantially among its members, the sheer number of RTAs combined with their cross-cutting memberships and varied coverage and rules are collectively inefficient.

One is reminded of John Maynard Keynes's insight showing that which is individually rational may also be collectively irrational. His "paradox of thrift" points out that as an economy slows, it makes economic sense for individuals to save in order to hedge against tougher economic times that are likely ahead. But if this rational act is followed by too many people, the economy will be faced with a sharper downturn than it would have otherwise had. Individual rationality can be collectively irrational. RTAs created in the name of economic liberalization may be individually rational but are collectively irrational in terms of efficiency.

Not all economic liberals would agree that the RTAs are collectively irrational because, as noted earlier, RTAs also may serve as stepping stones to greater liberalization by establishing standards for liberalizing areas not

covered or insufficiently covered by the WTO or by making a leap to multilateral liberalism seem less politically difficult. For these standard-making
and political consensus–building roles to be effective, not all RTAs are of
equal importance. The role of the large traders is of heightened importance as
they are the most significant economic and political weight in globalization.
The so-called quad—the EU, US, Japan, and Canada—combined with China,
account for over half of the world's trade.[1] Also of heightened importance are
large and rising developing-country exporters such Brazil, India, and Mexico
because of their significant economic weight and because of their traditional
leadership status in the developing world.

For the building-block economic liberals to be correct, there must be some
liberalization beyond RTAs toward which to build. There are two possibilities: broader RTAs that harmonize with existing RTAs and the multilateral
liberalization of WTO negotiations.

Shifting back to the spaghetti metaphor, geographically broader RTAs would
take thinner and highly varied spaghetti noodles and exchange them for wider
and more consistently shaped noodles, thus creating a more ordered spaghetti
bowl. There are many hemispheric or partial-hemispheric RTAs that seek to do
this. The problem thus far is that the wider the RTA in a given hemisphere, the
less successful at harmonizing across RTAs, with the EU as a prominent exception. The EU stands out in its degree of integration success and has harmonized
beyond the borders of its 27 members by forming the European Economic Area
(EEA), an RTA with most of the European Free Trade Association (EFTA)
member states. Elsewhere, hemispheric RTA efforts have not resulted in the
harmonized liberalization hoped for by building-block liberals. The FTAA in
the Americas, which includes nearly all countries in the Americas, has stalled.
So too has APEC in Asia. Pan-African free trade remains wildly unrealistic.
Subhemispheric RTAs, however, have met with more success than hemisphere-wide RTAs. Numerous African RTAs have successfully integrated despite the added pressures of poverty and artificial, often externally established,
national borders. In Asia the broader APEC has stalled, but the more focused
10-member ASEAN has harmonized and integrated much of Southeast Asia
and is increasingly the basis of Asia-wide integration plans through ASEAN
+ 3 (China, Japan, and South Korea) and the East Asian Summit, also called
ASEAN + 6 (ASEAN + 3 and Australia, India, and New Zealand).

Even smaller RTAs can also serve to harmonize disparate RTAs. The
Trans-Pacific Strategic Economic Partnership Agreement (TPP) is attempting to harmonize existing bilateral RTAs among its growing, albeit limited,
member states.[2]

Economic liberals that view RTAs as stumbling blocks toward liberalization point out that even those RTAs that attempt to harmonize existing

RTAs are piecemeal. The TPP, for instance, covers goods, not services or investment, and even if plans to extend the TPP to services and investment are successful, the TPP's limited membership—currently Brunei, Chile, New Zealand, and Singapore, possibly joined by Australia, Peru, the US, and Vietnam—severely limits its harmonizing role. In short, we are still left with a very confusing spaghetti bowl of overlapping RTAs and thus severely limited liberalization.

The skyscraper of liberalization that building-block economic liberals hope RTAs are building toward is another multilateral round of liberalizing WTO negotiations, the Doha Development Agenda (DDA). Architectural plans for the DDA have been scaled back a number of times already since DDA talks were launched in 2001. The long overdue building may still not be completed, and if it is, it will not be as tall nor as elaborate as originally intended. From the perspective of economic liberalization, many corners have been cut in building the DDA. The rise of RTAs increases the importance of the DDA's success to economic liberals. The DDA's relatively modest goals and even more modest success to date suggest that coordinating disparate RTAs will be of increasing importance to prevent RTAs from becoming stumbling blocks to liberalization.

Economic nationalists, of course, are less interested in what is collectively rational than in other goals. For instance, they point out that the above discussion is about economic efficiency, but states may have other goals that they deem as more important than efficiency. For instance, states may seek a degree of economic autonomy at the expense of efficiency, or they may be concerned about their economic performance compared with that of a rival. Economic policymakers' goals may be to protect employment in a given economic sector that is important to social stability or reelection.

RTAs and Globalization Critics

The gulf between economic liberals is wide indeed when economic liberals criticize RTAs because they may impede globalization, while globalization critics fear RTAs promote globalization altogether too much, or at least corporate-led consumption driven globalization that they fear harms the environment and fails to alleviate poverty. The current generation of RTAs certainly promotes globalization more than earlier generations. At the same time, however, the current generation of RTAs is also more open to influence from activist groups than previous RTAs. Thus RTAs today face, at least slightly, noncorporate goals as they are being shaped. There are provisions in many RTAs for environmental protection, a topic ignored in previous generations of RTAs. The EU is gaining as one of globalization's most potent regulators.

The EU has been slow to allow genetically modified organisms (GMOs) and recently passed a massive chemical regulation overhaul law requiring more environmental rigor than any other international organization or individual country. The 2007 REACH, or Registration, Evaluation, Authorisation, and Restriction of Chemical Substances, requires much more significant chemical safety testing and disclosure and seeks to find safer substitutes for many currently used chemicals.[3]

Globalization's critics might concede that the EU offers substantial governance that is significantly responsive to noncorporate interests, but would also contend correctly that the EU is atypical. Many RTAs have sought EU-like institutions, EU levels of integration, and thus, they hope, EU prosperity and stability. None has been successful at re-creating the EU's depth and success. Other examples of RTAs establishing international governance consistent with noncorporate interests are sparse. Perhaps more significantly, those provisions consistent with noncorporate interests, such as labor rights and environmental standards, tend to be cosmetic. So too is the access granted to shape RTAs.

Currently globalization critics are correct that this access is largely cosmetic and the provisions weak. In older RTAs, such access and provisions were simply absent. Newer RTAs are more likely to grant greater procedural access to noncorporate societal interests and have environmental and labor provisions, but these tend to have less bite than other RTA provisions. For instance, violations of NAFTA's environmental or labor provisions go through their own less-rigorous dispute settlement mechanisms than is the case for disputes involving violations of other NAFTA provisions.[4] NAFTA's member governments can more easily stop the dispute resolution process for environmental and labor violations than they can dispute resolution for other violations of NAFTA provisions. In short, NAFTA's environmental and labor dispute resolution mechanisms have fewer teeth than its other dispute resolution mechanisms. NAFTA does grant societal actors the ability to complain about environmental and labor violations, but governments retain a gatekeeper role in the complaint initiation process. Societal initiation of complaints can be halted by the government of the societal actor making the complaint. Since NAFTA's inclusion of the environment and labor provisions in side accords, it is now more common for the US to grant these areas their own "chapter" in RTAs, giving them at least symbolic equality with more traditional chapters on tariffs, investment, or a specific economic sector such as agriculture or textiles and apparel. Critics contend that these newer provisions remain inadequate. Cosmetic access and weak provisions are, to be sure, an improvement in balancing corporate with wider societal interests, but they will not hide globalization's scars from globalization critics.

RTAs and Economic Development

Globalization critics also argue that RTAs promote the interests of corporations rather than alleviate poverty. They rightly point out that economic growth isn't enough for economic development. For instance, a country that moves toward monocrop agriculture for export may be more efficient in its agricultural production but may also have more hunger than it had before export-oriented agriculture. Access to land and urban poverty are more important variables in alleviating hunger than marginal improvements in overall efficiency and are often sacrificed in the rush to increase exports.

While economic globalization is not enough to guarantee economic development, neither is simply turning away from it. No country has successfully developed by shielding itself from the rest of the world. The question for both RTAs and globalization more generally is how to ensure that economic openness leads to development, not just overall economic growth. It is well beyond the scope of this book to examine this with any depth, but the experiences of RTAs do point to some suggestions.

First, RTAs between rich and poor countries need to account for their radical development differences. Simply allowing trade access between unequally developed states is not helpful if, for instance, richer states continue to offer massive subsidies to their producers. RTAs between rich and poor also need to grant real openness in sectors important for the poor countries, typically agriculture and textiles and apparel. There is some controversy associated with sheltering poorer countries from fuller liberalization. Many economic liberals argue that any "special and different" provisions limiting the liberalization required of developing countries in RTAs will limit the degree of liberalization in those RTAs and in those poor countries, thus leading to continued inefficiency. Continued inefficiency will not help poor countries develop, they argue.

Second, RTAs need to lower barriers among poor countries themselves. Developing nations' barriers to other developing nations are higher than the barriers that developed countries have in place. This is true regarding tariff rates, lists of sensitive products that are excluded from freer trade, and non-tariff barriers such as excessively long administrative burdens at customs. A clear trend in RTAs is that developing countries are increasingly entering into them, so mutually lower barriers in developing-nation RTAs will be crucial in their efforts to develop.

Third, for lowered barriers to help economic development, infrastructure development must follow, and other so-called behind-the-border issues such as paperwork streamlining and corruption reduction must improve. These are typically issues that get little attention during most RTA negotiations. Commonly they are used to make the RTA more palatable for both domestic

and foreign audiences. Infrastructure requires capital and thus either governments with significant capacity, substantial foreign aid, or, ideally, private
investment. These all may be lacking in a given RTA. Behind-the-border
changes may require wholesale political and cultural shifts that are difficult
to negotiate or legislate into reality. The EU stands out in requiring a great
deal of change in acceding members' administrative practices and in the high
level of infrastructure funding that comes with pending membership. Contrast
this with infrastructure promises associated with NAFTA that were designed
largely to convince wavering legislators to vote for its passage. Subsequent
US government funding for infrastructure along the US-Mexico border has
not been negligible, but it has certainly been disappointing. Imagine RTAs
between much poorer countries with much less capacity, and one can gauge
the need for greater infrastructure in order to achieve both economic integration and development.

CONCLUDING THOUGHTS: RTAs AS MICROCOSMS OF GLOBALIZATION

RTAs are shaped by and in turn shape globalization. They are increasing in number, membership diversity, scope, and certainly importance and
controversy. Whether RTAs facilitate economic liberalization or economic
nationalism in the future and whether they promote a wider balance of societal interests than is currently the case remains to be seen. The interplay of
economics and politics will continue to be the center of determining these
future RTA, trade, and globalization trends.

Appendix A

The World Trade Organization

The WTO is among the most prominent of economic international organizations. Its lineage dates, indirectly, back to the 1944 Bretton Woods conference that established the International Monetary Fund (IMF) and the International Bank for Reconstruction and Development (IBRD), more commonly known as the World Bank. A third institution was also to be created, the International Trade Organization. The latter failed passage in the US Congress, and thus a provisional agreement, the General Agreement on Tariffs and Trade (GATT) became the de facto global trade organization. Despite this inauspicious beginning, the GATT successfully lowered barriers to trade through a series of "rounds" of trade agreements following the GATT principles of reciprocity (mutually lowered trade barriers) and nondiscrimination (also known as most favored nation, or MFN, whereby the lowest tariff offered to one GATT member will be offered to all GATT members). As tariffs were lowered on industrial goods, the GATT, in the Tokyo Round (1973–1979), began to focus on nontariff barriers (NTBs) such as quotas (numerical limits in imports), subsidies, and environmental and safety regulations. These so-called behind-the-border issues made many GATT actions more controversial. Also controversial was the fact that the two economic sectors most critical to developing nations were completely outside of the GATT: agriculture and textiles and apparel. Most workers in developing countries work in agriculture compared with only a few percent in developed countries. Apparel production is the most labor-intensive industry in the world, and thus poorer countries have a competitive advantage. As more developing nations joined the GATT, pressure continued to mount to include these sectors in GATT's liberalizing trade rules.

THE URUGUAY ROUND

The Uruguay Round of GATT negotiations (1986–1994) did bring agriculture and textiles and apparel into GATT rules. The Uruguay Round, which went into force in 1995, did much more than this, however: it marked the evolution of the GATT into the World Trade Organization, included trade in services through the General Agreement on Trade in Services (GATS), established regulations governing trade in intellectual property rights through the Agreement on Trade Related Aspects of Intellectual Property Rights (TRIPS), established rules on some investment laws through the Trade-Related Investment Measures Agreement (TRIMs), continued the increasing focus on behind-the-border issues, and established the Dispute Settlement Understanding (DSU), the WTO's dispute resolution mechanism that has more "teeth" than the GATT mechanism.

THE DOHA DEVELOPMENT AGENDA

The Uruguay Round changes were substantial, and developing nations were not pleased that many of the new elements to trade governance were favorable to developed countries. Intellectual property rights, for instance, are great for the owners of intellectual property but are of less interest to developing nations. Moreover, there are increased administrative costs to executing an increasing number of WTO regulations in increasing areas of the economy. True, agriculture had been brought into the WTO, a key developing nation demand, but it remained much protected and, in developed countries, highly subsidized. Thus the next round of global trade negotiations faced much difficulty getting started. The 1999 Seattle ministerial meeting was supposed to launch them, but the North-South divide between developed and developing countries proved too great (and were more of a problem than the riots outside the negotiations). When the round was finally launched in 2001, the negotiations were to focus on developing countries' needs to a greater degree than other trade rounds, including the name for the round: the Doha Development Agenda (DDA) (also named for the Doha Qatar, the site of the ministerial meeting in which the negotiations finally began). Developing nations, however, remain skeptical that the DDA will sufficiently promote developing nations' concerns. At the time of this writing, there were no breakthroughs in sight.

WTO MEMBERSHIP

The WTO has been increasing its membership steadily in recent years, and as of July 2008, it had 153 members (see box A.1).[1] WTO members account for

---

BOX A.1. COUNTRIES ACCEDING TO THE WTO

Afghanistan	Lebanon
Algeria	Liberia
Andorra	Libya
Azerbaijan	Montenegro
Bahamas	Russian Federation
Belarus	Samoa
Bhutan	Sao Tomé and Principe
Bosnia and Herzegovina	Serbia
Comoros	Seychelles
Equatorial Guinea	Sudan
Ethiopia	Tajikistan
Iran	Uzbekistan
Iraq	Vanuatu
Kazakhstan	Yemen
Laos	

Source: WTO, http://www.wto.org (January, 27, 2009).
Note: Currently, the WTO has 153 members and 29 acceding countries. Official accession listing in no way guarantees future WTO membership.

---

nearly all of the world trade. The primary trader not in the WTO is Russia. Russia still has to achieve bilateral agreements with a number of its trading partners and then, like other entrants, must sign a multilateral agreement with all WTO members. EU Trade Commissioner Peter Mandelson had predicted that Russia could possibly achieve WTO entry by early 2006, but Russia did not make a number of high-level political decisions sufficient to liberalize its economy to the liking of WTO members.[2] Like any country seeking to join the WTO, Russia's accession could be resolved quickly or slowly, or it could go on indefinitely. An explanation of the mechanics of the accession process and the politics that underpin WTO accession are both warranted.

The Mechanics of Joining the WTO

To accede to the WTO, applicants must have their economy examined by WTO members, negotiate agreements with WTO members, be voted in by WTO members, and accept the terms of entry. Specifically, it is necessary to establish a working party consisting of any interested WTO member and the applicant country to examine the applicant's economy and create terms of accession. Each WTO member must agree to the terms of accession in order for the applicant to move toward accession. The terms of accession regulate the phase-in period until WTO rules apply fully. For instance, how quickly will

WTO rules apply, and what will tariffs levels and other regulation be while WTO rules are being phased in? After the accession package is formally approved by the WTO (by all its members, meeting as the "General Council"), the acceding country must approve the accession package. Thirty days after doing so, it officially becomes a WTO member.

The Politics of Joining the WTO

What is really necessary to join the WTO is to make the political commitment to carry out the economic liberalization required by WTO rules and existing WTO members. In some cases, a lack of enthusiasm for liberalization in a country's leadership is the primary hurdle to WTO entry. Russian leader Vladimir Putin has been less than enthusiastic for the liberalization to move Russia's WTO membership bid forward rapidly. Indeed, he has been less than enthusiastic for the economic liberalization more generally, at least when it clashes with his other goals, be they domestic or international. He did, after all, break up one of Russia's largest companies—oil giant Yukos—and send its CEO, Mikhail Khodorkovsky, then Russia's wealthiest person, to jail as a warning to other "oligarchs" to not challenge him in the political arena. In other cases, a country's leadership may be more willing for the reforms. WTO accession requires the reforms, but the country needs to cultivate sufficient domestic consensus to engage in those reforms. Reforms, after all, mean change for domestic producers that are likely to be painful: the end of government subsidies and easy government contracts, reduced tariffs on competing imports, and greater investment in the country from competitors are all likely possibilities. True, there will be benefits—fewer barriers and more stable access to foreign markets being the most significant—but these benefits may not go to the same firms that will struggle the most with greater competition, and the benefits may be less tangible and immediate than the prospect of competing with the world's most efficient companies.

Last, accession may be delayed as a country negotiates with other WTO members for the terms of accession that will define that country's trading regulations during the phase-in period to membership. If the country is a significant trader, many WTO countries will be interested and drive a hard bargain, as was the case for trading giant China. More typically, a country's major trading partners and trading competitors will have sufficient interest to create additional stipulations for the phase-in period and thus require bilateral negotiations with the acceding country.

European Union Preferential Access Agreements

Table B.1. ACP-EU Economic Partnership Agreement Negotiating Groups

ACP Regional Group	Membership
West Africa	ECOWAS members and Mauritania
Central Africa	CEMAC members and São Tomé and Principe
Eastern and Southern African Region	COMESA members
Southern African Development Community	SADC members
Caribbean, or CARIFORUM	Fourteen ACP members of the Caribbean Community and the Dominican Republic
Pacific ACP States (PACPS)	Fourteen developing country members of the Pacific Islands Forum (PIF)

Table B.2. EU Preferential Access Agreements

Program Name	Acronym	Membership	Inception Dates of Operation and Description
Generalized System of Preferences (There are also subsets of the EU's GSP that provide incentives for good governance, labor rights, and sustainable development.)	GSP	Non-LDC* developing nations	1971. UNCTAD authorized and recommended the GSP in 1968 in which developed countries offer preferential access to their markets for developing-nation exports.
Everything But Arms	EBA	49 LDCs	2001. Some agricultural provisions phased in 2006–2009. This modifies the EU's GSP program for LDCs.
Africa, Caribbean, Pacific-European Union Partnership Agreement, a.k.a. the Cotonou Agreement	ACP-EU Partnership Agreement	78 developing nations. Includes both LDCs and non-LDC developing nations.	Nonreciprocal agreements, first begun in 1975. It evolved into the Cotonou program in 2000. This agreement was given an exception from WTO rules at the Doha Ministerial Meeting in 2001. Exemption expired January 1, 2008. With the exemption ending, there was the need to renegotiate the reciprocal EPAs.
Economic Partnership Agreements	EPAs	78 developing* nations. Includes both LDCs and non-LDC developing nations.	Reciprocal agreements, currently under negotiation. Negotiations were to be completed by December 31, 2007, but extensions were granted, and negotiations continue. There are six ACP regional groupings negotiating separately with the EU. Only the Caribbean region has reached an agreement with the EU on its EPA (as of April 2009).

Source: Mark Pearson, "Negotiating the Trade and Development Dimension of EPAs: A Way Forward," *Trade Negotiations Insights* 4 (30): 2; European Commission, "Generalised System of Preferences, Everything But Arms (EBA) Initiative," January 2004; "User's Guide to the European Union's Scheme of Generalized Tariff Preferences," September 2005, http://europa.eu.int/comm/trade/issues/global/gsp/gspguide.htm; and Melissa Julian, "EPA Update," *Trade Negotiations Insights* 8 (4) (April 2009).
* LDCs (least-developed countries) are those officially recognized by the UN as LDCs.

Appendix C

US Free Trade Agreements and Pending Free Trade Agreements

Table C.1. US FTAs Entered into Force

Agreement Name and/or Partner(s)	Date of Entry into Force, Other Details
Australia	2005
Bahrain	2006
CAFTA (or CAFTA-DR) (US-Central American Free Trade Agreement-Dominican Republic, popularly known as CAFTA): Costa Rica, El Salvador, Guatemala, Honduras, Nicaragua, Dominican Republic	2006 for El Salvador, Guatemala, Honduras, and Nicaragua. 2007 for the Dominican Republic. 2009 for Costa Rica. Negotiations ended in 2004 with congressional passage in the US in 2005. The agreement was supposed to enter into force on January 1, 2006, but was delayed because member countries had not passed implementing legislation acceptable to the US.
Chile	2004
Israel*	1985
Jordan*	2001. First US FTA with environmental provisions in main text of the agreement.
Morocco	2006
NAFTA (North American Free Trade Agreement): Canada and Mexico	1994. The US already had an FTA with Canada, which was signed in 1988. The controversial NAFTA included side negotiations on labor and the environment, resulting in supplemental chapters on labor and the environment.

Oman

2009. Approximately three years from the signing until passage and implementation.

Peru

2009. This FTA included the "enhanced labor and environmental standards" agreed upon by the Bush administration and congressional Democrats (the so-called May 10, 2007, agreement). This led to congressional approval in late 2007. The delay between approval and the agreement entering into force was due to Peruvian law having to meet agreed-upon standards regarding the environment and labor laws. Before implementation, Peru had to change labor and environmental standards sufficiently to gain certification from President Bush that it was meeting agreed-upon standards. Peru rushed regulatory changes to achieve certification in Bush's final week in office.

Singapore

2004

Source: US Department of Commerce, International Trade Administration, http://www.export.gov; US Department of Commerce, Trade Information Center, http://www.ita.doc.gov/td/tic/fta/ (March 3, 2005); Office of the United States Trade Representative (USTR), "Statement of US Trade Representative Susan C. Schwab Regarding Entry into Force of the US-Oman Free Trade Agreement," *USTR News*, December 29, 2008, www.ustr.gov; and "US, Peru Wrap Up Trade Pact despite Objections" *Reuters*, January 17, 2009.

*The US also has a Qualified Industrial Zone (QIZ) with Israel, Jordan, and Egypt that extends the preferential agreement to the US market to Palestinians in the Gaza Strip and West Bank.

Table C.2. US FTAs: Completed Negotiations, but Not Yet in Force

Agreement Partner and Agreement Name	Agreement Developments, Status, and Other Details
Colombia (US-Colombia FTA)	Negotiations began in 2004; the agreement was signed in 2006 and ratified by Colombia in 2007. As of May 2009, no US congressional approval. In 2008, the US Congress agreed to extend duty-free entry for most Colombian goods, pending a vote on the US-Colombia FTA. After the US-Colombia FTA was signed, congressional pressure led to the May 10, 2007, agreement between the Bush administration and congressional Democrats calling for revision to bolster environmental and labor provisions in exchange for passage of the US-Colombia FTA. In June 2007 the US-Colombia FTA was revised to include provisions on the environment and labor, ratified by Colombia in October 2007. Congressional Democrats continued their skepticism toward sufficient labor rights in Colombia, citing violence against labor activists, and thus have not approved the agreement.
Panama (US-Panama Trade Promotion Agreement)	Negotiations ran from 2004 to 2007, with the agreement signed in 2007 and ratified in Panama in 2007. As of March 2010, no passage in US Congress. Ratification held up in the US over concerns regarding Panamanian labor practices and health and safety standards on US exports to Panama.
South Korea KORUS FTA (Korea-US FTA)	Negotiations began in 2006, and an agreement was signed in 2007. This is the largest bilateral FTA (in economic terms) the US has negotiated since NAFTA. Sticking points to ratification have been the treatment of the Kaesong Industrial Complex—in which South Korean companies have set up production in Kaesong, North Korea, using cheap North Korean labor—and auto and beef trade. No congressional passage as of March 2010.

Source: Bridges Trade BioRes 6 (4) (March 3, 2006); Office of the United States Trade Representative (USTR), "Dates You Need to Know," April 2008; "US, South Korea to Launch Talks on Free-Trade Accord," *Associated Press*, February 2, 2006; Marcus Noland, "How North Korea Funds Its Regime" (testimony before the Subcommittee on Federal Financial Management, Government Information and International Security, Committee on Homeland Security and Governmental Affairs, US Senate, April 25, 2006); and "Freedom for Some Koreans," *Wall Street Journal*, May 2, 2006.
Note: According to the *Economist Intelligence Unit*, the two Koreas plan for the Kaesong Industrial Complex to eventually include 25 South Korean companies. See "South Korea Country Report, November 2005" and Office of the United States Trade Representative (USTR), "Free Trade Agreements," undated, http://www.ustr.gov/trade-agreements/free-trade-agreements (June 1, 2009).

Abbreviations

ACC	Arab Cooperation Council
ACP	Africa, Caribbean, Pacific-EU Partnership Agreement
ACP-EU	Africa, Caribbean, Pacific-European Union Partnership Agreements
ACS	Association of Caribbean States
AD	Antidumping provisions
AEC	African Economic Community
AEC	ASEAN Economic Community
AEUA	Arab Economic Unity Agreement
AFAS	ASEAN Framework Agreement of Services
AfDB	African Development Bank
AFTA	Andean Free Trade Agreement (US-Andean FTA)
AFTA	Arab Free Trade Agreement (a.k.a. PAFTA, Pan-Arab Free Trade Agreement)
AFTA	ASEAN Free Trade Area (*see* ASEAN)
AGOA	African Growth and Opportunity Act
AL	Arab League
ALADI	*Asociación Latinoamericana de Integración* (*see* LAIA)
ALALC	Latin American Free Trade Association (LAFTA) (*see* LAIA)
ALBA	*Alianza Bolivariana para las Américas*, or *Alternativa Bolivariana para las Américas* (Bolivarian Alternative for the Americas)
AMU	Arab Maghreb Union
ANC	African National Congress (South Africa)
ANZCERTA	Australia New Zealand Closer Economic Relations Trade Agreement
APEC	Asia Pacific Economic Corporation Forum

APRM	African Peer Review Mechanism (NEPAD)
APTA	Asia-Pacific Trade Agreement (Bangkok Agreement)
ASEAN	Association of South East Asian Nations
ASEAN + 3	ASEAN Plus Three Free Trade Area
ASEAN + 3 + 3	ASEAN Plus Three Plus Three Free Trade Area
ASEAN + 6	ASEAN Plus 6, same as ASEAN + 3 + 3
ATIGA	ASEAN Trade in Goods Agreement
ATPA	Andean Trade Preference Act (United States)
ATPDEA	Andean Trade Preference and Drug Eradication Act (United States)
AU	African Union
BCEAO	*Banque Centrale des états de l'Afrique de l'ouest*
BCIE	*Banco Centroamericano de Integración Económica*
BEAC	*Banque des états de l'Afrique Centrale*
BIMSTEC	Bangladesh Bay of Bengal Initiative for Multi-Sectoral Technical and Economic Cooperation, or the Bangladesh, India, Myanmar, Sri Lanka, Thailand Economic Cooperation
BIMSTEC-FTA	Bay of Bengal Initiative for Multi-Sectoral Technical and Economic Cooperation Free Trade Agreement, or the Bangladesh, India, Myanmar, Sri Lanka, Thailand Economic Cooperation FTA
BIT	Bilateral investment treaty
BSA	Bilateral swap arrangement(s)
BSEC	Black Sea Economic Cooperation
CACEU	Central African Customs and Economic Union
CACM	Central American Common Market
CACO	Central Asian Cooperation Organization
CAEC	Central Asian Economic Union
CAEMC	Central Africa Economic and Monetary Community
CAEU	Council of Arab Economic Unity
CAFE	Corporate Average Fuel Economy Standards
CAFTA	Central American Free Trade Agreement
CAFTA-DR	Central American Free Trade Agreement
CAN	Andean Community of Nations
CAP	Common Agriculture Policy (EU)
CARICOM	Caribbean Community and Common Market
CARIFTA	Caribbean Free Trade Association
CBERA	Caribbean Basin Economic Recovery Act (United States)
CBI	Caribbean Basin Initiative (United States)
CBI	Cross-border initiative (*see* RIFF)
CBTPA	Caribbean Basin Trade Partnership Act (United States)
CCIA	COMESA Common Investment Area
CEC	Commission for Environmental Cooperation (NAFTA)
CEEAC	*Communauté Économique des États d'Afrique Centrale*

CEFTA	Central Europe Free Trade Agreement (also CEFTA 2006)
CEPA	Comprehensive economic partnership agreement
CEPGL	*Communauté économique des Pays des Grands Lacs*
CER	Closer Economic Relations Agreement (Australia and New Zealand)
CERWARN	Conflict Early Warning and Response Mechanism (IGADD)
CET	Common external tariff
CFA	Central African Franc Zone (*Franc de la Communauté Financière d'Afrique* in the WAEMU and *franc de la Coopération Financière en Afrique Centrale* for the CAEMC. Originally had been *Colonies Françaises d'Afrique* in the original French colonial post–World War II currency zone, comprising both CFA franc zones.)
CILSS	The Permanent Inter-State Committee for Drought Control in the Sahel (*Comité Permanent Inter États de lutte contre la Sécheresse dans le Sahel*)
CIS	Commonwealth of Independent States
CLC	Commission for Labor Cooperation (of NAFTA)
CMA	Common Monetary Area
CMI	Chiang Mai Initiative
COBAC	*Commission Bancaire de l'Afrique Centrale* (of CAEMC)
COMESA	Common Market for Eastern and Southern Africa
CRNM	Caribbean Regional Negotiating Machinery
CSME	Caribbean Single Market and Economy
CSN	*Comunidad sudamericana de naciones*; SCN in English, now Union of South American Nations (UNASUR) Membership
CTC	Change of tariff classification
CTM	Confederation of Mexican Workers (*Confederación de Trabajadores de México*)
CU	Customs unions
CUSFTA	Canada-United States Free Trade Agreement (Sometimes CUFTA or CFTA)
CVD	Countervailing duties
DDA	Doha Development Agenda (Doha Round)
DSB	Dispute Settlement Body (WTO)
DSM	Dispute settlement mechanism
EAEC	East Asian Economic Caucus
EAI	Enterprise for the Americas Initiative (United States)
EAS	East Asian Summit
EBA	Everything But Arms
EC	European Communities
ECB	European Central Bank
ECCAS	Economic Community of Central African States

ECCB	Eastern Caribbean Central Bank
ECCM	East Caribbean Common Market
ECCU	Eastern Caribbean Currency Union
ECE	Evaluation Committee of Experts (within NAFTA's CLC)
ECE	United Nations Economic Commission for Europe
ECHR	European Court of Human Rights
ECJ	European Court of Justice
ECLAC	United Nations Economic Commission for Latin America and the Caribbean
ECO	Economic Cooperation Organization
ECOMOG	ECOWAS Monitoring Group
ECOTA	Economic Cooperation Organization Trade Agreement
ECOWAS	Economic Community of West African States
ECSC	European Coal and Steel Community
EEA	European Economic Area
EEC	Eurasian Economic Community
EFTA	European Free Trade Association
EHP	Early Harvest Program (ASEAN-India Regional Trade and Investment Area)
EMCP	ECOWAS Monetary Co-operation Programme
EMFTA	Euro-Mediterranean Free-Trade Area
EMS	European Monetary System
EP	European Parliament
EPA	Economic partnership agreements
EPL	Employment protection legislation
ERM	Exchange Rate Mechanism (also ERM II)
ESCWA	United Nations Economic and Social Commission for Western Asia
EU	European Union
FOC	Forum Officials Committee
FTA	Free trade agreement
FTAA	Free Trade Area of the Americas
FZ	Franc zone
G-3	Group of Three
GAFTA	Greater Arab Free Trade Area
GATS	General Agreement on Trade in Services
GATT	General Agreement on Tariffs and Trade
GCC	Gulf Cooperation Council
GSP	Generalized System of Preferences
GSTP	Global System of Trade Preferences
GUUAM	Georgia, Ukraine, Uzbekistan, Azerbaijan, and Moldova Organization
HCOM	Host country operational measures
HCT	High Commission territories
HIPC	Highly indebted poor countries

HS	Harmonized system
IADB	Inter-American Development Bank
IGADD	Intergovernmental Authority on Drought and Development
IIRSA	Integration of Regional Infrastructure of South America (of the UNASUR)
ILO	International Labour Organization
IMF	International Monetary Fund
IMU	Islamic Movement of Uzbekistan
IOC	Indian Ocean Commission
IORARC	Indian Ocean Rim Association for Regional Cooperation
IPE	International political economy
IPR	Intellectual property rights
ISI	Import substitution industrialization
ISLFTA	India–Sri Lanka Free Trade Agreement
JPAC	Joint Public Advisory Committee (within NAFTA's CEC)
LAC	Latin American and Caribbean
LAFTA	Latin American Free Trade Association
LAIA	Latin American Integration Association
LAS	League of Arab States
LDC	Least-Developed Countries (official UN designation, periodically changed)
LDC	Less-developed countries (loosely used term for poorer countries)
LDP	Liberal Democratic Party (Japan)
MEFTA	Middle East Free Trade Agreement
MENA	Middle East and North Africa
MEPI	Middle East Peace Initiative
MERCOSUL	*Mercado Comum do Sul* (Portuguese for Common Market of the South)
MERCOSUR	*Mercado Común del Sur* (Spanish for Common Market of the South)
MFN	Most-favored-nation (status)
MIRAB	Economies dependent upon migration, remittances, aid, and bureaucracy
MRU	Mano River Union
NAAEC	North American Agreement on Environmental Cooperation (NAFTA)
NAALC	North American Agreement on Labor Cooperation (NAFTA)
NAC	National Advisory Committee (within NAFTA's CEC)
NAFTA	North American Free Trade Agreement
NAO	National Administrative Offices (within NAFTA's CLC)
NATO	North Atlantic Treaty Organization
NEPAD	New Partnership for African Development (African Union)
NLD	National League for Democracy (Myanmar)

NTB(s)	Nontariff barrier(s)
OAU	Organization of African Unity
OECD	Organization for Economic Co-operation and Development
OECS	Organization of Eastern Caribbean States
OEEC	Organization for European Economic Cooperation
OPEC	Organization of Petroleum Exporting Countries
P-4	Pacific-4 (currently the TPP, or Trans-Pacific Strategic Economic Partnership Agreement)
PACER	Pacific Agreement on Closer Economic Relations
PACPS	Pacific ACP states
PAFTA	Pan-Arab Free Trade Area
PDVSA	*Petróleos de Venezuela*
PIC	Pacific Island countries
PICTA	Pacific Island Countries Trade Agreement
PIF	Pacific Island Forum
PNG	Papua New Guinea
PTA	Preferential trade agreement
QIZ	Qualified industrial zone
QMV	Qualified majority voting (European Union)
RCD	Regional Cooperation for Development
REC	Regional Economic Cooperation (AU)
RIA	Regional investment agency
RIFF	Regional Integration Facilitation Forum
RoO	Rules of origin
RTA	Regional trade agreement
RTFP	Regional Trade Facilitation Programme (PIF)
RUF	Revolutionary United Front (Sierra Leone)
SAARC	South Asian Association for Regional Cooperation
SACU	Southern African Customs Union
SADC	Southern African Development Community
SADCC	Southern African Development Coordination Conference
SAFTA	South Asian Free Trade Area
SAPTA	SAARC Preferential Trading Arrangement
SCN	South American Community of Nations, now Union of South American Nations (UNASUR)
SCO	Shanghai Cooperation Organization
SEA	Single European Act (European Union)
SES	Single Economic Space
SICA	*Sistema de Integración Centroamericana*
SIDS	Small Island Developing States (an official UN designation)
SIS	Small Island States
SLORC	State Law and Order Restoration Council (Myanmar/Burma)
SPARTECA	South Pacific Regional Trade and Economic Cooperation Agreement

SPDC	State Peace and Development Council (Myanmar/Burma)
SPP	Security and Prosperity Partnership (of North America) (NAFTA)
SPS	Sanitary and phytosanitary measures
SWAC	Sahel and West Africa Club
TDCA	Trade and Development and Cooperation Agreement (EU-South Africa)
TEU	Treaty on the European Union
TIFA	Trade and Investment Framework Agreement
TPL	Tariff preference levels
TPP	Trans-Pacific Strategic Economic Partnership Agreement (formerly the P-4)
TPR	Trade Policy Review (WTO)
TRIMs	Agreement on Trade Related Investment Measures
TRIPS	Trade-Related Aspects of Intellectual Property Rights Agreement
TRQ	Tariff rate quota
UAE	United Arab Emirates
UAR	United Arab Republic
UDEAC	*Union Douanière et Économique de l'Afrique Centrale*
UEMOA	*Union Économique et Monétaire de l'ouest Africaine* (French for WAEMU)
UMA	*Union du Maghreb Arabe* (Maghreb Union)
UNCTAD	United Nations Conference on Trade and Development
UNECA	United Nations Economic Commission for Africa
UNESCAP	United Nations Economic and Social Commission for Asia and the Pacific
USTR	Office of the United States Trade Representative
VAT	Value-added tax
WACB	West African Central Bank
WAEMU	West Africa Economic and Monetary Union
WAEU/CEAO	West Africa Economic Union
WAMI	West African Monetary Institute (ECOWAS)
WAMZ	West African Monetary Zone (ECOWAS)
WIPO	World Intellectual Property Organization
WISA	West Indies Associated States Council of Ministers
WTO	World Trade Organization

Glossary

acquis communautaire—The entire body of EU treaties, laws, judicial rulings, regulations, directives, and norms that aspiring EU members must incorporate in order to join the EU.

Agreement on Trade-Related Aspects of Intellectual Property (TRIPS)—Part of the Uruguay Round negotiations, TRIPS brought intellectual property rights (IPRs) into the GATT/WTO for the first time in 1995.

antidumping provisions (AD)—Government barriers to "dumped" imports—which is the selling of goods at less than the cost of production or for less than they are sold in a domestic market.

cartel—A group of producers that seek to manage production levels in order to control prices. The most famous of these is the Organization of Petroleum Exporting Countries (OPEC).

common external tariff (CET)—A shared tariff rate for all **customs union** members on all trade coming into the customs union.

common market—FTA in goods, services, investment, and labor. Internal trade barriers that limit trade (or mobility) for goods, services, investment, and labor are eliminated. A single market is a more robust form of a common market in which laws and regulations that influence prices are **harmonized**.

competitive liberalization—US RTA strategy articulated by US trade representative Robert Zoellick to expand trade liberalization by granting (reciprocal) preferential access to the US market in exchange for liberalization to Washington's liking (e.g., strong protections for IPRs) in order to pressure other countries into making similar RTAs with the US. This would slowly spread liberalization and would, he argued, create more support for the stalled DDA negotiations.

comprehensive free trade agreements—FTAs that remove tariffs and other trade restrictions in goods, services, and investment.

countervailing duties (CVDs)—Increased tariffs used to offset subsidies to industries given by foreign governments.[1]

critical perspectives of globalization—Broad grouping of schools of thought that focus on the economic, environmental, and social harm that flow from capitalism/globalization. These perspectives tend to focus on the massive inequality—between and within countries—that prevails and, in their view, is perpetuated by globalization. Roots include Karl Marx, and thus critical approaches are often associated with the political left. Most critical approaches do not call for communism but do argue that the international economic structure—its markets, institutions, and laws—unfairly favor the wealthy over the poor. Feminism and green perspectives fit within this rubric. Contrast with **economic liberalism** and **economic nationalism**.

customs union (CU)—An agreement that removes tariffs and other trade restrictions, as with an FTA, but also includes the adoption of a common external tariff (CET) and harmonized trade regulations for trade coming from outside of the CU.

Doha Development Agenda (DDA)—The current "round" of WTO negotiations, launched in Doha, Qatar, in 2001.

economic cooperation agreements—Agreements in one or more economic sectors to encourage trade or investment. These may grant most-favored-nation (MFN) status or clarify trade-related rules but do not grant greater than MFN status.

economic liberalism—A school of thought that generally believes in markets and relatively little government intervention in the economy: the government's primary role should be to enforce contracts and to prevent or correct market failures. Economic liberalism stresses efficiency, innovation, property rights, comparative advantage, and free trade. Roots in Adam Smith, but the modern version includes a larger governmental role, for instance as called for by John Maynard Keynes. Contrast with **economic nationalism** and **critical perspectives of globalization**.

economic nationalism—A school of thought that calls for a more robust government intervention in the economy to ensure that production and employment are maximized and so that a nation-state can maximize its economic autonomy and security. Specifically, economic nationalists stress that comparative advantage is dynamic and that government policies can alter comparative advantage. Contrast with **economic liberalism** and **critical perspectives of globalization**.

economic union—A **common market** in which economic institutions are unified by supranational policymaking institutions to promote economic policy coordination.

European Communities (EC)—The former name of what is currently the **European Union** and the continued name for the first pillar of the EU. It is also the name still used to describe the EU in official WTO language. *See* **European Union** for more.

European Community (EC)—Forerunner to the **European Union** (EU). The European Community was established by the Treaty of Rome in 1957, although it was then known as the European Economic Community (EEC) and popularly called the Common Market. *See* **European Union** for more.

fair trade—Movement to encourage fair wages to workers, good labor conditions, and production accomplished in an environmentally sustainable way.

framework agreements—Agreements to explore or negotiate the formation of an RTA. They typically establish the scope and timing of the negotiations.[2]

free trade agreement, free trade area (FTA)—FTAs include the removal of tariffs and other trade restrictions on a comprehensive array of either goods, services, or both. FTAs are more likely to concern goods than services. FTAs do have exceptions; some have so many exceptions that they look a lot like partial-scope preferential trade agreements/sectoral preferential trade arrangements.

GATS plus—RTAs that go beyond the **General Agreement on Trade in Services (GATS)** in liberalizing trade in services. GATS minus is also used to describe RTAs that do not create as much liberalization as found in the GATS.

General Agreement on Tariffs and Trade (GATT)—Forerunner to the WTO. Technically, its provisions are still operative within the 1995-established WTO (within the WTO, GATT provisions are known GATT 1994). Established in 1948, it lowered trade barriers through a series of negotiating rounds.

General Agreement on Trade in Services (GATS)—Created by the Uruguay Round negotiations, the GATS is the WTO's agreement to lower barriers in traded services. Established in 1995, the GATS is the first time trade in services has been brought within the GATT/WTO.

Generalized System of Preferences (GSP)—Established by the UN Conference on Trade and Development (UNCTAD) in 1968, the GSP allows developed countries to give unilateral asymmetrical (i.e., not reciprocated) preferential access to their markets to developing countries. This access, better than most-favored-nation status (MFN) access, is a WTO-approved violation of the MFN principle.[3]

harmonize, harmonization (of regulations)—Conformity (or at least aligning or mutually recognizing) of domestic regulations that affect prices and availability of goods and services, for example, ensuring that differences in health and safety regulations do not prohibit trade.

import safeguards—Temporary tariff barriers to protect surges of imports that have harmed an industry.[4]

intellectual property rights (IPRs)—The "rights to control use of . . . an invention or creative work." such as patents and copyrights. The IPR owner is granted exclusive or preferential rights over the protected item so that profits go to the inventor/creator.[5] IPRs are governed by individual countries, bilateral treaties, and multilateral treaties, including the **Agreement on Trade-Related Aspects of Intellectual Property (TRIPS)**.

intergovernmental—Decision making in an RTA (or other international organization) that is negotiated between governments. Negotiations focus on what the collective policy should be. Most RTAs and international organizations are intergovernmental in the majority of their decisions. This makes it easier for individual countries to guard their autonomy/sovereignty but makes arriving at collective decisions difficult. Contrast with **supranational**.

liberalization—The reduction of government regulations that interfere with markets' functioning, that is, letting efficiency guide economic outcomes. Sometimes called rationalization.

monetary union—In its strongest form, two or more countries with a single currency and a single central bank. There are, however, less robust levels of monetary integration.

most-favored-nation status (MFN)—A GATT norm in which GATT (now WTO) members grant the lowest tariff offered to any one member to all members. Also called **nondiscrimination**.

nondiscrimination—A GATT norm in which GATT (now WTO) members grant the lowest tariff offered any one member to all members. Also called **most-favored-nation status (MFN)**.

nonreciprocal preferential trade agreements—Unilateral trade preferences given by developed countries to developing countries, typically as part of the General System of Preferences (GSP).

nontariff barrier (NTB)—Barriers to trade other than a tariff (tax) on the exported item. Examples include quotas (numerical limits), health and safety standards, environmental standards, and customs administration procedures.

partial-scope preferential trade—Also called **sectoral preferential trading arrangements**, an agreement that gives preferential tariff rates between two or more countries in a limited number of sectors.

political union—Political decisions made primarily at the supranational level.

quota—A numerical limit on an import. These are no longer allowed under WTO rules (although **tariff quotas** are allowed).

reciprocity—A GATT norm in which GATT (now WTO) members mutually lowered trade barriers through negotiations.

regional trade agreement (RTA)—Broad term covering all types of economic integration agreements that grant some level of preference beyond **MFN** for two or more countries that may or may not be within a region. Agreements that fit within the RTA grouping include **nonreciprocal preferential trade agreements, sectoral preferential trading arrangements** (a.k.a. **partial-scope preferential trade agreements), free trade agreements, customs unions, common markets, monetary unions,** and **political unions**.

RTA—*See* **regional trade agreement**.

rules of origin (RoO)—Trade provisions that determine a product's country of origin. RoO are used to determine whether a sufficient percentage of a given product was produced within a given RTA to allow the product to receive the RTA's preferential tariff rate.

safeguards—*See* **import safeguards**.

sanitary and phytosanitary measures (SPS)—Laws and regulations regarding human health, animal and plant life, and food safety. These can be a technical barrier to trade (TBT) if they favor domestic over foreign producers.[6]

sectoral preferential trading arrangements—Also called **partial-scope preferential trade agreements**, agreements that give preferential tariff rates between two or more countries in a limited number of sectors.

Singapore issues—Four issues placed on the WTO negotiating agenda at the WTO's Singapore Ministerial Meeting in 1996: investment, competition policy (e.g., antitrust), government procurement transparency, and trade facilitation (customs administration). Subsequently removed from the DDA negotiations.[7]

supranational—Decision making in an RTA (or other international organization) that is above the national government level (at least in a specific issue area). The collective decision of the RTA members is made at the RTA, not in negotiation between the RTA and its members. For example, the European Union's executive, the European Commission, issued a fine against Intel Corporation for anticompetitive practices; individual EU countries gave up direct decision making in this issue area to the EU's European Commission. This makes arriving at collective decisions easier but at the cost of some national autonomy/sovereignty. Contrast with **intergovernmental**.

tariff—A tax on a traded good. This simple definition belies the complex way they can be applied and calculated. The simplest distinction is between between import tariffs on imported goods, by far the most common, and much rarer export tariffs. Other important and common tariff distinctions include bound tariffs (the highest tariff allowed by a trade agreement for an item), nominal tariffs (the written tariff in a country's tariff schedule), and applied tariffs (the actual tariff charged, which can be lower than the bound and nominal tariffs). Typical calculations of tariffs include ad valorem (a tariff charged as a percentage of the value of the good) and specific (a tariff charging a specific amount per unit of a good).[8]

tariff quotas—A lower tariff level is granted to a specified amount of an import (within the tariff quota), and a higher tariff level is granted to imports greater than the tariff quota amount.

trade creation—The efficiency gains flowing from freer trade in an RTA: as trade barriers are removed among RTA members, inefficient domestic production is replaced by more efficient production from other RTA members.

trade diversion—Efficiency losses from RTA rules creating production patterns such that less efficient production within an RTA replaces more efficient production from outside the RTA.

Trade-Related Investment Measures Agreement (TRIMs)—Part of the Uruguay Round, TRIMs regulates investment measures that distort trade (such as export requirements for foreign investors).

trade remedies—Government steps to protect against some unfair foreign trade practices or harmful trade outcomes. Trade remedies include **antidumping provisions (AD), countervailing duties (CVDs)**, and **import safeguards**.

TRIMs—*See* **Trade-Related Investment Measures Agreement**.

TRIPS—*See* **Agreement on Trade-Related Aspects of Intellectual Property**.

TRIPS plus—RTA provisions that grant stronger **intellectual property rights (IPRs)** than found in the WTO's **TRIPS** agreement. TRIPS minus also used to describe RTAs that grant less than TRIPS levels of IPRs.

Uruguay Round—The eighth GATT "round" of negotiations (1986 to 1994) that led to the establishment of the WTO in 1995.

variable geometry or variable speed—Regional trade agreement in which members determine for themselves the degree to which they lower barriers to one another.

Notes

PREFACE

1. "An Elder Challenges Outsourcing's Orthodoxy," *New York Times*, September 9, 2004.

CHAPTER 1
INTRODUCTION TO REGIONAL
TRADE AGREEMENTS

1. The term *regional trade agreement* will be used to broadly include all types of economic integration agreements that grant some level of preference beyond MFN for their members. This includes nonreciprocal preferential trade agreements, noncomprehensive free trade agreements, free trade agreements, customs unions, common markets, monetary unions, and political unions, all of which can be between two or more countries that may or may not be within a region. These terms are explained below.

2. Jagdish Bhagwati, *Termites in the Trading System: How Preferential Agreements Undermine Free Trade* (New York: Oxford University Press, 2008), 63.

3. "Don't Confuse Treaty with FTAs: Howard," *The Age* (Australia), November 11, 2004.

4. *New York Times*, May 15, 2002.

5. "PM's Parting Shot at WTO," *The Australian*, December 2, 2004.

6. Speech at North Carolina State University, Raleigh, North Carolina, October 4, 1992, as quoted by Leon V. Sigal, "The Last Cold War Election," *Foreign Affairs*, Winter 1992–1993, 14.

7. These issues were placed upon the WTO negotiating agenda at the WTO's Singapore ministerial meeting in 1996. They were subsequently kept out of the Doha Development Agenda (DDA) negotiations at the urging of developing nations and, with the "July Agreement" of 2004, officially kept out of the DDA negotiations. WTO, "Singapore WTO Ministerial Declaration," December 13, 1996, WT/MIN/(96)/DEC, http://www.wto.org.

8. See, for instance, chapter 5 of Supachai Panitchpakdi and Mark L. Clifford, *China and the WTO: Changing China, Changing World Trade* (Singapore: John Wiley & Sons, 2002).

9. Van Whiting, "The Dynamics of Regionalization: Roadmap to an Open Future" (paper presented at a conference "The Political Economy of North American Trade," at Claremont Graduate School, Claremont, California, March 12, 1993).

10. The PIF consists of the fourteen PIC and Australia and New Zealand. Greater international clout is nowhere near as important for the latter two PIF members than the PIF's 14 PIC members.

11. The quotation and the larger point about APEC are from C. Fred Bergsten, "Plan B for World Trade: Go Regional," *Financial Times*, August 16, 2006.

12. "Divisions Hobble EU in Talks with Russia," *Wall Street Journal*, November 18–19, 2006.

13. Jason McLure, "United States of Africa," *Newsweek online,* interview with AU Commission Chairman Jean Ping, December 1, 2008, http://www.newsweek.com/id/171588 (December 3, 2008).

14. US Department of State, "Middle East Partnership Initiative," undated, http://www.mepi.state.gov/ (June 2, 2006).

15. The antiglobalization movement includes both economic structuralists/radicals, environmentalists, and various other critics of economic liberalism. For excellent introductory coverage of these schools of thought, see David N. Balaam and Michael Veseth, eds., *Introduction to International Political Economy*, 3rd ed. (Prentice Hall, 2004). For more advanced coverage, see Robert Gilpin, *The Political Economy of International Relations*, 1987; *Global Political Economy: Understanding the International Economic Order*, 2001; and *The Challenge of Global Capitalism: The World Economy in the 21st Century*, 2002, all from Princeton University Press.

16. With greater economies of scale, the per-unit cost of production goes down. For instance, building an auto assembly plant in order to produce just one car would obviously be monumentally inefficient. Assembling one hundred autos there would be more efficient—the building and machinery are already in place. Building a thousand or ten thousand cars would further decrease the per-car costs of production, and so on. There are limits to this. Eventually, the capacity of the auto plant would be reached, and a larger building or different machinery would be needed. Economies of scale is one reason why people double a recipe for cookies; besides getting to eat more cookies, the time it takes to get the ingredients out of the cupboard and clean up does not change noticeably. The cost in time per cookie decreases.

17. United Nations Economic and Social Commission for Asia and the Pacific (UNESCAP), Trade and Investment Division, "Multilateralizing Regionalism: Towards an Integrated and Outward-Oriented Asia-Pacific Economic Area" (paper presented at "Delivering on the WTO Round: A High-Level Government-Business Dialogue for Development," October 4–6, 2005, Macao, China), 8.

18. A small number of bananas are also produced in La Conchita, California, but nowhere else in the "Lower 48."

19. Robert Z. Lawrence, "Emerging Regional Arrangements: Building Blocks or Stumbling Blocks?" in *Finance and the International Economy*, vol. 5, ed. Richard O'Brien (Oxford University Press, 1991).

20. Jeffrey J. Schott, "Free Trade Agreements: Boon or Bane of the World Trading System?" in *Free Trade Agreements, US Strategies and Priorities*, ed. Jeffrey J. Schott (Washington, DC: Institute for International Economics, 2004), 12.

21. GATT Article XXIV and Article 5 of the General Agreement on Trade in Services (GATS) allow for free trade agreements and customs unions. The GATT Enabling Clause also allows developing nations to form nonreciprocal preferential trade agreements among themselves. See Bart Kerremans and Bob Switky, "Introduction," in *The Political Importance of*

Regional Trading Blocs, eds. Bart Kerremans and Bob Switky (Aldershot, England: Ashgate, 2000), 5.

22. Consultative Board to WTO Director-General Supachai Panitchpakdi, "The Future of the WTO: Addressing Institutional Challenges in the New Millennium," January 2005, WTO, http://www.wto.org.

23. WTO, *2003 Annual Report*, November 15, 2002, 11, http://www.wto.org/english/res_e/booksp_e/anrep_e/anrep03_e.pdf.

24. Roberto V. Fiorentino, Luis Verdeja, and Christelle Toqueboeuf, "The Changing Landscape of Regional Trade Agreements: 2006 Update," Regional Trade Agreements Section, Trade Policies Review Division, WTO Secretariat, *WTO Discussion Paper* no. 12 (May 2007), 1, http://www.wto.org.

25. Fiorentino et al., "The Changing Landscape," 5.

26. Fiorentino et al., "The Changing Landscape," 5.

27. Fiorentino et al., "The Changing Landscape," 3.

28. Fiorentino et al., "The Changing Landscape," 1–2.

29. Economic Commission for Africa (UNECA), "Assessing Regional Integration in Africa," *Economic Commission for Africa (UNECA) Policy Research Report*, May 2004, http://www.uneca.org/aria/.

30. Consultative Board, "Future of the WTO," paragraphs 60, 74.

31. Consultative Board, "Future of the WTO," paragraphs 60, 105.

32. Rodrigo de Rato and Paul Wolfowitz, "Time to Get Back to Business on Doha," *Le Figaro*, September 18, 2006.

33. As quoted by P. Brusick in "Special and Different Treatment of Developing Countries" (PowerPoint presentation by P. Brusick, UNCTAD Secretariat, at WTO Public Symposium, May 26, 2004), WTO, http://www.wto.org.

34. Brusick, "Special and Different." Brusick argues this to be the case for competition policy, which is but one of the Singapore issues. "Previous" refers to before the failure at the WTO's Cancún meeting to reach agreement on key points in the DDA negotiations, including competition policy.

35. Juan A. Marchetti and Martin Roy, *Opening Markets for Trade in Services, Countries and Sectors in Bilateral and WTO Negotiations* (Cambridge University Press, 2008), 82–89.

36. These exclusions are found in GATS Article I:3b and c. WTO Secretariat, "The General Agreement on Trade in Services, an Introduction," March 29, 2006 (3776.4), http://www.wto.org/english/tratop_e/serv_e/serv_e.htm; and Marchetti and Roy, *Opening Markets*, 707.

37. A more technical way of saying this is that the usage of the term *RTA* goes beyond agreements covered by the GATT/WTO's Article XXIV and the GATS. For more on this, see Kerremans and Switky, eds., *The Political Importance of Regional Trading Blocs*.

38. "Pakistan Gets Praise, But No U.S. Trade Deal," *Wall Street Journal*, May 2, 2006; and Bilateral Investment Treaty List, US Trade Compliance Center, US Department of Commerce's International Trade Administration, undated, http://tcc.export.gov/Trade_Agreements/Bilateral_Investment_Treaties/index.asp (May 25, 2006).

39. This definition draws upon Walter Goode, *Dictionary of Trade Policy Terms*, 4th ed. (Cambridge University Press/WTO, 2003).

40. "A New U.S.-ASEAN Trade Tack," Commentary in the *Wall Street Journal*, February 9, 2006.

41. It should also be noted that some TIFAs will be superseded by RTAs once the RTAs are in force. Office of the United States Trade Representative (USTR), "Trade and Investment Framework Agreements (TIFAs)," USTR, http://www.ustr.gov/ (May 25, 2006).

42. See Marc Santucci, "Free Trade and the Auto Pact" (proceedings of a seminar, Centre for Canadian-American Studies, Windsor, Ontario, February 13, 1987), in *U.S.-Canadian Trade and Technology Transfer*, ed. James Chacko (Windsor, Ontario: University of Windsor Press, 1988); Keith Acheson, "Power Steering the Canadian Automotive Industry: The 1965 Canada-USA Auto Pact and Political Exchange," *Journal of Economic Behavior and Organization* 11 (2) (1989); and David A. Lynch, "National & International Sources of American Foreign Economic Policy: The North American Free Trade Agreement (NAFTA)" (PhD diss., University of California, Santa Barbara, 1995).

43. UN Conference on Trade and Development (UNCTAD), "About GSP" and "Generalized System of Preferences, List of Beneficiaries," 2005, UNCTAD/ITCD/TSB/Misc.62/Rev.1, both from UNCTAD, http://www.unctad.org.

44. UNCTAD, "About GSP."

45. Guido Glania and Jurgen Matthes, *Multilateralism or Regionalism? Trade Policy Options for the European Union* (Brussels: Centre for European Policy Studies, 2005), 6; and Fiorentino et al.,"The Changing Landscape," 8.

46. See, for instance, Miles Kahler, "Legalization as Strategy: The Asia-Pacific Case," in *Legalization and World Politics*, eds. Judith Goldstein, Miles Kahler, Robert O. Keohane, and Anne-Marie Slaughter (MIT Press, 2001).

47. Bernhard Zangl, "Judicialization Matters! A Comparison of Dispute Settlement under GATT and the WTO," *International Studies Quarterly* (2008): 52.

48. Goldstein, Kahler, Keohane, and Slaughter, *Legalization and World Politics*, esp. 3 and 20.

49. Zangl, "Judicialization Matters!" 831.

50. Frederick M. Abbott, "NAFTA and the Legalization of World Politics: A Case Study," in *Legalization and World Politics*, eds. Judith Goldstein, Miles Kahler, Robert O. Keohane, and Anne-Marie Slaughter (MIT Press, 2001), 135–37.

51. Another example within NAFTA is that companies that have lost antidumping or countervailing duties cases may initiate a challenge using a NAFTA chapter 19 panel and may participate in the proceedings. Abbott, "NAFTA and the Legalization of World Politics," 152.

52. Gary Clyde Hufbauer and Jeffrey J. Schott, *NAFTA Revisited: Achievements and Challenges* (Washington, DC: Institute for International Economics, 2005), chapter 4.

53. See Public Citizen, "NAFTA Chapter 11 Investor-to-State Cases: Bankrupting Democracy," undated, http://www.citizen.org/publications/release.cfm?ID=7076 (June 10, 2005).

54. *Inside US Trade*, September 16, 2005.

55. UNESCAP, "Multilateralizing Regionalism," 4. Of course, if a country is not in the WTO, it may or may not receive less than MFN access to any country, including APEC members.

56. Antoni Estevadeordal and Kati Suominen, "Rules of Origin in FTAs: A World Map" (paper presented at the seminar "Regional Trade Agreements in Comparative Perspective: Latin America and the Caribbean and Asia-Pacific," organized by the Pacific Economic Cooperation Council [PECC] and the Latin America/Caribbean and Asia/Pacific Economic and Business Association [LAEBA], an initiative of the Inter-American Development Bank and the Asian Development Bank Institute, Washington, DC, April 22–23, 2003), http://www.pecc.org.

57. Lynch, "NAFTA," chapter 4; and David Lynch, "Negotiating with Goliath: Crossnational and Cross-level Interactions in NAFTA's Auto and Textile Sectors," in *The Political Importance of Regional Trading Blocs*, eds. Bob Switky and Bart Kerremans (Aldershot, England: Ashgate, 2000).

58. In fact, in the CUSFTA, TPLs were called tariff rate quotas (TRQs); the name was changed by government officials to prevent associating TRQs with a true quota, which is a numerical limit on an import. Lynch, "NAFTA," chapter 5.

59. Seven percent of the portion of the good that gives the product its "essential character" may be non-NAFTA material. Allan I. Mendelowitz, "NAFTA: Issues Related to Textile/ Apparel and Auto and Auto Parts Industries," Government Accountability Office testimony, Subcommittee on Commerce, Consumer and Monetary Affairs of the Committee on Governmental Operations, US House of Representatives, May 34, 1993), 11 (of prepared statement), 23 (of hearing proceedings), http://archive.gao.gov/d43t14/149165.pdf.

60. Pablo Sanguinetti and Eduardo Bianchi, "Implementing PTAs in the Southern Cone Region of Latin America," in *The Origin of Goods: Rules of Origin in Regional Trade Agreements*, eds. Olivier Cadot, Antoni Estevadeordal, Akiko Suwa-Eisenmann, and Thierry Verdier (Oxford University Press and the Centre for Economic Policy Research, 2006), 227.

61. For examples of such indices, see Antoni Estevadeordal and Kati Suominen, "Rules of Origin in the World Trading System" (paper for Seminar on Regional Trade Agreements & the WTO, Geneva, Switzerland, November 11, 2003), 33–35, http://www.wto.org/english/tratop_e/ region_e/sem_nov03_e/estevadeordal_paper_e.pdf; and Antoni Estevadeordal and Kati Suominen, "Mapping and Measuring Rules of Origin around the World," in *The Origin of Goods*, ed. Olivier Cadot et al., 92–98. Methodology for the indices can be found in these sources.

62. WTO, http://www.wto.org.

63. Ross Singleton, "Knowledge and Technology: The Basis of Wealth and Power," in *Introduction to International Political Economy*, eds. David N. Balaam and Michael Veseth (Pearson/Prentice Hall, 2005), 222.

64. WTO, http://www.wto.org/english/thewto_e/glossary_e/glossary_e.htm. There are numerous other types of IPRs. See the WTO's Intellectual Property (TRIPS) gateway page, http://www.wto.org/english/tratop_e/TRIPS_e/TRIPS_e.htm, and "Understanding the WTO: The Agreements; Intellectual Property: Protection and Enforcement," http://www.wto.org/ english/thewto_e/whatis_e/tif_e/agrm7_e.htm.

65. Singleton, "Knowledge and Technology," 222.

66. World Intellectual Property Organization (WIPO), "WIPO Member States," undated, http://www.wipo.int/members/en/ (May 30, 2006).

67. Laurence R. Helfer, "Regime Shifting: The TRIPS Agreement and New Dynamics of International Intellectual Property Lawmaking," *Yale Journal of International Law* 29 (1) (2004).

68. "U.S. Reaches Patent Compromise to Provide Drugs to Poor Nations," *Wall Street Journal*, August 28, 2003.

69. Marchetti and Roy, *Opening Markets*, 72. They note that this excludes notification regarding EU enlargement and counts the US-Central American Free Trade Agreement (CAFTA) as one notification.

70. Marchetti and Roy, *Opening Markets*, 72.

71. Marchetti and Roy, *Opening Markets*, xix, 1–2. Services GDP data comes from World Bank Development indicators as reported by Marchetti and Roy, with no date given for the data. As they note, "measured" services trade (measured in the balance of payments) vastly underestimates actual services trade. For instance, it does not include local sales by companies that have established a presence in that foreign market (i.e., "foreign affiliates" trade).

72. Mode four of GATS Article 1. (See more on the GATS and GATS mode in the following section.)

73. Note that the GATS does not cover all services. Air-traffic rights and services directly related to these rights are specifically excluded from the GATS. More importantly, so too are services from any sector if they are considered "supplied in the exercise of governmental authority," meaning they are supplied on a noncommercial basis and do not have competition with other suppliers. Examples of this are police, fire, mandatory social security systems, and administration of tax and customs policy. These exclusions are found in GATS Article I:3b and

c, WTO Secretariat, "The General Agreement on Trade in Services: An Introduction," March 29, 2006 (3776.4), http://www.wto.org/english/tratop_e/serv_e/serv_e.htm; and Marchetti and Roy, *Opening Markets*, 707.

74. These are found in GATS Article 1.3. WTO Secretariat, specifically "The General Agreement on Trade in Services (GATS): Objectives, Coverage and Disciplines," undated, http://www.wto.org/english/tratop_e/serv_e/gatsqa_e.htm (February 15, 2009); WTO, "GATS: An Introduction"; and Marchetti and Roy, *Opening Markets*, 708–9.

75. Marchetti and Roy, *Opening Markets*, esp. 78–82.

76. Marchetti and Roy, *Opening Markets*, 72–73.

77. Marchetti and Roy, *Opening Markets*, 89. They found GATS-style positive-list RTAs had an average score of just under 50 compared with just over 69 for NAFTA-style negative-list RTAs.

78. "Illegal" here means not consistent with WTO, RTA, or other commitments. WTO Secretariat, http://www.wto.org/english/thewto_e/glossary_e/glossary_e.htm. There are also "special safeguards" for agriculture. For more on the trade remedies, see Michael J. Trebilcock and Robert Howse, *The Regulation of International Trade*, 2nd ed. (London and New York: Routledge, 2002).

79. The RTAs studied were a geographically diverse set of most recent RTAs, all but four notified to the WTO, which account for approximately half of world trade. Robert Teh, Thomas J. Prusa, and Michele Budetta, "Trade Remedy Provisions in Regional Trade Agreements," *WTO Staff Working Paper* ERSD-2007-3, WTO Economic Research and Statistics Division.

80. This is typically done by shortening the length of the period in which AD actions may be filed or by changing the thresholds associated with initiating an AD case—increasing the dumping margin needed (the difference between the "fair" price and actual dumped price) or the dumping volume (the amount of dumping needed to trigger an initiation). Teh, Prusa, and Budetta, "Trade Remedy Provisions," 19.

81. Teh, Prusa, and Budetta, "Trade Remedy Provisions," 21.

82. Teh, Prusa, and Budetta, "Trade Remedy Provisions," 22.

83. Teh, Prusa, and Budetta, "Trade Remedy Provisions," 21–22.

84. Teh, Prusa, and Budetta, "Trade Remedy Provisions," 24–26.

85. "French Auto Aid Prompts EU Competition Inquiry," *Wall Street Journal*, February 11, 2009; and the European Commission, http://ec.europa.eu/competition/index_en.html.

CHAPTER 2
AFRICA

1. Yongzheng Yang and Sanjeev Gupta, "Regional Trade Arrangements in Africa: Past Performance and the Way Forward" (IMF working paper, February 2005, WP/05/36).

2. Paul Masson and Catherine Pattillo, "A Single Currency for Africa?" *Finance and Development* (2004), IMF, http://www.imf.org/external/pubs/ft/fandd/2004/12/pdf/masson.pdf.

3. "West Africa Opts for Currency Union," BBC, April 21, 2000, http://news.bbc.co.uk/2/hi/africa/721707.stm.

4. "Countdown to the Monetary Union," West African Monetary Institute (WAMI), February 23, 2003, http://www.wami-imao.org.

5. "What Does the Future Hold for Currency Blocs in Africa?" *IMF Survey*, August 29, 2005.

6. Masson and Pattillo, *Monetary Geography of Africa*, 2.

7. Some would add Liberia to a list of uncolonized African countries. Others do not because Liberia was dominated by American blacks who settled there.

8. "List of Landlocked Developing Countries," UN Office of the High Representative for the Least Developed Countries, Landlocked Developing Countries and Small Island Developing States, http://www.un.org/special-rep/ohrlls/lldc/list.htm.

9. Kimberly Process, http://www.kimberlyprocess.com; and European Commission, "EU & the Kimberly Process (Conflict Diamonds)," updated November 2005.

10. Ian Gary and Terry Lynn Karl, "Bottom of the Barrel: Africa's Oil Boom and the Poor," Catholic Relief Services (June 2003), 9.

11. Gary and Lynn Karl, "Bottom of the Barrel," 12.

12. Margaret C. Lee, *The Political Economy of Regionalism in Southern Africa* (Lynne Rienner and University of Cape Town Press, 2003).

13. "Country Profile: Comoros" BBC, November 17, 2005, http://news.bbc.co.uk/2/hi/africa/country_profiles/1070727.stm.

14. Stephen Ellis, "How to Rebuild Africa," *Foreign Affairs*, September/October 2005. One of the countries described here as moving toward democracy, Kenya, faced widespread political and ethnic violence in 2008.

15. "United Nations Peacekeeping Operation, Background Note: 31 August 2008," UN Department of Peacekeeping Operations, http://www.un.org/Depts/dpko/dpko/bnote.htm (November 3, 2008). These figures do not include civilian personnel or local personnel working within UN missions.

16. AGOA was amended by the Trade and Development Act of 2000 (AGOA II) and AGOA Acceleration Act of 2004 (AGOA III). Hereafter, AGOA as amended is "AGOA." AGOA, http://www.agoa.gov (March 3, 2005).

17. William Tordoff, "Regional Groupings and the Organization of African Unity," in *Government and Politics in Africa*, 4th ed. (Indiana University Press, 2002), 250–51.

18. For examples of Qaddafi's volatility, see chapter 7's section on the Arab League. His rule in Libya has included some quirky things such as repeatedly changing the calendar system and calling himself "the dean of Arab rulers, the king of kings of Africa and the imam of Muslims" at the 2009 Arab League Summit. "Gaddafi Storms Out of Arab League," BBC, March 30, 2009. There are multiple spellings for "Qaddafi." (This one is used by the *New York Times*, the *Economist*, and many others.)

19. "Country Profile: Cameroon," BBC, November 3, 2005, http://news.bbc.co.uk/2/hi/africa/country_profiles/1042937.stm.

20. Esther Pan, "Q & A: African Peacekeeping Operations," *New York Times*, December 7, 2005.

21. European Commission, "Africa and the European Union," May 2003, 7; and Masson and Pattillo, *Monetary Geography of Africa*, 2.

22. "NEPAD in Brief," NEPAD Secretariat, November 27, 2005, http://www.nepad.org.

23. Masson and Pattillo, *Monetary Geography of Africa*.

24. "Africa Economic Summit, 2005: Strategic Insight, the Agenda Review for Global Leaders," World Economic Forum (May 2005), 5, http://www.weforum.org/africa.

25. T. Ademola Oyejide, "Policies for Regional Integration in Africa," Economic Research Papers no. 62, African Development Bank, 2000; and Margaret C. Lee, *The Political Economy of Regionalism in Southern Africa* (Lynne Rienner and the University of Cape Town Press, 2003), 29.

26. Oyejide, "Policies for Regional Integration," 15.

27. Oyejide, "Policies for Regional Integration," 16.

28. Lee, *Political Economy of Regionalism*, 29.

29. "African Leaders Agree to Work toward 26-Country Trade Bloc," *Bridges Weekly Trade News Digest* 12 (36) (October 30, 2008), by the International Centre for Trade and Sustainable Development, http://www.ictsd.net/i/news/bridgesweekly/32373.

30. McLure, "United States of Africa."

31. McLure, "United States of Africa."

32. "Central African Economic and Monetary Community: Selected Issues," IMF Country Report no. 05/390, 63, November 11, 2005, http://www.imf.org/external/pubs/cat/longres. cfm?sk=18676.0.

33. Jeffrey Frankel, *Regional Trading Blocs in the World Economic System* (Washington, DC: Institute for International Economics, 1997), 274; and Jo-Ann Crawford and Robert V. Fiorentino, "The Changing Landscape of Regional Trade Agreements," *WTO Discussion Paper* no. 8, 2005.

34. "Central African Economic and Monetary Community: Selected Issues," IMF Country Report.

35. "Overview of African RTAs," South Africa Department of Foreign Affairs, February 12, 2004, http://www.dfa.gov.za/foreign/Multilateral/africa/caemc.htm.

36. "Current Peace, Peacebuilding and Crisis Prevention Operations," Center for International Peace Operations (Germany), June 2005, http://www.zif-berlin.org/en/home.html.

37. South Africa Department of Foreign Affairs, "Overview of African RTAs."

38. "CFA franc zone" means *franc de la Communauté Financière d'Afrique* in the WAEMU and *franc de la Coopération Financière en Afrique Centrale* in the CAEMC. Originally it had meant *Colonies Françaises d'Afrique* in the original French post–World War II currency zone, comprising both CFA franc zones. Masson and Pattillo, *Monetary Geography of Africa*.

39. "What Does the Future Hold for Currency Blocs in Africa?" *IMF Survey*, August 29, 2005; Masson and Pattillo, *Monetary Geography of Africa*.

40. *World Factbook* (Central Intelligence Agency, 2003).

41. Masson and Pattillo, *Monetary Geography of Africa*.

42. "Give Us Our Notes, the CFA Franc and the Euro," *Economist*, February 9, 2002.

43. Masson and Pattillo, *Monetary Geography of Africa*, 1.

44. Masson and Pattillo, *Monetary Geography of Africa*, 7.

45. Masson and Pattillo, *Monetary Geography of Africa*, 8.

46. Masson and Pattillo, "Single Currency for Africa?"

47. Masson and Pattillo, "Single Currency for Africa?"

48. Masson and Pattillo, *Monetary Geography of Africa*, 6.

49. Masson and Pattillo, *Monetary Geography of Africa*, 8.

50. Masson and Pattillo, "Single Currency for Africa?"

51. Masson and Pattillo, "Single Currency for Africa?"

52. CEN-SAD, http://www.cen-sad.org/new/index.php?option=com_content&task=view& id=173&Itemid=181 (November 23, 2008).

53. "Common Market for Eastern and Southern Africa (COMESA)," US Department of State Fact Sheet.

54. COMESA Secretariat website. Angola had been a member but suspended its membership.

55. Lee, *Political Economy of Regionalism*.

56. "Mauritius Trade Policy Review," World Trade Organization, April 2008, WT/TPR/198, 21; Lee, *Political Economy of Regionalism*; COMESA website; and Lee, *Political Economy of Regionalism*, as updated by the author.

57. *Agence France Presse*, May 21, 2001, and October 31, 2001.

58. Lee, *Political Economy of Regionalism*.

59. COMESA website.

60. *Agence France Presse*, May 21, 2001, and October 31, 2001; "Ministers Push for COMESA Customs Union," *East African Standard*, September 22, 2006; "Trade Policy Review: Madagascar," 16; and "COMESA Records Increased Trade After Customs Union," *Post* (Zambia), May 11, 2009. The latter was posted on the COMESA website.

61. "Trade Policy Review: Madagascar."

62. "Trade Policy Review: Madagascar," 16.

63. Lee, *Political Economy of Regionalism*. The COMESA secretariat agrees that there is more to be done to reduce NTBs. The WTO secretariat notes that NTBs inhibit the establishment of the CET. Specifically, COMESA-FTA members do not recognize one another's certificates of origin. "Trade Policy Review: Madagascar,"16.

64. "Trade Policy Review: Mauritius," World Trade Organization, 23.

65. Lee, *Political Economy of Regionalism*.

66. Lee, *Political Economy of Regionalism*; and "Common Market for Eastern and Southern Africa (COMESA)," US Department of State Fact Sheet.

67. Lee, *Political Economy of Regionalism*.

68. Lee, *Political Economy of Regionalism*.

69. "Tanzania Quits COMESA Trading Bloc," BBC, September 2, 2000, http://news.bbc .co.uk/2/hi/africa/908008.stm; and *Agence France Presse*, May 21, 2001.

70. "Dar Forum Divided on COMESA," *Daily News* (Tanzania), July 13, 2006; and "Business Sector Offers to Pay Government's COMESA Subscription," IPP Media, July 13, 2006, http://www.ippmedia.com.

71. Lee, *Political Economy of Regionalism*.

72. "Trade Policy Review: Madagascar," World Trade Organization, 15.

73. "Common Market for Eastern and Southern Africa (COMESA)," US Department of State Fact Sheet.

74. East Africa Community, http://www.eac.int.

75. "East Africa Trade Pact Gets Date," BBC, June 11, 2004, http://news.bbc.co.uk/2/hi/ business/3798439.stm; "East Africa Trade Accord Launched," BBC, January 1, 2005, http:// news.bbc.co.uk/2/hi/africa/4139635.stm; and "East Africa Living Encyclopedia," University of Pennsylvania African Studies Center, undated (December 16, 2005).

76. Yang and Gupta, "Regional Trade Arrangements in Africa," 24.

77. Various other arrangements—including one dating to 1917—can also be considered forerunners to the EAC. "EAC History," EAC, 2004, http://www.eac.int/ (December 16, 2005).

78. EAC, http://www.eac.int; and COMESA, http://www.comesa.int/.

79. "Kenya-Uganda Row Mars Trade Pact," BBC, September 5, 2005, http://news.bbc .co.uk/2/hi/africa/4216610.stm.

80. Masson and Pattillo, *Monetary Geography of Africa*, 2. The East African Currency Board operated from 1919 to 1972, although the board closed its offices in Kenya, Tanzania, and Uganda when these countries each established central banks. See Wambui Mwangi, "The Order of Money: Colonialism and the East African Currency Board" (PhD diss., University of Pennsylvania, 2003), 17.

81. *Agence France Presse*, November 30, 2001, and March 25, 2002; and "East Africa Trade Accord Launched," BBC, January 1, 2005, http://news.bbc.co.uk/2/hi/africa/4139635.stm.

82. "East Africa Trade Accord Launched."

83. "Two Months After Customs Union Started, Bottlenecks Still Plague Regional Trade," *Daily Monitor* (Uganda), March 2, 2010, http://www.monitor.co.ug/Business/

Business%20Power/-/688616/871502/-/l3uvx4/-/index.html; and "Cross-Border Trade Gains as Union Lifts Barriers," *Standard* (Kenya), January 26, 2010, http://www.standardmedia. co.ke/InsidePage.php?id=2000001678&catid=457&a=1.

84. "Kenya-Uganda Row Mars Trade Pact," BBC, September 5, 2005, http://news.bbc. co.uk/2/hi/africa/4216610.stm.

85. Todd J. Moss, *African Development: Making Sense of the Issues and Actors* (Boulder, CO: Lynne Rienner, 2007), 195.

86. EAC, http://www.eac.int/ and "East African Trade Policy Review," WTO Secretariat Report, September 20, 2006, WT/TPR/171, 3.

87. South Africa Department of Foreign Affairs, "Overview of African RTAs."

88. South Africa Department of Foreign Affairs, "Overview of African RTAs."

89. "Profile: Economic Community of Central African States (ECCAS-CEEAC)," African Union Secretariat, undated, http://www.africa-union.org/root/au/recs/eccas.htm (January 22, 2006).

90. "Congo: Peace at Last?" *Economist*, February 2, 2008 and "Rwanda Arrests Congo Rebel Leader," BBC, January 23, 2009, http://news.bbc.co.uk/2/hi/7846339.stm.

91. "Great Lakes: Ministers Move to Revive Economic Cooperation," IRIN (UN Office for the Coordination of Humanitarian Affairs), July 12, 2004, http://www.irinnews.org/print .asp?ReportID=42116.

92. "Mali Trade Policy Review," WTO Secretariat, May 24, 2004, WT/TPR/133.

93. "New ECOWAS Economic Tariff Takes Effect," *Tide* (Nigeria), October 3, 2005.

94. "Ghana Trade Policy Review," WTO Secretariat, January 2008, WT/TPR/S/194, 15.

95. "Mali Trade Policy Review," 20.

96. "Ghana Trade Policy Review," 15.

97. All but one of the non-WAEMU ECOWAS members pledged to create the WAMZ. Liberia was interested but has not officially agreed to WAMZ. The remaining non-WAEMU ECOWAS members are Gambia, Ghana, Guinea, Nigeria, and Sierra Leone. "Market Integration Programme," ECOWAS Secretariat, http://www.sec.ecowas.int/sitecedeao/english/ achievements-1.htm (November 19, 2008); and "Ghana Trade Policy Review," 16.

98. "Countdown to the Monetary Union," West African Monetary Institute (WAMI), February 23, 2003, http://www.wami-imao.org.

99. "West African Economic and Monetary Union: Recent Economic Developments and Regional Policy Issues," *IMF Country Report* no. 03/07 (March 2003), 5.

100. "What Does the Future Hold for Currency Blocs in Africa?" *IMF Survey* (August 29, 2005).

101. "Ghana Trade Policy Review," 16; and "ECOWAS Sets New Date for WAMZ Monetary Union," GhanaWeb, June 24, 2009, http://www.ghanaweb.com/GhanaHomePage/ economy/artikel.php?ID=164263.

102. "ECOWAS Sets New Date."

103. "Ghana Trade Policy Review," 15.

104. "A Continuing Abomination," *Economist*, November 1, 2008.

105. "ECOWAS Secretariat Briefs the Press," *Concord Times* (Sierra Leone), September 14, 2005.

106. "Economic Community of West African States, ECOWAS," US Department of State Fact Sheet, November 22, 2002.

107. "ECOWAS," US Department of State.

108. Esther Pan, "Q & A: African Peacekeeping Operations," *New York Times*, December 7, 2005.

109. "ECOWAS," US Department of State; "Profile: ECOMOG," BBC, June 17, 2004, http:// news.bbc.co.uk/2/hi/africa/country_profiles/2364029.stm; and Moss, *African Development*, 197.

110. On the latter point, see Moss, *African Development*, 197.

111. Nelson O. Magbagbeola, "The Quest for a West Africa Monetary Union: Implementation Issues, Progress and Prospects" (conference by the Council for the Development of Social Science Research in Africa, Cotonou, Benin, September 6–7, 2003), http://www.codesria .org/Links/conferences/cotonou/cotonou_papers.htm.

112. "Destitution Not Dearth," *Economist*, August 20, 2005.

113. "Ghana Powerless against Nigeria's Imports Ban," *Ghana News Agency*, September 13, 2005.

114. "Military 'Seizes Power' in Guinea," BBC, December 23, 2008, http://news.bbc .co.uk/2/hi/africa/7796902.stm; and "West African Bloc Suspends Guinea," BBC, January 10, 2009, http://news.bbc.co.uk/2/hi/africa/7822167.stm.

115. "And Still They Starve; Mali," *Economist*, July 28, 2005.

116. "Intergovernmental Authority on Development (IGAD) Factsheet," US Department of State, July 16, 2003.

117. "IGAD Profile," Institute for Security Studies (South Africa), http://www.iss.co.za/AF/ RegOrg/unity_to_union/igadprof.htm#.

118. US Department of State, "IGAD Factsheet"; Moss, *African Development*, 198; and "IGAD Set to Become Free Trade Area in 2009—Chief," *East African Business Week* (Uganda), November 2, 2008.

119. "IGAD Set to Become Free Trade Area in 2009—Chief."

120. "IGAD Set to Become Free Trade Area in 2009—Chief."

121. Richard E. Mshomba, *Africa in the Global Economy* (Boulder, CO: Lynne Rienner, 2000), 195–96.

122. "IGAD Set to Become Free Trade Area in 2009—Chief."

123. Indian Ocean Commission Secretariat, http://www.coi-info.org; "Indian Ocean Secretariat," *Courier ACP-EU*; and Donald Sparks, "Indian Ocean Region," in *Oxford Companion to Politics of the World*, 2nd ed., ed. Joel Krieger (Oxford University Press, 2001), 388–90.

124. "Indian Ocean Commission: Regional Solidarity in the Face of Globalisation," *Courier ACP-EU*, November–December 2003, http://www.europa.eu.int/comm/development/body/ publications/courier/courier201/pdf/en_018.pdf.

125. Sparks, "Indian Ocean Region," 388–90.

126. "Indian Ocean Rim Association for Regional Cooperation," Australian Government Department of Foreign Affairs and Trade, undated, http://www.dfat.gov.au/trade/iorarc (January 1, 2006).

127. Mshomba, "Africa in the Global Economy," 177.

128. Moss, *African Development*, 198.

129. CILSS, http://www.cilss.bf/htm/mandat.htm (November 23, 2008); and OECD, "Framework for Cooperation between CILSS and SWAC," October 2006, http://www.oecd .org/dataoecd/15/22/38460920.pdf (November 23, 2008).

130. Nicolas Gorjestani, "Africa Cross Border Initiative: Trade and Investment Facilitation," *World Bank Info Brief* 58 (2000); and Henri Mutai, "The Regional Integration Facilitation Forum: A Simple Answer to a Complicated Problem?" Trade Law Centre for Southern Africa, 2003, http://www.tralac.org/pdf/WP3_2003.pdf.

131. Jose Fajgenbaum, Robert Sharer, Kamau Thugge, and Hema DeZoysa, "The Cross-Border Initiative in Eastern and Southern Africa," International Monetary Fund, July 14, 1999, http://www.imf.org/external/np/cross/INDEX.HTM.

132. Gorjestani, "Africa Cross Border Initiative."

133. Nicolas Gorjestani, "Cross-Border Initiative in Eastern and Southern Africa: Regional Integration by Emergence," *World Bank Findings* no. 166, September 2000.

134. Gorjestani, "Africa Cross Border Initiative."

135. Lee, *Political Economy of Regionalism*.

136. Lee, *Political Economy of Regionalism.*
137. Lee, *Political Economy of Regionalism,* 74.
138. Lee, *Political Economy of Regionalism,* 75.
139. Frankel, *Regional Trading Blocs,* 270.
140. Mshomba, *Africa in the Global Economy,* 177.
141. Frankel, *Regional Trading Blocs,* 270.
142. The Seychelles joined the SADC but pulled out in 2003 for financial reasons. Madagascar became an SADC member in 2005, bringing SADC membership back up to 14. SADC, http://www.sadc.int/index.php?action=a1001&page_id=about_corp_profile.
143. In 2000, SADC Trade Protocol members also adopted and entered into force an amendment protocol to the SADC Trade Protocol. Hereafter, no distinction will be made between the amended and original SADC Trade Protocol. "Factual Presentation: Protocol on Trade in the Southern African Development Community (SADC)," Committee on Regional Trade Agreements, WTO Secretariat, March 12, 2007, WT/REG176/4, 5.
144. "Protocol on Trade," 5.
145. SADC, http://www.sadc.int/index.php?action=a1001&page_id=about_corp_profile.
146. Mshomba, "Africa in the Global Economy," 187; and Lee, *Political Economy of Regionalism,* 44.
147. Lee, *Political Economy of Regionalism,* 44.
148. Lee, *Political Economy of Regionalism,* 45.
149. Mshomba, "Africa in the Global Economy," 187.
150. Lee, *Political Economy of Regionalism,* 47.
151. Lee, *Political Economy of Regionalism,* 48–49.
152. Lee, *Political Economy of Regionalism,* 48–49; and Mshomba, "Africa in the Global Economy," 187.
153. Lee, *Political Economy of Regionalism,* 63.
154. Lee, *Political Economy of Regionalism,* 62.
155. Masson and Pattillo, "Single Currency for Africa?"; and WTO, "Madagascar Trade Policy Review," 17.
156. "Assessing Regional Integration in Africa," United Nations Economic Commission for Africa, 2004, http://www.uneca.org, 30.
157. "Protocol on Trade," 6.
158. "Protocol on Trade," 10–11. This is using a simple average (not weighted for the volume of trade) counting each SADC member equally except SACU members, which are together counted as one member for this measurement.
159. "Protocol on Trade." Most CTC require change at the tariff heading level (four-digit), with some at the subheading level (six-digit). The HS is a way to classify products in a standardized way to facilitate the administration of trade moving across borders and ensure uniformity in customs administration. See Trebilcock and Howse, "Regulation of International Trade," 127.
160. "Protocol on Trade," 17.
161. "Protocol on Trade," 19.
162. "Protocol on Trade," 23.
163. OECD, "Framework."
164. OECD, "Sahel and West Africa Club," undated, http://www.oecd.org/document/62/0,3343,en_38233741_38242551_38257982_1_1_1_1,00.html (December 2005).
165. South Africa Department of Foreign Affairs, "West African Economic and Monetary Union (WAEMU)/*Union Économique et Monétaire de l'ouest Africaine (UEMOA)*" February 12, 2004, http://www.dfa.gov.za/foreign/Multilateral/africa/waemu.htm.
166. "Mali Trade Policy Review."
167. "Mali Trade Policy Review," 22–23.

CHAPTER 3
THE AMERICAS

1. For more on ISI, see "The Context of Economic Integration in South America: Statism, Economic Liberalism, and Its Critics," in this chapter.

2. APEC began in 1989 but was not seen as a vehicle for economic integration until President Clinton's 1993 call for APEC to be central to US trade policy in the Pacific Rim.

3. Jeffrey Schott, "Does the FTAA Have a Future?" Institute of International Economics, 2005, http://www.iie.com/publications/papers/schott1105.pdf.

4. Schott, "Does the FTAA Have a Future?"

5. Stephen Cohen, Joel Paul, and Robert Blecker, *Fundamentals of US Foreign Trade Policy: Economics, Politics, Laws, and Issues* (Boulder, CO: Westview, 1996), 224–25.

6. Trade remedies include antidumping and countervailing duties. See chapter 1 and the glossary for more detail.

7. Initially this was known as the South American Community of Nations (SCN).

8. FARC stands for *Fuerzas Armadas Revolucionarias de Colombia*, or the Revolutionary Armed Forces of Colombia, a Marxist guerrilla organization that has been fighting Colombia's government since 1964. See http://www.globalsecurity.org or "Profiles: Colombia's Armed Groups," BBC, November 19, 2007, http://news.bbc.co.uk/2/hi/americas/4528631.stm.

9. Fernando Henrique Cardoso and Enzo Faletto, *Dependency and Development in Latin America* (University of California Press, 1979). This was an update of the original 1971 work, *Dependencia y desarrollo en América Latina*.

10. "Chávez Claims Victory at Americas Summit," *New York Times*, November 8, 2005.

11. "A Storm Brews," *Economist*, April 3, 2008.

12. "Chávez' Oil-Fueled Revolution," *Business Week*, October 10, 2005.

13. "Uncle Sam Visits His Restive Neighbors," *Economist*, November 3, 2005.

14. "Chávez' Oil-Fueled Revolution."

15. "Chávez' Oil-Fueled Revolution."

16. ACS, http://www.acs-aec.org/.

17. "Country Profile: Haiti," BBC, http://news.bbc.co.uk/2/hi/americas/1202857.stm.

18. CIA, *2005 World Factbook*, as measured by PPP; the data is for 2004. www.cia.gov/cia/publications/factbook/rankorder/2004rank.html.

19. United Nations Population Fund, *State of the World Population 2005*, 111–14.

20. "Haiti Clashes Mar Dominican Talks," BBC, December 13, 2005, http://news.bbc.co.uk/2/hi/americas/4523294.stm.

21. "OECD's Project on Harmful Tax Practices: 2004 Progress Report," OECD, http://www.oecd.org/dataoecd/60/33/30901115.pdf.

22. "Monaco: Tax Haven and Playground," BBC, April 6, 2005, http://news.bbc.co.uk/2/hi/business/4416075.stm. As of May 2009, there were no countries listed as uncooperative tax havens.

23. "Economic Partnership Agreements: EU and Caribbean Region Launch Third Phase of Negotiations," *European Commission News*, September 28, 2005, http://www.europa.eu.int/comm/issues/bilateral/regional/acp/pr28095_en.htm.

24. "European Commission Disappointed with WTO Arbitrators' Ruling against Proposed Banana Import Tariff," European Commission news release, October 27, 2005, http://europa.eu/rapid/pressReleasesAction.do?reference=IP/05/1359&format=HTML&aged=0&language=EN&guiLanguage=en.

25. "Caribbean Basin Initiative," Office of the United States Trade Representative, USTR website, undated (March 15, 2010).

26. Eamon Courtney, former foreign trade minister from Belize, as quoted in "Region Seeks Fair WTO Hearing," BBC, November 11, 2005, http://www.bbc.co.uk/caribbean/news/story/2005/11/051111_wto-special.shtml.

27. 1962 is sometimes given as the date. The sanctions were instituted in 1961 and made tougher in 1962.

28. *New York Times*, February 21, 1997.

29. "Trade with Cuba Steadily Rising," CBS News, November 4, 2005, http://www.cbs news.com/stories/2005/11/04/politics/main1009953.shtml?tag=mncol;lst;1.

30. "Overwhelming UN Vote against US Blockade of Cuba," *New York Times*, November 8, 2005.

31. Keen Haynes, *A History of Latin America*, 6th ed. (Boston: Houghton Mifflin, 2000), 98, 457–59.

32. It was also known as the Central American Union. "Central American Federation," *Columbia Encyclopedia*, 6th ed. (New York: Columbia University Press, 2001–2005).

33. "Central American Federation."

34. "Honduras," Library of Congress Country Studies Index, http://countrystudies.us/.

35. "Cooperation in Central America," *New York Times*, October 13, 2005.

36. Inter-American Development Bank (IADB), *Beyond Borders: The New Regionalism in Latin America: Economic and Social Progress in Latin America* (Inter-American Development Bank, 2008), http://www.iadb.org/iadbstrore 28.

37. "Andean Community," in *Guide to Latin American and Caribbean Integration* (Latin American Economic System [SELA], 1999).

38. Inter-American Development Bank (IADB), *Beyond Borders*, 28.

39. *Europa Directory of International Organizations*, 4th ed. (London and New York: Europa Publications 2002), 220; IADB, *Beyond Borders*, 28; and "Andean Community."

40. IADB, *Beyond Borders*, 28; and *Europa Directory of International Organizations*, 221.

41. *Europa Directory of International Organizations*, 221.

42. Organization of American States Foreign Trade Information System (SICE), *Trade and Integration Arrangements in the Americas: An Analytical Compendium*, June 10, 1996.

43. "Peru Fully Incorporated into the Andean Free Trade Area," Andean Community press release, January 10, 2006, http://www.comunidadandina.org/ingles/press/np10-1-06.htm; *Europa Directory of International Organizations*, 221; and IADB, *Beyond Borders*, 28.

44. "Electoral Uncertainties," *Economist*, October 1, 2005.

45. "Americas: Border Dispute Ends with Treaty"; BBC, October 24, 1998, http://news.bbc.co.uk/2/hi/americas/200348.stm; and "Americas: Peru and Ecuador Sign Border Treaty," BBC, October 27, 1998, http://news.bbc.co.uk/2/hi/americas/201442.stm.

46. "Andean Community."

47. Office of the United States Trade Representative (USTR), "Andean Trade Preference Act," undated, "New Andean Trade Benefits," September 25, 2005, and "Second Report to Congress on the Operation of the Andean Trade Preference Act as Amended," April 30, 2005, http://www.ustr.gov/Trade_Development/Preference_Programs/ATPA/Section_Index.html (November 17, 2005).

48. Jacqueline Ann Braveboy-Wagner, "English-Speaking Caribbean," in *Oxford Companion to Politics of the World*, 2nd ed., ed. Joel Krieger (Oxford University Press, 2001), 243–45.

49. ACS Secretariat, http://www.acs-aec.org/.

50. "Association of Caribbean States," in *Guide to Latin American and Caribbean Integration* (Latin American Economic System [SELA], 1999).

51. ALBA voted last summer to change its name to the Bolivarian Alliance for the Americas (*Alianza Bolivariana para las Américas*), or more formally, the Bolivarian Alliance for the Peoples of the Americas (*Alianza Bolivariana Para Los Pueblos de Nuestra Américas*) but will still be known as ALBA. "New ALBA Trading Currency Dawns at Bolivia Summit," Americas Society and the Council of the Americas website, October 16, 2009, http://www.as-coa.org/article.php?id=1948 and ALBA-TCP Portal (March 15, 2010) http://www.alianzabolivariana.org/index.php.

52. "Ecuador Joins ALBA This Week, Announced President Chávez," MercoPress, June 22, 2009, http://en.mercopress.com/2009/06/22/ecuador-joins-alba-this-week-announced-president-chavez.

53. "Zelaya Plays the Chávez Card," *Economist*, November 1, 2008; "Honduran Congress Votes to Leave ALBA," January 13, 2010, bilaterals.org, http://www.bilaterals.org/article.php3?id_article=16597; and "El Parlamento de Honduras Ratifica Su Salida de la Alba," *El Tiempo* (Colombia), undated (March 15, 2010), http://www.eltiempo.com/mundo/latinoamerica/honduras-sale-de-la-alba_6939247-1.

54. "Leftist Trio Seals American Pact, BBC, April 29, 2006, http://news.bbc.co.uk/2/hi/americas/4959008.stm; "Caribbean Ponders Venezuela's ALBA," BBC, January 29, 2008, http://www.bbc.co.uk/caribbean/news/story/2008/01/080129_albastory.shtml; and "Is ALBA Alright for CARICOM?" BBC, February 4, 2008, http://www.bbc.co.uk/caribbean/news/story/2008/01/080125_albaforum.shtml.

55. "Zelaya Plays the Chávez Card."

56. "Proposed ALBA Currency, the Sucre Poses Dilemma for Dominica Government," Dominican.net, April 18, 2009, http://www.thedominican.net/2009/04/proposed-alba-currency-sucre-poses.html; "Caribbean Countries Against New ALBA Currency," *Antigua Sun*, October 21, 2009, http://www.antiguasunonline.com/news/local/251433-caribbean-countries-against-new-alba-currency.html; and "New ALBA Trading Currency Dawns at Bolivia Summit," Americas Society and the Council of the Americas website, October 16, 2009, http://www.as-coa.org/article.php?id=1948.

57. "Caribbean Basin Initiative," Office of the United States Trade Representative, USTR website, undated (March 15, 2010); and US Department of Commerce, "Caribbean Basin Initiative," Department of Commerce Market Access and Compliance, http://www.mac.doc.gov.CBI/webmain/intro.htm.

58. CARICOM, http://www.caricom.org/index.jsp.

59. CARICOM Secretariat, "History of the Caribbean Community," http://www.caricom.org/jsp/community/history.jsp?menu=community; and Jacqueline Ann Braveboy-Wagner, "English-Speaking Caribbean," in *Oxford Companion to Politics of the World*, 2nd ed., ed. Joel Krieger (Oxford University Press, 2001), 243–45.

60. Statement by Patrick Manning, prime minister of Trinidad and Tobago, CARICOM press release 233/2005, December 31, 2005; "Caricom Leaders Meet for Talks," "Caricom Heads Discuss CSME," BBC, July 4, 2005, http://www.bbc.co.uk/caribbean/news/story/2005/07/050704_singlemarketjagdeo.shtml; and "Six Join Caribbean Single Market," BBC, January 3, 2006, http://www.bbc.co.uk/caribbean/news/story/2006/01/060103_newcaricommembers.shtml.

61. CARICOM, http://www.caricom.org/index.jsp.

62. WTO, "Trade Policy Review, Barbados," 2008, http://www.wto.org/english/tratop_e/tpr_e/tp303_e.htm; "Heads to Re-evaluate CARICOM Single Economy Deadlines," *ZIZ* (St. Kitts), March 13, 2010, http://www.zizonline.com/news/?57119784-2219-22DB-AB44E1F9F0C43614; and CSME Unit of Trinidad and Tobago, "CARICOM Single Market and Economy," March 15, 2010, http://76.162.14.12/index.shtml.

63. Thomas A. O'Keefe, "The Role the Organization of Eastern Caribbean States (OECS) Plays within the Caribbean Common Market and Community (CARICOM) and in the Caribbean's Relationship with the World Economy" (paper delivered at the International Studies Association Annual Conference, New Orleans, February 19, 2010); International Studies Association, http://www.isanet.org/neworleans2010/isa-2010-paper-archive.html; and Mercosur Consulting Group, http://mercosurconsulting.net/mmix/index.php?blog=11.

64. Statement by Patrick Manning, CARICOM press release; "Caricom Heads Discuss CSME"; and "Six Join Caribbean Single Market."

65. Statement by Patrick Manning, CARICOM press release.

66. Caribbean Regional Negotiating Machinery, http://www.crnm.org.

67. See the discussion of Cariforum below.

68. European Commission, "The European Union, Latin America and the Caribbean," May 2002, 1.

69. Crawford and Fiorentino, "The Changing Landscape"; and "US Free Trade Agreements," US International Trade Administration, http://export.gov/fta/.

70. "Tariff Changes Have Little Effect," *Congressional Quarterly Weekly*, August 1, 2005.

71. "Bush Signs Latin Free Trade Pact," BBC, August 2, 2005, http://news.bbc.co.uk/2/hi/business/4739803.stm.

72. "Nothing's Free in This World," *Economist*, August 6, 2005.

73. Markus Rodlauer and Alfred Schipke, "Introduction and Overview," in *Central America: Global Integration and Regional Cooperation*, eds. Markus Rodlauer and Alfred Schipke (International Monetary Fund, July 2005), 3, http://www.imf.org/external/pubs/ft/op/243/index.htm.

74. Roman Macaya, "Economic and Social Consequences of an Overprotection of Intellectual Property Rights in CAFTA," National Chamber of Generic Products (Costa Rica), April 2005.

75. "'Big Pharma' vs. Generic in CAFTA Drug War," *Congressional Quarterly Weekly*, July 25, 2005.

76. "Nothing's Free in This World."

77. "Diplomacy in Latin America," testimony by Roger Noriega, Assistant US Secretary of State, Bureau of Western Hemisphere Affairs, before the Subcommittee on the Western Hemisphere Committee on International Relations, July 27, 2005, www.usinfo.state/gov/wh/Archive/2005/Jul/27-535072.html.

78. *Europa Directory of International Organizations*; SICA Secretariat, http://www.sgsica.org; and Goode, *Dictionary of Trade Policy Terms*, 316–17.

79. *2001 WTO Annual Report*, 38; and IADB, *Beyond Borders*, 28.

80. "Central American Common Market," in *Columbia Encyclopedia* (Columbia University Press, 2008).

81. IADB, *Beyond Borders*, 28.

82. "Central American Common Market."

83. "Honduras," Library of Congress Country Studies Index, http://countrystudies.us/.

84. "Honduras."

85. "Central American Common Market," in *Guide to Latin American and Caribbean Integration*.

86. IADB, *Beyond Borders*, 28.

87. IADB, *Beyond Borders*, 28.

88. IADB, *Beyond Borders*, 28; and Rodlauer and Schipke, *Central America: Global Integration and Regional Cooperation*, 3.

89. World Bank, *2005 World Development Indicators*.

90. "Gutierrez Pushes for Free Trade Talks," *Associated Press*, November 2, 2005.

91. "Uncle Sam Visits His Restive Neighbors."

92. "Name Calling Erodes Ties between Fox and Chávez," *New York Times*, November 15, 2005.

93. "Hemisphere Meeting Ends without Trade Consensus," *New York Times*, November 6, 2005.

94. Andreas Oppenheimer, "The Final Outcome of Summit: Two Americas," *Miami Herald*, November 6, 2005.

95. Goode, *Dictionary of Trade Policy Terms*, 161.

96. "Group of Three," in *Guide to Latin American and Caribbean Integration*; and "Trade Policy Review: Mexico, 2008," WTO, WT/TPR/S/195, http://www.wto.org/english/tratop_e/tpr_e/tp295_e.htm, 27. The automotive sector is due to be fully phased in by 2011.

97. ALADI, http://www.aladi.org/nsfaladi/arquitec.nsf/VSITIOWEBi/aviso_jur%EDdicoI.

98. IADB, *Beyond Borders*, 28.

99. Lia Valls Pereira, "Toward the Common Market of the South," in *MERCOSUR: Regional Integration, World Markets*, ed. Riordan Roett (Lynne Rienner, 1999), 8.

100. ALADI, http://www.aladi.org/nsfaladi/arquitec.nsf/VSITIOWEBi/aviso_jur%EDdicoI; and Goode, *Dictionary of Trade Policy Terms*, 211.

101. Lia Valls Pereira, "Toward the Common Market of the South," 8.

102. WTO Secretariat, "Brazil Trade Policy Review," March 2009, WT/TPR/S/212, http://www.wto.org/english/tratop_e/tpr_e/tp312_e.htm, 21.

103. "Mercosur Eludes Chavez as Paraguay Demurs," United Press International, January 7, 2010. Posted on bilaterals.org, http://www.bilaterals.org/article.php3?id_article=16569; "Paraguayan Senate 'Freezes' Venezuela's Mercosur Incorporation," MercoPress, December 5, 2009 http://en.mercopress.com/2009/11/30/paraguayan-senate-freezes-venezuelas-mercosur-incorporation; "The Brazilian Senate Approves the Entry of Venezuela into Mercosur," Momento 24 (Argentina), December 15, 2009, http://momento24.com/en/2009/12/15/the-brazilian-senate-approves-the-entry-of-venezuela-into-mercosur/; and "Brazil Senators Approve Venezuela Entry into Mercosur," Bloomberg, December 15, 2009, http://www.bloomberg.com/apps/news?pid=20601086&sid=aKMncefxQsq4.

104. "Improbable Allies," *Economist*, October 1, 2005.

105. "An Ominous Step: MERCOSUR and Venezuela," *Economist*, December 10, 2005.

106. IADB, *Beyond Borders*, 28.

107. Lia Valls Pereira, "Toward the Common Market of the South," 10; IADB, *Beyond Borders*, 28.

108. IADB, *Beyond Borders*, 29.

109. IADB, *Beyond Borders*, 29.

110. "An Ominous Step: MERCOSUR and Venezuela," *Economist*, December 10, 2005.

111. Roberto Bouzas, "MERCOSUR's External Trade Negotiations: Dealing with a Congested Agenda," in *MERCOSUR: Regional Integration, World Markets*, ed. Riordan Roett (Boulder, CO: Lynne Rienner, 1999).

112. Bouzas, "MERCOSUR's External Trade Negotiations."

113. "South America Trade Bloc Expands," BBC, July 8, 2004, http://news.bbc.co.uk/2/hi/americas/3878817.stm; and WTO, "Mexico Trade Policy Review," 27.

114. "South American Unity Still a Distant Dream," *Financial Times*, December 9, 2004.

115. Riordan Roett, ed., *MERCOSUR: Regional Integration, World Markets*, (Boulder, CO: Lynne Rienner, 1999), 3.

116. Lia Valls Pereira, "Toward the Common Market of the South," 16.

117. "Paper Dreams," *Economist*, October 8, 2005.

118. "Paper Dreams"; and "Paraguay Threatens to Walk Out of MERCOSUR," *Financial Times*, July 3, 2006.

119. "Improbable Allies."

120. "Improbable Allies."

121. "Paraguay Threatens to Walk Out of MERCOSUR."

122. "Improbable Allies."

123. "Improbable Allies."

124. IADB, *Beyond Borders*, 29.

125. Office of the United States Trade Representative (USTR), "Softwood Lumber," http://www.ustr.gov/World_Regions/Americas/Canada/Softwood_Lumber/Section_Index. html; "Softwood Lumber Dispute," CBC News, August 23, 2006, http://www.cbc.ca/news/ background/softwood_lumber/; and "Softwood Lumber," Foreign Affairs and International Trade Canada, http://www.dfait-maeci.gc.ca/eicb/softwood/background-en.asp.

126. Canadian perceptions of US capriciousness stem from pre-CUSFTA US antidumping procedures, which Canada felt were used as veiled protectionism, and from a number of clashes over implementation of the CUSFTA. The most prominent regarded Canadian-produced Hondas, which Canada deemed to be North American under the CUSFTA rules but the US deemed non–North American and therefore subject to a duty. One prominent Canadian negotiator called Americans "bastards" and "thugs" over the issue. Simon Reisman, as quoted in the *New York Times*, February 2, 1992.

127. Because the provincial governments have jurisdiction over labor issues and joint jurisdiction with the federal government over environmental issues, each province must be a party to the supplemental agreements in order for their provisions to apply to the provinces. It is also necessary for the provinces to seek remedy against Mexican, US, or state governments' failure to enforce their own environmental and labor laws. From the *Globe and Mail,* August 14, 1993.

128. See *Globe and Mail*, August 14, 1993.

129. The text of NAFTA's environmental and labor side agreements can be found, respectively, at http://www.cec.org/pubs_info_resources/law_treat_agree/naaec/index. cfm?varlan=english and http://www.naalc.org/naalc/naalc-full-text.htm. The CEC and CLC's websites are, respectively, http://www.cec.org/home/index.cfm?varlan=english and http:// www.naalc.org//index.cfm?page=137.

130. The CEC secretariat had approximately 25 professional staff and a $9 million annual budget in its initial years, and the CLC began with 15 professional staff (five from each NAFTA nation). CEC, *Environmental Performance Reviews, Mexico* (OECD, 1998), 183; Public Citizen, *NAFTA's Broken Promises: The Border Betrayed* (Washington, DC: Public Citizen 1996); and International Labor Rights Forum, "Faulting US Labor Laws, Mexican Unions File 'Broadest' NAFTA Labor Complaint on Washington State Apple Industry," May 27, 1998, http://www.laborrights.org/creating-a-sweatfree-world/changing-global-trade-rules/1385.

131. In the US, the NAO is part of the Labor Department's Bureau of International Labor Affairs.

132. Public Citizen, *NAFTA's Broken Promises*.

133. Office of the United States Trade Representative (USTR), *Study on the Operation and Effect of the North American Free Trade Agreement*, 1997; International Labor Rights Forum, "Faulting US Labor Laws."

134. Public Citizen, *NAFTA's Broken Promises*.

135. See Public Citizen, *NAFTA's Broken Promises*, for more on the NAC. The NAC advises the US Environmental Protection Agency on implementation of the CEC and the BECC.

John J. Audley, *Green Politics and Global Trade: NAFTA and the Future of Environmental Politics* (Washington, DC: Georgetown University Press, 1997), 125.

136. "JPAC Report to Council," Mérida, Yucatán, June 24–26, 1998.

137. Gary Clyde Hufbauer and Jeffrey J. Schott, *NAFTA: An Assessment*, rev. ed. (Washington, DC: Institute for International Economics, 1993), 160.

138. The advisory committee has 12 members: three each from labor organizations, employers, and academia. USTR, *Study on the Operation and Effect.*

139. Hufbauer and Schott, *NAFTA: An Assessment*, 161.

140. Hufbauer and Schott, *NAFTA: An Assessment*, 161.

141. Public Citizen, *NAFTA's Broken Promises.*

142. US Department of Homeland Security, "Fact Sheet: Security and Prosperity Partnership," June 27, 2005, http://www.dhs.gov/xnews/releases/press_release_0695.shtm. See also the SPP website, http://www.spp.gov/index.asp.

143. Originally from David A. Lynch, "NAFTA, 10 Years Later," in *A Global Agenda: Issues Before the 59th General Assembly of the United Nations*, 2004–2005 ed., ed. Angela Drakulich (New York: United Nations Association of the United States, 2004). Permission granted by the UNA-USA, http://www.unausa.org.

144. "Free Trade on Trial," *Economist*, December 30, 2003; and "10 Years Later, NAFTA Harvests a Stunted Crop," *Chicago Tribune*, December 14, 2003.

145. "Free Trade on Trial," *Economist*, December 30, 2003; "10 Years Later NAFTA Harvest Falls Short for Rural Mexicans," *Chicago Tribune*, December 13, 2003; and "As China Gallops, Mexico Sees Factory Jobs Slip Away," *New York Times*, September 3, 2003.

146. John Audley, Sandra Polaski, Demetrios G. Papademetriou, and Scott Vaughan, *NAFTA's Promise and Reality: Lessons from Mexico for the Hemisphere* (Carnegie Endowment for International Peace, 2003), http://www.carnegieendowment.org. For a debate on NAFTA's economic legacy, see Gary Clyde Hufbauer and Jeffrey J. Schott, "Slanting the NAFTA Story," Peterson Institute for International Economics' Realtime Economic Issues Watch, December 18, 2009, http://www.piie.com/realtime/?p=1105; and Eduardo Zepeda, Timothy Wise, and Kevin Gallagher, "Rethining Trade Policy for Development: Lessons from Mexico under NAFTA," Carnegie Endowment for Peace Policy Outlook, December 2009, http://www.carnegie endowment.org/publications/index.cfm?fa=view&id=24271.

147. OECS, http://www.oecs.org/mission.html.

148. "Draft of the New Treaty," OECS, July 14, 2009, http://www.oecs.org/; Thomas A. O'Keefe, "The Role the Organization of Eastern Caribbean States (OECS) Plays within the Caribbean Common Market and Community (CARICOM) and in the Caribbean's Relationship with the World Economy" (paper delivered at the International Studies Association Annual Conference, New Orleans, February 19, 2010), International Studies Association, http://www .isanet.org/neworleans2010/isa-2010-paper-archive.html and Mercosur Consulting Group, http://mercosurconsulting.net/mmix/index.php?blog=11.

149. Jacqueline Braveboy-Wagner, "English-Speaking Caribbean," in *Oxford Companion to Politics of the World*, 2nd ed., ed. Ed. Joel Krieger (Oxford University Press, 2001), 243–45.

150. This eventually did lead to independence for the seven states in the 1970s and 1980s: Grenada (1974), Dominica (1978), St. Lucia and St. Vincent (1979), Antigua and Barbuda (1981), and St. Kitts/Nevis (1983). The three states that did not enter into the federation gained their independence during this same era: Guyana (1966), Bahamas (1974), and Belize (1981). Braveboy-Wagner, "English-Speaking Caribbean," 243–45.

151. OECS, http://www.oecs.org/.

152. ECCB, http://www.eccb-centralbank.org/Money/index.asp; and IMF, "Eastern Caribbean Currency Union: 2005 Article IV Consultation—Staff Report and Public Information Notice

on the Executive Board Discussion on the Eastern Caribbean Currency Union," August 2005, IMF Country Report no. 05/304, http://www.imf.org/external/pubs/cat/longres.cfm?sk=18518.0.

153. European Commission, "The European Union, Latin America and the Caribbean," May 2002, 1.

154. "A Dream with Many Hurdles," BBC, December 9, 2004, http://news.bbc.co.uk/2/hi/business/4082027.stm.

155. Andean Community, "Cusco Declaration on the South American Community of Nations," December 8, 2004, http://www.communidadandina.org/ingles/document/cusco8-12-04.htm.

156. "South America Launches Trading Bloc," BBC, December 9, 2004, http://news.bbc.co.uk/2/hi/americas/4079505.stm.

157. "Country Profile: Chile," BBC, September 16, 2005, http://news.bbc.co.uk/2/hi/americas/country_profiles/1222764.stm.

158. "Chávez Accuses Colombia of Coup Conspiracy," *Associated Press*, November 2, 2005.

159. Roberto Bouzas, "MERCOSUR's External Trade Negotiations: Dealing with a Congested Agenda," in *MERCOSUR: Regional Integration, World Markets*, ed. Riordan Roett (Boulder, CO: Lynne Rienner, 1999), 84–85.

160. Bouzas, "MERCOSUR's External Trade Negotiations," 84–85.

161. "South American Unity Still a Distant Dream," *Financial Times*, December 9, 2004.

162. "A Dream with Many Hurdles."

163. "South American Unity Still a Distant Dream."

CHAPTER 4
ASIA

1. For greater depth on Asian RTAs, see *Currency and Contest in East Asia: The Great Power Politics of Financial Regionalism* (Ithaca, NY: Cornell University Press, 2009), and Ellen L. Frost, *Asia's New Regionalism* (Boulder, CO: Lynne Rienner, 2008).

2. Chalmers Johnson, *Japan: Who Governs? The Rise of the Developmental State* (New York: W. W. Norton, 1995). Don't confuse the Japanese government's role with more heavy-handed government approaches, such as the command economies of the Soviet Union or pre–Deng Xiaoping China, in which there was no private ownership and thus no capitalism, or with the mixed economy approach of Great Britain after World War II and before Margaret Thatcher, in which many industries were state run in an otherwise highly capitalist economy. See "Inside Japan Inc.," in *The Pacific Century* documentary series, Frank Gibney producer (The Pacific Basin Institute, 1992).

3. OECD, "China Could Become World's Largest Exporter by 2010," *Economic Survey of China 2005*, September 9, 2005. This counts EU countries individually, not as a bloc. Indeed, China has become the world's largest exporter of goods, but in goods and services exports, the US is the largest exporter.

4. "China Cancels Talks with Japan," BBC, December 9, 2005, http://news.bbc.co.uk/2/hi/asia-pacific/4512806.stm.

5. "South Korean Tells Japan's Leader to Stop Visiting Shrine," *New York Times*, November 19, 2005; "US Frustrated over Japan's Strained Ties," *Reuters*, November 19, 2005; and "APEC Takes Aim at Bird Flu," *Reuters*, November 19, 2005.

6. Mary Somers Heidhues, *Southeast Asia: A Concise History* (London: Thames & Hudson, 2000), 157–60.

7. "Friction on the Thai-Malay Fault Line," *Far Eastern Economic Review*, November 2005.

8. Somers Heidhues, *Southeast Asia: A Concise History*, 152.

9. "Indonesia Timeline," BBC, April 22, 2009, http://news.bbc.co.uk/1/hi/world/asia-pacific/country_profiles/1260546.stm.

10. There was some liberalization under Prime Minister Rajiv Gandhi in the 1980s, but it was far less extensive than the liberalization in and since the 1990s.

11. Somers Heidhues, *Southeast Asia: A Concise History*, 182.

12. Mari Pangestu and Sudarshan Gooptu, "New Regionalism: Options for China and East Asia," in *East Asia Integrates* (World Bank, 2003).

13. Somers Heidhues, *Southeast Asia: A Concise History*, 182.

14. "Clashes on Thai-Cambodian Border," BBC, April 3, 2009, http://news.bbc.co.uk/2/hi/asia-pacific/7980535.stm.

15. Somers Heidhues, *Southeast Asia: A Concise History*, 174–177; and "Burma Timeline," BBC, http://news.bbc.co.uk/1/hi/world/asia-pacific/1300082.stm.

16. "Profile: Aung San Suu Kyi," BBC, May 14, 2009, http://news.bbc.co.uk/1/hi/world/asia-pacific/1950505.stm; and Somers Heidhues, *Southeast Asia: A Concise History*, 174–77.

17. "Burma Timeline," BBC, May 14, 2009, http://news.bbc.co.uk/1/hi/world/asia-pacific/1300082.stm.

18. "China Cancels Talks with Japan."

19. "ASEAN and Its Free Trade Agreements," in *Bridges Asia*, May 2005, 12; and Pangestu and Gooptu, *New Regionalism*.

20. Mia Mikic, "ASEAN and Trade Integration," *UNESCAP, Trade and Investment Division Staff Working Paper* 01/09, April 8, 2009, 11.

21. Pangestu and Gooptu, *New Regionalism*. Numerous other studies concur.

22. Mikic, "ASEAN and Trade Integration," 23–24.

23. Mikic, "ASEAN and Trade Integration," 7.

24. Mikic, "ASEAN and Trade Integration," 14.

25. "ASEAN and Its Free Trade Agreements," 12.

26. "ASEAN and Its Free Trade Agreements," 12.

27. ASEAN, "ASEAN Media Statement on the Signing of the Agreement Establishing the ASEAN-Australia-New Zealand Free Trade Area," February 27, 2009, http://www.aseansec.org/.

28. "ASEAN and Its Free Trade Agreements," 12.

29. "The Japan Syndrome," *Economist*, May 12, 2007.

30. "The Japan Syndrome."

31. "ASEAN and Its Free Trade Agreements," 12.

32. "APEC Seeks Trade Talk Flexibility," BBC, November 16, 2005, http://news.bbc.co.uk/2/hi/business/4442448.stm.

33. APEC, http://www.apecsec.org.sg/apec/about_apec.html.

34. "APEC Takes Aim at Bird Flu," *Reuters*, November 19, 2005.

35. UNESCAP's forerunner was the UN Economic Commission for Asia and the Far East (ECAFE) until the UN's economic commissions were reorganized.

36. Trade in Investment Division of UNESCAP, "Facts about the Bangkok Agreement (Asia-Pacific Trade Agreement)," June 2005, and "The Asia-Pacific Trade Agreement," undated, http://www.unescap.org/tid/apta.asp (November 28, 2005).

37. UNESCAP, "Facts about the Bangkok Agreement"; and "China, India to Extend Tariff Cuts," *China Daily*, November 3, 2005.

38. "India's Current Engagements in RTAs," Indian Department of Commerce, http://www.commerce.nic.in/india_rta_main.htm; and BIMST-EC, http://www.bimstec.org.

39. "BIMSTEC Trade Meeting Begins in Dhaka with Focus on FTA," *Mizzima News*, October 10, 2005; "Long Road from BIMSTEC to BOBCOM," *Financial Express* (India), August 5, 2004; and WTO, "Trade Policy Review: Bangladesh," September 2006.

40. "India's Current Engagements in RTAs."

41. "Long Road from BIMSTEC."

42. "Manmohan Pitches for Early Conclusion of BIMSTEC Trade Pact," *The Hindu* (India), November 13, 2008.

43. "BIMSTEC Trade Negotiating Meeting Held," press release, India Ministry of Commerce and Industry, Department of Commerce, June 12, 2009, http://commerce.nic.in/pressrelease/pressrelease_detail.asp?id=2416 and "BIMSTEC Ministerial Joint Statement, Twelfth BIMSTEC Ministerial Meeting, December 2009," BIMSTEC Newsletter, December 2009, http://www.bimstec.org/Newsletter_XXXIV.pdf.

44. World Trade Organization, "Trade Policy Review, Thailand," November 2007, WT/TPR/S/191, http://www.wto.org/english/tratop_e/tpr_e/tp291_e.htm.

45. "BIMSTEC Trade Meeting Begins."

46. "India's Current Engagements in RTAs"; "Demand for Short FTA Sensitive List," *The Hindu*, July 20, 2005.

47. WTO, "Trade Policy Review, Thailand," November 2007. WT/TPR/S/191, http://www.wto.org/english/tratop_e/tpr_e/tp291_e.htm.

48. "Demand for Short FTA Sensitive List."

49. C. Randall Henning, "The Future of the Chiang Mai Initiative: An Asian Monetary Fund?" *Peterson Institute for International Economics Policy Brief*, February 2009, www.petersoninstitute.org.

50. See Henning, "The Future of the Chiang Mai Initiative."

51. Nagesh Kumar, "China-India Strategic Partnership and East Asian Integration," *Bridges Asia*, May 2005, 3.

52. "South Korean Tells Japan's Leader to Stop Visiting Shrine," *New York Times*, November 19, 2005.

53. Bernard K. Gordon, "Asia's Trade Blocs Imperil the WTO," *Far Eastern Economic Review*, November 2005.

54. "As an Asian Century Is Planned, US Power Stays in the Shadows," *New York Times*, December 13, 2005.

55. "As an Asian Century Is Planned"; and "ASEAN: Leaders Gather with Focus on Upcoming East Asia Summit," *Radio Free Europe/Radio Liberty*, December 12, 2005.

56. "East Asia Summit's Birthing Pains," *Straits Times* (Singapore), February 22, 2005.

57. "India Backs Asian Free Trade Area," BBC, December 12, 2005, http://news.bbc.co.uk/2/low/south_asia/4522154.stm; and Mohan Malik, "The East Asia Summit: More Discord Than Accord," *Yale Global Online*, December 20, 2005, http://www.yaleglobal.yale.edu.

58. Robert Broadfoot, Political and Economic Risk Consultancy, as quoted in "ASEAN: Leaders Gather," *Radio Free Europe/Radio Liberty*.

59. "Summit or Trough? The Enigma of SAARC," *Economist*, November 17, 2005.

60. "Can SAARC Come of Age?" BBC, November 11, 2005, http://news.bbc.co.uk/2/hi/south_asia/4427244.stm.

61. SAARC Secretariat press release, April 28, 2005, www.saarc-sec.org; *Dow Jones Newswires*, December 30, 2005; and WTO, "Trade Policy Review: Bangladesh."

62. "The Enigma of SAARC"; and WTO, "Trade Policy Review: Bangladesh."

63. "Can SAARC Come of Age?"

64. WTO, "Trade Policy Review: Bangladesh."

65. "The Enigma of SAARC"; "Singhing in a New Free Trade Zone," *Economic Times*, October 27, 2005.

66. "The Enigma of SAARC"; "Pak to Push for China's SAARC Membership," *Indian Express*, November 15, 2005.

67. "The Enigma of SAARC."

68. "Japan's Observer Status to SAARC," Japanese Ministry of Foreign Affairs press release, November 15, 2005.

69. "Trade Facts: United States to Negotiate Participation in Trans-Pacific Strategic Economic Partnership," Office of the United States Trade Representative (USTR), September 2008, http://www.ustr.gov; and "Trans-Pacific Strategic Economic Partnership Agreement," New Zealand Ministry of Foreign Affairs and Trade, http://www.mfat.govt.nz/Trade-and-Economic-Relations/Trade-Agreements/Trans-Pacific/index.php.

70. "Trans-Pacific Strategic Economic Partnership Agreement"; and "Bush Pushes Trans-Pacific Free Trade," *Wall Street Journal*, November 24, 2008.

CHAPTER 5
EUROPE

1. "Q & A: The Lisbon Treaty," BBC, May 6, 2009, http://news.bbc.co.uk/2/hi/europe/6901353.stm.

2. WTO, http://www.wto.org/, with population update from the CIA *World Factbook*, https://www.cia.gov/library/publications/the-world-factbook/geos/ee.html.

3. "Rendezvous in Versailles," *Economist*, January 22, 2003.

4. UN Economic Commission for Europe, "Black Sea Economic Cooperation (BSEC)," UN Economic Commission for Europe's "Regional Trade Agreements for Europe" Blog, undated, http://ecetrade.typepad.com//BSEC%20basic%20information.doc (January 3, 2006).

5. CEFTA Secretariat, http://www.cefta2006.com/ (March 16, 2010); and Borko Handjiski, Robert Lucas, Philip Martin, and Selen Sarisoy Guerin, "Enhancing Regional Trade Integration in Southeast Europe," World Bank Working Paper no. 185, January 2010.

6. Robert Teh, Thomas J. Prusa, and Michele Budetta, "Trade Remedy Provisions in Regional Trade Agreements," *WTO Staff Working Paper* ERSD-2007-3, WTO Economic Research and Statistics Division, 19.

7. Teh, Prusa, and Budetta, "Trade Remedy Provisions," 28–29.

8. Derek W. Urwin, *The Community of Europe: A History of European Integration Since 1945* (London and New York: Longman, 1991), 101–15.

9. Dick Leonard, *Economist Guide to the European Union*, 8th ed. (Bloomberg Press, 2002), 6.

10. Leonard, *Economist Guide to the European Union*, 6.

11. Urwin, *The Community of Europe*, 101–15; and Leonard, *Economist Guide to the European Union*, 6.

12. Leonard, *Economist Guide to the European Union*, 28.

13. European Commission, "Africa and the European Union," May 2003, 4.

14. European Union, "Introducing the European Union," http://europa.eu.int/institutions/index_en.htm (March, 13, 2006).

15. "What the Charter Means for the EU," *Wall Street Journal*, April 22, 2005; "Dutch Lean toward Sinking EU Charter," *Wall Street Journal*, May 19, 2005; and "Germany Approves EU Constitution," *Deutsche Welle*, May 5, 2005.

16. EU Commission, "Treaty of Lisbon," EU Commission, http://europa.eu/isbon_treaty/index_en.htm.

17. "The Treaty of Lisbon," Euractive.com, April 27, 2007, http://www.euractiv.com.

18. The procedures for codecision, the European Parliament and the EU Council jointly legislating, are complex. The EU Council has a 50-page guide for those who want more detail,

available at the EU Council's website, http://www.consilium.europa.eu/uedocs/cmsUpload/
code_EN.pdf.

19. Roger Scully, "The European Parliament," in *European Union Politics*, 2nd ed., ed.
Michelle Cini (Oxford University Press, 2007), 178–79.

20. CIA, "July 2009 Population Estimates," *World Factbook*, https://www.cia.gov/library/
publications/the-world-factbook/rankorder/2119rank.html.

21. CIA, "July 2009 Population Estimates."

22. "European Union, "European Institutions and Other Bodies, The Council of the European Union," undated, http://europa.eu/institutions/inst/council/index_en.htm (May 11, 2009);
and Jeffrey Lewis, "The Council of the European Union," in *European Union Politics*, 2nd ed.,
ed. Michelle Cini (Oxford University Press, 2007).

23. The council president can be removed by QMV also, per Article 9b of the Lisbon
Treaty.

24. Hugo Brady and Katinka Barysch, "CER Guide to the Reform Treaty," October 2007,
Centre for European Reform, http://www.cer.org.uk; and Article 9.C.9 of the Lisbon Treaty.

25. Brady and Barysch, "CER Guide to the Reform Treaty."

26. Brady and Barysch, "CER Guide to the Reform Treaty."

27. European Commission, http://ec.europa.eu/index_en.htm.

28. In technical language, acceding members must incorporate the EU's *acquis communautaire*—the entire body of EU treaties, laws, judicial rulings, regulations, directives, and norms. (*Acquis* is French for "that which has been agreed.") There are 35 chapters of *acquis* negotiations for
accession. European Commission, "How Does a Country Join the EU?" undated, http://ec.europa.
eu/enlargement/enlargement_process/accession_process/how_does_a_country_join_the_eu/
negotiations_croatia_turkey/index_en.htm (May 31, 2009); and European Commission, http://
ec.europa.eu/enlargement/the-policy/process-of-enlargement/mandate-and-framework_en.htm,
undated (May 31, 2009).

29. "Macedonia Faces Possible EU Delay," BBC, December 12, 2005, http://news.bbc.co
.uk/2/hi/europe/4522234.stm.

30. "EU Postpones Croatia Entry Talks," BBC, March 16, 2005, http://news.bbc.co.uk/2/hi/
europe/4351357.stm.

31. "Commission Delivers Opinion on Iceland's Accession Bid," European Commission Press
Release IP/10/186, February 24, 2010, http://europa.eu/rapid/pressReleasesAction.do?reference=
IP/10/186&format=HTML&aged=0&language=EN&guiLanguage=en; "Commission Gives
Green Light to Iceland's EU Bid," Euractive.com, February 25, 2010, http://www.euractiv.com/en/
enlargement/commission-gives-green-light-icelands-eu-bid-news-286007; Iceland's Preparation
for Accession to the EU—The Next Steps," European Commission, undated (February 26, 2010),
http://ec.europa.eu/enlargement/pdf/key_documents/2010/100224_next_steps.pdf; and "Key Findings of the Commission's Opinion on Iceland," European Commission press release MEMO/10/48,
February 24, 2010, http://europa.eu/rapid/pressReleasesAction.do?reference=MEMO/10/48.

32. Various *Economist* and BBC online articles.

33. *Economist*, "Caught between Two Worlds," October 10, 2005.

34. In 1997 the ERM-II began.

35. European Central Bank, "Frequently Asked Questions: EU Enlargement and Economic
and Monetary Union (EMU)," undated (March 18, 2010), http://www.ecb.eu/ecb/history/
enlargement/html/faqenlarge.en.html#l2; and "Euro in an Enlarged European Union," EU Commission, 2005, http://ec.europa.eu/economy_finance/euro/adoption/index_en.htm.

36. European Central Bank, "Your Country and the Euro," updated May 4, 2009 (March
18, 2010), http://ec.europa.eu/economy_finance/euro/countries/index_en.htm; and Reuters,
"Germany Sees Estonia on Way to Euro," January 13, 2010, http://www.reuters.com/article/
idUSLDE60C2LX20100113?type=marketsNews.

37. "Euro: New Member States Need to Step Up Efforts," *Europa Newsletter*, November 17, 2005, http://europa.eu.int/newsletter/index_en.htm; and European Commission, "Second Report on the State of Practical Preparations for the Future Enlargement of the Euro Area," press conference by Joaquín Almunia, European Commissioner for Economic and Monetary Affairs, November 4, 2005.

38. "The Farmers' Friend," *Economist*, November 3, 2005.

39. "The Farmers' Friend."

40. Justice and Home Affairs Ministry of the European Commission, "Freedom to Travel: Abolition of Internal Borders and Creation of a Single EU External Frontier," updated September 2008, http://ec.europa.eu/justice_home/fsj/freetravel/schengen/fsj_freetravel_schengen_en.htm.

41. "Passport-Free Travel in Europe, Burning Bridges," *Economist*, October 22, 2007.

42. Justice and Home Affairs Ministry of the European Commission, "Freedom to Travel."

43. "Passport-Free Travel in Europe, Burning Bridges."

CHAPTER 6
RUSSIA AND THE FORMER SOVIET REPUBLICS

1. "Poverty-Hit Armenia Yearns for Change," BBC, March 5, 2003, http://news.bbc.co.uk/2/hi/europe/2820907.stm.

2. "Regions and Territories: Nagorno-Karabakh," BBC, November 20, 2005, http://news.bbc.co.uk/2/hi/europe/country_profiles/3658938.stm; and "Turkey Edges towards Armenia Ties," BBC, April 29, 2005, http://news.bbc.co.uk/2/hi/europe/4497519.stm.

3. "Country Profile: Azerbaijan," BBC, December 14, 2005, http://news.bbc.co.uk/2/hi/europe/country_profiles/1235976.stm.

4. "Fearing Ukrainian-Style Uprising, Belarus Cracks Down," *New York Times*, October 18, 2005.

5. "Country Profile: Georgia," BBC, December 20, 2005, http://news.bbc.co.uk/2/hi/europe/country_profiles/1102477.stm.

6. "Regions and Territories: Trans-Dniester," BBC, February 12, 2009, http://news.bbc.co.uk/2/hi/europe/country_profiles/3641826.stm; and "Country Profile: Moldova," BBC, December 11, 2005, http://news.bbc.co.uk/2/hi/europe/country_profiles/3038982.stm.

7. "Country Profile: Ukraine," BBC, November 2, 2005, http://news.bbc.co.uk/2/hi/europe/country_profiles/1102303.stm.

8. Martha Brill Olcott, "The New Nations of Central Asia," in *The Successor States to the USSR*, ed. John W. Blaney (Washington, DC: CQ Press, 1995).

9. Brill Olcott, "The New Nations of Central Asia"; and "Guide to Central Asia," BBC, undated, http://news.bbc.co.uk/2/shared/spl/hi/guides/456900/456938/html/nn1page1.stm (December 1, 2005).

10. "Guide to Central Asia."

11. "Uzbekistan and America, Evicted," *Economist*, August 6, 2005; "Uzbekistan, Punishment Please," *Economist*, August 27, 2005; "Uzbekistan, a Show Trial," *Economist*, October 1, 2005; "US Told That Kyrgyz Base Will Stay Open," Associated Press, October 11, 2005; and "European Union Bars Visits by 12 Senior Uzbek Officials," *New York Times*, November 14, 2005.

12. "Uzbekistan and America, Evicted"; "Uzbekistan, Punishment Please"; "Uzbekistan, a Show Trial"; "US Told That Kyrgyz Base Will Stay Open"; and "European Union Bars Visits by 12 Senior Uzbek Officials."

13. "Guide to Central Asia."

14. "Guide to Central Asia."

15. Olcott, "The New Nations of Central Asia."

16. "Country Profile: Kyrgyzstan," BBC, December 20, 2005, http://news.bbc.co.uk/2/hi/asia-pacific/country_profiles/1296485.stm.

17. "Hanging Separately: The Heavy Costs of Non-co-operation," *Economist*, July 26, 2003.

18. Baktybek Abdrisaev, "The Russification of Kyrgyzstan," *Foreign Policy*, April 2009, http://www.foreignpolicy.com.

19. "Country Profile: Kyrgyzstan."

20. Abdrisaev, "The Russification of Kyrgyzstan."

21. Mark R. Beissinger, "Commonwealth of Independent States," in *Oxford Companion to Politics of the World*, 2nd ed., ed. Joel Krieger (Oxford University Press, 2001), 155–56.

22. "Guide to Central Asia."

23. "Guide to Central Asia."

24. *Columbia Encyclopedia*, "Commonwealth of Independent States"; and "Guide to Central Asia."

25. "Guide to Central Asia."

26. "Guide to Central Asia."

27. "Guide to Central Asia."

28. "Guide to Central Asia."

29. "Hanging Separately."

30. UN Economic Commission for Europe, "The Russia Belarus Union," UN Economic Commission for Europe's "Regional Trade Agreements in the ECE" Blog, undated, http://ecetrade.typepad.com//russie%20belarus%20union%20basic%20information.doc (January 4, 2006); and "Russia-Belarus Gas Deal Reached," BBC, December 31, 2006, http://news.bbc.co.uk/2/hi/europe/6221835.stm.

31. "Russia Joins CACO," *RFE/RL Newsline* 8 (198), Part I, October 19, 2004.

32. UN Economic Commission for Europe, "Central Asian Cooperation Organization" Blog, undated, http://ecetrade.typepad.com//Central%20Asian%20Cooperation%20Organization%20basic%20info.doc (January 4, 2006).

33. UN Economic Commission for Europe, "CACO and EEC Are Merging," UN Economic Commission for Europe's "Regional Trade Agreements in the ECE" Blog, November 2, 2005, http://ecetrade.typepad.com.

34. For more on Central Asian stability and development, see Frederick S. Starr, "A Partnership for Central Asia," *Foreign Affairs*, July/August 2005.

35. Starr, "A Partnership for Central Asia."

36. Beissinger, "Commonwealth of Independent States," 155–56.

37. Walter Goode, *Dictionary of Trade Policy Terms*, 4th ed. (Cambridge University Press/WTO, 2003), 71; and Beissinger, "Commonwealth of Independent States," 155–56.

38. Beissinger, "Commonwealth of Independent States," 155–56.

39. *Columbia Encyclopedia*, "Commonwealth of Independent States." See the discussion of the EEC in this chapter for more.

40. Sean Kay, *Global Security in the Twenty-First Century* (Lanham, MD: Rowman & Littlefield, 2006), 159; and Beissinger, "Commonwealth of Independent States," 155–56.

41. UN Economic Commission for Europe, "CACO and EEC Are Merging."

42. *Columbia Encyclopedia*, "Commonwealth of Independent States."

43. *Columbia Encyclopedia*, "Commonwealth of Independent States."

44. WTO, "Trade Policy Review, Kyrgyz Republic," October 2006, WT/TPR/S/170.

45. UN Economic Commission for Europe, "CIS System," UN Economic Commission for Europe's "Regional Trade Agreements in the ECE" Blog, undated, http://ecetrade.typepad.com/CIS%20systm.doc (January 4, 2006); and "Eurasian Economic Community," UN Economic Commission for Europe's "Regional Trade Agreements in the ECE" Blog, undated, http://ecetrade.typepad.com//Eurasian%20Economic%20Community%20Basic%20info.doc (January 4, 2006).

46. "Eurasian Economic Community," *Eurasian Home Analytical Resource*, undated, http://www.eurasianhome.org/xml/t/databases.xml?lang=en&nic=databases&intorg=3&pid=25 (June 11, 2009); "Russia Proposes to Join WTO with New Bloc," *Journal of Commerce*, June 10, 2009; and WTO, "Trade Policy Review: Kyrgyz Republic," October 9 and 11, 2006.

47. UN Economic Commission for Europe, "Eurasian Economic Community"; and Harry G. Broadman, ed., *From Disintegration to Reintegration: Eastern Europe and the Former Soviet Union in International Trade* (World Bank, 2005).

48. UN Economic Commission for Europe, "Eurasian Economic Community."

49. UN Economic Commission for Europe, "Eurasian Economic Community."

50. Broadman, *From Disintegration to Reintegration*.

51. Johannes Linn, "Central Asia Human Development Report," United Nations Development Programme, Regional Bureau for Europe and the Commonwealth of Independent States, http://europeandcis.undp.org, 56.

52. UN Economic Commission for Europe, "CACO and EEC Are Merging."

53. UN Economic Commission for Europe, "Economic Cooperation Organization (ECO)."

54. Sean Kay, *Global Security in the Twenty-First Century*, 159; and "The GUUAM Organization," UN Economic Commission for Europe's "Regional Trade Agreements for Europe" Blog, undated, http://ecetrade.typepad.com//GUUAM%20basic%20info.doc (January 3, 2006).

55. Adam Weinstein, "Russian Phoenix: The Collective Security Treaty Organization," *Whitehead Journal of Diplomacy and International Relations* (Winter–Spring 2007), http://www.journalofdiplomacy.org.

56. Andres Scheineson, "The Shanghai Cooperation Organization," Council of Foreign Relations Backgrounder, March 24, 2009, http://www.cfr.org/publication/10083/.

57. "Uzbekistan and America, Evicted"; "Uzbekistan, Punishment Please"; "Uzbekistan, a Show Trial"; "US Told That Kyrgyz Base Will Stay Open"; and "European Union Bars Visits by 12 Senior Uzbek Officials."

58. Baktybek Abdrisaev, "The Russification of Kyrgyzstan," *Foreign Policy*, April 2009, http://www.foreignpolicy.com.

59. S. Frederick Starr, as quoted by Andres Scheineson, "The Shanghai Cooperation Organization," *Council of Foreign Relations Backgrounder*, March 24, 2009, http://www.cfr.org/publication/10083/.

60. UN Economic Commission for Europe, "The Single Economic Space," UNECE's "Regional Trade Agreements in the ECE" Blog, undated, http://ecetrade.typepad.com//Single%20Economic%20Space%20Initiative%20basic%20information.doc.

61. "SES Presidents Sign Agreement on VAT," *RFE/RL Newsline* 8 (177), Part I (September 16, 2004).

62. "SES Meeting May 2004," *RFE/RL Newsline* 8 (98), Part 1 (May 25, 2004).

63. "SES Meeting May 2004." With an FTA, the VAT would change from a country of origin VAT to a country of destination VAT.

64. "SES Meeting May 2004."

65. UN Economic Commission for Europe, "Ukrainian President Visits Kazakhstan," August 25, 2005, and "SES RTA," UN Economic Commission for Europe, undated, "Regional Trade Agreements in the ECE" Blog, http://www.ecetrade.typepad.com.

66. "SES Meeting May 2004."

67. UN Economic Commission for Europe, "The Single Economic Space."

CHAPTER 7
THE MIDDLE EAST AND NORTH AFRICA

1. Mohsin S. Khan, "The GCC Monetary Union: Choice of Exchange Rate Regime," *Peterson Institute for International Economic Working Paper Series* 09-1, April 2009; and "UAE Quits Gulf Monetary Union," *Wall Street Journal*, May 21, 2009.

2. "China, GCC Agree to Start FTA Talks," *People's Daily Online*, July 7, 2004, http://english.peopledaily.com.cn/; and Jo-Ann Crawford and Robert V. Fiorentino, "The Changing Landscape of Regional Trade Agreements," *WTO Discussion Paper* no. 8, 2005.

3. Qatar had been negotiating with the US but stopped the negotiations, disliking provisions in fellow GCC members' bilateral FTAs with the US. Negotiations with the UAE stopped after the controversy of a UAE company's attempting to "buy" US ports. The US was reportedly displeased with a lack of Egyptian political reforms. "Egyptian Cotton Makers Fight to Survive," BBC, December 7, 2004, http://news.bbc.co.uk/2/hi/business/4073365.stm.

4. See, for instance, Kemal Dervi, Peter Bocock, and Julia Delvin, "Intraregional Trade among Arab Countries: Building a Competitive Economic Neighborhood" (paper presented at the Middle East Institute 52nd Annual Conference, Panel on "Arab Economic Market," Washington, DC, October 17, 1998).

5. UN Economic and Social Commission for Western Asia (ESCWA), "Analysis of Performance and Assessment of Growth and Productivity in the ESCWA Region," E/ESCWA/EAC/2004/2, January 12, 2004, 15, http://www.escwa.org.lb/information/publications/ead/docs/Ead04e2.pdf.

6. Samiha Fawzy, "The Economics and Politics of Arab Economic Integration," in *Arab Economic Integration: Between Hope and Reality*, eds. Ahmed Galal and Bernard Hoekman (Cairo and Washington, DC: Egyptian Center for Economic Studies and the Brookings Institution Press, 2003), 23–25.

7. Fawzy, "Arab Economic Integration," 23–25. Tariffs measured were "trade weighted" averages.

8. Fawzy, "Arab Economic Integration," 30.

9. "WTO General Council Successfully Adopts Saudi Arabia's Terms of Accession," WTO press release, Press/420, November 11, 2005.

10. Fawzy, "Arab Economic Integration."

11. Marcus Noland and Howard Pack, "Islam, Globalization and Economic Performance in the Middle East," *Peterson Institute for International Economics Policy Brief* 04-4, June 2004, http://www.petersoninstitute.org/publications/pb/pb04-4.pdf. Specifically, Noland and Pack argue that Arab societies, compared with those in other regions, demonstrate less willingness to close inefficient factories and a greater need to protect one's local way of life against foreign influences and are more doubtful of the desirability of society's accepting homosexuality. In short, they are averse to change. These survey questions were originally asked by the Pew Center for the People and the Press and reported in its 2003 "Views of a Changing World."

12. Fawzy, "Arab Economic Integration," 23.

13. UN Economic and Social Commission for Western Asia (ESCWA), "Analysis of Performance," 15.

14. "Conference of Arab Leaders Yields Little of Significance," *New York Times*, March 24, 2005.

15. "Conference of Arab Leaders Yields Little of Significance."

16. The criticism stemmed from Egypt's support of the Fatah faction of the Palestinian Authority, which governs the West Bank, and from Egypt's criticism of Fatah's rival, Hamas, which governs the Gaza Strip and which is supported by Qatar.

17. "Gaddafi Storms Out of Arab League," BBC, March 30, 2009.

18. African Union, "Profile: Arab Maghreb Union (AMU)," http://www.africa-union.org/root/au/recs/AMUOverview.pdf.

19. Jeffrey Frankel, *Regional Trading Blocs in the World Economic System* (Washington, DC: Institute for International Economics, 1997), 277.

20. Frankel, *Regional Trading Blocs*, 277.

21. African Union, "Profile: Arab Maghreb Union (AMU)."

22. Fawzy, "Arab Economic Integration," 30.

23. Michael Moran, "Q & A: The Arab League and Iraq," *Council on Foreign Relations*, October 10, 2005.

24. Moran, "Q & A: The Arab League and Iraq."

25. "Summits That Showcase Arab Disunity," BBC, March 23, 2005, http://news.bbc.co.uk/2/hi/middle_east/4376599.stm.

26. "Saudis and Syrians Cement Détente," BBC, March 10, 2009, http://news.bbc.co.uk/2/hi/7934607.stm; and "Wide Rifts on Show at Arab Summit," January 19, 2009, BBC, http://news.bbc.co.uk/2/hi/middle_east/7837582.stm.

27. Frankel, *Regional Trading Blocs*, 277; and CAEU, http://www.caeu.org.eg/English/Intro/.

28. Frankel, *Regional Trading Blocs*, 277; and Ahmed Galal and Bernard Hoekman, "Overview of Arab Economic Integration," in *Arab Economic Integration: Between Hope and Reality*, eds. Ahmed Galal and Bernard Hoekman (Cairo and Washington, DC: Egyptian Center for Economic Studies and the Brookings Institution Press, 2003), 3.

29. The convergence criteria include a budget deficit cap (as a percentage of GDP), an overall debt cap (as a percentage of GDP), inflation and interest rate targets, and foreign exchange reserve minimums. WTO, "Trade Policy Review: Oman," June, 2008, http://www.wto.org/english/tratop_e/tpr_e/tp301_e.htm, 16; and Khan, "The GCC Monetary Union."

30. "Profile: Gulf Co-operation Council," BBC, July 23, 2005, http://news.bbc.co.uk/2/hi/middle_east/country_profiles/4155001.stm.

31. "UAE Quits Gulf Monetary Union."

32. GCC, http://www.gccsg.org/eng/index.php; WTO, "Report of the Working Party on the Accession of the Kingdom of Saudi Arabia to the World Trade Organization," WT/ACC/SAU/61, 97; and "Profile: Gulf Co-operation Council."

33. Frankel, *Regional Trading Blocs*, 277–78.

34. Frankel, *Regional Trading Blocs*, 277–78.

35. WTO, "Report of the Working Party, Saudi Arabia," 97–98.

36. Bahrain and Oman have implemented bilateral FTAs with the US. FTA talks with Qatar and the UAE each ended unsuccessfully.

37. "Profile: Gulf Co-operation Council."

38. European Commission, "The Euro-Mediterranean Partnership," undated, http://ec.europa.eu/external_relations/euromed/index_en.htm (November 21, 2005).

39. European Commission, "The Euro-Mediterranean Partnership."

40. European Commission, "The Euro-Mediterranean Partnership."

41. European Commission, "The Euro-Mediterranean Partnership."

42. European Commission, "Commissioner Patten Attends Signature of Agadir Agreement," European Commission press release, February 24, 2004, IP/04/256, http://europa.eu.int/comm/external_relations/euromed/news/ip04_256.htm.

43. Arab League, "Declaration Pan-Arab Free Trade Area," Resolution No. 1317-P/S/ 59, February 19, 1997, www.medea.be/files/Declaration_PanArab_Free_Trade_Area.doc; Fawzy, "Arab Economic Integration," 33; and World Bank, *Trade, Investment, and Development in the Middle East and North Africa: Engaging with the World* (World Bank, August 2003), http://web.worldbank.org/WBSITE/EXTERNAL/COUNTRIES/MENAEXT/ 0,,contentMDK:20261801~pagePK:146736~piPK:146830~theSitePK:256299,00.html.

44. European Institute for Research on Mediterranean and Euro-Arab Cooperation and the World Bank, "Arab Free Trade Area (AFTA)" (European Institute for Research on Mediterranean and Euro-Arab Cooperation and the World Bank, 2003), 215, www.medea.be.

45. European Institute, "Arab Free Trade Area (AFTA)."

46. "Free Trade Zone Kicks Off Today," *Gulf Times* (Qatar), January 1, 2005; and "Arab Free Trade Zone Goes into Effect," *Yemen Observer*, January 8, 2005.

47. European Institute, "Arab Free Trade Area (AFTA)."

48. European Institute, "Arab Free Trade Area (AFTA)."

49. European Institute, "Arab Free Trade Area (AFTA)."

50. Ahmed Galal and Bernard Hoekman, "Between Hope and Reality: An Overview of Arab Economic Integration," in *Arab Economic Integration: Between Hope and Reality*, eds. Ahmed Galal and Bernard Hoekman, 5; and Fawzy, "Arab Economic Integration," 33.

51. Inter-Arab Investment Guarantee Corporation, *2004 Report* (Inter-Arab Investment Guarantee Corporation, 2005), 11–12, http://www.iaigc.org/index_e.html.

52. World Bank, *Trade, Investment, and Development in the MENA*, 215.

53. WTO, "Trade Policy Review: Oman," 17.

CHAPTER 8
THE PACIFIC ISLANDS

1. Originally from Geoff Bertram and Ray Watters, "The MIRAB Economy in South Pacific Microstates," *Pacific Viewpoints* 26, no. 3 (1985), 497–519, as quoted in Francis X. Hezel, "Is That the Best You Can Do? A Tale of Two Micronesian Economies," *Pacific Islands Policy* no. 1 (2006), 24–25.

2. "The Unpacific Pacific: Australia and the Island-States," *Economist*, August 23, 2003.

3. Pacific Islands Forum Secretariat, "PICTA and PACER Frequently Asked Questions," Pacific Islands Secretariat website, undated, http://www.forumsec.org.fj/resources/uploads/ attachments/documents/FAQs%20PICTA%20PACER.pdf (May 2005).

4. WTO, http://www.wto.org/.

5. Australian Department of Foreign Affairs and Trade, http://www.dfat.gov.au/geo/new_ zealand/anz_cer/anz_cer.html; and Australian Department of Foreign Affairs, "Guide to the CER" (1997).

6. Robert Tehe, Thomas J. Prusa, and Michele Budetta, "Trade Remedy Provisions in Regional Trade Agreements," *WTO Staff Working Paper* ERSD-2007-3, WTO Economic Research and Statistics Division, 18, 28.

7. US Department of the Interior, Office of Insular Affairs, "Definitions of Insular Area Political Organizations" and "Tariff Treatment of Imports from the Freely Associated States Under Public Law 99-239"; Hezel, "Is That the Best You Can Do?"; and Pacific Islands Secretariat, "PICTA and PACER Frequently Asked Questions."

8. "Forum: Leaders Defer Campaign on Labour Mobility," *Island Business* (Fiji), October 26, 2005.

9. "Palau Ponders End of US Gravy Train," *Marianas Variety*, February 18, 2009, http://www.mvariety.com. Hawaii also received Compact Impact money.

10. There are, of course, numerous caveats to these general rules. US Department of the Interior, Office of Insular Affairs, "Tariff Treatment of Imports—US Insular Areas, Harmonized Tariff Schedule General Note 3(a)(iv)," http://www.doi.gov/oia/.

11. "4 US Retailers Settle Saipan Labor Suit," *Los Angeles Times*, August 10, 1999.

12. "With Abramoff in Jail, Saipan Loses Its Fight," *Washington Post*, May 8, 2008.

13. Fiji Foreign Affairs and External Trade Ministry, http://www.foreignaffairs.gov.fj/.

14. "Melanesia Signs Trade Agreement with Forum," *Solomon Star News*, October 31, 2005.

15. Pacific Islands Forum Secretariat, "PICTA and PACER Frequently Asked Questions."

16. "Plan Must Be for Pacific," *Fiji Times*, August 20, 2005.

17. Goode, *Dictionary of Trade Policy Terms*, 226.

18. PIF Secretariat, "Pacific Plan, Frequently Asked Questions," "Forum Communiqué, Thirty-Sixth Pacific Islands Forum" (Papua New Guinea, October 25–27, 2005, PIFS [05] 12); "Toward a New Pacific Regionalism," vol. 1, September 28, 2005, and vol. 2, May 5, 2005; and Ron Crocombe, "Toward a New Pacific Regionalism," vol. 3, April 20, 2005, http://www.forumsec.org.fj/.

19. PIF Secretariat, "Forum Communiqué, Thirty-Sixth Pacific Islands Forum."

20. "Regional Trade Wars Raise Questions over Greater Integration," *Pacific Beat* on Radio Australia, October 20, 2005, as posted on Small Island Developing States Network, http://www.SIDSnet.org.

21. "Country Profile: Solomon Islands," BBC, October 24, 2004, http://news.bbc.co.uk/2/hi/asia-pacific/country_profiles/1249307.stm; and "Timeline: Solomon Islands," BBC, October 24, 2004, http://news.bbc.co.uk/2/hi/asia-pacific/country_profiles/1249397.stm.

22. "Country Profile: Papua New Guinea," BBC, September 16, 2005, http://news.bbc.co.uk/2/hi/asia-pacific/country_profiles/1246074.stm; and "Timeline: Papua New Guinea," BBC, September 16, 2005, http://news.bbc.co.uk/2/hi/asia-pacific/country_profiles/3028825.stm.

23. "Country Profile: Papua New Guinea"; and "Timeline: Papua New Guinea."

24. "NZ and Fiji Each Expel Diplomats," BBC, December 23, 2008, http://news.bbc.co.uk/2/hi/7797482.stm.

25. "Pacific Leaders Set Fiji Deadline," *BBC online*, January 27, 2009, http://news.bbc.co.uk/2/hi/asia-pacific/7852636.stm.

26. "Pacific Leaders Set Fiji Deadline."

27. "Forum: Leaders Defer Campaign on Labour Mobility," *Island Business* (Fiji), October 26, 2005.

28. UN Office of the High Representative for the Least Developed Countries, Landlocked Developing Countries and Small Island Developing States, "List of Small Island Developing States," www.un.org/special-rep/ohrlls/sid/list.htm.

29. *Europa Directory of International Organizations*, 491.

30. "Audio and Images: PIF Small Island States Meeting," *Scoop Independent News* (New Zealand), October 25, 2005.

31. "Regional Trade Wars Raise Questions over Greater Integration."

32. PIF Secretariat, "Pacific Forum Appoints National Planner for Nauru," PIF press release, August 26, 2005; "Country Profile: Nauru," BBC September 24, 2005, http://news.bbc.co.uk/2/hi/asia-pacific/country_profiles/1134221.stm; and "Timeline: Nauru," BBC, October 13, 2005, http://news.bbc.co.uk/2/hi/asia-pacific/1134774.stm.

33. Tokelau is a self-governing territory of New Zealand with approximately 1,400 people. It is moving toward free association with New Zealand. CIA, *2005 World Factbook*.

34. Australia Department of Foreign Affairs and Trade, "Pacific Islands Forum," undated, http://www.dfat.gov.au/geo/spacific/regional_orgs/spf.html (December 12, 2005).

35. Australian Broadcasting Corporation, "Pacific Islands Forum Considers Entry of Non-Independent Territories," October 4, 2005; and Australia Department of Foreign Affairs and Trade, "Pacific Islands Forum."

36. *Europa Directory of International Organizations*, 494.

37. PIF Secretariat, "Papua New Guinea Ratifies Trade Agreements," PIF Secretariat press statement 85/03, August 8, 2003; and Goode, *Dictionary of Trade Policy Terms*, 226.

38. PIF Secretariat, "Forum Trade Ministers Meeting," PIF press statement 20-04, April 2, 2004.

39. PIF Secretariat, "Papua New Guinea Ratifies Trade Agreements."

40. PIF Secretariat, "Press Statement by Secretary General W. Noel Levi, at the Launching of the PICTA," April 15, 2003; and "PICTA and PACER Frequently Asked Questions."

41. PIF Secretariat, "PICTA and PACER Frequently Asked Questions."

42. PIF Secretariat, "Key Features of PICTA and PACER."

43. PIF Secretariat, "PICTA and PACER Frequently Asked Questions."

44. United Nations Economic and Social Commission for Asia and the Pacific (UNESCAP), Trade and Investment Division, http://www.unescap.org/tid/aptiad/viewagreement.aspx?id=PATCRA.

45. New Zealand Ministry of Foreign Trade, http://www.mfat.govt.nz/Foreign-Relations/Pacific/Trade/index.php; and WTO Secretariat, http://www.wto.org.

CHAPTER 9
CONCLUSION

1. Specifically, they accounted for 48.6 percent of global merchandise exports in 2008 and 54.3 percent of merchandise imports. They are more dominant in services trade, accounting for 58.6 and 52.1 percent of 2008 global services exports and imports, respectively. This counts only extra-EU 27 exports. If intra-EU trade were included, their importance would appear notably larger. *International Trade Statistics, 2009* (World Trade Organization), tables I.9 and I.11.

2. Jeffrey J. Schott, "APEC and Trade Liberalization: Towards Greater Integration," *Business Times* (Singapore), November 10, 2009; and Peterson Institute for International Economics, http://www.piie.com/publications/opeds/oped.cfm?ResearchID=1324 (November 11, 2009).

3. European Commission, "The REACH in Brief," October 2007, http://ec.europa.eu/environment/chemicals/reach/pdf/2007_02_reach_in_brief.pdf (January 8, 2010); and European Commission, "REACH: What Is REACH?" undated, http://ec.europa.eu/environment/chemicals/reach/reach_intro.htm (January 8, 2010).

4. There is no one NAFTA environmental dispute resolution mechanism nor one labor dispute resolution mechanism; rather, there are sets of each between pairs of NAFTA's three members.

APPENDIX A
THE WORLD TRADE ORGANIZATION

1. WTO, "Cape Verde to Join WTO on 23 July 2008." *WTO News Item*, June 23, 2008. The next most recent member to join the WTO was Ukraine, in May 2008.

2. Mandelson, as quoted in "Russia Has Chance to Join WTO in 2006—EU," *Reuters*, May 9, 2005.

GLOSSARY

1. WTO, http://www.wto.org.

2. This definition draws upon Walter Goode, *Dictionary of Trade Policy Terms*, 4th ed. (Cambridge University Press, 2003).

3. GSPs cannot be negotiated, nor can they require developing nations to make concessions to receive them. In order to offer a GSP or a GSP-like program, a developed country must receive a waiver from the WTO's rules on nondiscrimination. Examples of GSP-like programs include the US's AGOA, and the EU's Everything But Arms Initiative. European Commission, "User's Guide to the European Union's Tariff Preferences," February 2003; and WTO, "Differential and More Favorable Treatment Reciprocity."

4. WTO, http://www.wto.org.

5. Ross Singleton, "Knowledge and Technology: The Basis of Wealth and Power," in *Introduction to International Political Economy*, eds. David N. Balaam and Michael Veseth (Pearson/Prentice Hall, 2005), 222; and WTO, http://www.wto.org.

6. WTO, "WTO Glossary," http://www.wto.org/english/theWTO_e/glossary_e/glossary_e.htm.

7. WTO, "Singapore WTO Ministerial Declaration," December 13, 1996, WT/MIN/(96)/DEC, http://www.wto.org.

8. There are nuances well beyond this overview, but this covers the most commonly referred to tariff terminology. For more detail, see Walter Goode, *Dictionary of Trade Policy Terms*, 4th ed. and http://www.wto.org.

Bibliography

Abbott, Frederick M. "NAFTA and the Legalization of World Politics: A Case Study." In *Legalization and World Politics,* edited by Judith Goldstein, Miles Kahler, Robert O. Keohane, and Anne-Marie Slaughter. MIT Press, 2001.

Abdrisaev, Baktybek. "The Russification of Kyrgyzstan." *Foreign Policy* (April 2009), http://www.foreignpolicy.com.

Acheson, Keith. "Power Steering the Canadian Automotive Industry: The 1965 Canada-USA Auto Pact and Political Exchange." *Journal of Economic Behavior and Organization* 11, no. 2 (1989).

African, Caribbean and Pacific Group (ACP) Secretariat. http://www.acpsec.org.

African Growth and Opportunity Act. "2004 Comprehensive Report on U.S. Trade and Investment Policy toward Sub-Saharan Africa and Implementation of the African Growth and Opportunity Act." African Growth and Opportunity Act. http://ustraderep.gov/assets/Trade_Development/Preference_Programs/AGOA/asset_upload_file679_3741.pdf (accessed March 3, 2005).

African Union. "Profile: Arab Maghreb Union (AMU)." http://www.africa-union.org/root/au/recs/AMUOverview.pdf (accessed January 1, 2006).

———. "Profile: Economic Community of Central African States (ECCAS-CEEAC)." http://www.africa-union.org/Recs/ECCASoverview.pdf (accessed January 22, 2006).

Age (Australia). November 11, 2004.

Agence France-Presse. May 21, 2001–March 7, 2004.

ALBA-TCP Portal. http://www.alianzabolivariana.org/index.php (accessed March 15, 2010).

Americas Society and the Council of the Americas. "New ALBA Trading Currency Dawns at Bolivia Summit," October 16, 2009. http://www.as-coa.org/article.php?id=1948.

Andean Community. "Cusco Declaration on the South American Community of Nations." http://www.comunidadandina.org/ingles/documentos/documents/cusco8-12-04.htm.

———. "Peru Fully Incorporated into the Andean Free Trade Area." Andean Community press release. http://www.comunidadandina.org/ingles/press/press/np10-1-06.htm.

Antigua Sun (Antigua and Barbuda). October 21, 2009.

Arab League. http://www.arableagueonline.org/arableague/index_en.jsp.

———. "Declaration Pan-Arab Free Trade Area." Resolution No. 1317-P/S/ 59. http://www.medea.be/files/Declaration_PanArab_Free_Trade_Area.doc.

Asia-Pacific Economic Cooperation. "About APEC." http://www.apecsec.org.sg/apec/about_apec.html.

Associated Press. October 11, 2005–February 2, 2006.

Association of Caribbean States (ACS). http://www.acs-aec.org/.

Association of South Eastern Asian Nations (ASEAN). "Joint Media Statement on the Signing of the Agreement Establishing the ASEAN-Australia-New Zealand Free Trade Area." http://www.aseansec.org/22255.htm.

Audley, John J. *Green Politics and Global Trade: NAFTA and the Future of Environmental Politics*. Washington, DC: Georgetown University Press, 1997.

Audley, John, Sandra Polaski, Demetrios G. Papademetriou, and Scott Vaughan. "NAFTA's Promise and Reality: Lessons from Mexico for the Hemisphere." Carnegie Endowment for International Peace (2003). http://www.carnegieendowment.org/files/nafta1.pdf.

Australia Department of Foreign Affairs and Trade. "Guide to the CER." http://www.dfat.gov.au/geo/new_zealand/anz_cer/anz_cer.html.

———. "Indian Ocean Rim Association for Regional Cooperation." http://www.dfat.gov.au/trade/iorarc (accessed January 1, 2006).

———. "Pacific Islands Forum." http://www.dfat.gov.au/geo/spacific/regional_orgs/spf.html (accessed December 12, 2005).

Australian. December 2, 2004.

Australian Broadcasting Corporation. October 4, 2005.

Balaam, David N., and Michael Veseth, eds. *Introduction to International Political Economy*. 3rd ed. Prentice Hall, 2004.

Bay of Bengal Initiative for Multi-Sectoral Technical and Economic Cooperation (BIMSTEC). http://www.bimstec.org.

BBC. October 24, 1998–February 5, 2010.

Beissinger, Mark R. "Commonwealth of Independent States." In *Oxford Companion to Politics of the World*, 2nd ed., edited by Joel Krieger. Oxford University Press, 2001.

Bergsten, C. Fred. "Plan B for World Trade: Go Regional." *Financial Times*, August 16, 2006.

Bhagwati, Jagdish. *Termites in the Trading System: How Preferential Agreements Undermine Free Trade*. Oxford University Press, 2008.

Bilaterals.org. January 13, 2010.

Bloomberg. December 15, 2009.

Bomberg, Elizabeth, and Alexander Stubb, eds. *The European Union: How Does It Work?* Oxford University Press, 2004.

Bouzas, Roberto. "MERCOSUR's External Trade Negotiations: Dealing with a Congested Agenda." In *MERCOSUR: Regional Integration, World Markets*, edited by Riordan Roett. Boulder, CO: Lynne Reinner, 1999.

Brady, Hugo, and Katinka Barysch. "CER Guide to the Reform Treaty." October 2007. Centre for European Reform (October 2007). http://www.cer.org.uk/pdf/briefing_reform_treaty_17oct07.pdf.

Braveboy-Wagner, Jacqueline Ann. "English-Speaking Caribbean." In *Oxford Companion to Politics of the World*, 2nd ed., edited by Joel Krieger. Oxford University Press, 2001.

Bridges Asia (May 2005).

Bridges Trade BioRes (March 3, 2006).

Bridges Weekly (October 30, 2008).

Brill Olcott, Martha. "The New Nations of Central Asia." In *The Successor States to the USSR*, edited by John W. Blaney. Washington, DC: Congressional Quarterly Press, 1995.

Broadman, Harry G., ed. *From Disintegration to Reintegration: Eastern Europe and the Former Soviet Union in International Trade*. World Bank, 2005.

Brusick, P. "Special and Different Treatment of Developing Countries." PowerPoint presentation at the WTO Public Symposium, May 26, 2004.

Business Times (Singapore). November 10, 2009.

Business Week. October 10, 2005.

Canadian Government, Foreign Affairs and International Trade Canada. "Softwood Lumber." http://www.dfait-maeci.gc.ca/eicb/softwood/background-en.asp.

Cardoso, Fernando Henrique, and Enzo Faletto. *Dependency and Development in Latin America*. University of California Press, 1979.

Caribbean Community and Common Market (CARICOM) Secretariat. http://www.caricom.org/ (accessed March 15, 2010).

———. "History of the Caribbean Community." http://www.caricom.org/jsp/community/history .jsp?menu=community.

Caribbean Regional Negotiating Machinery. http://www.crnm.org.

CARICOM Single Market and Economy (CSME). http://www.csmeonline.org/cms/.

CBC News. August 23, 2006. http://www.cbc.ca/news/.

CBS News. November 4, 2005. http://www.cbsnews.com.

Center for International Peace Operations (ZIF, Germany). "Current Peace, Peacebuilding and Crisis Prevention Operations" (June 2005). http://www.zif-berlin.org/en/home.html.

Central European Free Trade Agreement (CEFTA) Secretariat. http://www.cefta2006.com/ (accessed March 16, 2010).

Central Intelligence Agency. "July 2009 Population Estimates." In *World Factbook*. https:// www.cia.gov/library/publications/the-world-factbook/rankorder/2119rank.html.

———. *World Factbook*, 2003–2009.

Chicago Tribune. December 14, 2003.

China Daily. November 3, 2005.

Cini, Michelle, ed. *European Union Politics*. 2nd ed. Oxford: Oxford University Press, 2003.

Coastweek (Kenya). September 22–28, 2006.

Cohen, Benjamin J. *The Geography of Money*. Ithaca, NY: Cornell University Press, 1998.

Cohen, Stephen, Joel Paul, and Robert Blecker. *Fundamentals of US Foreign Trade Policy: Economics, Politics, Laws and Issues*. 2nd ed. Boulder, CO: Westview, 2003.

Columbia Encyclopedia. 6th ed. 2001–2005.

Comité Permanent Inter États de lutte contre la Sécheresse dans le Sahel (CILSS). http://www .cilss.bf/htm/mandat.htm (accessed November 23, 2008).

Commission for Environmental Cooperation (CEC). http://www.cec.org/home/index.cfm ?varlan=english.

Commission for Labor Cooperation (CLC). http://www.naalc.org//index.cfm?page=137.

Common Market for Eastern and Southern Africa (COMESA) Secretariat. "COMESA in Figures." http://about.comesa.int/attachments/060_COMESA%20In%20Figures.pdf (accessed November 2, 2008).

Commonwealth Secretariat/World Bank Joint Task Force on Small States. "Small States: Meeting Challenges in the Global Economy." Report of the Commonwealth Secretariat/ World Bank Joint Task Force on Small States. April 2000. http://www.worldbank.org/smallstates/ and http://www.thecommonwealth.org.

Community of Sahel-Saharan States (CEN-SAD). http://www.cen-sad.org/new/index .php?option=com_content&task=view&id=173&Itemid=181.

Concord Times (Sierra Leone). September 14, 2005.

Congressional Quarterly Weekly. August 1, 2005–July 25, 2005.

Consultative Board to WTO Director-General Supachai Panitchpakdi. "The Future of the WTO: Addressing Institutional Challenges in the New Millennium." http://www.wto.org/english/ thewto_e/10anniv_e/future_wto_e.htm.

Council of Arab Economic Unity. http://www.caeu.org.eg/English/Intro/.

Council of Europe. http://www.coe.int/DEFAULTEN.ASP.

Crawford, Jo-Ann, and Robert V. Fiorentino. "The Changing Landscape of Regional Trade Agreements." WTO Discussion Paper No. 8, 2005.

Crocombe, Ron. "Toward a New Pacific Regionalism." Vol. 3 Working Papers (April 20, 2005), http://www.adb.org/Documents/Reports/Pacific-Regionalism/vol3/wp01.pdf.

CSME Unit of Trinidad and Tobago. CARICOM Single Market and Economy (CSME). http://76.162.14.12/index.shtml (accessed March 15, 2010).

Daily Monitor (Uganda). March 2, 2010.

Daily News (Tanzania). July 13, 2006.

Delegation of the European Commission to the USA. http://www.eurunion.org/.

de Rato, Rodrigo, and Paul Wolfowitz. "Time to Get Back to Business on Doha." *Le Figaro*, September 18, 2006.

Destler, I. M. *American Trade Politics*. 3rd ed. Washington, DC: Institute for International Economics, 1995.

Deutsche Welle. May 5, 2005.

Dominican.net (Dominica). April 18, 2009.

Dow Jones Newswires. December 30, 2005.

East African Business Week (Uganda). November 2, 2008.

East African Community (EAC). http:// www.eac.int.

Eastern Caribbean Central Bank (ECCB). http://www.eccb-centralbank.org/Money/index.asp.

Economic Commission for Africa (UNECA). "Assessing Regional Integration in Africa." Economic Commission for Africa (UNECA) Policy Research Report (May 2004). http://www.uneca.org/aria/.

Economic Community of Central African States/*Communauté Économique des États d'Afrique Centrale* (ECCAS/CEEAC). http://www.ceeac-eccas.org/.

Economic Times (India). October 27, 2005.

Economist. January 22, 2004–November 1, 2008.

Economist Intelligence Unit. "South Korea Country Report, November 2005."

ECOWAS Secretariat. "Market Integration Programme." http://www.sec.ecowas.int/sitecedeao/english/achievements-1.htm (accessed November 19, 2008).

Ellis, Stephen. "How to Rebuild Africa." *Foreign Affairs*, September/October 2005.

Estevadeordal, Antoni, and Kati Suominen. "Rules of Origin in FTAs: A World Map." Paper presented at the seminar "Regional Trade Agreements in Comparative Perspective: Latin America and the Caribbean and Asia-Pacific," organized by the Pacific Economic Cooperation Council (PECC) and the Latin America/Caribbean and Asia/Pacific Economic and Business Association (LAEBA), an initiative of the Inter-American Development Bank and the Asian Development Bank Institute, Washington, DC, April 22–23, 2003. http://www.pecc.org.

———. "Rules of Origin in the World Trading System." Paper for Seminar on Regional Trade Agreements and the WTO, Geneva, Switzerland, November 11, 2003. http://www.wto.org/english/tratop_e/region_e/sem_nov03_e/estevadeordal_paper_e.pdf.

Euractive.com. "Commission Gives Green Light to Iceland's EU Bid," February 25, 2010. http://www.euractiv.com/en/enlargement/commission-gives-green-light-icelands-eu-bid-news-286007.

———. "The Treaty of Lisbon," April 27, 2007. http://www.euractiv.com.

Eurasian Home Analytical Resource. "Eurasian Economic Community (EAEC)." http://www.eurasianhome.org/xml/t/databases.xml?lang=en&nic=databases&intorg=3&pid=25.

Europa Directory of International Organizations 2002. 4th ed. London and New York: Routledge, 2002.

European Central Bank. http://www.ecb.eu/ecb/orga/escb/html/index.en.html (accessed April 14, 2008).

———. "Frequently Asked Questions: EU Enlargement and Economic and Monetary Union (EMU)." http://www.ecb.eu/ecb/history/enlargement/html/faqenlarge.en.html#l2 (accessed March 18, 2010).

———. "Your Country and the Euro," May 4, 2009. http://ec.europa.eu/economy_finance/euro/countries/index_en.htm (accessed March 18, 2010).

European Commission. "Africa and the European Union." May 2003.

———. "Bilateral Trade Relations: ACP and EU, a Long and Preferential Relationship."

———. "Commission Delivers Opinion on Iceland's Accession Bid." European Commission press release IP/10/186, February 24, 2010. http://europa.eu/rapid/pressReleasesAction.do?reference=IP/10/186&format=HTML&aged=0&language=EN&guiLanguage=en.

———. "Commissioner Patten Attends Signature of Agadir Agreement." European Commission press release, February 24, 2004. http://europa.eu.int/comm/external_relations/euromed/news/ip04_256.htm.

———. "Cotonou Agreement."

———. "Economic Partnership Agreements: EU and Caribbean Region Launch Third Phase of Negotiations." *European Commission News*, September 28, 2005. http://www.europa.eu.int/comm/issues/bilateral/regional/acp/pr28095_en.htm.

———. "Enlargement: The Policy." http://ec.europa.eu/enlargement/the-policy/process-of-enlargement/mandate-and-framework_en.htm (accessed May 31, 2009).

———. "EU & the Kimberly Process (Conflict Diamonds)." Updated November 2005.

———. "Euro in an Enlarged European Union," 2005. http://ec.europa.eu/economy_finance/euro/adoption/index_en.htm.

———. "Euro-Mediterranean Partnership" (accessed November 21, 2005).

———. "Euro: New Member States Need to Step Up Efforts." *Europa Newsletter*, November 17, 2005. http://europa.eu.int/newsletter/index_en.htm.

———. "European Commission Disappointed with WTO Arbitrators' Ruling against Proposed Banana Import Tariff." News release, October 27, 2005.

———. "European Neighbourhood Policy; Partners" (accessed November 21, 2005).

———. "Generalised System of Preferences, Everything But Arms (EBA) Initiative." January 2004.

———. "How Does a Country Join the EU?" http://ec.europa.eu/enlargement/enlargement_process/accession_process/how_does_a_country_join_the_eu/negotiations_croatia_turkey/index_en.htm (accessed May 31, 2009).

———. "Iceland's Preparation for Accession to the EU—the Next Steps," undated. http://ec.europa.eu/enlargement/pdf/key_documents/2010/100224_next_steps.pdf (accessed February 26, 2010).

———. "Indian Ocean Commission: Regional Solidarity in the Face of Globalisation." *Courier ACP-EU*, November–December 2003. http://www.europa.eu.int/comm/development/body/publications/courier/courier201/pdf/en_018.pdf.

———. "Information Note on the Revision of the Cotonou Agreement."

———. "Introducing the European Union." http://europa.eu.int/institutions/index_en.htm, (accessed March 13 2006).

———. "Key Findings of the Commission's Opinion on Iceland." European Commission Press Release MEMO/10/48, February 24, 2010. http://europa.eu/rapid/pressReleasesAction.do?reference=MEMO/10/48.

———. "REACH: What Is REACH?" http://ec.europa.eu/environment/chemicals/reach/reach_intro.htm (accessed January 8, 2010).

———. "Second Report on the State of Practical Preparations for the Future Enlargement of the Euro Area." Press conference by Joaquín Almunia, European Commissioner for Economic and Monetary Affairs, November 4, 2005.

———. "The European Union, Latin America and the Caribbean." May 2002.

———. "The REACH in Brief." http://ec.europa.eu/environment/chemicals/reach/pdf/2007_02_reach_in_brief.pdf (accessed January 8, 2010).

———. "Treaty of Lisbon." http://europa.eu/lisbon_treaty/index_en.htm.

———. "User's Guide to the European Union's Scheme of Generalized Tariff Preferences." September 2005.

European Commission Justice and Home Affairs Ministry. "Freedom to Travel: Abolition of Internal Borders and Creation of a Single EU External Frontier," updated September 2008. http://ec.europa.eu/justice_home/fsj/freetravel/schengen/fsj_freetravel_schengen_en.htm.

European Institute for Research on Mediterranean and Euro-Arab Cooperation and the World Bank. "Arab Free Trade Area (AFTA)." http://www.medea.be.

European Union Council. "Co-Decision Guide." http://www.consilium.europa.eu/uedocs/cmsUpload/code_EN.pdf.

———. "European Institutions and Other Bodies." http://europa.eu/institutions/inst/council/index_en.htm, (accessed May 11, 2009).

Fajgenbaum, Jose, Robert Sharer, Kamau Thugge, and Hema DeZoysa. "The Cross-Border Initiative in Eastern and Southern Africa." International Monetary Fund, July 14, 1999, http://www.imf.org/external/np/cross/INDEX.HTM.

Far Eastern Economic Review. November 2005.

Fawzy, Samiha. "The Economics and Politics of Arab Economic Integration." In *Arab Economic Integration, Between Hope and Reality*, edited by Ahmed Galal and Bernard Hoekman. Cairo and Washington, DC: Egyptian Center for Economic Studies and the Brookings Institution Press, 2003.

Fiji Foreign Affairs and External Trade Ministry. http://www.foreignaffairs.gov.fj/.

Fiji Times. August 20, 2005.

Financial Express (India). August 5, 2004.

Financial Times. December 9, 2004–August 16, 2006.

Fiorentino, Roberto V., Luis Verdeja, and Christelle Toqueboeuf. "The Changing Landscape of Regional Trade Agreements: 2006 Update." WTO Discussion Paper No. 12 (May 2007), 1. http://www.wto.org.

Frankel, Jeffrey. *Regional Trading Blocs in the World Economic System.* Washington, DC: Institute for International Economics, 1997.

Franko, Patrice. *The Puzzle of Latin American Economic Development.* 3rd ed. Lanham, MD: Rowman & Littlefield, 2007.

Frost, Ellen L. *Asia's New Regionalism.* Boulder, CO: Lynne Rienner, 2008.

G-77. http://www.g77.org/gstp/index.htm.

Galal, Ahmed, and Bernard Hoekman. "Between Hope and Reality: An Overview of Arab Economic Integration." In *Arab Economic Integration, Between Hope and Reality*, edited by Ahmed Galal and Bernard Hoekman. Cairo and Washington, DC: Egyptian Center for Economic Studies and the Brookings Institution Press, 2003.

Gar, Ian, and Terry Lynn Karl. "Bottom of the Barrel: Africa's Oil Boom and the Poor." Catholic Relief Services, June 2003.

Georgia, Ukraine, Uzbekistan, Azerbaijan, Moldova (GUUAM). http://www.guuam.org.

Ghana Web. June 24, 2009.

Gibney, Frank. "Inside Japan Inc." *The Pacific Century* documentary series, Pacific Basin Institute, 1992.

Gilpin, Robert. *Global Political Economy: Understanding the International Economic Order*. Princeton University Press, 2001.

———. *The Challenge of Global Capitalism: The World Economy in the 21st Century*. Princeton University Press, 2002.

———. *The Political Economy of International Relations*. Princeton University Press, 1987.

GlobalSecurity.org. http://www.globalsecurity.org.

Globe and Mail. August 14, 1993.

Goldstein, Judith, Miles Kahler, Robert O. Keohane, and Anne-Marie Slaughter, eds. *Legalization and World Politics*. MIT Press, 2001.

Goode, Walter, *Dictionary of Trade Policy Terms*. 4th ed. Cambridge University Press/WTO, 2003.

Gorjestani, Nicolas. "Africa Cross Border Initiative: Trade and Investment Facilitation." *World Bank Info Brief* 58 (2000).

———. "Cross-Border Initiative in Eastern and Southern Africa: Regional Integration by Emergence." *World Bank Findings* no. 166 (September 2000).

Grimes, William W. *Currency and Contest in East Asia: The Great Power Politics of Financial Regionalism*. Ithaca, NY: Cornell University Press, 2009.

Gulf Cooperation Council (GCC). http://www.gccsg.org/eng/index.php.

Gulf Times (Qatar). January 1, 2005.

Handjiski, Borko, Robert Lucas, Philip Martin, and Selen Sarisoy Guerin. "Enhancing Regional Trade Integration in Southeast Europe." World Bank Working Paper No. 185, January 2010.

Haynes, Keen. *A History of Latin America*. 6th ed. Boston: Houghton Mifflin, 2000.

Helfer, Laurence R. "Regime Shifting: The TRIPS Agreement and New Dynamics of International Intellectual Property Lawmaking. *Yale Journal of International Law* 29 (1) (2004).

Henning, C. Randall. "The Future of the Chiang Mai Initiative: An Asian Monetary Fund?" Peterson Institute for International Economics Policy Brief, February 2009. http://www.petersoninstitute.org.

Hezel, Francis X. "Is That the Best You Can Do? A Tale of Two Micronesian Economies." East-West Center, *Pacific Islands Policy* 1 (2006).

Hindu (India). July 20, 2005–November 13, 2008.

Hufbauer, Gary Clyde, and Jeffrey J. Schott. *NAFTA: An Assessment*. Rev. ed. Washington, DC: Institute for International Economics, 1993.

———. *NAFTA Revisited: Achievements and Challenges*. Washington, DC: Institute for International Economics, 2005.

———. "Slanting the NAFTA Story." Peterson Institute for International Economics Realtime Economic Issues Watch, December 18, 2009. http://www.piie.com/realtime/?p=1105.

Indian Express. November 15, 2005.

Indian Ministry of Commerce and Industry, Department of Commerce. "BIMSTEC Trade Negotiating Meeting Held." Press release, June 12, 2009. http://commerce.nic.in/pressrelease/pressrelease_detail.asp?id=2416.

———. "India's Current Engagements in RTAs." http://www.commerce.nic.in/india_rta_main.htm.

Indian Ocean Commission Secretariat. http://www.coi-info.org.

Inside US Trade. September 16, 2005.

Institute for Security Studies (South Africa). "IGAD Profile." http://www.iss.co.za/AF/RegOrg/unity_to_union/igadprof.htm#.

Inter-American Development Bank (IADB). *Beyond Borders: The New Regionalism in Latin America: Economic and Social Progress in Latin America*. Inter-American Development Bank (2008). http://www.iadb.org/iadbstrore.

Inter-Arab Investment Guarantee Corporation. *2004 Report*. Inter-Arab Investment Guarantee Corporation. http://www.iaigc.org/index_e.html.

International Labor Rights Forum. "Faulting US Labor Laws, Mexican Unions File 'Broadest' NAFTA Labor Complaint on Washington State Apple Industry," May 27, 1998. http://www.laborrights.org/creating-a-sweatfree-world/changing-global-trade-rules/1385.

International Monetary Fund. "Central African Economic and Monetary Community: Selected Issues." November 11, 2005. *IMF Country Report* No. 05/390, 63. http://www.imf.org/external/pubs/cat/longres.cfm?sk=18676.0.

———. "Eastern Caribbean Currency Union: 2005 Article IV Consultation—Staff Report and Public Information Notice on the Executive Board Discussion on the Eastern Caribbean Currency Union." *IMF Country Report* No. 05/304, August 2005. http://www.imf.org/external/pubs/cat/longres.cfm?sk=18518.0.

———. "West African Economic and Monetary Union: Recent Economic Developments and Regional Policy Issues." *IMF Country Report* No. 03/07, March 2003.

———. "What Does the Future Hold for Currency Blocs in Africa?" *IMF Survey*, August 29, 2005.

IPP Media (Tanzania). July 13, 2006.

Island Business (Fiji). October 26, 2005.

Japanese Ministry of Foreign Affairs. "Japan's Observer Status to SAARC." Press release, November 15, 2005.

Johnson, Chalmers. *Japan: Who Governs? The Rise of the Developmental State*. New York: W. W. Norton, 1995.

Joint Public Advisory Committee. "JPAC Report to Council." Mérida, Yucatán, June 24–26, 1998, Commission for Environmental Cooperation. http://www.cec.org.

Journal of Commerce. June 10, 2009.

Kahler, Miles. "Legalization as Strategy: The Asia-Pacific Case." In *Legalization and World Politics*, edited by Judith Goldstein, Miles Kahler, Robert O. Keohane, and Anne-Marie Slaughter. MIT Press, 2001.

Kay, Sean. *Global Security in the Twenty-First Century*. Lanham, MD: Rowman & Littlefield, 2006.

Kemal, Dervi, Peter Bocock, and Julia Delvin. "Intraregional Trade among Arab Countries: Building a Competitive Economic Neighborhood." Paper presented at the Middle East Institute 52nd Annual Conference, panel on "Arab Economic Market," Washington, DC, October 17, 1998.

Kerremans, Bart, and Bob Switky. "Introduction." In *The Political Importance of Regional Trading Blocs*, edited by Bart Kerremans and Bob Switky. Aldershot, England: Ashgate, 2000.

Khan, Mohsin S. "The GCC Monetary Union: Choice of Exchange Rate Regime." Peterson Institute for International Economic Working Paper Series 09-1, April 2009.

Kimberly Process. http://www.kimberlyprocess.com.

Laffan, Brigid, and Alexander Stubb. "Member States." In *The European Union: How Does It Work?* edited by Elizabeth Bomberg and Alexander Stubb. Oxford University Press, 2004.

Lanoszka, Anna. *The World Trade Organization: Changing Dynamics in the Global Political Economy*. Boulder, CO: Lynne Rienner, 2009.

Latin American Economic System (SELA). *Guide to Latin American and Caribbean Integration*. SELA, 1999.

Lawrence, Robert Z. "Emerging Regional Arrangements: Building Blocks or Stumbling Blocks?" In *Finance and the International Economy*, vol. 5, edited by Richard O'Brien. Oxford University Press, 1991.

Le Figaro (France). September 18, 2006.

Lee, Margaret C. *The Political Economy of Regionalism in Southern Africa.* Lynne Rienner and University of Cape Town Press, 2003.

Leonard, Dick. *Economist Guide to the European Union.* 8th ed. Bloomberg Press, 2002.

Lewis, Jeffrey. "The Council of the European Union." In *European Union Politics,* 2nd ed., edited by Michelle Cini. Oxford University Press, 2007.

Library of Congress Countries Studies Index. http://countrystudies.us/.

Linn, Johannes. "Central Asia Human Development Report." United Nations Development Programme, Regional Bureau for Europe and the Commonwealth of Independent States. http://europeandcis.undp.org.

Los Angeles Times. August 10, 1999.

Lynch, David A. "NAFTA, 10 Years Later." In *A Global Agenda, Issues before the 59th General Assembly of the United Nations,* 2004–2005, edited by Angela Drakulich. New York: United Nations Association of the United States, 2004.

———. "National & International Sources of American Foreign Economic Policy: The North American Free Trade Agreement (NAFTA)." PhD diss., University of California, Santa Barbara, 1995.

———. "Negotiating with Goliath: Cross-National and Cross-Level Interactions in NAFTA's Auto and Textile Sectors." In *The Political Importance of Regional Trading Blocs,* edited by Bob Switky and Bart Kerremans. Aldershot, England: Ashgate, 2000.

Macaya, Roman. "Economic and Social Consequences of an Overprotection of Intellectual Property Rights in CAFTA." National Chamber of Generic Products (Costa Rica), April 2005.

Magbagbeola, Nelson O. "The Quest for a West Africa Monetary Union: Implementation Issues, Progress and Prospects." Conference by the Council for the Development of Social Science Research in Africa, Cotonou, Benin, September 6–7, 2003. http://www.codesria.org/Links/conferences/cotonou/cotonou_papers.htm.

Malik, Mohan. "The East Asia Summit: More Discord Than Accord." *Yale Global Online,* December 20, 2005. http://www.yaleglobal.yale.edu.

Manning, Patrick. "Statement of Patrick Manning PM of Trinidad and Tobago." CARICOM press release 233/2005, December 31, 2005.

Marchetti Juan A., and Martin Roy. *Opening Markets for Trade in Services, Countries and Sectors in Bilateral and WTO Negotiations.* Cambridge University Press, 2008.

Marianas Variety. February 18, 2009.

Masson, Paul, and Catherine Pattillo. "A Single Currency for Africa?" *Finance and Development* (2004).

———. *Monetary Geography of Africa.* Washington, DC: Brookings Institution, 2003. http://www.brookings.edu/views/papers/masson/20030410.htm.

McIntyre, Meredith A. "Trade Integration in the East Africa Community: An Assessment for Kenya." IMF Staff Working Paper 143, WP/05/143.

McLure, Jason. "United States of Africa." Interview with AU Commission Chairman Jean Ping. *Newsweek,* December 1, 2008. http://www.newsweek.com/id/171588.

Mendelowitz, Allan I. "NAFTA: Issues Related to Textile/Apparel and Auto and Auto Parts Industries." Government Accountability Office testimony, Subcommittee on Commerce, Consumer and Monetary Affairs of the Committee on Governmental Operations, US House of Representatives, May 3–4, 1993. http://archive.gao.gov/d43t14/149165.pdf.

MercoPress. June 22, 2009–December 5, 2009.

Miami Herald. November 6, 2005.

Mikic, Mia. "ASEAN and Trade Integration." UNESCAP, Trade and Investment Division Staff Working Paper 01/09, April 8, 2009.

Mizzima News (India). October 10, 2005.

Momento 24 (Argentina). December 15, 2009.

Moran, Michael. "Q & A: The Arab League and Iraq." Council on Foreign Relations, October 10, 2005.

Moss, Todd J. *African Development: Making Sense of the Issues and Actors*. Boulder, CO: Lynne Rienner, 2007.

Mshomba, Richard E. *Africa in the Global Economy*. Boulder, CO: Lynne Rienner, 2000.

Mutai, Henry. "The Regional Integration Facilitation Forum: A Simple Answer to a Complicated Problem?" Trade Law Centre for Southern Africa, 2003. http://www.tralac.org/pdf/WP3_2003.pdf.

Mwangi, Wambui. "The Order of Money: Colonialism and the East African Currency Board." PhD diss., University of Pennsylvania, 2003.

NEPAD Secretariat. "NEPAD in Brief," November 27, 2005. http://www.nepad.org.

New York Times. February 2, 1992–November 15, 2005.

New Zealand Ministry of Foreign Affairs and Trade. "Pacific." http://www.mfat.govt.nz/Foreign-Relations/Pacific/Trade/index.php.

———. "Trans-Pacific Strategic Economic Partnership Agreement." http://www.mfat.govt .nz/Trade-and-Economic-Relations/Trade-Agreements/Trans-Pacific/index.php.

Noland, Marcus. "How North Korea Funds Its Regime." Testimony before the Subcommittee on Federal Financial Management, Government Information and International Security, Committee on Homeland Security and Governmental Affairs, US Senate, April 25, 2006.

Noland, Marcus, and Howard Pack. "Islam, Globalization and Economic Performance in the Middle East." Peterson Institute for International Economics Policy Brief 04-4, June 2004. http://www.petersoninstitute.org/publications/pb/pb04-4.pdf.

Noriega, Roger. "Diplomacy in Latin America." Testimony before the Subcommittee on the Western Hemisphere Committee on International Relations, July 27, 2005. http://www .usinfo.state/gov/wh/Archive/2005/Jul/27-535072.html.

North American Agreement on Environmental Cooperation (NAAEC). http://www.cec.org/pubs_info_resources/law_treat_agree/naaec/index.cfm?varlan=english.

North American Agreement on Labor Cooperation (NAALC). http://www.naalc.org/naalc/naalc-full-text.htm.

O'Keefe, Thomas A. "The Role the Organization of Eastern Caribbean States (OECS) Plays within the Caribbean Common Market and Community (CARICOM) and in the Caribbean's Relationship with the World Economy." Paper delivered at the International Studies Association Annual Conference, New Orleans, LA, February 19, 2010. International Studies Association, http://www.isanet.org/neworleans2010/isa-2010-paper-archive.html and Mercosur Consulting Group, http://mercosurconsulting.net/mmix/index .php?blog=11.

Organisation for Economic Co-operation and Development (OECD). "China Could Become World's Largest Exporter by 2010." *Economic Survey of China 2005*, September 9, 2005.

———. *Environmental Performance Reviews, Mexico*. OECD, 1998.

———. "Framework for Cooperation between CILSS and SWAC." October 2006. http://www .oecd.org/dataoecd/15/22/38460920.pdf.

———. "OECD's Project on Harmful Tax Practices: 2004 Progress Report." http://www.oecd .org/dataoecd/60/33/30901115.pdf.

———. "Regionalism and the Multilateral Trading System." 2003.

———. "Sahel and West Africa Club." http://www.oecd.org/document/62/0,3343,en_38233741_ 38242551_38257982_1_1_1_1,00.html (accessed December 2005).

Organisation of Eastern Caribbean States (OECS). http://www.oecs.org/mission.html.

Organization of American States Foreign Trade Information System (SICE). *Trade and Integration Arrangements in the Americas: An Analytical Compendium.* June 10, 1996.

Oyejide, T. Ademola. "Policies for Regional Integration in Africa." Economic Research Papers no. 62, African Development Bank, 2000.

Pacific Islands Secretariat. "PICTA and PACER Frequently Asked Questions" (accessed May 2005).

Pan, Esther. "Q & A: African Peacekeeping Operations." Council of Foreign Relations, December 7, 2005.

Pangestu, Mari, and Sudarshan Gooptu. "New Regionalism: Options for China and East Asia." In *East Asia Integrates.* World Bank, 2003.

Panitchpakdi, Supachai, and Mark L. Clifford. *China and the WTO: Changing China, Changing World Trade.* Singapore: John Wiley & Sons, 2002.

Pastor, Robert A. *Toward a North American Community: Lessons from the Old World for the New.* Washington, DC: Institute for International Economics, 2001.

People's Daily Online. July 7, 2004–October 26, 2005.

Pereira, Lia Valls. "Toward the Common Market of the South." In *MERCOSUR: Regional Integration, World Markets,* edited by Riordan Roett. Boulder, CO: Lynne Rienner, 1999.

PIF Secretariat. "Forum Communiqué, Thirty-Sixth Pacific Islands Forum." PIFS (05) 12, October 25–27, 2005. http://www.forumsec.org.fj/.

———. "Pacific Forum Appoints National Planner for Nauru." PIF press release, August 26, 2005.

———. "Papua New Guinea Ratifies Trade Agreements." PIF Secretariat press statement 85/03, August 8, 2003.

———. "Press Statement by Secretary General W. Noel Levi, at the Launching of the PICTA." April 15, 2003.

———. "Toward a New Pacific Regionalism." Vol. 1, September 28, 2005; vol. 2, May 5, 2005. http://www.forumsec.org.fj/.

Post (Zambia). May 11, 2009.

Public Citizen. "NAFTA Chapter 11 Investor-to-State Cases: Bankrupting Democracy." http://www.citizen.org/publications/release.cfm?ID=7076 (accessed June 10, 2005).

———. *NAFTA's Broken Promises: the Border Betrayed.* Washington, DC: Public Citizen, 1996.

Radio Australia. October 20, 2005.

Radio Free Europe/Radio Liberty. December 12, 2005.

Ravenhill, John. "Regionalism." In *Global Political Economy,* 2nd ed., edited by John Ravenhill. Oxford: Oxford University Press, 2007.

Reuters. May 9, 2005–January 13, 2010.

RFE/RL Newsline. May 25, 2004.

Riordan, Roett, ed. *MERCOSUR: Regional Integration, World Markets.* Boulder, CO: Lynne Reinner, 1999.

Rodlauer, Markus, and Alfred Schipke. "Introduction and Overview." In *Central America: Global Integration and Regional Cooperation,* edited by Markus Rodlauer and Alfred Schipke. International Monetary Fund, July 2005. http://www.imf.org/external/pubs/ft/op/243/index.htm.

Sanguinetti, Pablo, and Eduardo Bianchi. "Implementing PTAs in the Southern Cone Region of Latin America." In *The Origin of Goods: Rules of Origin in Regional Trade Agreements,* edited by Olivier Cadot, Antoni Estevadeordal, Akiko Suwa-Eisenmann, and Thierry Verdier. Oxford University Press and the Centre for Economic Policy Research, 2006.

Santucci, Marc. "Statement." In *Free Trade and the Auto Pact*, edited by James Chacko. Proceedings of a Seminar, Centre for Canadian-American Studies, February 13, 1987, Windsor, Ontario. Windsor, Ontario: University of Windsor Press, 1988.

Scheineson, Andres. "The Shanghai Cooperation Organization." Council of Foreign Relations Backgrounder, March 24, 2009. http://www.cfr.org/publication/10083/.

Schott, Jeffrey J. "APEC and Trade Liberalization: Towards Greater Integration." *Business Times* (Singapore), November 10, 2009. Peterson Institute for International Economics, November 11, 2009. http://www.piie.com/publications/opeds/oped.cfm?ResearchID=1324.

———. "Does the FTAA Have a Future?" Institute for International Economics, 2005. http://www.iie.com/publications/papers/schott1105.pdf.

———. "Free Trade Agreements: Boon or Bane of the World Trading System?" In *Free Trade Agreements, US Strategies and Priorities*. Washington, DC: Institute for International Economics, 2004.

———. *Prospects for Free Trade in the Americas*. Washington, DC: Institute for International Economics, 2001.

———. *WTO After Seattle*. Washington, DC: Institute for International Economics, 2000.

Scoop Independent News (New Zealand). October 25, 2005.

Scully, Roger. "The European Parliament." In *European Union Politics*, 2nd ed., edited by Michelle Cini. Oxford University Press, 2007.

Security and Prosperity Partnership of North America (SPP). http://www.spp.gov/index.asp.

Sigal, Leon V. "The Last Cold War Election." *Foreign Affairs*, Winter 1992–1993.

Singleton, Ross. "Knowledge and Technology: The Basis of Wealth and Power." In *Introduction to International Political Economy*, edited by David N. Balaam and Michael Veseth. Pearson/Prentice Hall, 2005.

Sistema de Integración Centroamericana (SICA) Secretariat. http://www.sgsica.org.

Solomon Star News. October 31, 2005.

Somers Heidhues, Mary. *Southeast Asia: A Concise History*. London: Thames & Hudson, 2000.

South Africa Department of Foreign Affairs. "Overview of African RTAs." February 12, 2004. http://www.dfa.gov.za/foreign/Multilateral/africa/caemc.htm.

———. "West African Economic and Monetary Union (WAEMU)/Union Économique et Monétaire de l'ouest Africaine (UEMOA)," February 12, 2004. http://www.dfa.gov.za/foreign/Multilateral/africa/waemu.htm.

South Asian Association for Regional Cooperation (SAARC). http://www.saarc-sec.org.

Southern African Development Community (SADC). http://www.sadc.int/index.php?action=a1001&page_id=about_corp_profile.

Sparks, Donald. "Indian Ocean Region." In *Oxford Companion to Politics of the World*, 2nd ed., edited by Joel Krieger. Oxford University Press, 2001.

Standard (Kenya). January 26, 2010.

Starr, Frederick S. "A Partnership for Central Asia." *Foreign Affairs* (July/August 2005).

Straits Times (Singapore). February 22, 2005.

Teh, Robert, Thomas J. Prusa, and Michele Budetta. "Trade Remedy Provisions in Regional Trade Agreements." WTO Staff Working Paper ERSD-2007-3, WTO Economic Research and Statistics Division.

Tide (Nigeria) October 3, 2005.

Tiempo (Colombia). Undated (accessed March 15, 2010).

Tordoff, William. "Regional Groupings and the Organization of African Unity." In *Government and Politics in Africa*. 4th ed. Indiana University Press, 2002.

Trade Negotiations Insights. May/June 2005—April 2009.

Trade News Digest. October 30, 2008.

Trebilcock, Michael J., and Robert Howse. *The Regulation of International Trade*. 2nd ed. London and New York: Routledge, 2002.

"UK EU Presidency 2005." http://www.eu2005.gov.

United Nations Conference on Trade and Development (UNCTAD). "About GSP." http://www.unctad.org.

———. "Generalized System of Preferences, List of Beneficiaries." UNCTAD/ITCD/TSB/Misc.62/Rev.1. http://www.unctad.org.

———. "Developing Countries Launch New Round of Trade Negotiations." UNCTAD press release, UNCTAD/PRESS/PR/SPA/2004/010, June 17, 2004.

———. "Global System of Trade Preferences." UNCTAD press release, UNCTAD/PRESS/IN/SPA/2004/001, June 16, 2004.

United Nations Department of Peacekeeping Operations. "United Nations Peacekeeping Operation, Background Note: 31 August 2008." http://www.un.org/Depts/dpko/dpko/bnote.htm.

United Nations Economic and Social Commission for Asia and the Pacific (UNESCAP), Trade and Investment Division. "Analysis of Performance and Assessment of Growth and Productivity in the ESCWA Region." E/ESCWA/EAC/2004/2, January 12, 2004. http://www.escwa.org.lb/information/publications/ead/docs/Ead04e2.pdf.

———. "Facts about the Bangkok Agreement (Asia-Pacific Trade Agreement)." June 2005.

———. "Multilateralizing Regionalism: Towards an Integrated and Outward-Oriented Asia-Pacific Economic Area." Paper presented at "Delivering on the WTO Round: A High-Level Government-Business Dialogue for Development," Macao, China, October 4–6, 2005.

———. "The Asia-Pacific Trade Agreement." November 28, 2005.

United Nations Economic Commission for Africa. "Assessing Regional Integration in Africa," 2004. http://www.uneca.org.

United Nations Economic Commission for Europe. "Black Sea Economic Cooperation (BSEC)." UN Economic Commission for Europe's "Regional Trade Agreements for Europe" Blog. http://ecetrade.typepad.com//BSEC%20basic%20information.doc (accessed January 3, 2006).

———. "CACO and EEC Are Merging." UN Economic Commission for Europe's "Regional Trade Agreements in the ECE" Blog, November 2, 2005. http://ecetrade.typepad.com.

———. "Central Asian Cooperation Organization." UN Economic Commission for Europe's "Regional Trade Agreements in the ECE" Blog. http://ecetrade.typepad.com//Central%20Asian%20Cooperation%20Organization%20basic%20info.doc (accessed January 4, 2006).

———. "CIS System." UN Economic Commission for Europe's "Regional Trade Agreements in the ECE" Blog. http://ecetrade.typepad.com/CIS%20systm.doc (accessed January 4, 2006).

———. "Eurasian Economic Community." UN Economic Commission for Europe's "Regional Trade Agreements in the ECE" Blog. http://ecetrade.typepad.com//Eurasian%20Economic%20Community%20Basic%20info.doc (accessed January 4, 2006).

———. "The GUUAM Organization." UN Economic Commission for Europe's "Regional Trade Agreements in the ECE" Blog. http://ecetrade.typepad.com//GUUAM%20basic%20info.doc (accessed January 3, 2006).

———. "The Russia Belarus Union." UN Economic Commission for Europe's "Regional Trade Agreements in the ECE" Blog. http://ecetrade.typepad.com//russie%20belarus%20union%20basic%20information.doc (accessed January 4, 2006).

———. "The Single Economic Space." UNECE's "Regional Trade Agreements in the ECE" Blog. http://ecetrade.typepad.com//Single%20Economic%20Space%20Initiative%20basic%20information.doc.

United Nations Economic Commission for Latin America and the Caribbean (ECLAC). *Latin America and the Caribbean in the World Economy: 2005 Trends*. ECLAC, 2004.

United Nations Office for the Coordination of Humanitarian Affairs' IRINnews.org. "Great Lakes: Ministers Move to Revive Economic Cooperation." July 12, 2004. http://www .irinnews.org/print.asp?ReportID=42116.

United Nations Office of the High Representative for the Least Developed Countries, Land-locked Developing Countries and Small Island Developing States. "List of Small Island Developing States." http://www.un.org/special-rep/ohrlls/sid/list.htm.

United Nations Population Fund. *State of the World Population 2005*.

United Press International. January 7, 2010.

United States Department of Commerce. "Caribbean Basin Initiative." Department of Commerce's Market Access and Compliance. http://www.mac.doc.gov.CBI/webmain/intro.htm.

United States Department of Commerce, Trade Information Center. http://www.ita.doc.gov/td/ tic/fta/, (accessed March 3, 2005).

United States Department of Homeland Security. "Fact Sheet: Security and Prosperity Partnership." June 27, 2005. http://www.dhs.gov/xnews/releases/press_release_0695.shtm.

United States Department of State. "Common Market for Eastern and Southern Africa (COMESA)." Fact sheet, undated.

———. "Economic Community of West African States, ECOWAS." Fact sheet, November 22, 2002.

———. "Intergovernmental Authority on Development (IGAD) Factsheet." July 16, 2003.

———. "Middle East Partnership Initiative." http://www.mepi.state.gov/ (accessed June 2, 2006).

United States Department of the Interior, Office of Insular Affairs. "Definitions of Insular Area Political Organizations." http://www.doi.gov/oia/Islandpages/political_types.htm, http:// www.doi.gov/oia/, and http://www.doi.gov/oia/Firstpginfo/islandfactsheet.htm.

———. "Tariff Treatment of Imports from the Freely Associated States Under Public Law 99-239."

———. "Tariff Treatment of Imports-US Insular Areas, Harmonized Tariff Schedule General Note 3(a)(iv)." http://www.doi.gov/oia/.

United States International Trade Administration. "Bilateral Investment Treaty List." US Trade Compliance Center. http://tcc.export.gov/Trade_Agreements/Bilateral_Investment_Treaties/ index.asp (accessed May 25, 2006).

———. "US Free Trade Agreements."

United States Trade Representative, Office of (USTR). "Andean Trade Preference Act."

———. "Caribbean Basin Initiative." http://www.ustr.gov/Trade_Development/Preference_ Programs/CBI/Section_Index.html.

———. "Dates You Need to Know." April 2008.

———. "Free Trade Agreements." http://www.ustr.gov/trade-agreements/free-trade-agreements (accessed June 1, 2009).

———. "New Andean Trade Benefits." September 25, 2005.

———. "Second Report to Congress on the Operation of the Andean Trade Preference Act as Amended." April 30, 2005. http://www.ustr.gov/Trade_Development/Preference_Programs/ ATPA/Section_Index.html.

———. "Softwood Lumber." http://www.ustr.gov/World_Regions/Americas/Canada/Softwood_ Lumber/Section_Index.html.

———. "Statement of US Trade Representative Susan C. Schwab Regarding Entry into Force of the US-Oman Free Trade Agreement." *USTR News*, December 29, 2008. http://www .ustr.gov.

———. *Study on the Operation and Effect of the North American Free Trade Agreement.* 1997.

———. "Trade and Investment Framework Agreements (TIFAs)." http://www.ustr.gov/ (accessed May 25, 2006).

———. "Trade Facts: United States to Negotiate Participation in Trans-Pacific Strategic Economic Partnership." September 2008. http://www.ustr.gov.

University of Pennsylvania African Studies Center. "East Africa Living Encyclopedia" (accessed December 16, 2005).

Urwin, Derek W. *The Community of Europe: A History of European Integration since 1945.* London and New York: Longman, 1991.

Wall Street Journal. September 5, 2003–May 21, 2009.

Washington Post. May 8, 2008.

Weinstein, Adam. "Russian Phoenix: The Collective Security Treaty Organization." *Whitehead Journal of Diplomacy and International Relations*, Winter–Spring 2007. http://www.journalofdiplomacy.org.

West African Monetary Institute (WAMI). "Countdown to the Monetary Union." February 23, 2003. http://www.wami-imao.org.

Whiting, Van. "The Dynamics of Regionalization: Roadmap to an Open Future." Paper presented at a conference, "The Political Economy of North American Trade," at Claremont Graduate School, Claremont California, March 12, 1993.

Woolcock, Stephen, ed. *Trade and Investment Rule-Making: The Role of Regional and Bilatearal Agreements.* Tokyo: United Nations University Press, 2006.

World Bank. *2005 World Development Indicators.*

———. *Trade, Investment, and Development in the Middle East and North Africa: Engaging with the World.* World Bank, 2003. http://web.worldbank.org/WBSITE/EXTERNAL/COUNTRIES/MENAEXT/0,,contentMDK:20261801~pagePK:146736~piPK:146830~theSitePK:256299,00.html.

World Economic Forum. "Africa Economic Summit, 2005: Strategic Insight, the Agenda Review for Global Leaders." May 2005. http://www.weforum.org/africa.

World Intellectual Property Organization (WIPO). "WIPO Member States." http://www.wipo.int/members/en/ (accessed May 30, 2006).

World Trade Organization. *2001 WTO Annual Report.* 2000.

———. *2003 Annual Report.* November 25, 2002.

———. *2009 Annual Report.* 2008.

———. "Barbados, Trade Policy Review." 2008. http://www.wto.org/english/tratop_e/tpr_e/tp303_e.htm.

———. "Brazil Trade Policy Review." WT/TPR/S/212, March 2009. http://www.wto.org/english/tratop_e/tpr_e/tp312_e.htm.

———. "Cape Verde to Join WTO on 23 July 2008." WTO News Item, June 23, 2008.

———. "East African Trade Policy Review." WT/TPR/171, September 20, 2006.

———. "Factual Presentation: Protocol on Trade in the Southern African Development Community (SADC)." Committee on Regional Trade Agreements. WT/REG176/4, March 12, 2007.

———. "The General Agreement on Trade in Services: An Introduction." March 29, 2006. http://www.wto.org/english/tratop_e/serv_e/serv_e.htm.

———. "The General Agreement on Trade in Services (GATS): Objectives, Coverage and Disciplines." http://www.wto.org/english/tratop_e/serv_e/gatsqa_e.htm (accessed February 15, 2009).

———. "Ghana: Trade Policy Review." WT/TPR/S/194, 15 (January 2008).

———. Intellectual Property (TRIPS) Gateway Page. http://www.wto.org/english/tratop_e/ TRIPS_e/TRIPS_e.htm.

———. *International Trade Statistics 2009.* http://www.wto.org/english/res_e/statis_e/its2009_ e/its09_toc_e.htm.

———. "Jordan: Trade Policy Review." WT/TPR/S/206, November 2008. http://www.wto .org/english/tratop_e/tpr_e/tp306_e.htm.

———. "Kyrgyz Republic: Trade Policy Review." WT/TPR/S/170, October 2006.

———. "Mali: Trade Policy Review." WT/TPR/133, 24 May 2004. http://www.wto.org/english/ res_e/booksp_e/anrep_e/anrep03_e.pdf.

———. "Mauritius: Trade Policy Review." WT/TPR/198, April 2008.

———. "Mexico: Trade Policy Review." WT/TPR/S/195, February 2008. http://www.wto.org/ english/tratop_e/tpr_e/tp295_e.htm.

———. "Oman: Trade Policy Review." June 2008. http://www.wto.org/english/tratop_e/tpr_e/ tp301_e.htm.

———. "Regional Trade Agreements Notified to the GATT/WTO and in Force as of March 1, 2006." http://www.wto.org.

———. "Report of the Working Party on the Accession of the Kingdom of Saudi Arabia to the World Trade Organization." WT/ACC/SAU/61, November 1, 2005.

———. "Singapore WTO Ministerial Declaration." WT/MIN/(96)/DEC, December 13, 1996. http://www.wto.org.

———. "Thailand: Trade Policy Review." WT/TPR/S/191, November 2007. http://www.wto .org/english/tratop_e/tpr_e/tp291_e.htm.

———. "Understanding the WTO: The Agreements: Intellectual Property: Protection and Enforcement," February 2007. http://www.wto.org/english/thewto_e/whatis_e/tif_e/agrm7_ e.htm.

———. "WTO General Council Successfully Adopts Saudi Arabia's Terms of Accession." WTO press release, Press/420, November 11, 2005.

———. "WTO Glossary." http://www.wto.org/english/thewto_e/glossary_e/glossary_e.htm.

Xinhua News Service. December 6, 2005.

Yang, Yongzheng, and Sanjeev Gupta. "Regional Trade Arrangements in Africa: Past Performance and the Way Forward." IMF Working Paper WP/05/36, February 2005.

Yemen Observer. January 8, 2005.

Zangl, Bernhar. "Judicialization Matters! A Comparison of Dispute Settlement under GATT and the WTO." *International Studies Quarterly* (2008): 52.

Zepeda, Eduardo, Timothy Wise, and Kevin Gallagher. "Rethining Trade Policy for Development: Lessons from Mexico under NAFTA." Carnegie Endowment for Peace Policy Outlook, December 2009. http://www.carnegieendowment.org/publications/index .cfm?fa=view&id=24271.

ZIZ (St. Kitts). March 13, 2010.

Index

Venezuela, xv, *26*, 87–88, *88*, 90–91, 98–99, *100–101*, 101–2, *109*, 110–11, *112–13*, 114–15, 127–28, *127*, 233
Vietnam, *131*, 137, *137*, 139, *141*, 151, 237
Virgin Islands. *See* British Virgin Islands; US Virgin Islands

WAEU/CEAO (West Africa Economic Union). *See* West African Economic and Monetary Union
WAEMU/UEMOA. *See* West African Economic and Monetary Union (WAEMU/UEMOA)
WAMU/UMOA (first) West African Monetary Union. *See* West African Economic and Monetary Union (WAEMU/UEMOA)
WAMZ (West African Monetary Zone). *See* ECOWAS
West Africa Economic Union (WAEU/CEAO). *See* West African Economic and Monetary Union (WAEMU/UEMOA)
West African Economic and Monetary Union (WAEMU/UEMOA), 8, *27*, 42, *48*, 49, 59, 62, 64, 72–73, 83, *83*, 275n38, 278n97
West African Monetary Union (first West African Monetary Union *or* WAMU/UMOA). *See* West African Economic and Monetary Union (WAEMU/UEMOA)

West African Monetary Union (second West African Monetary Union). *See* ECOWAS
West African Monetary Zone (WAMZ). *See* ECOWAS
Western Samoa. *See* Samoa
West Indies Associated States Council of Ministers (WISA). *See* Organisation of Eastern Caribbean States
WISA (West Indies Associated States Council of Ministers). *See* Organisation of Eastern Caribbean States
World Trade Organization (WTO): accession to, 243–44, *243*; establishment of, 30, 241; GATT and, 241; norms, 24–25, 241, 264–65. *See also* Doha Development Agenda (DDA); Uruguay Round
WTO. *See* World Trade Organization

Yeltsin, Boris, 185–86
Yemen, *76*, *204*, 210–13, *210*, *212*, 216, *216*, *243*
Yushchenko, Viktor, 188, 195, 201

Zambia, *48*, 54, *55*, *60*, 65, *65*, 67, *78*, 80–81, *80*
Zapatista, 123
Zelaya, Fernando, 101
Zimbabwe, *48*, 57, *60*, *65*, 67, *78*, 80–81, *80*
Zoellick, Robert, 4, 147, 261

About the Author

David A. Lynch is professor and chair, Department of Social Science, at Saint Mary's University of Minnesota, where he teaches international relations, international political economy, and other political science courses. He received his PhD in political science from the University of California, Santa Barbara, and his BA in political science from Iowa State University. He has written over a dozen chapters on trade, economics, and foreign policy in edited books, including the chapter on global trade for the United Nations Association of the United States of America's annual *A Global Agenda* from 1996 to 2005. He lives in Winona, Minnesota, with his wife and two children.